CCSP® (ISC)²®
Certified Cloud Security Professional
Official Study Guide

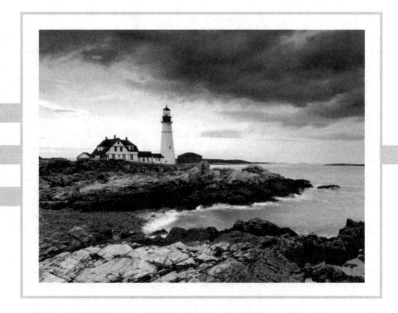

Brian T. O'Hara

Ben Malisow

SYBEX®
A Wiley Brand

Development Editor: Kelly Talbot
Technical Editors: Tom Updegrove, Jerry K. Rayome, Valerie Nelson, Jordan Pike
Production Editor: Rebecca Anderson
Copy Editor: Elizabeth Welch
Editorial Manager: Mary Beth Wakefield
Production Manager: Kathleen Wisor
Executive Editor: Jim Minatel
Book Designers: Judy Fung and Bill Gibson
Proofreader: Josh Chase, Word One New York
Indexer: J & J Indexing
Project Coordinator, Cover: Brent Savage
Cover Designer: Wiley
Cover Image: ©Getty Images Inc./Jeremy Woodhouse

Copyright © 2017 by John Wiley & Sons, Inc., Indianapolis, Indiana

Published simultaneously in Canada

ISBN: 978-1-119-27741-5
ISBN: 978-1-119-27742-2 (ebk.)
ISBN: 978-1-119-27743-9 (ebk.)

Manufactured in the United States of America

For general information on our other products and services or to obtain technical support, please contact
our Customer Care Department within the U.S. at (877) 762-2974, outside the U.S. at (317) 572-3993 or
fax (317) 572-4002.

Wiley publishes in a variety of print and electronic formats and by print-on-demand. Some material
included with standard print versions of this book may not be included in e-books or in print-on-demand.
If this book refers to media such as a CD or DVD that is not included in the version you purchased, you
may download this material at http://booksupport.wiley.com. For more information about Wiley products, visit www.wiley.com.

Library of Congress Control Number: 2017936608

Acknowledgments

The authors would like to thank (ISC)^2 for making this work possible, and the sublime publishing and editing team at Sybex, including Jim Minatel, Kelly Talbot, Rebecca Anderson, and Christine O'Connor. This book is dedicated to all the candidates seeking CCSP certification. We hope it helps.

About the Authors

Brian T. O'Hara, CISA, CISM, CCSP, and CISSP, is the Information Security Officer for Do It Best Corp. With over 20 years of experience providing security and audit services, he has served as the information security officer for Fortune 500 companies and has worked in PCI, healthcare, manufacturing, and financial services, providing audit and security advisory services. Prior to entering the field of IS audit, Brian served as program chair for information technology at the largest community college in the country, where he helped develop the first NSA Two-Year Center of Academic Excellence in Information Security. In addition to co-authoring the *CISA Study Guide*, he has served as a technical editor on books for Wiley, Sybex, and (ISC)². Brian has been an active member both locally and internationally of the Information Security Systems Association (ISSA) for over 10 years and is an ISSA Fellow. He currently serves as the past president of the Indiana chapter of ISACA and president of the InfraGard Indiana Members Alliance, a public–private partnership with the FBI aimed at protecting the United States' critical infrastructures.

Ben Malisow, CISSP, CISM, CCSP, and Security+, is an instructor for (ISC)², teaching prep classes for the CISSP and CCSP certifications. He has been in the information technology and information security field for almost 25 years. He wrote the internal IT security policy for DARPA, served as the Information System Security Manager for the FBI's most-classified counterterror intelligence-sharing network, and helped develop the IT security architecture for the Department of Homeland Security's Transportation Security Administration. Ben has taught courses at many schools and universities, including Carnegie Mellon's CERT/SEI, UTSA, the College of Southern Nevada, and grades 6–12 at a school for troubled youths in Las Vegas. He is widely published in the field, having written for SecurityFocus.com, *ComputerWorld*, and various other publications, as well as several books.

About the Technical Editors

Tom Updegrove, CCSP and EC-Council security trainer, is the CEO of Internetwork Service, an AWS and Microsoft Azure partner. With over 20 years of experience providing technical and security services, he has worked in PCI, healthcare, manufacturing, and financial services, providing security consulting services. In addition to contributing to the *CCSP (ISC)² Study Guide*, he has served as a technical editor on security-related books for Wiley and Sybex, as well as presenting the Social Engineering course for ITProTV. He has helped develop the Liberty University MIS lab infrastructure and currently serves as a technical editor for *Hakin9* and *Pen Testing* magazines.

Jerry K. Rayome, BS/MS Computer Science, CISSP, is a member of the Cyber Security Program at Lawrence Livermore National Laboratory. He has over 20 years of experience providing cybersecurity services, including software development, penetration testing, incident response, firewall implementation, firewall auditing, cyber forensic investigations, NIST 800-53 control implementation/assessment, cloud risk assessment, and cloud security auditing.

Contents at a Glance

Contents

Introduction

Cloud computing has been transforming the way the world conducts business for some time now. Organizations are rethinking their IT strategies and embracing the concepts and practices of cloud computing as a way to be competitive in today's global markets. In addition, the information security industry has begun to recognize the uniqueness of this specialized, new, disruptive force and the need for trained professionals with the right cloud security knowledge and skill sets.

The Certified Cloud Security Professional (CCSP) certification was developed by (ISC)^2 in partnership with the Cloud Security Alliance (CSA) to satisfy the growing demand for trained and qualified cloud security professionals.

The *CCSP (ISC)^2 Certified Cloud Security Professional Official Study Guide* offers the cloud professional a solid foundation for taking and passing the Certified Cloud Security Professional (CCSP) exam.

This book targets students and professionals attempting to further their professional lives by studying for and passing this challenging exam.

(ISC)^2

The CCSP exam is governed by the International Information Systems Security Certification Consortium (ISC)^2. (ISC)^2 is a global not-for-profit organization with four primary mission goals:

- Maintain the Common Body of Knowledge (CBK) for the field of information systems security
- Provide certification for information systems security professionals and practitioners
- Conduct certification training and administer the certification exams
- Oversee the ongoing accreditation of qualified certification candidates through continued education

A board of directors elected from the ranks of its certified practitioners operates the (ISC)^2.

(ISC)^2 supports and provides a wide variety of certifications, including the CISSP, SSCP, CAP, CSSLP, CCFP, HCISPP, and CCSP. These certifications are designed to verify the knowledge and skills of IT security professionals across all industries. You can obtain more information about the organization and its other certifications by visiting www.isc2.org.

Topical Domains

The CCSP certification covers material from the six topical domains. They are as follows:

- Architectural Concepts and Design Requirements
- Cloud Data Security

- Cloud Platform and Infrastructure Security
- Cloud Application Security
- Operations
- Legal and Compliance

These domains, created in conjunction with the Cloud Security Alliance (CSA), cover all of the pertinent areas of security related to the cloud. Computing knowledge and understanding of each ensures the cloud security professional is prepared to provide sound advice and best practices regarding all functional and security-related aspects of cloud computing.

Candidates may find more information regarding each of these by visiting the (ISC)² website at www.isc2.org/ccsp.

Prequalifications

(ISC)² has defined the qualifications and requirements you must meet to become a CCSP as follows:

- A minimum of five years of cumulative, paid, full-time information technology experience of which three years must be in information security and one year in one of the six domains of the CCSP examination.
- Earning the Cloud Security Alliance's CCSK certificate may be substituted for one year of experience in one of the six domains of the CCSP examination.
- Earning the CISSP credential may be substituted for the entire CCSP experience requirement.

Candidates who do not meet these requirements may still sit for the exam and become an Associate of (ISC)². You must also adhere to the (ISC)² formal code of ethics, which can be found on the (ISC)² website at www.isc2.org/ethics.

Overview of the CCSP Exam

The CCSP exam consists of 125 multiple-choice questions covering the following six domains of the CCSP CBK:

Domain 1: Architectural Concepts and Design Requirements

Domain 2: Cloud Data Security

Domain 3: Cloud Platform and Infrastructure Security

Domain 4: Cloud Application Security

Domain 5: Operations

Domain 6: Legal and Compliance

You will have four hours to complete the exam. Twenty-five of the questions will be beta or test questions used for research purposes in trying out new questions and answers, and they will not be calculated in your final score. So be sure to answer every single question, as you will not know which is beta and which is not, and you will receive 0 points for unanswered questions. Look at it this way: If you do not even have a clue as to the answer, you have a 1 in 4 chance of guessing it right. If you can eliminate at least two of the answers as incorrect, you have a 50/50 chance of getting it right. So answer each question.

CCSP Exam Question Types

Most of the questions on the CCSP exam are multiple-choice questions, with four options and a single correct answer. Some are straightforward, such as asking you to identify a definition. In addition, other questions will ask you to identify an appropriate concept or best practice. Here is one example:

1. The convoluting of code to the point that even if the source code were obtained it would not be easily decipherable is known as:

    A. Randomization

    B. Elasticity

    C. Obfuscation

    D. Masking

You must select the one correct or best answer. Sometimes the answer will seem obvious to you, and other times, it will be harder to discriminate between two good answers and pick the best. Watch out for general, specific, universal, superset, and subset answer selections. In other cases, none of the answers will seem correct. In these instances, you will want to select the least incorrect answer. There are also questions that are scenario based, where you must answer several questions given a specific situation.

 The correct answer to the question above is option C, obfuscation. Obfuscation is the convolution of code to protect it from unauthorized viewing.

In addition to the standard multiple-choice question format, (ISC)[2] has added a new question format that uses a drag-and-drop approach. For instance, you may see a list of items on one side of the screen that you need to drag and drop onto their appropriate counterparts on the other side of the screen. Other interactive questions may include matching terms with definitions and clicking on specific areas of a chart or graphic. These interactive questions are weighted with a higher point value than the multiple-choice type, so you should pay extra attention when answering them.

Study and Exam Preparation Tips

We recommend planning for at least 30 days of nightly intensive studying for the CCSP exam. We have compiled a list of practices that should speed you along on your journey.

- Take one or two evenings to read each chapter thoroughly and work through the review material at the end.

- Think about joining a study group.

- Answer all the review questions and take the practice exam.

- Complete the written labs from each chapter.

- Before you move on to the next section of work, be sure to review the previous day's work to be sure you are retaining the information.

- Take study breaks but stay on track.

- Put together a study plan.

- Review the (ISC)² Exam Outline: Candidate Information Bulletin from www.isc2.org.

- Use the flashcards included with the study tools to reinforce your understanding of the concepts.

 We recommend spending almost as much time with the practice exam and flashcards as with reading and reviewing concepts. You might also consider visiting other online resources such as www.csa.org and other CCSP- or cloud-focused websites.

Exam Format and Scoring

The CCSP exam consists of 125 multiple-choice questions with four choices each. There may be scenario-based questions also, which may have one or more multiple choice questions associated with them. There will also be 25 sample questions that are not used to score your exam; these are included for research purposes only. This is how (ISC)² develops new questions for the exam to keep them fresh and up to date. You will not know which is which, so answer all the questions. You get no points for unanswered questions.

Advice on Taking the Exam

Here are some test taking tips and general guidelines:

- Answer easy questions first. You can mark all of the questions you are unsure of and go back over them after you have completed the exam.

- Eliminate incorrect answers first.

- Be careful of double negatives in the language of the question.

- Read the questions carefully to ensure you fully understand them.

- *Take your time.* Do not hurry. Rushing leads to test anxiety and loss of focus.

- Take a bathroom break and a breather if you need to, but keep it short. You want to maintain your focus.

Manage your time. You have four hours to answer 125 questions. That equates to about two minutes per question, which in most cases is more than enough time.

Make sure you get plenty of sleep the night before and try to go easy on the caffeine so that you do not get the jitters the day of the exam. Be sure to bring any food or drink you think you might need, although they will be stored while you are taking the exam. Also, remember to bring any medications you need to take and alert the staff of any condition that might interfere with your test taking, such as diabetes or heart disease. No test or certification is worth your health.

You may not wear a watch into the test lab. There are timers on the computers and in the testing labs. You must also empty your pockets with the exception of your locker key and ID.

You must bring at least one picture ID with a signature, such as a driver's license, with you to the testing center, and you should have at least one more form of ID with a signature. Arrive at least 30 minutes early to the testing site to make sure you have everything you need. Bring the registration form that you received from the testing center along with your IDs.

If English is not your first language, you can register for one of several other versions of the exam. A translation dictionary is allowed if you need one, but you must be able to prove your need.

Completing the Certification Process

Once you have successfully completed the CCSP exam, there are a few more things to do before you have "earned" your new credential. First, transmission of your (ISC)² score happens automatically. You will receive instructions on the printed results from your test as you leave the testing center. They will include instructions on how to download your certification form, which will ask you for things such as whether you already have a CISSP and similar questions. Once completed, you will need to sign and submit the form to (ISC)² for approval. Usually, you will receive notice of your official certification within a few days. Once you are fully certified, you can use the CCSP designation in your signatures and other places of importance per (ISC)² usage guidelines.

Notes on This Book's Organization

This book covers all of the six CCSP Common Body of Knowledge (CBK) domains in sufficient depth to provide you with a clear understanding of the material. The main body of the book is composed of 11 chapters that are arranged as follows:

Chapter 1: Architectural Concepts

Chapter 2: Design Requirements

Chapter 3: Data Classification

Chapter 4: Cloud Data Security

Chapter 5: Security in the Cloud

Chapter 6: Responsibilities in the Cloud

Chapter 7: Cloud Application Security

Chapter 8: Operations Elements

Each chapter includes elements designed to assist you in your studies and to test your knowledge of the material presented in the chapter. It is recommended that you read Chapter 1 first to best orient yourself in the subject matter before moving on to the other chapters.

 Please see the table of contents and chapter introductions for more detailed domain topics covered in each chapter.

Elements of This Study Guide

This study guide contains several core elements that will help you prepare for the CCSP exam and the real world beyond it:

Real World Scenarios: The book has several real-world scenarios laid out to help you further assimilate the information by seeing where and under what circumstances certain solutions have worked (or not) in the real world and why.

Summaries: The summary is a quick overview of important points made in the chapter.

Exam Essentials: Exam Essentials highlight topics that could appear on the exam in some form. While we do not know exactly what will be included on a particular exam, this section reinforces significant concepts that are key to understanding the CBK and the test specs for the CCSP exam.

Written Labs: Each chapter includes written labs that bring together various topics and concepts brought up in the chapter. The scenarios and questions raise considerations to assist you in assimilating the material in such a way as to help you better understand and propose potential security strategies or solutions.

Chapter Review Questions: Each chapter includes practice questions designed to measure your knowledge of key ideas discussed in the chapter. After you finish each chapter, answer the questions; if some of your answers are incorrect, it is an indication that you need to spend more time studying the corresponding topics. The answers to the practice questions are at the end of the book.

What Is Included with the Additional Study Tools

Beyond all of the information provided in the text, this book comes with a helpful array of additional study tools.

The Sybex Test Preparation Software

The test preparation software, made by the experts at Sybex, can help prepare you for the CCSP exam. In this test engine, you will find all the review and assessment questions from the book and additional bonus practice exam questions that are included with the study tools. You can take the assessment test, test yourself by chapter, take the practice exam, or take a randomly generated exam consisting of all the questions.

Electronic Flashcards

Sybex's electronic flashcards include hundreds of questions designed to challenge you further for the CCSP certification exam. Between the review questions, practice exam, and flashcards, you should have more than enough practice for the exam.

Glossary of Terms in PDF

Sybex offers a robust glossary of terms in PDF format. This comprehensive glossary includes key terms you should understand for the CCSP certification exam, in a searchable format.

Bonus Practice Exams

Sybex includes two practice exams; these contain questions meant to survey your understanding of the essential elements of the CCSP CBK. Both tests are 250 questions long, twice the length of the actual certification exam. The exams are available online at http://sybextestbanks.wiley.com.

 Readers can gain access to the following tools by visiting sybextestbanks.wiley.com.

How to Use This Book's Study Tools

This book has a number of features designed to guide you through your studies for the CCSP certification exam. At the beginning of each chapter, we have created a list of the CCSP topics covered in the chapter, giving you a quick view into what lies inside each. In addition, we have created summaries at the end of each chapter followed by Exam Essentials designed to provide you with quick tips on items to which you should pay special attention. Lastly, we have provided you with both written labs that will expose you to real-world examples of cloud issues and technology and review questions that will further assist you in assimilating the material presented. We have also created some suggestions that will help you get even more out of your study efforts:

- Take the assessment test before you start reading the material. This will give you an idea of the areas on which you need to spend additional study time as well as those areas in which you may just need a brief refresher.

- Answer the review questions after you have read each chapter. If you answer any incorrectly, go back to the chapter and review the topic, or use one of the additional resources if you need more information.

- Download the flashcards to your mobile device, and review them when you have a few minutes during the day.

- Take every opportunity to test yourself. In addition to the assessment test and review questions, bonus practice exam questions are included with the additional study tools. Take the exam without referring to the chapters and see how well you have done. Then go back and review the topics, concepts, definitions, and so on that you have missed until you fully understand and can apply the concepts.

Finally, find a study partner or group if possible. Studying for and taking the exam with someone else can be a great motivator. In addition, you can learn from each other.

Assessment Test

1. What type of solutions enable enterprises or individuals to store their data and computer files on the Internet using a storage service provider rather than storing the data locally on a physical disk, such as a hard drive or tape backup?

   A. Online backups

   B. Cloud backup solutions

   C. Removable hard drives

   D. Masking

2. When using an Infrastructure as a Service (IaaS) solution, what is the key benefit for the customer?

   A. Scalability

   B. Metered service

   C. Energy and cooling efficiencies

   D. Transfer of ownership cost

3. _____ focuses on security and encryption to prevent unauthorized copying and limitations on distribution to only those who pay.

   A. Digital rights management (DRM)

   B. Enterprise digital rights management

   C. Bit splitting

   D. Degaussing

4. Which of the following represents the correct set of four cloud deployment models?

   A. Public, Private, Joint and Community

   B. Public, Private, Hybrid, and Community

   C. Public, Internet, Hybrid, and Community

   D. External, Private, Hybrid, and Community

5. What is a special mathematical code that allows encryption hardware/software to encode and then decipher an encrypted message called?

   A. PKI

   B. Encryption key

   C. Public key

   D. Masking

6. Which of the following lists the correct six components of the STRIDE threat model?

   A. Spoofing, Tampering, Repudiation, Information Disclosure, Denial of Service, and Elevation of Privilege

   B. Spoofing, Tampering, Repudiation, Information Disclosure, Denial of Service, and Social Engineering Elasticity

    C. Spoofing, Tampering, Repudiation, Information Disclosure, Distributed Denial of Service, and Elevation of Privilege

    D. Spoofing, Tampering, Nonrepudiation, Information Disclosure, Denial of Service, and Elevation of Privilege

7. What is the term for the assurance that a specific author actually created and sent a specific item to a specific recipient, and that the message was successfully received?

    A. PKI

    B. DLP

    C. Nonrepudiation

    D. Bit splitting

8. What is the correct term for the process of deliberately destroying the encryption keys used to encrypt data?

    A. Poor key management

    B. PKI

    C. Obfuscation

    D. Crypto-shredding

9. In a federated environment, who is the relying party, and what do they do?

    A. The relying party is the service provider and they would consume the tokens generated by the identity provider.

    B. The relying party is the service provider and they would consume the tokens generated by the customer.

    C. The relying party is the customer and they would consume the tokens generated by the identity provider.

    D. The relying party is the identity provider and they would consume the tokens generated by the service provider.

10. What is the process of replacing sensitive data with unique identification symbols that retain all the essential information about the data without compromising its security?

    A. Randomization

    B. Elasticity

    C. Obfuscation

    D. Tokenization

11. Which of the following data storage types are associated or used with Platform as a Service (PaaS)?

    A. Databases and Big Data

    B. SaaS application

    C. Tabular

    D. Raw and block

12. What is the term used for software technology that encapsulates application software from the underlying operating system on which it is executed?

    A. Hypervisor

    B. Application virtualization

    C. VMWare

    D. SaaS

13. Which of the following represents the legislation enacted to protect shareholders and the public from enterprise accounting errors and fraudulent practices?

    A. PCI

    B. Gramm-Leach-Bliley Act (GLBA)

    C. Sarbanes-Oxley Act (SOX)

    D. HIPAA

14. What is a device called that can safely store and manage encryption keys and is used in servers, data transmission, and log files?

    A. Private key

    B. Hardware security module (HSM)

    C. Public key

    D. Trusted Operating System Module (TOS)

15. What is a type of cloud infrastructure that is provisioned for open use by the general public and is owned, managed, and operated by a business, academic, or government organization and exists on the premises of the cloud provider called?

    A. Private cloud

    B. Public cloud

    C. Hybrid cloud

    D. Personal cloud

16. When using transparent encryption of a database, where does the encryption engine reside?

    A. Within the database application itself

    B. At the application using the database

    C. On the instances attached to the volume

    D. In a key management system

17. What is a type of assessment called that employs a set of methods, principles, or rules for assessing risk based on non-numerical categories or levels?

    A. Quantitative assessment

    B. Qualitative assessment

    C. Hybrid assessment

    D. SOC 2

18. What best describes the Cloud Security Alliance Cloud Controls Matrix?

    A. A set of regulatory requirements for cloud service providers

    B. A set of software development life cycle requirements for cloud service providers

    C. A security controls framework that provides mapping/cross relationships with the main industry-accepted security standards, regulations, and controls frameworks such as the ISO 27001/27002, ISACA's COBIT, and PCI-DSS

    D. An inventory of cloud service security controls that are arranged into separate security domains

19. When a conflict of laws occurs, _____ determines the jurisdiction in which the dispute will be heard.

    A. Tort law

    B. Doctrine of Proper Law

    C. Common law

    D. Criminal law

20. Which one of the following is the *most* important security consideration when selecting a new computer facility?

    A. Local law enforcement response times

    B. Location adjacent to competitor's facilities

    C. Aircraft flight paths

    D. Utility infrastructure

21. Which of the following is *always* safe to use in the disposal of electronic records within a cloud environment?

    A. Physical destruction

    B. Overwriting

    C. Encryption

    D. Degaussing

22. Which of the following describes a SYN flood attack?

    A. Rapid transmission of Internet Relay Chat (IRC) messages

    B. Creating a high number of partially open TCP connections

    C. Disabling the Domain Name Service (DNS) server

    D. Excessive list linking of users and files

23. Which of the following is an example of a form of cloud storage that applies to storing an individual's mobile device data in the cloud and providing the individual with access to the data from anywhere?

    A. Raw storage

    B. Flash storage

    C. Obfuscation archiving

    D. Mobile cloud storage

24. Which of the following terms best describes a distributed model where software applications are hosted by a vendor or cloud service provider and made available to customers over network resources?

    A. Infrastructure as a Service (IaaS)

    B. Public cloud

    C. Software as a Service (SaaS)

    D. Private cloud

25. Which of the following is a federal law enacted in the United States to control the way that financial institutions deal with private information of individuals?

    A. PCI

    B. ISO/IEC

    C. Gramm-Leach-Bliley Act (GLBA)

    D. Consumer Protection Act

26. The typical function of Secure Sockets Layer (SSL) in securing Wireless Application Protocol (WAP) is to protect transmissions that exist:

    A. Between the WAP gateway and the wireless endpoint device

    B. Between the web server and the WAP gateway

    C. From the web server to the wireless endpoint device

    D. Between the wireless device and the base station

27. What is an accounting report on controls at a service organization that replaces older SAS70 type reports?

    A. SOC 1

    B. SSAE16

    C. GAAP

    D. SOC 2

28. What is a company that purchases hosting services from a cloud server hosting or cloud computing provider who then resells to its own customers?

    A. Cloud broker

    B. Cloud computing reseller

    C. Cloud proxy

    D. VAR

29. What is a type of computing comparable to grid computing that relies on sharing computing resources rather than having local servers or personal devices to handle applications?

    A. Server hosting

    B. Legacy computing

    C. Cloud computing

    D. Intranet

30. What is a set of technologies designed to analyze application source code and binaries for coding and design conditions that are indicative of security and vulnerabilities?

    A. Dynamic application security testing (DAST)

    B. Static application security testing (SAST)

    C. Secure coding

    D. OWASP

Answers to Assessment Test

1. **B.** Cloud backup solutions enable enterprises to store their data and computer files on the Internet using a storage service rather than storing data locally on a hard disk or tape backup. This has the added benefit of providing access to data should the primary business location be damaged in some way that prevents accessing or restoring data locally due to damaged infrastructure or equipment. Online backups and removable hard drives are other options but do not by default supply the customer with ubiquitous access. Masking is a technology used to partially conceal sensitive data.

2. **D.** The primary benefit to the customer of using Infrastructure as a Service (IaaS) is the transfer of cost of ownership. In a cloud environment, the customer uses and is billed only for what they use as opposed to the full cost of implementation, saving them a significant amount in terms of cost of ownership. While scalability, metered service, and energy and cooling efficiencies are a part of the benefit of a cloud computing environment, they are not the primary benefit or business driver behind IaaS adoption.

3. **A.** Digital rights management (DRM) was designed to focus on security and encryption as a means of preventing unauthorized copying and limitations on distribution of content to only those authorized (purchasers). Enterprise digital rights management, also known as information rights management (IRM), is a subset of DRM and typically refers to business-to-business securing of information rights. Bit splitting is a method of hiding information across multiple geographical boundaries, and degaussing is a method of deleting data permanently from magnetic media.

4. **B.** The only correct answer for this is Public, Private, Hybrid, and Community. Joint, Internet, and External are not cloud models.

5. **B.** An encryption key is just that: a key used to encrypt and decrypt information. It is mathematical code that supports either hardware- or software-based encryption used to encode or decode information.

6. **A.** The letters in STRIDE threat model represent Spoofing of identity, Tampering with data, Repudiation, Information disclosure, Denial of service, and Elevation of privilege. The other options are simply mixed up or incorrect versions of the same.

7. **C.** Nonrepudiation means that a specific author or user cannot refute or repudiate that he or she created and/or sent a message and the receiver of the data or message cannot deny they received it.

8. **D.** The act of crypto-shredding means destroying the key that was initially used to encrypt the data, thereby making it forever unrecoverable.

9. **A.** The identity provider would hold all of the identities and generate a token for known users. The relying party (RP) would be the service provider and would consume the tokens. All other answers are incorrect.

10. **D.** Replacing sensitive data with unique identification symbols is known as tokenization, a simple and only somewhat effective way of hiding or concealing sensitive data with the

replacement of unique identification symbols. It is not considered as strong as encryption but can be effective in keeping prying eyes off of sensitive information. While randomization and obfuscation are also means of concealing information, they are done quite differently.

11. A. PaaS uses databases and Big Data storage types.

12. B. Application virtualization encapsulates application software from the underlying operating system on which it is executed.

13. C. The Sarbanes-Oxley Act (SOX) was enacted in response to the 2000 accounting scandal that caused the bankruptcy of Enron. At that time, top executives laid the claim that they were unaware of the accounting practices that led to the company's demise. SOX not only forces executives to oversee all accounting practices, but holds them accountable should such activity occur again.

14. B. A hardware security module is a device that can safely store and manage encryption keys. These can be used in servers, workstations, and so on. Once common type is called the Trusted Platform Module (TPM) and can be found on enterprise workstations and laptops. There is no such term as a trusted operating system, and public and private keys are terms used with PKI.

15. B. This is the very definition of public cloud computing.

16. A. In transparent encryption, the encryption key for a database is stored in the boot record of the database itself.

17. B. A qualitative assessment is a set of methods or rules for assessing risk based on non-mathematical or categories or levels. One that uses those mathematical categories or levels is called a quantitative assessment. There is no such thing as a hybrid assessment, and an SOC 2 is an accounting report regarding control effectiveness.

18. C. The CCM cross-references many industry standards, laws, and guidelines.

19. B. The Doctrine of Proper Law is used when a dispute occurs over which jurisdiction will hear a case. Tort law refers to civil liability suits. Common law refers to laws regarding marriage, and criminal law refers to violations of state or federal criminal code.

20. D. Of the answers given, option D is the most important. It is vital that any datacenter facility be close to sound facility resources such as power, water, and connectivity.

21. C. Encryption can always be used in a cloud environment, but physical destruction, overwriting, and degaussing may not be available due to access and physical separation factors.

22. B. A SYN flood is where a TCP connection attempt is made and then cut short just prior to completion, thereby leaving a server waiting for a response. If enough of these connection attempts are made, a "flood" occurs, causing the end unit to consume resources to the point that either services and/or the system itself become unavailable for use. The other options have no connection with a flood of any kind.

23. D. Mobile cloud storage is defined as a form of cloud storage that applies to storing an individual's mobile device data in the cloud and providing the individual with access to the data from anywhere.

24. C. This is the definition of the Software as a Service (SaaS) service model. Public and private are cloud deployment models, and Infrastructure as a Service (IaaS) does not provide applications of any type.

25. C. The Gramm-Leach-Bliley Act targets U.S. financial institutions and requires them to deal specifically with protecting account holders' private information. PCI refers to credit card processing requirements, ISO/IEC is a standards organization, and the Consumer Protection Act, while providing oversight for the protection of consumer private information, is limited in scope.

26. C. The purpose of SSL is to encrypt the communication channel between two end points. In this example, it is the end user and the server.

27. A. The correct answer is the SOC 1 report, which is designed to assess the controls primarily revolving around financial reporting, formerly found in the SAS 70. The SOC 2 is a report that provides information related to one or more of the AICPA five security principles.

28. B. The cloud computing reseller purchases hosting services and then resells them.

29. C. Cloud computing is built on the model of grid computing whereby resources can be pooled and shared rather than having local devices do all the compute and storage functions.

30. B. Static application security testing (SAST) differs from dynamic application security testing (DAST) in that it looks at source code and binaries to see if it can detect problems before the code is loaded into memory and run.

 Additional CCSP practice questions, videos and resources are available on the website at sybextestbanks.wiley.com.

Chapter

1

Architectural Concepts

THE OBJECTIVE OF THIS CHAPTER IS TO ACQUAINT THE READER WITH THE FOLLOWING CONCEPTS:

✓ **Domain 1: Architectural Concepts and Design Requirements**

- A. Understand Cloud Computing Concepts
  - A.1 Cloud Computing Definitions
  - A.2 Cloud Computing Roles
  - A.3 Key Cloud Computing Characteristics
  - A.4 Building Block Technologies
- B. Describe Cloud Reference Architecture
  - B.1 Cloud Computing Activities
  - B.2 Cloud Service Capabilities
  - B.3 Cloud Service Categories
  - B.4 Cloud Deployment Models
  - B.5 Cloud Cross-Cutting Aspects
- D. Understanding Design Principles of Secure Cloud Computing
  - D.3 Cost/Benefit Analysis

✓ **Domain 3: Cloud Platform and Infrastructure Security**

- D. Plan Disaster Recovery and Business Continuity Management
  - D.1 Understanding the Cloud Environment
  - D.2 Understanding the Business Requirements

✓ **Domain 6: Legal and Compliance**

- B. Understand Privacy Issues, Including Jurisdictional Variation
  - B.3 Difference Among Confidentiality, Integrity, Availability, and Privacy

This chapter is the foundation for all the other chapters in this study guide. You may find it useful to review this material before reading other chapters.

The CCSP is not a certification of basic computer skills or training; it is a professional certification for practitioners with some background in the field. (ISC)² expects that those who want to earn this particular certification already have experience in the industry, have been employed in an InfoSec position in some professional capacity, and have a thorough understanding of many basic areas related to computers, security, business, risk, and networking. Many people taking the test already have other certifications that validate their knowledge and experience such as the CISSP. Therefore, this book will not contain many of the basics that, while testable, you are already expected to know. If you aren't coming from a CISSP background, it would be good to supplement your knowledge with CISSP-focused materials as well.

However, the CCSP Common Body of Knowledge (CBK) contains terminology and concepts that may be expressed in specific ways to include perspectives and usages that may be unique to the CCSP and different from what you are used to dealing with in your normal operations. This chapter is therefore intended as a guide, laying down the foundation for understanding the rest of the material and the CBK as a whole.

Cloud computing has come to mean many things, but the following characteristics have become part of the generally accepted definition:

- Broad network access

- On-demand services

- Resource pooling

- Measured or "metered" service

These traits are expressed succinctly in the NIST definition of cloud computing.

NIST 800-145 Cloud Computing Definition

The official NIST definition of cloud computing says, "Cloud Computing is a model for enabling ubiquitous, convenient, on-demand network access to a shared pool of configurable computing resources (e.g., networks, servers, storage, applications, and services) that can be rapidly provisioned and released with minimal management effort or service provider interaction."

You can expect to see mention of each of these throughout this book, the CBK, and the exam.

Broad network access means that there should never be network bandwidth bottlenecks. This is generally accomplished with the use of such technologies as advanced routing techniques, load balancers, multisite hosting, and other technologies.

On-demand services refer to the model that allows customers to scale their compute and/or storage needs with little or no intervention from or prior communication with the provider. The services happen in real time.

Resource pooling is the characteristic that allows the cloud provider to meet various demands from customers while remaining financially viable. The cloud provider can make capital investments that greatly exceed what any single customer could provide on their own and can apportion these resources, as needed, so that the resources are not underutilized (which would mean a wasteful investment) or overtaxed (which would mean a decrease in level of service).

Finally, measured or metered service simply means that the customer is charged for only what they use and nothing more. This is much like how a water or power company might charge you each month for the services used.

The ISO/IEC standard that provides an overview and vocabulary for cloud computing (ISO/IEC 17788, www.iso.org/iso/catalogue_detail?csnumber=60544) includes these traits, and it also adds the characteristic of multitenancy. While it is true that multitenancy is quite often an aspect of most cloud service offerings, it is not exactly a defining element of the field. There are cloud services that do not include multitenancy, as customers can purchase, rent/lease, and stand-alone resources.

Rest assured—we will be going into more detail regarding all of these concepts in the chapters to come.

 Real World Scenario

Online Shopping

Think of retail demand during the pre-holiday crush toward the end of the year. The sheer volume of customers and transactions greatly exceeds all normal operations throughout the rest of the year. When this happens, retailers who offer online shopping can see great benefit from hosting their sales capability in the cloud. The cloud provider can apportion resources necessary to meet this increased demand and will charge for this increased usage at a negotiated rate, but when shopping drops off after the holiday, the retailers will not continue to be charged at the higher rate.

It is a great business model, which is why some people say that cloud computing is not a technology but rather a business enabler.

Business Requirements

The IT department is not a profit center; it provides a support function. This is even truer for the security department. Security activities actually hinder business efficiency (because generally the more secure something is, be it a device or a process, the less efficient it will be). This is why the business needs of the organization drive security decisions, and not the other way around.

A successful organization will gather as much information about operational business requirements as possible; this information can be used for many purposes, including several functions in the security realm (we'll touch on this throughout the book, but a few examples include the business continuity/disaster recovery effort, the risk management plan, and data categorization). Likewise, the astute security professional needs to understand as much as possible about the operation of the organization. Operational aspects of the organization can help security personnel better perform their tasks no matter what level or role they happen to be assigned to. For example:

- A network security administrator has to know what type of traffic to expect based on the business of the organization.

- The intrusion detection analyst has to understand what the organization is doing and why and how and where to better understand the nature and intensity of external attacks and how to adjust baselines accordingly.

- The security architect has to understand the various needs of the organizational departments to enhance their operation without compromising their security profile.

Functional requirements: Those performance aspects of a device, process, or employee that are necessary for the business task to be accomplished. Example: A salesperson in the field must be able to connect to the organization's network remotely.

Nonfunctional requirements: Those aspects of a device, process, or employee that are not necessary for accomplishing a business task but are desired or expected. Example: The salesperson's remote connection must be secure.

Many organizations are currently considering moving their network operations to a cloud-based motif. This is not a decision made lightly, and the business requirements must be supported by this transition. As described in the previous paragraphs, there are also different service and delivery models of cloud computing, and an organization must decide which one will optimize success.

Existing State

In this initial effort, a true evaluation and understanding of the business processes, assets, and requirements is essential. Failing to properly capture the full extent of the business needs could result in not having an asset or capability in the new environment, after the migration.

At the start of this effort, however, the intent is not to determine what will best fulfill the business requirements, but to determine what those requirements are. A full inventory of assets, processes, and requirements is necessary, and there are various methods for collecting this data. Typically several methods are used jointly, as a means to reduce the possibility of missing something.

Possible methods for gathering business requirements include

- Interviewing functional managers
- Interviewing users
- Interviewing senior management
- Surveying customers
- Collecting network traffic
- Inventorying assets
- Collecting financial records
- Collecting insurance records
- Marketing data collection
- Collecting regulatory mandates

After sufficient data has been collected, a detailed analysis is necessary. This is the point where a business impact analysis (BIA) takes place.

The BIA is an assessment of the priorities given to each asset and process within the organization. A proper analysis should consider the effect ("impact") any harm or loss of each asset might mean to the organization overall. During the BIA, special care should be paid to identifying critical paths and single points of failure. You also need to determine the costs of compliance—that is, the legislative and contractual requirements mandated for your organization. Your organization's regulatory restrictions will be based on many variables, including the jurisdictions where your organization operates, the industry the organization is in, the types and locations of your customers, and so on.

Assets can be tangible or intangible. They can include hardware, software, intellectual property, personnel, processes, and so on. An example of tangible assets would be things like routers and servers, whereas intangible assets are generally something you cannot touch, such as patents, trademarks, copyrights, and business methodologies.

Quantifying Benefits and Opportunity Cost

Once you have a clear picture of what your organization does in terms of lines of business and processes, you can get a better understanding of what benefits the organization might derive from cloud migration, as well as the costs associated with the move.

Obviously, the greatest driver pushing organizations toward cloud migration at the moment is cost savings, and that is a significant and reasonable consideration. The next few sections describe some of those considerations.

Reduction in Capital Expenditure

If your organization buys a device for use in its internal environment, the capacity of that device will either be fully utilized or (more likely) not. If the device is used at its fullest capacity, then it's quite likely that the function for which it is needed may experience inefficiencies at some point. Even a small uptick in demand for that device will overload its capacity. However, if the device is not fully utilized, then the organization has paid for something for which it is getting no value. The unused or excess capacity goes to waste. In effect, the organization has overpaid for the device unless the organization uses the device to the point where it is dangerously close to overload—you just cannot buy part of a device.

In the cloud, however, the organization is only paying for what it uses (regardless of the number of devices, or fractions of devices, necessary to handle the load), and no more. This is the *metered service* model described earlier. As a result, the organization does not overpay for these assets. However, cloud providers do have excess capacity available to be apportioned to cloud customers, so your organization is always in a position to experience increased demand (even dramatic, rapid, and significant demand) and not be overwhelmed.

One way an organization can use hosted cloud services is to augment internal, private datacenter capabilities with managed services during times of increased demand. We refer to this as "cloud bursting." The organization might have datacenter assets it owns, but it can't handle the increased demand during times of elevated need (crisis situations, heavy holiday shopping periods, and so on), so it rents the additional capacity as needed from an external cloud provider. See Figure 1.1.

FIGURE 1.1 On-demand scalability allows the customer to dictate the volume of resource usage

Therefore, with deployment to a cloud environment, the organization realizes cost savings immediately (not paying for unused resources) and avoids a costly risk (the possibility of loss of service due to increased demand).

Reduction in Personnel Costs

For most organizations (other than those that deliver IT services), managing data is not a core competency, much less a profitable line of business. Data management is also a specialized skill, and people with IT experience and training are relatively expensive (compared to employees in other departments). The personnel required to fulfill the needs of an internal IT environment represent a significant and disproportionally large investment for the organization. In moving to the cloud, the organization can largely divest itself of a large percentage, if not a majority, of these personnel.

Reduction in Operational Costs

Maintaining and administering an internal environment takes a great deal of effort and expense. When an organization moves to the cloud, the cost becomes part of the price of the service, as calculated by the cloud provider. Therefore, costs are lumped in with the flat-rate cost of the contract and will not increase in response to enhanced operations (scheduled updates, emergency response activities, and so on).

Transferring Some Regulatory Costs

Some cloud providers may offer holistic, targeted regulatory compliance packages for their customers. For instance, the cloud provider might have a set of controls that can be applied to a given customer's cloud environment to ensure the mandates of Payment Card Industry (PCI) are met. Any customer wanting that package can specify so in a service contract, instead of trying to delineate individual controls a la carte. In this manner, the cloud customer can decrease some of the effort and expense they might otherwise incur in trying to come up with a control framework for adhering to the relevant regulations.

We will go into more detail about service-level agreements or service contracts in later chapters.

It is, however, crucial to note here (and we'll repeat it throughout the book) that under current laws, no cloud customer can transfer risk or liability associated with the inadvertent or malicious disclosure of personally identifiable information (PII). This is very, very important to understand: your organization, if it holds PII of any kind, is ultimately responsible for any breaches or releases of that data, even if you are using a cloud service and the breach/release results from negligence or attack on the part of the cloud provider. Legally and financially, in the eyes of the court, your organization is always responsible for any unplanned release of PII.

PII is a major component of regulatory compliance, whether the regulation comes in the form of statutes or contractual obligation. Protection of PII will be a large part of our security concern in the cloud.

Reduction in Costs for Data Archival/Backup Services

Offsite backups are standard practice, for both long-term data archival and disaster recovery purposes. Having a cloud-based service for this purpose is sensible and cost-efficient even if the organization does not conduct its regular operations in the cloud. However, moving operations into the cloud can create an economy of scale when combined with the archiving/backup usage; this can lead to an overall cost savings for the organization. As we'll discuss later in the book, this can enhance the business continuity/disaster recovery (BC/DR) strategy for the organization as well.

Intended Impact

All of these benefits can be enumerated according to dollar value: each potential cost-saving measure can be quantified. Senior management—with input from subject matter experts—needs to balance the potential financial benefits against the risks of operating in the cloud. It is this cost-benefit calculation, driven by business needs but informed by security concerns, that will allow senior management to decide whether a cloud migration of the organization's operational environment makes sense.

A great many risks are associated with cloud migration as well. We will be addressing these in detail throughout this book.

Cloud Evolution, Vernacular, and Definitions

The arrival of the cloud and its related technology has provided a lot of advantages. To incorporate the cloud and these advantages, it is necessary to understand new terminology and how it relates to the terminology of traditional models. This new technology and its terminology are an integral part of understanding cloud computing service models and cloud computing deployment models.

New Technology, New Options

Fifteen, or even ten years ago, suggesting that organizations hand off their data and operations to a third party that is geographically distant and run by people that most managers in the organization will never meet would have seemed absurd, especially from a security perspective. The risk would have been seen as insurmountable, and ceding that level of control to an outside vendor would have been daunting. Today, a combination of technological capabilities and contractual trust make cloud computing not only appealing but almost a foregone conclusion, in terms of financial viability.

There are specific characteristics that are emblematic of cloud computing. We're going to define them here and offer examples of how each might be demonstrated.

- **Elasticity:** This is the flexibility of allocating resources as needed for immediate usage, instead of purchasing resources according to other variables. For instance, a traditional organization might purchase one desktop for every employee. In that model, the organization would be paying for the entire capacity of the desktop computer—its processing power, its storage capacity, etc.—even though individual users would probably not be using the full capacity of each device at all times.

  In the cloud environment, the organization is paying not for a device, but for the use of a service, when it is being used. The ability of the cloud vendor to offer this type of service (while remaining profitable) is based on the elasticity and the flexibility offered by recent enhancements in technology, including virtualization (we will discuss virtualization further in upcoming chapters). With virtualization, the cloud provider can allocate partial usage of each resource to every user and customer, when those users and customers require it, and nothing more, thereby avoiding wasted, underutilized resources and excess, nonproductive costs.

  In a virtualized environment, users can also access their data from almost any device or platform, and almost any location. This allows portability, availability, and accessibility that exceed previous enterprise environments.

- **Simplicity:** Usage and administration of cloud services ought to be transparent to cloud customers and users; from their perspective, a digital data service is paid for and can be used, with very little additional input other than what is necessary to perform their duties. Proper cloud implementations should not require constant or even frequent interaction between the cloud provider and cloud customer.

- **Scalability:** The organization's computing needs won't remain static: there will be new (and hopefully more) users, customers, and data as the organization continually matures. A cloud service can easily meet those needs, either temporarily or long-term, in a much more cost-efficient manner than a traditional environment, because new computing resources can be assigned and allocated without any significant additional capital investment on the part of the cloud provider, and at an incremental cost to the cloud customer.

The Difference between a Cloud Customer and a Cloud User

A *cloud customer* is anyone who is purchasing a cloud service (which could be an individual or a company), whereas a *cloud user* is just someone using cloud services. It could be an employee of a company who is a cloud customer or just a private individual.

For instance, Company A purchases SaaS services from Cloud Provider X. Company A is a cloud customer. All employees of Company A are cloud users, because they're using the cloud services their employer, a cloud customer, has purchased for their usage.

> Not all cloud users are staff of cloud customers, though. Many cloud users are simply individuals who are using publicly available cloud services for their personal purposes, such as a person who has a Gmail account or someone who syncs their smartphone to a free online backup service.

Cloud Computing Service Models

Cloud services are usually offered in terms of three general models, based on what the vendor offers and the customer needs, and the responsibilities of each according to the service contract. These models are Infrastructure as a Service (IaaS), Platform as a Service (PaaS), and Software as a Service (SaaS), as shown in Figure 1.2. In this section, we'll review each of them in turn.

FIGURE 1.2   Cloud Service Models

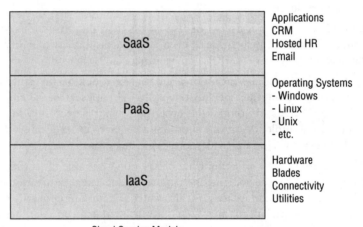

SaaS — Applications / CRM / Hosted HR / Email

PaaS — Operating Systems / - Windows / - Linux / - Unix / - etc.

IaaS — Hardware / Blades / Connectivity / Utilities

Cloud Service Models

Some vendors and consultants demonstrate a lot of zeal in capitalizing on the popularity of the "cloud" concept and incorporate the word into every term they can think of in order to make their products more appealing. We see a broad proliferation of such labels as Networking as a Service (NaaS), Compliance as a Service (CaaS), and Data Science as a Service (DSaaS), but they're mostly just marketing techniques. The only service models you'll need to know for both the exam and your use as a practitioner are IaaS, PaaS, and SaaS.

Infrastructure as a Service (IaaS)

The most basic of cloud service offerings, IaaS allows the customer to install all software, including operating systems (OSs) on hardware housed and connected by the cloud vendor.

In this model, the cloud provider has a datacenter with racks and machines and cables and utilities, and administers all these things. However, all logical resources such as software are the responsibility of the customer.

In traditional terms, we might think of this as what used to be considered a "warm site" for BC/DR purposes: the physical space exists, the connectivity exists, and it is available for the customer organization to fill with any type of baseline configuration and populate with any data the customer requires.

IaaS might be optimum for organizations that want enhanced control over the security of their data, or are looking to the cloud for a limited purpose, such as BC/DR or archiving.

Some examples of IaaS would include datacenters that offer Infrastructure as a Service, allowing clients to load whatever operating system and applications they choose. The cloud provider simply supplies the compute, storage, and networking functions.

Platform as a Service (PaaS)

PaaS contains everything included in IaaS, with the addition of OSs. The cloud vendor usually offers a selection of OSs, so that the customer can use any or all of the available choices. The vendor will be responsible for patching, administering, and updating the OS as necessary, and the customer can install any software they deem useful.

This model is especially useful for software development operations (DevOps), as the customer can test their software in an isolated environment without risk of damaging production capabilities, and determine the viability of the software across a range of OS platforms.

Some examples of PaaS include hosting providers that offer not only infrastructure but systems already loaded with a hardened operating system such as Windows Server or Linux.

Software as a Service (SaaS)

SaaS includes everything listed in the previous two models, with the addition of software programs. The cloud vendor becomes responsible for administering, patching, and updating this software as well. The cloud customer is basically only involved in uploading and processing data on a full production environment hosted by the provider.

There are many examples of SaaS configurations, ranging across a spectrum of functionality. Google Docs, Microsoft's Office 365, and QuickBooks Online are all examples of SaaS products.

Some examples of SaaS would include things like customer relationship manager (CRM) software or accounting software hosted in the cloud. The provider takes care of all the infrastructure, compute, and storage needs as well as providing the underlying operating systems and the application itself. All of this is completely transparent to the end user who only sees the application they have purchased.

Cloud Deployment Models

In addition to viewing cloud offerings in terms of what levels of service are involved, another perspective has to do with ownership. You'll be expected to know the facets of both sets of models.

Public

The public cloud is what we typically think of when discussing cloud providers. The resources (hardware, software, facilities, and staff) are owned and operated by a vendor and sold, leased, or rented to anyone (offered to the public—hence the name).

Examples of public cloud vendors include Rackspace, Microsoft's Azure, and Amazon Web Services (AWS).

Private

Private clouds are owned and operated by independent organizations, for the exclusive use of their customers and users. A private cloud can be thought of as the traditional legacy IT environment, with connections made via the web and with remote access capabilities. If your organization hosts a web server and allows access via remote services, that can be considered a private cloud instance.

Examples of private clouds include such things as what used to be called intranets. These often host shared internal applications, storage, and compute resources. One example is an internally hosted SharePoint site.

> The terms "public" and "private" can be confusing, because we might think of them in the context of who is offering them instead of who is using them. Remember: A public cloud is owned by a specific company and is offered to anyone who contracts its provided services, whereas a private cloud is owned by a specific organization but is only available to users authorized by that organization.

Community

A community cloud features infrastructure and processing owned and operated by an affinity group; disparate pieces might be owned or controlled by individuals or distinct organizations, but they come together in some fashion to perform joint tasks and functions.

Gaming communities might be considered community clouds. For instance, the PlayStation network involves many different entities coming together to engage in online gaming: Sony hosts the identity and access management (IAM) tasks for the network, a particular game company might host a set of servers that run digital rights management (DRM) functions and processing for a specific game, and individual users conduct some of their own processing and storage locally on their own PlayStations.

Hybrid

A hybrid cloud, of course, contains elements of the other models. For instance, an organization might want to retain some private cloud resources (say, their legacy production environment, which is accessed remotely by their users), but also lease some public cloud space as well (maybe a PaaS function for DevOps testing, away from the production environment so that there is much less risk of crashing systems in operation).

An example of a hybrid cloud environment might include a hosted internal cloud such as a SharePoint site with a portion carved out for external partners who need to access a shared service. To them it would appear as an external cloud; therefore, it would be operating as a hybrid.

Cloud Computing Roles and Responsibilities

Various entities are involved in cloud service arrangements:

Cloud Service Provider (CSP)   The vendor offering cloud services. The CSP will own the datacenter, employ the staff, own and manage the resources (hardware and software), monitor service provision and security, and provide administrative assistance for the customer and the customer's data and processing needs. Examples include Amazon Web Services, Rackspace, and Microsoft's Azure.

Cloud Customer   The organization purchasing, leasing, or renting cloud services.

Cloud Access Security Broker (CASB)   A third-party entity offering independent identity and access management (IAM) services to CSPs and cloud customers, often as an intermediary. This can take the form of a variety of services, including single sign-on, certificate management, and cryptographic key escrow.

Regulators   The entities that ensure organizations are in compliance with the regulatory framework for which they're responsible. These can be government agencies, certification bodies, or parties to a contract. Regulations include the Health Information Portability and Accountability Act (HIPAA), the Graham-Leach-Bliley Act (GLBA), the Payment Card Industry Data Security Standards (PCI-DSS), the International Organization for Standardization (ISO), the Sarbanes–Oxley Act (SOX), and so forth. Regulators include the Federal Trade Commission (FTC), the Securities and Exchange Commission (SEC), and auditors commissioned to review compliance with contracted or asserted standards (such as PCI-DSS and ISO), among many others.

Cloud Computing Definitions

Because cloud definitions are at the heart of understanding the following chapters and applying security fundamentals for the Certified Cloud Security Professional, we have included some of those definitions here.

Apache Cloud Stack   An open source cloud computing and IaaS platform developed to help make creating, deploying, and managing cloud services easier by providing a complete "stack" of features and components for cloud environments.

Business Requirement   An operational driver for decision making and input for risk management.

Cloud App (Cloud Application)   The phrase used to describe a software application accessed via the Internet; may include an agent or applet installed locally on the user's device.

Cloud Architect   Subject matter expert for cloud computing infrastructure and deployment.

Cloud Backup   Backing up data to a remote, cloud-based server. As a form of cloud storage, cloud backup data is stored in an accessible form from multiple distributed resources that comprise a cloud.

Cloud Computing   A type of computing, compared to grid computing, that relies on ensuring computing resources rather than having local server or personal devices to handle applications. The goal of cloud computing is to apply traditional supercomputing or high-performance computing power, normally used by military and research facilities, to perform tens of trillions of computations per second and consumer-oriented applications such as financial portfolios, or even to deliver personalized information or power immersive computer games.

Cloud Computing Reseller   A company that purchases hosting services from a cloud server hosting or computing provider and then resells them to its own customers.

Cloud Migration   The process of transitioning all or part of a company's data, applications, and services from onsite premises to the cloud, where the information can be provided over the Internet on an on-demand basis.

Cloud OS   A phrase frequently used in place of PaaS to denote an association to cloud computing.

Cloud Portability   The ability to move applications and associated data between one cloud provider and another, or between legacy and cloud environments.

Cloud Provider   A service provider that offers customer storage or software solutions available via a public network, usually the Internet. The cloud provider dictates both the technology and operational procedures involved.

Cloud Services Broker (CSB)   Typically a third-party entity or company that looks to extend or enhance value to multiple customers of cloud-based services through relationships with multiple cloud service providers. It acts as a liaison between cloud services customers and cloud service providers, selecting the best provider for each customer and monitoring the services.

Cloud Storage   The storage of data online in the cloud, wherein a company's data is stored in an accessible form from multiple distributed and connected resources that comprise a cloud.

Cloud Testing   Load and performance testing conducted on the applications and services provided by a cloud provider, particularly the capability to access the services, in order to ensure optimal performance and scalability under a wide variety of conditions.

Community Cloud A model where the cloud infrastructure is designed for use by a specific community. Generally, this is a community of users or consumers with shared concerns, missions, and/or security requirements.

Enterprise Application The term used to describe applications or software that a business would use to assist the organization in solving enterprise problems.

Eucalyptus An open source cloud computing and Infrastructure as a Service (IaaS) platform for enabling private clouds.

FIPS 140-2 A NIST document that lists accredited and outmoded cryptosystems.

Hybrid Cloud A cloud solution that mixes elements of public, private, and community cloud models.

Infrastructure as a Service (IaaS) One of three main categories of cloud computing services, alongside Software as a Service (SaaS) and Platform as a Service (PaaS). Offers only hardware and administration, leaving the customer responsible for the OS and other software.

Managed Service Provider An IT service where the customer dictates both the technology and operational procedures, and an external party executes administration and operational support according to a contract.

Multi-Tenant Multiple customers using the same public cloud (and often the same hosts, in a virtualized cloud environment).

NIST 800-53 A guidance document with the primary goal of ensuring that appropriate security requirements and controls are applied to all U.S. federal government information in information management systems.

Platform as a Service (PaaS) A way for customers to rent hardware, operating systems, storage, and network capacity over the Internet from a cloud service provider. PaaS is one of three main categories of cloud computing services, alongside Software as a Service (SaaS) and Infrastructure as a Service (IaaS).

Private Cloud The phrase used to describe a cloud computing platform that is implemented within the organization. A private cloud is designed to offer the same features and benefits of public cloud systems but removes a number of objections to the cloud computing model, including control over enterprise or customer data, worries about security, and issues connected to regulatory compliance or contractual agreements.

Software as a Service (SaaS) SaaS is a software delivery method that provides access to software and its functionality remotely as a web-based service. Software as a Service allows organizations to access business functionality at a cost typically less than paying for licensed application because SaaS pricing is based on a monthly fee. SaaS is one of three main categories of cloud computing services, alongside Platform as a Service (PaaS) and Infrastructure as a Service (IaaS).

Trusted Cloud Initiative (TCI) Reference Model The TCI reference model is a guide for cloud providers, allowing them to create a holistic architecture (including the physical facility of the datacenter, the logical layout of the network, and the processes necessary to utilize both) that cloud customers can purchase and use with comfort and confidence. For more information, visit https://cloudsecurityalliance.org/wp-content/uploads/2011/10/TCI-Reference-Architecture-v1.1.pdf.

Vendor Lock-in   Vendor lock-in occurs in a situation where a customer may be unable to leave, migrate, or transfer to an alternate provider due to technical or nontechnical constraints.

Vendor Lock-out   Vendor lock-out occurs when a customer is unable to recover or access their own data due to the cloud provider going into bankruptcy or otherwise leaving the market.

Virtualization   Creating a virtual (a logical vs. a physical) version of something, including virtual computer hardware platforms, operating systems, storage devices, and computer network resources. Computer hardware virtualization is a way of improving overall efficiency. It involves CPUs that provide support for virtualization in hardware, and other hardware components that help improve the performance of a guest environment.

The successful CCSP candidate will be familiar with each of these terms. We will go into more detail regarding these terms over the course of the book.

Back to Basics

It's also important to remember all the security fundamentals used throughout the industry. For instance, the familiar CIA triad will be mentioned extensively throughout the CBK, the exam, and this book.

- **Confidentiality:** Protecting information from unauthorized access/dissemination

- **Integrity:** Ensuring that information is not subject to unauthorized modification

- **Availability:** Ensuring that authorized users can access the information when they are permitted to do so

---

Foundational Concepts of Cloud Computing

There are some aspects of cloud computing that are pervasive throughout all discussion of the topic. We're introducing them here, and you should become familiar with them. These concepts will be included in various discussions throughout the book.

Sensitive Data

Each organization will have its own risk appetite and desire for confidentiality. No matter how each cloud customer makes their own determination for these aspects of their data, the cloud provider must offer some way for the customer to categorize data according to its sensitivity, and sufficient controls to ensure these categories are protected accordingly.

Virtualization

Virtualization is one of the technologies that has made cloud services a financially viable business model. Cloud providers can purchase and deploy a sufficient number of hosts for a respective number of customers and users without wasting capacity or letting resources go idle.

In a virtualized environment, a cloud user can log onto the cloud network and boot up a synthetic version of a desktop computer. To the user, there is no appreciable difference between the virtual machine (VM) and a traditional computer. However, from the provider's perspective, the VM being offered to the user is just a piece of software, not an actual, dedicated piece of hardware being exclusively operated by the user. Indeed, there may be several, or even dozens, of VMs operating on a single host in the cloud space concurrently. When the user logs off or shuts down, the cloud network takes a snapshot of the user's VM, capturing it as a single file that can be stored somewhere else in the cloud until the user next requests access, when the VM can be restored exactly as they left it.

In this way, the cloud provider can offer services to any number of customers and users, and not be required to purchase a new hardware device for each new user. This economy of scale allows the cloud provider to offer the same basic IT services that the users expect from traditional networks with much less cost and at an enhanced level of service.

There are many virtualization product vendors, including VMware and Microsoft. There are also a variety of implementation strategies, and two fundamental virtualization types (Type 1 and Type 2).

Encryption

As an IT security professional, you should already be familiar with the basic concepts and tools of encryption. However, in terms of cloud services, encryption plays an enhanced role and presents some additional challenges.

Because your cloud data will be in an environment controlled and operated by personnel other than your organization, encryption offers a degree of assurance that nobody without authorization will be able to access your data in a meaningful way. You can encrypt your data before it reaches the cloud, and only decrypt it as necessary.

Another concern related to cloud operation is that it necessitates remote access. As with any remote access, there will always be a risk (however great or slight) of interception of data, eavesdropping, and man-in-the-middle attacks. Encryption also assists in alleviating this concern by mitigating this threat to some degree; if data in motion is encrypted, it is that much more difficult to access even if it is intercepted.

Auditing and Compliance

Cloud services pose specific challenges and opportunities for regulatory compliance and auditing.

From a compliance perspective, service providers may be able to offer holistic solutions for organizations under particular regulatory schema. For instance, the cloud provider may have an extant, known, tested control set and procedural outline for PCI, HIPAA, or GLBA. This could be extremely appealing to potential customers, as the difficulty and effort expended in trying to stay compliant can now be shifted out of the customer organization and over to the provider.

Conversely, auditing becomes more difficult. Cloud providers are extremely reluctant to allow physical access to their facilities or to share network diagrams and lists of controls; maintaining confidentiality of these things enhances the provider's overall security. However, these are essential elements of an audit. Also, as you'll see in upcoming chapters, it is difficult to determine exactly where in the cloud environment a given organization's data is located at any moment, or which devices contain a certain customer's data, making auditing even more difficult. Audits will require the cooperation of the cloud provider, and providers have thus far disallowed the requisite level of access for the purpose. Instead, cloud providers often offer an assertion of their own audit success (often in the form of a Statement on Standards for Attestation Engagements and Service Organization Controls Type 3 report). Any organization considering cloud migration should confer with the regulatory agencies that provide oversight for them in order to determine whether this limited audit insight will be sufficient for the regulators.

Cloud Service Provider Contracts

The business arrangement between the cloud provider and the cloud customer will usually take the form of a contract and a service-level agreement (SLA). The contract will spell out all the terms of the agreement: what each party is responsible for, what form the services will take, how issues will be resolved, and so on. The SLA will set specific, quantified goals for these services and their provision over a certain timeframe.

For instance, the contract might stipulate "The Provider will ensure the Customer has constant, uninterrupted access to the Customer's data storage resources." The SLA will then explicitly define the metrics for what "constant, uninterrupted access" will mean: "There will be no interruption of connectivity to data storage longer than three (3) seconds per calendar month." The contract will also state what the penalties are (usually financial) when the cloud provider fails to meet the SLA for a given period: "Customer's monthly fee will be waived for any period following a calendar month in which any service level has not been attained by Provider."

These are obviously rough examples, but they demonstrate the relationship between the contract, the SLA, the cloud provider, and the cloud customer. The book will continually refer to the contract and the SLA based on the relationship explained here.

Summary

In this chapter, we have explored business requirements, cloud definitions, cloud computing roles and responsibilities, and foundational concepts of cloud computing. As this is the introductory chapter, we will explore each of these topics in more detail as we move ahead.

Exam Essentials

Understand business requirements.   Always bear in mind that all management decisions are driven by business needs, including security and risk decisions. Security and risk should be considered before these decisions are made, and may not take precedence over the business and operational requirements of the organization.

Understand cloud vernacular and definitions.   Make sure you have a clear understanding of the definitions introduced in Chapter 1. A great deal of the CCSP exam focuses on terms and definitions.

Be able to describe the cloud service models.   It is vitally important that you understand the differences between the three cloud service models, IaaS, PaaS, and SaaS, and the different features associated with each.

Understand cloud deployment models.   It is also important for you to understand the features of each of the four cloud deployment models, Public, Private, Community, and Hybrid, as well as their differences.

Be familiar with cloud computing roles and the associated responsibilities.   Make sure you know and understand the different roles and the responsibilities of each of the roles. We will explore roles in more detail in the chapters that follow.

Written Labs

1. Go to the CSA website and watch the video titled "Intro to Cloud Computing" at https://cloudsecurityalliance.org/education/white-papers-and-educational-material/courseware/. When you are done, spend some time exploring the site.

2. Write down three things you can think of that might be legitimate business drivers for an organization considering cloud migration.

3. List the three cloud computing service models and the advantages and disadvantages of each.

Review Questions

You can find the answers in Appendix A.

1. Which of the following is *not* a common cloud service model?
   A. Software as a Service
   B. Programming as a Service
   C. Infrastructure as a Service
   D. Platform as a Service

2. All of these technologies have made cloud service viable except:
   A. Virtualization
   B. Widely available broadband
   C. Cryptographic connectivity
   D. Smart hubs

3. Cloud vendors are held to contractual obligations with specified metrics by:
   A. SLAs
   B. Regulations
   C. Law
   D. Discipline

4. _____ drive security decisions.
   A. Customer service responses
   B. Surveys
   C. Business requirements
   D. Public opinion

5. If a cloud customer cannot get access to the cloud provider, this affects what portion of the CIA triad?
   A. Integrity
   B. Authentication
   C. Confidentiality
   D. Availability

6. Cloud Access Security Brokers (CASBs) might offer all the following services EXCEPT:
   A. Single sign-on
   B. BC/DR/COOP
   C. IAM
   D. Key escrow

7. Encryption can be used in various aspects of cloud computing, including all of these except:

   A. Storage

   B. Remote access

   C. Secure sessions

   D. Magnetic swipe cards

8. All of these are reasons an organization may want to consider cloud migration except:

   A. Reduced personnel costs

   B. Elimination of risks

   C. Reduced operational expenses

   D. Increased efficiency

9. The generally accepted definition of cloud computing includes all of the following characteristics except:

   A. On-demand services

   B. Negating the need for backups

   C. Resource pooling

   D. Measured or metered service

10. All of the following can result in vendor lock-in except:

   A. Unfavorable contract

   B. Statutory compliance

   C. Proprietary data formats

   D. Insufficient bandwidth

11. The risk that a cloud provider might go out of business and the cloud customer might not be able to recover data is known as:

   A. Vendor closure

   B. Vendor lock-out

   C. Vendor lock-in

   D. Vending route

12. All of these are features of cloud computing except:

   A. Broad network access

   B. Reversed charging configuration

   C. Rapid scaling

   D. On-demand self-service

13. When a cloud customer uploads PII to a cloud provider, who becomes ultimately responsible for the security of that PII?

    A. Cloud provider

    B. Regulators

    C. Cloud customer

    D. The individuals who are the subjects of the PII

14. We use which of the following to determine the critical paths, processes, and assets of an organization?

    A. Business requirements

    B. BIA

    C. RMF

    D. CIA triad

15. The cloud deployment model that features organizational ownership of the hardware and infrastructure, and usage only by members of that organization, is known as:

    A. Private

    B. Public

    C. Hybrid

    D. Motive

16. The cloud deployment model that features ownership by a cloud provider, with services offered to anyone who wants to subscribe, is known as:

    A. Private

    B. Public

    C. Hybrid

    D. Latent

17. The cloud deployment model that features joint ownership of assets among an affinity group is known as:

    A. Private

    B. Public

    C. Hybrid

    D. Community

18. If a cloud customer wants a secure, isolated sandbox in order to conduct software development and testing, which cloud service model would probably be best?

    A. IaaS

    B. PaaS

    C. SaaS

    D. Hybrid

19. If a cloud customer wants a fully-operational environment with very little maintenance or administration necessary, which cloud service model would probably be best?

   A. IaaS

   B. PaaS

   C. SaaS

   D. Hybrid

20. If a cloud customer wants a bare-bones environment in which to replicate their own enterprise for BC/DR purposes, which cloud service model would probably be best?

   A. IaaS

   B. PaaS

   C. SaaS

   D. Hybrid

Chapter

2

Design Requirements

THE OBJECTIVE OF THIS CHAPTER IS TO ACQUAINT THE READER WITH THE FOLLOWING CONCEPTS:

✓ **Domain 1: Architectural Concepts and Design Requirements**

■ D. Understand Design Principles of Secure Cloud Computing

■ D.4 Functional Security Requirements

✓ **Domain 2: Cloud Data Security**

■ C. Design and Apply Data Security Strategies

■ C.1 Encryption

■ C.6 Emerging Technologies

✓ **Domain 3: Cloud Platform and Infrastructure Security**

■ B. Analyze Risks Associated To Cloud Infrastructure

■ B.1 Risk Assessment/Analysis

■ D. Plan Disaster Recovery and Business Continuity Management

■ D.1 Understanding of the Cloud Environment

■ D.2 Understanding of the Business Requirements

■ D.3 Understanding of the Risks

We mentioned the asset inventory and BIA in Chapter 1, "Architectural Concepts." It bears repeating: security decisions are driven by business requirements. This is neither new nor unique to the cloud—it's the manner in which security should always be provided. In this chapter, we will discuss many of the inputs for those security decisions, and the business activities we undertake to determine the requirements.

Business Requirements Analysis

Security does not happen in stasis; we need information in order to conduct security activities in a proper and efficient manner. There are certain things we need to know in order to decide how we will handle risks within our organization. These include the following:

- An inventory of all assets
- A valuation of each asset
- A determination of critical paths, processes, and assets
- A clear understanding of risk appetite

Inventory of Assets

To protect our assets, we first have to know what they are. Everything owned or controlled by the organization can be considered an asset, and assets take many different forms. Assets can be tangible items, such as IT hardware, retail inventory, buildings, and vehicles. Assets can also be intangible, such as intellectual property, public perception, and goodwill with business partners and vendors. Personnel can also be considered assets, because of the skills, training, and productivity they provide to the organization.

In order to protect all our assets, we have to know what they are and, to a lesser extent, where they are and what they do. If we lose track of something under our control, it becomes impossible to secure it.

Therefore, the first step in creating a sound security program would be to perform a thorough, comprehensive inventory. There are many methods and tools for doing so, such as surveys, interviews, audits, and so forth. In performing an IT inventory, we can also incorporate automation into the process, enhancing our capabilities and efficiency.

Valuation of Assets

While we are ascertaining the number, location, and type of assets, we also want to determine the value of each. We need to be able to know which of the assets provide the intrinsic value of our organization, and which support this value.

We need to know the value of the assets we protect, so we know how much time, money, and effort to expend to protect them. We do not put a $10 lock on a $5 bicycle.

This is a process known as the business impact analysis (BIA). We determine a value for every asset (usually in terms of dollars), what it would cost the organization if we lost that asset (either temporarily or permanently), what it would cost to replace or repair that asset, and any alternate methods for dealing with that loss.

There are various ways to assign cost: we can use the insured value, the replacement cost, or some other method of making that valuation. Usually, we allow the data owners—that is, the individual line-of-business managers responsible for their respective data—to determine the value of the information under their control.

Usually, the data owner for a given data set is the business manager in charge of that data. This is generally the head of the department that collected or created that data.

There are some risks associated with letting the data owners assign value to their assets. The most significant of these is the tendency of data owners to overvalue assets that belong to them. Ask anyone in the organization which department is the most important, and they will say that it is theirs.

The data owner is also tasked with assigning a category and/or classification to their data, usually when it is created. We will discuss this in Chapter 3, "Data Classification."

Determination of Criticality

Once the inventory and valuation is complete, the BIA effort continues with a determination made by senior management regarding criticality. Criticality denotes those aspects of the organization without which the organization could not operate or exist. These could include tangible assets, intangible assets, specific business processes, data pathways, or even key personnel.

Real World Scenario

Criticality Examples

Here are some examples of critical aspects in organizations:

- Tangible assets: The organization is a rental car company; cars are critical to its operations—if it has no cars to rent to customers, it can't do business.

- Intangible assets: The organization is a music production firm; music is the intellectual property of the company—if the ownership of the music is compromised (for instance, if the copyright is challenged and the company loses ownership, or the encryption protecting the music files is removed and the music can be copied without protection), the company has nothing of value and will not survive.

- Processes: The organization is a fast-food restaurant noted for its speed; the process of taking orders, preparing and delivering food, and taking payment is critical to its operations—if the restaurant cannot complete the process for some reason (for instance, the registers fail so that the restaurant cannot accept payment), the restaurant cannot function.

- Data paths: The organization is an international shipping line; matching orders to cargo carriers is critical to its operations. If the company cannot complete its logistical coordination—assigning cargo requests to carriers with sufficient capacity—it cannot provide its services, and will not survive.

- Personnel: The organization is a surgical provider; the surgeon is critical to the existence of the company—if the surgeon cannot operate, there is no company.

Senior management has the correct perspective for making determinations of criticality. The security professional, however, should have a good understanding of the overall mission and function of the organization, in order to better serve and advise the organization in securing critical elements.

Another function of the BIA process that can support the security effort is the identification of single points of failure (SPOFs). If there is any chokepoint in a process, procedure, or production chain—a place where an entire workflow would halt because of the loss of a single element—that's a SPOF. SPOFs, especially in critical paths, pose a significant risk to the organization and ought be addressed as soon as they are identified. Like critical aspects, SPOFs can be caused by hardware, software, processes, or personnel.

Methods for dealing with SPOFs include the following:

- Adding redundancies so that if the SPOF goes out of service, a replacement is immediately available

- Creating alternative processes to take the place of SPOFs in times of outage

- Cross-training personnel so that they can fill many roles
- Consistently and thoroughly backing up data in a manner from which it can be easily and quickly restored
- Load sharing/balancing for the IT assets

In a cloud environment, customers should expect that the provider has no SPOFs within their facilities and architecture; part of the benefit of moving to the cloud is the ability of cloud providers to offer a robust and resilient service that is not susceptible to failures due to SPOFs. The customer can therefore focus on attenuating any SPOFs on their own side of the operation: accessing and using the data in the cloud.

Don't get confused: not all SPOFs are part of critical aspects, and not all critical aspects of an organization contain SPOFs.

Risk Appetite

Again, this is not a new concept, and the use of cloud services does not significantly change anything about it. It bears mentioning here because of the importance of the concept to the overall practice of security, and its inclusion in the CCSP Common Body of Knowledge (CBK).

Risk appetite is the level, amount, or type of risk that the organization finds acceptable. This varies wildly from organization to organization, based on innumerable factors both internal and external, and can change over time.

Here's a quick review of some risk fundamentals:

- Risk is the likelihood an impact will be realized.
- Risk can be reduced but never eliminated.
- Organizations accept a level of risk that allows operations to continue in a successful manner.
- It is legal and defensible to accept risks higher than the norm, or greater than your competitors, except risks to health and human safety; these risks *must* be addressed to the industry standard or whatever regulatory motif to which your organization adheres.

 Real World Scenario

Health and Human Safety Risks

An organization cannot accept risks to health and human safety that are beyond industry standards and known best practices; to do so would be unethical, and it would expose the organization to a great deal of liability (which creates its own risk, which must also be considered). There are a few exceptions to this rule; the military is one example, where loss of life and limb are an expected outcome from operations and an acceptable risk.

However, individuals can accept such risks on their own behalf. For instance, commercial fishing has consistently been among the professions with the highest fatality rates in the United States for the past 100 years (in terms of number of hours worked per death), yet there is no shortage of people willing to engage in that industry. For the individual workers, the level of risk is both known and acceptable. From an organizational perspective, however, the relatively high possibility of fatal accidents does not obviate the need for ensuring adherence to industry best practices (perhaps life vests, tether lines, and so forth), and does not remove all liability.

Organizations have four main ways to address risk:

Avoidance   This isn't really a method for handling risk; it means leaving a business opportunity because the risk is simply too high and cannot be compensated for with adequate control mechanisms—a risk that exceeds the organization's appetite.

Acceptance   The opposite of avoidance; the risk falls within the organization's risk appetite, so the organization continues operations without any additional efforts regarding the risk.

Transference   The organization pays someone else to accept the risk, at a lower cost than the potential impact that would result from the risk being realized; this is usually in the form of insurance. This type of risk is often associated with things that have a low probability of occurring but a high impact should they occur.

Mitigation   The organization takes steps to decrease the likelihood or the impact of the risk (and often both); this can take the form of controls/countermeasures, and is usually where security practitioners are involved.

Risk is involved in every activity. We can manage risk, attenuate it, even minimize it, but there is always an element of risk in operations. When we choose to mitigate risk by applying countermeasures and controls, the remaining, leftover risk is called *residual risk*. The task of the security program is to reduce residual risk until it falls within the acceptable level of risk according to the organization's risk appetite.

The risk appetite of an organization is set by senior management, and is the guide for all risk-management activities in the organization. The security practitioner must have a thorough understanding of the risk appetite of the organization in order to perform their functions properly and efficiently.

Once the business requirements have been determined, and the BIA has been completed, the information acquired can and should be reused throughout many of the organization's security-related efforts. For instance, the BIA results can be utilized in the risk assessment, the selection of specific security controls throughout the environment, and the Business Continuity/Disaster Recovery plan(s) (BC/DR); knowing the critical aspects of the organization and the values of all assets is essential to accomplishing these tasks.

Boundaries of Cloud Models

In legacy environments, we had bright-line definitions of the organization's IT perimeter: everything inside the perimeter belonged to the organization, including data, hardware, and risk; everything outside was someone else's problem. We could even point at a specific location, a given cable leaving the facility or campus, and know that it, there, was the place where our control ended and someone else's began. We could armor our defenses at the interface between the internal environment and external factors, building up a demilitarized zone (DMZ).

This is not readily the case with cloud computing. In the cloud motif, our data resides inside an IT environment owned by someone else, riding on a hardware infrastructure that does not belong to us, and largely outside our control. Our users operate programs and machines that we have limited access to and knowledge of. It is therefore difficult to know exactly where the boundaries exist in cloud models, where our risks are, and how far they extend.

In this section, we'll apply a notional perspective of cloud computing boundaries. But it is extremely important to remember this: under the current legal and regulatory regime, the cloud customer **is always ultimately legally liable for any loss of data**. This is true even if the cloud provider demonstrates negligence or malice.

WARNING
The cloud customer can seek restitution if the cloud provider fails in some way, causing damage to the customer. For instance, if the cloud provider hires an administrator who then illegally sells access to data belonging to the cloud customer, the customer can sue the provider for damages. *However, the cloud customer is still legally responsible for all mandates applicable to the loss, such as complying with data breach notification laws in that jurisdiction.* This requirement does not cease just because the cloud customer has outsourced operations to the cloud provider.

So what do these boundaries look like, in the different cloud models?

IaaS Boundaries

In Infrastructure as a Service (IaaS), the cloud customer has the most responsibility and authority of all the possible cloud models. The provider is responsible for the buildings and land that compose the datacenter; must provide connectivity and power; and creates and administers the hardware assets the customer's programs and data will ride on. The customer, however, is in charge of everything from the operating system and up; all software will be installed and administered by the customer, and the customer will supply and manage all the data.

In terms of security, the cloud customer is still losing some of the control featured in the legacy environment. For instance, the customer obviously does not get to select the specific IT assets, so the security of the acquisition process (during which we normally vet vendors and suppliers) must be entrusted to the cloud provider. The cloud customer may also lose some ability to monitor network traffic inside the datacenter—the cloud provider might not be willing to allow the customer to place monitoring equipment or sensors on the provider's infrastructure, and also might refuse to share traffic data they, the provider, have collected themselves.

This makes auditing difficult, which also affects security policy and regulatory compliance. An organization migrating to the cloud will necessarily have to drastically adapt its security policy to reflect the new constraints, and will have to find some way to provide the requisite deliverables to appease regulators. This must be negotiated at the outset of migration, and early communication with regulators is highly advisable. For instance, if regulators insist on scheduled audits of the environment where data processing takes place, what form will those audits take, if the organization cannot now directly audit network traffic and event logs?

In IaaS, though, the cloud customer may still collect and review event logs from the software, including the OS, which still lends a great deal of insight into the usage and security of the data.

PaaS Boundaries

With Platform as a Service (PaaS), the cloud customer loses still more control of the environment, because the cloud provider is now responsible for installing, maintaining, and administering the OS(s). This will entail further modification of the security policy and additional efforts to ensure regulatory compliance.

The cloud customer still, however, gets to monitor and review software events, since the programs running on the OS will belong to the customer. The responsibilities for updating and maintaining the software will also be the customer's. However, updates and administration of the OS now fall to the provider, which, while posing a loss of control for operational and security purposes on the customer's part, will also represent a cost savings and increase of efficiency.

SaaS Boundaries

With Software as a Service (SaaS), of course, most of the control of the environment is ceded to the provider. The cloud customer will not have ownership of the hardware, the software, or the administration of either; the customer only supplies and processes data to and in the system.

For all relevant intents and purposes, the cloud customer, as an organization, has taken the role and responsibilities of what a common user would have in a legacy environment: few administrative rights, few privileged accounts, and very few permissions and responsibilities.

To repeat what we've mentioned earlier: the customer remains liable for all statutory and contractual obligations related to the safeguarding of the data but, in this case, has little control over how that data is protected. The cloud provider is now almost exclusively responsible for all system maintenance, all security countermeasures, and the vast majority of policy (and implementation of that policy) affecting the data.

In all three models, the customer is giving up an essential form of control: physical access to the devices on which the data resides. This is a massive and serious increase of risk and loss of assurance; anyone who can physically access the location of the data can eventually take it, with or without permission.

Can we implement means to reduce the likelihood of breaches as a result of this risk? Of course—and we need to do so, in order to demonstrate due diligence. Such measures might include ensuring the cloud provider performs strict background checks and continual monitoring of all personnel with access to the datacenter, extreme physical security measures at the datacenter location, encryption of data processed and stored in the cloud, assignment of contractual liability to the provider (bearing in mind that legal liability remains with the customer, however), and so forth. It is important to remember, though, that the residual risk of loss of data to physical access will always remain, even if attenuated. We will cover these at length in the next section.

Figure 2.1 shows a notional visual depiction of the areas of responsibilities and authority, and how they relate and blend, in the various cloud models, derived from Cloud Security Alliance material. It is worth noting that there are no defined mandates or detailed uniformity ubiquitous throughout the industry; each provider will be different, and each contract will be different, so each set of rights and responsibilities will vary according to what the customer and provider negotiate.

FIGURE 2.1   Defense-in-depth layers

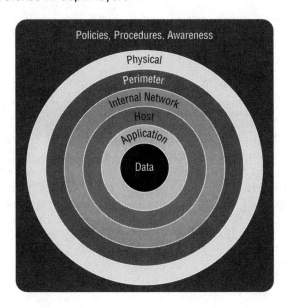

Design Principles for Protecting Sensitive Data

The following section reviews some basic secure architectural methods. Bear in mind that this is not an exhaustive list, and these techniques alone will not suffice to protect an organization and its data, but they can serve as a guideline for IT infrastructure controls.

Hardening Devices

In the legacy environment, devices in the DMZ (that notional area where the internal network connects with the outside world) were secured as a matter of practice; we knew and understood that these boxes were more likely to suffer intrusion attempts, and we hardened them accordingly.

For the cloud environment, it is probably best to adhere to this same practice, both from the cloud provider side of the equation and as cloud users. In treating all cloud-related devices as if they are in the DMZ, we are forming good habits and a conceptual way of viewing the cloud.

The cloud provider should ensure that all devices in the datacenter are secured such that

- All guest accounts are removed
- All unused ports are closed
- No default passwords remain
- Strong password policies are in effect
- Any admin accounts are significantly secured and logged
- All unnecessary services are disabled
- Physical access is severely limited and controlled
- Systems are patched, maintained, and updated according to vendor guidance and industry best practices

These concepts should not be in any way new to security practitioners, but they continue to have a significant value in the cloud motif.

The cloud customer has a similar and related, but different, list of tasks. Customers must bear in mind the risks related to the way they access the cloud, which often takes the form of a BYOD (bring-your-own-device) environment and always involves remote access. BYOD existed before the current ubiquity of cloud computing, and many of those known security practices can be employed to good effect in our current models.

For instance, cloud customers should ensure that all assets in their BYOD infrastructure that access the cloud should

- Be protected with some form of antimalware/security software

- Have remote wipe/remote lock capability in the event of loss/theft, with the user granting written permission to the organization to wipe/lock via a signed authorized use policy

- Utilize some form of local encryption

- Be secured with strong access controls (a password, or perhaps a biometric) in a multi-factor configuration

- Have and properly employ VPN solutions for cloud access

- Have some sort of data loss, leak prevention, and protection (DLP) solution installed

The organization may also want to consider containerization software options for personally owned user devices as a means to isolate their personal data from the organization's information.

 It's not only physical devices that need to be hardened—we have to think of virtual devices in the same manner we'd consider their physical counterparts. Because cloud computing relies so heavily on virtualization for load balancing and scalability, it is important to remember that virtual instances will require strong protection both when active (so that data being processed can't be detected by other instances/users) and while stored (as files, because they contain so much material attackers would like to acquire, and they are so portable). In terms of configuration, they also have to be hardened in all the same ways we secure physical machines.

Encryption

We've mentioned encryption already, and you can expect to see more references throughout the book; it's impossible to divest modern security practices from various uses of encryption. This is as true in the cloud as it was in the legacy environment.

We will cover cloud data security, and the associated encryption mechanisms, in an upcoming chapter. For the purposes of this specific discussion (basic cloud design requirements), suffice it to say that encryption should be utilized:

- In the cloud datacenter, for

  - Long-term storage/archiving

  - Protecting near-term stored files, such as snapshots of virtualized instances

  - Preventing unauthorized access to specific datasets by authorized personnel (for instance, securing fields in databases so that database admins can manage software but not modify/view content)

- In communications between cloud providers and users, for

  - Creating secure sessions

  - Ensuring the integrity and confidentiality of data in transit

Eventually, we'd like to be able to process data in the cloud while it's encrypted, without having to decrypt it, so that it is never exposed, even temporarily, to anyone other than the authorized user(s). Although this capability is not currently available, ongoing research shows promise. This technology is known as *homomorphic encryption*, and it's worth knowing the term and understanding the possibility, even though it's still in the experimental stages.

Layered Defenses

This again is not a new concept, but one that carries over into the cloud. Also referred to as "defense-in-depth," it is the practice of having multiple overlapping means of securing the environment with a variety of methods. These should include a blend of administrative, logical, technical, and physical controls.

From a cloud provider perspective, a layered defense should entail

- Strong personnel controls, involving background checks and continual monitoring
- Technological controls such as encryption, event logging, and access control enforcement
- Physical controls related to both the overall campus, the various facilities, the areas within the datacenter where data is processed and stored, individual racks and particular devices, and portable media entering and leaving the campus
- Governance mechanisms and enforcement, such as strong policies and regular, thorough audits

From a cloud customer perspective, similar efforts should include

- Training programs for staff and users that include good coverage of security topics
- Contractual enforcement of policy requirements
- Use of encryption and logical isolation mechanisms on BYOD assets, as mentioned earlier in this chapter
- Strong access control methods, perhaps including multifactor authentication

When considering secure architectures and designs, it is often helpful to refer to existing guidance; there is no reason to rediscover and reinvent every aspect of security for yourself when many publications and tools already exist. Some you might find useful:

- The Cloud Security Alliance Cloud Controls Matrix (https://cloudsecurityalliance.org/group/cloud-controls-matrix/)

- The National Institute of Standards and Technology (NIST)'s Risk Management Framework (SP 800-37) (http://nvlpubs.nist.gov/nistpubs/SpecialPublications/NIST.SP.800-37r1.pdf)

- ISACA's ITIL

Summary

In this chapter, we have gone into some depth in discussing how an organization determines its business requirements and critical paths, and what that information is used for, in terms of security. We also covered the nominal boundaries of the various cloud service models, and the rights and responsibilities related to each, from both the customer and provider perspectives. In addition, we touched on basic cloud architectural and design concepts for protecting sensitive data. In upcoming chapters, we will explore the latter topic in more detail.

Exam Essentials

Know how to determine business requirements.   Understand the function and purpose of the business impact analysis, and how it enables the organization to ascertain the inventory, value, and criticality of organizational assets.

Be familiar with the boundaries of each of the cloud service models.   Know which models assign typical control and dependence to the parties involved in a cloud service relationship. Realize that there is a significant amount of room to negotiate contractual definitions of the responsibilities and rights of both the cloud provider and cloud customer for all of the models.

Understand how cloud architecture and design supports sensitive data security.   Be familiar with how hardening devices, encryption, and defense in depth enhances the protection of data in the cloud. Know where to find frameworks, models, and guidance for secure cloud design.

Written Labs

1. Download FEMA's Business Impact Analysis Worksheet at `https://www.fema`
   `.gov/media-library-data/1388776348838-b548b013b1cfc61fa92fc4332b615e05/`
   `Business_ImpactAnalysis_Worksheet_2014.pdf`.

2. Choose a department/function within your organization to use for this exercise; it can be anything you want, whether or not it has to do with IT provision or cloud computing.

3. Choose a hypothetical risk/threat to use in the exercise; this might be a natural disaster, or it could be an attack by malicious actors, or anything else you prefer.

4. Fill out the form using the business function and risk/threat, using information as accurately and realistically as possible.

Review Questions

You can find the answers in Appendix A.

1. Gathering business requirements can aid the organization in determining all of this information about organizational assets, except:
   A. Full inventory
   B. Usefulness
   C. Value
   D. Criticality

2. The BIA can be used to provide information about all the following, except:
   A. Risk analysis
   B. Secure acquisition
   C. BC/DR planning
   D. Selection of security controls

3. In which cloud service model is the customer required to maintain the OS?
   A. CaaS
   B. SaaS
   C. PaaS
   D. IaaS

4. In which cloud service model is the customer required to maintain and update only the applications?
   A. CaaS
   B. SaaS
   C. PaaS
   D. IaaS

5. In which cloud service model is the customer only responsible for the data?
   A. CaaS
   B. SaaS
   C. PaaS
   D. IaaS

6. The cloud customer and provider negotiate their respective responsibilities and rights regarding the capabilities and data of the cloud service. Where is the eventual agreement codified?
   A. RMF
   B. Contract

   C. MOU

   D. BIA

7. In attempting to provide a layered defense, the security practitioner should convince senior management to include security controls of which type?

   A. Technological

   B. Physical

   C. Administrative

   D. All of the above

8. Which of the following is considered an administrative control?

   A. Access control process

   B. Keystroke logging

   C. Door locks

   D. Biometric authentication

9. Which of the following is considered a technological control?

   A. Firewall software

   B. Fireproof safe

   C. Fire extinguisher

   D. Firing personnel

10. Which of the following is considered a physical control?

   A. Carpets

   B. Ceilings

   C. Doors

   D. Fences

11. In a cloud environment, encryption should be used for all the following, except:

   A. Long-term storage of data

   B. Near-term storage of virtualized images

   C. Secure sessions/VPN

   D. Profile formatting

12. The process of hardening a device should include all the following, except:

   A. Improve default accounts

   B. Close unused ports

   C. Delete unnecessary services

   D. Strictly control administrator access

13. The process of hardening a device should include which of the following?

   A. Encrypting the OS

   B. Updating and patching the system

   C. Using video cameras

   D. Performing thorough personnel background checks

14. What is an experimental technology that is intended to create the possibility of processing encrypted data without having to decrypt it first?

   A. Homomorphic

   B. Polyinstantiation

   C. Quantum-state

   D. Gastronomic

15. Risk appetite for an organization is determined by which of the following?

   A. Appetite evaluation

   B. Senior management

   C. Legislative mandates

   D. Contractual agreement

16. What is the risk left over after controls and countermeasures are put in place?

   A. Null

   B. High

   C. Residual

   D. Pertinent

17. All the following are ways of addressing risk, except:

   A. Acceptance

   B. Reversal

   C. Mitigation

   D. Transfer

18. To protect data on user devices in a BYOD environment, the organization should consider requiring all the following, except:

   A. DLP agents

   B. Local encryption

   C. Multifactor authentication

   D. Two-person integrity

19. Devices in the cloud datacenter should be secure against attack. All the following are means of hardening devices, except:

   A. Using a strong password policy

   B. Removing default passwords

    C. Strictly limiting physical access

    D. Removing all admin accounts

20. Which of the following best describes risk?

    A. Preventable

    B. Everlasting

    C. The likelihood that a threat will exploit a vulnerability

    D. Transient

Chapter

3

Data Classification

THE OBJECTIVE OF THIS CHAPTER IS TO ACQUAINT THE READER WITH THE FOLLOWING CONCEPTS:

✓ **Domain 1: Architectural Concepts and Design Requirements**

- C. Understand Security Concepts Relevant to Cloud Computing
  - C.3 Data and Media Sanitization
- D. Understand Design Principles of Secure Cloud Computing
  - D.1 Cloud Secure Data Lifecycle

✓ **Domain 2: Cloud Data Security**

- A. Understand Cloud Data Lifecycle
  - A.1 Phases
  - A.2 Relevant Data Security Technologies
- D. Understand and Implement Data Discovery and Classification Technologies
  - D.1 Data Discovery
  - D.2 Classification
- E. Design and Implement Relevant Jurisdictional Data Protections for Personally Identifiable Information (PII)
  - E.2 Implementation of Data Discovery
  - E.3 Classification of Discovered Sensitive Data
- F. Design and Implement Data Rights Management
  - F.1 Data Rights Objectives
  - F.2 Appropriate Tools
- G. Plan and Implement Data Retention, Deletion, and Archiving Policies
  - G.1 Data Retention Policies
  - G.2 Data Deletion Procedures and Mechanisms
  - G.3 Data Archiving Procedures and Mechanisms

- ■ H. Design and Implement Auditability, Traceability, and Accountability of Data Events
  - ■ H2. Data event logging
  - ■ H.3 Storage and Analysis of Data Events
  - ■ H.4 Continuous Optimizations

✓ **Domain 3: Cloud Platform and Infrastructure Security**

- ■ C. Design and Plan Security Controls
  - ■ C.5 Audit Mechanisms

✓ **Domain 5: Operations**

- ■ D. Manage Physical Infrastructure for Cloud Environment
  - ■ D.8 Log Capture and Analysis
- ■ G. Manage Logical Infrastructure for Cloud Environment
  - ■ G.7 Log Capture and Analysis

✓ **Domain 6: Legal and Compliance**

- ■ A. Understand Legal Requirements and Unique Risks within the Cloud Environment
  - ■ A.3 Legal Controls
  - ■ A.4 eDiscovery
- ■ C. Understand Audit Process, Methodologies, and Required Adaptions for a Cloud Environment
  - ■ C.1 Internal and External Audit Controls
  - ■ C.3 Assurance Challenges of Virtualization and Cloud
  - ■ C.7 Audit Plan
- ■ D. Understand Implications of Cloud to Enterprise Risk Management
  - ■ D.1 Assess Providers Risk Management

As with all other assets, knowing what data you have, as well as its relative value and need for protection, is absolutely essential for properly apportioning security resources. In this chapter, we will discuss how data is categorized and classified, why the location of the data matters, intellectual property concepts and practices, and various aspects of data retention and deletion requirements.

Data Inventory and Discovery

In the previous chapter, we discussed the importance of creating an asset inventory; part of that effort will require identifying all the data owned by the organization.

Data Ownership

When we talk about data, we must assign responsibilities for that data according to who has possession and legal ownership of that data. In the cloud computing motif, we tend to assign roles to allocate those responsibilities.

In most cases:

- The *data owner* is the organization that has collected or created the data, in general terms. Within the organization, we often assign a specific data owner as being the individual with rights and responsibilities for that data; this is usually the department head or business unit manager for the office that has created or collected a certain dataset. From a cloud perspective, the cloud customer is usually the data owner. Many international treaties and frameworks refer to the data owner as the *data controller.*

- The *data custodian* is any organization or person who manipulates, stores, or moves the data on behalf of the data owner. Within the organization, a data custodian might be a database administrator. In the cloud context, the data custodian is usually the cloud provider. From an international perspective, the data custodian is also known as the *data processor.*

Here are essential points to remember about the rights and responsibilities of data ownership and custody:

- Data custodians do not necessarily all have direct relationships with data owners; custodians can be third parties, or even further removed down the supply chain.

- Data owners remain legally responsible for all data they own. This is true even if data is compromised by a data custodian several times removed from the data owner.

- Ownership, custody, rights, responsibilities, and liability are all relative to the dataset in question, and therefore are only specific to that data in that circumstance. For instance, a cloud provider is usually the data processor for a cloud customer's data, but the provider is the data owner for information that the provider collects and creates, such as the provider's own customer list, asset inventory, and billing information.

The Data Life Cycle

The data life cycle is represented in Figure 3.1.

FIGURE 3.1   Data life cycle

It is important to know the phases of the data life cycle, in order, both for the CCSP exam and for your understanding of data security concepts. In this section of the chapter, we're mostly concerned with the first phase: Create.

The data owner will be identified in the Create phase. Many data security and management responsibilities require action on the part of the data owner at this point of the life cycle.

Data Categorization

The data owner will be in the best position to understand how the data is going to be used by the organization. This allows the data owner to appropriately categorize the data. The organization can have any number of categories or types of information; these might be clearly defined and reused throughout the organization, or they might be arbitrarily assigned by data owners during the Create phase.

Here are some ways an organization might categorize data:

Regulatory Compliance   Different business activities are susceptible to different regulations. The organization may want to create categories based on which regulation(s) apply to a specific dataset. This might include Graham-Leach-Bliley Act (GLBA), Payment Card Industry (PCI), Sarbanes-Oxley (SOX), and/or Health Insurance Portability and Accountability Act (HIPAA) compliance.

Business Function   The organization might want to have specific categories for different uses of data. Perhaps the data is tagged based on its use in billing, marketing, or operations.

Functional Unit   Each department or office might have its own category, and keep all data it controls within its own category.

By Project   Some organizations might define datasets by the projects they are associated with, as a means of creating discrete, compartmentalized projects.

There is literally no limit to how an organization might categorize data. Whatever motif the organization uses, however, should be adopted and enforced uniformly throughout the organization. Ad hoc categorization is tantamount to having no categorization at all.

Data Classification

Much like categorization, data classification is the responsibility of the data owner, takes place in the Create phase, and is assigned according to an overall organizational motif based on a specific characteristic of the given dataset. The classification, like the categorization, can take any form defined by the organization and should be uniformly applied.

Types of classification might include the following:

Sensitivity   This is the classification model used by the military. Data is assigned a classification according to the sensitivity of the data, based on the negative impact an unauthorized disclosure would cause. In models of this kind, classification must be assigned to all data, even in the negative, so material that is not deemed to be sensitive must be assigned the "unclassified" label. We will discuss labeling shortly.

Jurisdiction   The geophysical location of the source or storage point of the data might have significant bearing on how that data is treated and handled. For instance, Personally Identifiable Information (PII) data gathered from citizens of the European Union (EU) is subject to the EU privacy laws, which are much more strict and comprehensive than privacy laws in the United States.

Criticality   Data that is deemed critical to organizational survival might be classified in a manner distinct from trivial, basic operational data. As we know from previous chapters, the BIA helps us determine which material would be classified this way.

There are no industry-defined, statutory-mandated definitions for "categorization" versus "classification" of data, except in those areas covered by specific regulations (for instance, the military uses classification constructs defined by federal law). The terms can often be used interchangeably. For the purposes of discussion in this book, we will try to adhere to this understanding of the terms: data is categorized by its use and classified by a certain trait. Again, this is not an industry standard, and the International Information System Security Certification Consortium, or (ISC)[2], does not create a bright-line distinction between the terms.

Data Labeling

When the data owner creates, categorizes, and classifies the data, it also needs to be labeled. The label should indicate who the data owner is, usually in terms of the office or role, instead of an individual name or identity (because, of course, personnel can change roles with an organization, or leave for other organizations). The label should take whatever form is necessary for it to be enduring, understandable, and consistent; for instance, labels on data in hardcopy might be printed headers and footers, whereas labels on electronic files might be embedded in the filename and nomenclature. Labels should be evident and communicate the pertinent concepts without necessarily disclosing the data they describe.

Depending on the needs of the organization and the nature of its operations, labels might include the following kinds of information:

- Date of creation
- Date of scheduled destruction/disposal
- Confidentiality level
- Handling directions
- Dissemination/distribution instructions
- Access limitations
- Source
- Jurisdiction
- Applicable regulation

 Real World Scenario

Labels Work Both Ways

Labels can aid in security efforts by readily indicating the nature of certain information and how it should be handled and protected. For instance, in the U.S. military and federal government, classified data in hardcopy is labeled in a number of ways, including the use of cover sheets. Cover sheets convey only one characteristic of the data: the sensitivity of the material (in military taxonomy, this is called "classification," with a somewhat different meaning than we're using in this book). Sensitivity is indicated in at least two ways: the title of the class (e.g., "Secret," "Top Secret") in large, bold letters, and the color of the sheet and markings: blue for Confidential, red for Secret, and so forth. This reminds the user (the person carrying or reading the documents) in a very simple fashion how to secure the material when it is not in use or is unattended. It also informs anyone else how to react if they come across such material unattended; a manager leaving the office at the end of the workday might do one last walkthrough of the workspace, and a red cover sheet left on a desk will immediately catch the eye.

Of course, this also has the same effect for malicious actors: the cover sheet lets someone with ill intent instantly know the potential value of specific material: the pages with the red cover sheet are more valuable than the ones with the blue cover sheet.

Data Discovery Methods

To determine and accurately inventory the data under its control, the organization can employ various tools and techniques. "Data discovery" is a term that can be used to refer to several kinds of tasks: it might mean that the organization is attempting to create that initial inventory of data it owns, or that the organization is involved in electronic discovery ("ediscovery," the legal term for how electronic evidence is collected as part of an investigation or lawsuit; we'll discuss this in more depth in Chapter 11, "Legal and Compliance Part 2"), and it can also mean the modern use of datamining tools to discover trends and relations in the data already in the organization's inventory.

Label-Based Discovery

Obviously, the labels created by data owners in the Create phase of the data life cycle will greatly aid any data discovery effort. With accurate and sufficient labels, the organization can readily determine what data it controls, and what amounts of each kind. This is another reason why the habit and process of labeling is so important.

Labels can be especially useful when the discovery effort is undertaken in response to a mandate with a specific purpose, such as a court order or a regulatory demand: if all data related to "X" is required, and all such data is readily labeled, it is easy to collect and disclose all the appropriate data, and only the appropriate data.

Metadata-Based Discovery

In addition to labels, metadata can be useful for discovery purposes. Colloquially referred to as "data about data," metadata is a listing of traits and characteristics about specific data elements or sets. Metadata is often automatically created at the same time as the data, often by the hardware or software used to create the parent data. For instance, most modern digital cameras create a vast amount of metadata every time a photograph is taken, such as date, time, and location where the photo was shot, make and model of the camera, and so forth; all that metadata is embedded in the picture file, and is copied and transferred whenever the image itself is copied or moved.

Data discovery can therefore use metadata in the same way labels might be used; specific fields of the metadata might be scanned for particular terms, and all matching data elements collected for a certain purpose.

Content-Based Discovery

Even without labels or metadata, discovery tools can be used to locate and identify specific kinds of data by delving into the content of datasets. This technique can be as basic as term searches or can use sophisticated pattern-matching technology.

 NOTE   Content analysis can also be used for more specific security controls, as well as discovery; we will discuss data loss, leak protection, and prevention solutions in Chapter 4, "Cloud Data Security."

Data Analytics

Current technological options provide additional options for finding and typing data. In many cases, these modern tools create new data feeds from sets of data already existing within the environment. These include the following:

Datamining   The term for the family of activities that the other options on this list derive from. This kind of data analysis is an outgrowth of the possibilities offered by regular use of the cloud, also known as "big data." When the organization has collected various data streams and can run queries across these various feeds, the organization can detect and analyze previously unknown trends and patterns that can be extremely useful.

Real-time Analytics   In some cases, tools can provide datamining functionality concurrently with data creation and use. These tools rely on automation and require efficiency to perform properly.

Agile Business Intelligence   State-of-the-art datamining involves recursive, iterative tools and processes that can detect trends in trends, and identify even more oblique patterns in historical and recent data.

It's worth your time to understand data analytics options, both for purposes of the exam as well as possible security implications in your organization.

Jurisdictional Requirements

Various legal constructs exist across the globe, and being in the cloud means your organization may be subject to many simultaneously. This can create additional risks for your organization, and more complications for you as a security practitioner. It will be your duty to be aware which laws affect the organization, and you must have a general idea of how to ensure your organization can comply with them all.

Unfortunately, the use of cloud computing comes with some challenges in terms of awareness and compliance with specific jurisdictions. For instance, because of the way resources are dynamically assigned, the cloud user might not know exactly where, in terms of both datacenters and geographic locations, the organization's data is physically present at any given moment; the data may cross city limits, state lines, or even national borders as the cloud provider manages virtualized images, stored data, and operational data. (Indeed, depending on the level of automation and datacenter design, the cloud provider might not even know, moment by moment, which city, state, or country specific data is located in.)

So for both the CCSP exam and for the protection of your organization, you should be familiar with several legal constructs that may significantly affect the data in your charge. The book addresses many of these in some detail in Chapters 11 and 12; we're simply going to list some of them here, with brief notes, to introduce the concepts.

The United States   Strong intellectual property protections, including stringent, multiple legal frameworks. No singular, overarching federal privacy statute; instead, the United States tends to address privacy with industry-specific legislation (GLBA, HIPAA, and so forth), or with contractual obligations (PCI). Many strong, granular data breach notification laws exist that are enforced by states and localities.

Europe   Good intellectual property protections. Massive, exhaustive, comprehensive personal privacy protections, including the EU Data Directive and the General Data Protection Regulation.

Asia   Disparate levels of intellectual property protection. Data privacy protection levels differ greatly by country, with Japan adhering to the EU model, and other countries following much-reduced guidance.

South/Central America   Various intellectual property mechanisms. Generally lax privacy protection frameworks, with the notable exception of Argentina, which is in direct correlation with the EU legislation.

Australia/New Zealand   Strong intellectual property protections. Very strong privacy protections, with the Australian Privacy Act mapping directly to the EU statutes.

   The EU privacy laws will be a big driver for any organization wanting to do business in or with Europe. For exam purposes, you should be versed in both the original guidance (the EU Data Directive), and the recently updated law (the EU General Data Regulation), as well as the mechanisms used in the United States to comply with these laws (the Safe Harbor program and the Privacy Shield, respectively). These are all addressed further in Chapters 11 and 12.

Data Rights Management

The industry has taken to referring to technology solutions that protect intellectual property as digital rights management (DRM) tools. In this section, we'll review intellectual property protections and discuss the traits of DRM tools.

Intellectual Property Protections

Intellectual property is that class of valuable belongings that are intangible; literally, assets of the mind. There are many legal protections for intellectual property, and you should be familiar with them.

Copyright

The legal protection for expressions of ideas is known as "copyright." In the United States, copyright is granted to anyone who first creates an expression of an idea. Usually, this involves literary works, films, music, software, and artistic works.

Oddly, copyright does not include titles of works. For instance, while you cannot copy and sell the film *Star Wars*, you could, theoretically, write, produce, and sell a new movie that you call *Star Wars*, as long as it does not cover the same material as the other film with that name. We don't, however, recommend it.

Copyright does not cover ideas, specific words, slogans, recipes, or formulae. Those things can often be secured with other intellectual property protections; we'll discuss them later in this section.

 Copyright protects the tangible expression of an idea, not the form of an idea. For instance, copyright protects the content of a book, not the hardcopy version of a book itself; illegal copying of content of a book would be a copyright infringement, whereas stealing a physical book would be theft. The copyright belongs to the author or whomever the author sells or grants the rights to, not to someone who currently holds the physical copy of the book.

The duration of copyrights vary based on the terms under which they were created, depending on if an individual created the work themselves or if the work was created under contract (a "work-for-hire"). Typically, copyright lasts for either 70 years after the author's death, or 120 years after the first publication of a work for hire.

Copyright gives exclusive use of the work to the creator, with some exceptions. The creator is the only entity legally allowed to:

- Perform the work publically
- Profit from the work
- Make copies of the work
- Make derivative works from the original
- Import or export the work
- Broadcast the work
- Sell or otherwise assign these rights

There are exceptions to the exclusivity of these rights. Exceptions include:

Fair Use   There is a family of exceptions to copyright exclusivity, known as "fair use." Fair use includes:

Academic Fair Use   Instructors can make limited copies or presentations of copyrighted works for educational purposes.

Critique   The work may be reviewed or discussed for purposes of assessing its merit, and portions of the work may be used in these critical reviews.

News Reporting   Because an informed populace is essential to a free society, we have waived some intellectual property protections for reporting purposes.

Scholarly Research   Similar to academic fair use, but among researchers instead of teachers and students.

Satire   A mocking sendup of the work may be created using a significant portion of the original work.

Library Preservation   Libraries and archives are allowed to make limited numbers of copies of original works in order to preserve the work itself.

Personal Backup   Someone who has legally purchased a licensed work may make a single backup copy for themselves, for use if the original fails. This explicitly includes computer programs.

Versions for People with Physical Disabilities   It is legal to make specialized copies of licensed works for use by someone with a disability. This could, for instance, include making a Braille or audio copy of a book for use by the blind.

These exceptions are not unlimited; anyone making use of a copyright exception has to take into account many subjective factors, including the possible commercial market for the work and the size, scope, and nature of the original work.

Copyright infringement is usually dealt with as a civil case: the copyright owner has to bring a lawsuit against someone they believe has illegally copied or used their work. However, in some cases, demonstrated willful infringement can be investigated by the government as a criminal matter.

In the United States, copyright is assigned the moment an expression is put into a tangible medium; the creator automatically holds the copyright when the work is created. However, enforcing these rights in a lawsuit against infringement will require some proof of the creator's claim. The U.S. Copyright Office allows copyright holders to register their works as means of securing this proof. It is not mandatory to register works in order to own them. The fact that something is copyrighted is often communicated by attaching the copyright symbol to it, sometimes with additional text that emphasizes this fact. See Figure 3.2.

FIGURE 3.2   The copyright symbol

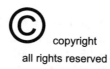

Different countries view copyrights in various ways. Although the creator automatically owns the copyright in the United States, in some jurisdictions the copyright belongs to the person who first registers that work in that jurisdiction.

Real World Scenario

The DMCA

The Digital Millennium Copyright Act (DMCA) is a notorious piece of legislation ostensibly created to provide additional protections to creative works in digital formats. It is generally viewed as both crafted for too specific a purpose and also used in an overly broad manner. It also puts the burden of proof on those accused of copyright infringement and requires presumptive action upon accusation.

Basically, the story goes like this: The Hollywood film industry was using an electronic encryption mechanism known as CSS—the Content Scramble System—to protect content on DVDs from being illegally copied. A group of people created a program to remove this encryption from DVDs; this program was known as DeCSS. Lobbyists for content producers, under specific direction from the Motion Picture Association of America and eventually with the participation of the Recording Industry Association of America, convinced Congress to pass the DMCA to make DeCSS and programs like it illegal; this would include writing, distributing, and publishing anti-encryption software. The intent was to protect copyrighted material (movies and songs, for the most part) from piracy.

In practice, however, the effect has been quite different. Certain provisions of the DMCA, namely the "takedown notice" process, have been abused as a matter of course. Under the takedown notice clause, any web hosting service must remove content from the Internet if anyone accuses that content as being or including copyrighted material, and that material has to remain off the web until whoever published it can prove either that the material is not copyrighted or that they own the copyright. This has led to a significant use of the takedown notice for frivolous or malicious reasons. And this is just one of many unintended consequences of the DMCA.

Trademarks

Unlike copyrights, trademark protection is intended to be applied to specific words and graphics. Trademarks are representations of an organization—its brand. A trademark is meant to protect the esteem and goodwill that an organization has built among the marketplace, especially in public perception.

A trademark can be the name of an organization, or a logo, a phrase associated with an organization, even a specific color or sound, or some combination of these.

In order to have a trademark protected by law, it must be registered within a jurisdiction. Commonly, that is the U.S. Patent and Trademark Office (USPTO), the federal entity for registering trademarks. Trademarks registered with the USPTO can use the ® symbol to signify registration. States also offer trademark registration, and trademarks registered with state offices often use the ™ symbol.

Trademarks last into perpetuity, as long as the trademark owner continues to use them for commercial purposes. Trademark infringement is actionable, and trademark owners can sue in court for remedy for infringement.

Patents

The USPTO, as the name indicates, is also responsible for registering patents. Patents are the legal mechanism for protecting intellectual property in the form of inventions, processes, materials, decorations, and plant life. In securing a patent, the patent owner gains exclusivity in the production, sale, and importation of the patented property.

Patents typically last for 20 years from the time of the patent application. There is some provision for extension, since the process of getting a patent can take many months, or even years. Some kinds of patented properties, such as pharmaceuticals, can also gain additional extensions; conversely, the exclusivity of marketing some pharmaceuticals under a particular name is granted not by the USPTO, but by the FDA, and this period of marketing exclusivity is much shorter in duration.

Patent infringement, as with the other intellectual property protections, is cause to sue for relief in federal court.

Trade Secrets

Trade secrets are intellectual property that involve many of the same aspects as patented material: processes, formulas, commercial methods, and so forth. They can also include some things that aren't patentable, such as aggregations of information (this might include lists of clients or suppliers, for instance).

Trade secrets are also somewhat like copyrights in the United States, in that protections for them exist upon creation, without any additional requirement for registration.

However, unlike other intellectual property protections, material considered trade secrets must be just that: secret. They cannot be disclosed to the public, and efforts must be made to maintain secrecy in order to keep this legal protection.

Trade secrets are then provided legal protection from illicit acquisition; anyone who tries to acquire trade secrets by theft or misappropriation can be sued in civil court (similar to other forms of intellectual property), but can also be prosecuted in federal court for this crime.

Trade secret protection does not, however, confer the exclusivity granted by other intellectual property protections. Anyone other than the owner of the trade secret who discovers or invents the same or similar methods, processes, and information through legal means is justified and legally free to use that knowledge to their own benefit. In fact, someone who discovers someone else's trade secret through legitimate means is also free to patent it (assuming there is no existing patent on the same material or concept).

Like a trademark, a trade secret lasts into perpetuity, as long as the owner is still using it in commercial activity.

DRM Tool Traits

Digital rights management (DRM) solutions are used to protect intellectual property, in order to comply with the relevant protections, and to maintain ownership rights. DRM can be implemented in enterprises, by manufacturers, vendors, or content creators. Usually, material protected by DRM solutions need some form of labeling or metadata associated with the material in order for the DRM tool to function properly.

DRM implementations can vary in technological sophistication and technique. Here are some ways that DRM has been or could be applied:

Rudimentary Reference Checks   The content itself can automatically check for proper usage or ownership. For instance, in many vintage computer games, the game would pause in operation until the player entered some information that could only have been acquired with the purchase of a licensed copy of the game, like a word or a phrase from the manual that shipped with the game.

Online Reference Checks   Microsoft software packages, including Windows operating systems and Office programs, are often locked in the same manner, requiring users to enter a product key at installation; the program would then later check the product key against an online database when the system connected to the Internet.

Local Agent Checks   The user installs a reference tool that checks the protected content against the user's license. Again, gaming engines often work this way, with gamers having to download an agent of Steam or GOG.com when installing any games purchased from those distributors; the agents check the user's system against the online license database to ensure the games are not pirated.

Presence of Licensed Media   Some DRM tools require the presence of licensed media, such as disks, in the system while the content is being used. The DRM engine is on the media, often installed with some cryptographic engine that identifies the unique disk and the licensed content, and allowing usage based on that relationship.

Support-Based Licensing   Some DRM implementations are predicated on the need of continual support for content; this is particularly true of production software. Licensed software might be allowed ready access to updates and patches, while the vendor could prevent unlicensed versions from getting this type of support.

DRM implementations usually include adding another layer of access control (beyond what the enterprise employs for its own operational purposes) on files and objects containing protected material. DRM can also be used to implement localized information security policies; specific users or groups of users might have all content they create specially tagged and marked with appropriate access restrictions, for instance.

Employing DRM in the cloud poses some challenges, though. These include the following:

Replication Restrictions   Because DRM often involves preventing unauthorized duplication, and the cloud necessitates creating, closing, and replicating virtualized host instances (including user-specific content stored locally on the virtual host), DRM might interfere with automatic resources allocation processes.

Jurisdictional Conflicts   The cloud extends across boundaries and borders, often in a manner unknown or uncontrolled by the data owner, which can pose problems when intellectual property rights are restricted by locale.

Agent/Enterprise Conflicts   DRM solutions that require local installation of software agents for enforcement purposes might not always function properly in the cloud environment, with virtualization engines, or with the various platforms used in a bring your own device (BYOD) enterprise.

Mapping Identity and Access Management (IAM) and DRM   Because of the extra layer of access control (often involving content-specific Access Control Lists (ACLs), the DRM IAM processes might conflict or not work properly with the enterprise/cloud IAM. This is even truer when cloud IAM functions are outsourced to a third party, such as a cloud access security broker (CASB).

API Conflicts   Because the DRM tool is often incorporated into the content, usage of the material might not offer the same level of performance across different applications, such as content readers or media players.

In general terms, DRM should provide the following functions, regardless of type of content or format:

Persistent Protection   The DRM should follow the content it protects, regardless of where that content is located, whether it is a duplicate copy or the original file, or how it is being utilized. The protection should not be rendered useless through simple operation in the production environment.

Dynamic Policy Control   The DRM tool should allow content creators and data owners to modify ACLs and permissions for the protected data under their control.

Automatic Expiration   Because of the nature of some legal protections of intellectual property (described earlier in this chapter), a significant amount of digital content will not be protected in perpetuity. The DRM protections should cease when the legal protections cease. Conversely, licenses also expire; access and permissions for protected content should likewise expire, no matter where that content exists at the end of the license period.

Continuous Auditing   The DRM should allow for comprehensive monitoring of the content's use and access history.

Replication Restrictions   Much of the purpose of DRM is to restrict illegal or unauthorized duplication of protected content. Therefore, DRM solutions should enforce these restrictions across the many forms of copying that exist, to include screen-scraping, printing, electronic duplication, email attachments, and so on.

Remote Rights Revocation   The owner of the rights to specific intellectual property should have the ability to revoke those rights at any time; this capability might be used as a result of litigation or infringement.

Data Control

The organization also needs to protect data in life-cycle phases other than Create. Industry standards and best practices require the creation, use, and enforcement of a host of data management policies and practices, including the areas of data retention, audit, and disposal. In this section, we'll address each of those in turn.

Each aspect of data management—retention, audit, and disposal—will need a specific policy addressing it. There is no reason, however, that you cannot include all three policies under one overarching policy, such as a data management policy. Just be sure each area is addressed thoroughly and with sufficient granularity; don't let any individual subpolicy slip in quality or comprehensiveness simply because you're aggregating your required governance.

Data Retention

As with all matters involving our profession, the organization's data retention program should start with and be based on a strong, coherent policy. The data retention policy should include the following:

Retention Periods   How long the data should be kept by the organization. This usually refers to data that is being archived for long-term storage—that is, data not currently being used in the production environment. The retention period is often expressed in a number of years and is frequently set by regulation or legislation (see the next item). Data retention periods can also be mandated or modified by contractual agreements.

Applicable Regulation   As we just mentioned, the retention period can be mandated by statute or contract; the retention policy should refer to all applicable regulatory guidance. This is especially true in cases where there is conflicting regulation; the policy should then also highlight any such disparity, and include mention of senior management's decision for how to approach and resolve this conflict with the policy as an appropriate mechanism. For instance, states may impose different retention periods for specific kinds of data, and the organization might operate in states with differing mandated periods; the policy should then explicitly state the conflicting periods, as well as the period senior management determined as the solution.

Retention Formats   The policy should contain a description of how the data is actually archived—that is, what type of media it is stored on, and any handling specifications particular to the data. For example, some types of data are required by regulation to be kept encrypted while in storage. In these cases, the policy should include a description of the encryption engine, key storage and retrieval procedures, and reference to the applicable regulation(s) (see earlier).

Data Classification   The organization should have an overarching data classification policy that serves as guidance for data creators, owners, curators, and users, describing how and when data should be classified, and security procedures and controls for handling the various classifications (as well as enforcement mechanisms for dealing with policy infractions). In addition to the main policy, the data retention policy should include specific mention of how the various classes of data will be archived and retrieved.

Archiving and Retrieval Procedures   Having data in storage is useful; stored data can be used to correct production errors, can serve as business continuity and disaster recovery (BC/DR) backups, and can be datamined for business intelligence purposes. But stored data is only useful if it can be retrieved and put back into production in an efficient and cost-effective manner. The policy should include a detailed description of the processes both for sending data into storage and for recovering it. This element of the policy (the detailed processes) might be included as an attachment or mentioned by reference to the actual documentation for the processes; the processes might require more frequent updates and editing than the policy and could be kept separate.

Monitoring, Maintenance, and Enforcement   As with all policies in the organization, the policy should list, in detail, how often the policy will be reviewed and amended, by whom, consequences for failure to adhere to the policy, and which entity within the organization is responsible for enforcement.

Backups are great; a lot of organizations do regular, thorough backups. However, all too often, these same organizations don't practice recovery from backup, so they are unprepared for those situations where recovery is necessary, and recovery efforts are hampered or fail. It is useful, and in some cases required by regulation, to test your organization's recovery from backup in order to ensure this won't happen to you.

Managing data retention in the cloud can be especially tricky; it may be difficult to ensure, for instance, that the cloud provider is not retaining the organization's data beyond the retention period (part of the appeal of the cloud is how good cloud providers are at retaining data, and not losing; purposefully getting rid of data is a wholly other matter). When considering cloud migration, and during negotiations with potential cloud providers, the organization should make a point of ensuring the provider can support the organization's retention policy.

The data retention policy addresses the activities that take place in the Archive phase of the data life cycle.

Data Audit

As with all other assets, the organization needs to regularly review, inventory, and inspect usage and condition of the data it owns. Data audit is a powerful tool for effecting these efforts.

As with the other elements of data management, the organization should have a policy for conducting audits of its data. The policy should include detailed descriptions of

- Audit periods
- Audit scope
- Audit responsibilities (internal and/or external)
- Audit processes and procedures
- Applicable regulations
- Monitoring, maintenance, and enforcement

As with all types of audits, the organization should be particularly careful about ensuring that auditors do not report to anyone in the management structure that owns or is affected by the data they are auditing; conflicts of interest must be avoided for the audits to have validity and utility.

In most organizations and enterprises, audit is predicated on logging. Logging can happen in many forms: event logging, security logging, traffic logging, and so forth. Logs can be generated by applications, OSs, and devices, and for general or specific purposes (e.g., devices that collect logs as a byproduct of operations, such as servers, or devices that do logging as their main purpose, such as IDSs and SEIMs).

Log review and audit is a specialized task for personnel with specific training and experience. Logging is fairly easy; most software and devices in modern enterprises can effectively log anything and everything the organization might want to capture. Reading and analyzing these logs, however, can prove challenging:

Log review and analysis is not often a priority.   Most organizations do not have the wherewithal to dedicate the personnel required to effectively analyze log data. Usually, log review becomes an additional duty for someone tasked to another office (the security department, for instance). And many additional duties do not get accomplished because the personnel assigned to them become task-saturated with their other, regular job tasks.

Log review is mundane and repetitive.   Reviewing logs takes a certain kind of person: someone who can sift through loads of data in order to spot the minute portion that might vary from the norm. This is not exciting work, and even the best analyst can become lax through repetition.

Log review requires someone both new to the field and experienced.   This can become a management quandary: the log reviewer must be someone junior enough that they can be assigned to perform log reviews without incurring too much trade-off cost to the organization (that is, other functions they might be performing are not more expensive or valuable than the log reviews), yet the person needs to have sufficient experience and training to perform the activity in a worthwhile manner.

The reviewer needs to have an understanding of the operation.   If the reviewer cannot distinguish between what is authorized activity and what is not, they are not adding security value to the process.

It might serve the organization well for log reviews to only be a part-time function of a specific individual. If a person is only doing log analysis and has no other duties, repetition and boredom might lead to the person missing something in the review that would have otherwise been noticed. However, the person assigned to review logs must perform the task often enough that they recognize baseline activity, and therefore deviations from it; long periods between analysis sessions might lead to the analyst losing institutional knowledge and some atrophy of the skillset.

Logs are like data backups, though: many organizations perform logging; logs are easy to set, acquire, and store. The challenge, then, is to determine how often logs will be reviewed or audited, by whom, the processes for doing so, and so forth. Having the logs is one thing: reviewing the logs you have is something else.

A natural inclination of a security practitioner might be to log every-thing; people in our field notoriously loathe to part with data, and want to know everything about everything. The problem with doing so? Log-ging everything creates additional risks and costs. Having so much log data aggregated creates additional vulnerabilities, and requires additional protections, and the storage required for logging everything will entail a wholesale duplication of storage systems and space.

Data audit in the cloud can pose some almost insurmountable challenges. The cloud pro-vider may not want (or, indeed, even be able, for operational or contractual reasons) to dis-close log data with the customer, for security, liability, or competitive reasons. Therefore, the organization must consider, again, specific audit requirements when opting for cloud migration, and include any such specifications in the contract with the cloud provider.

The data audit policy addresses activities that take place in *all* phases of the data life cycle.

Data Destruction/Disposal

In the legacy environment, where the organization has ownership and control of all the infrastructure, including the data, hardware, and software, data disposal options are direct and straightforward. In the cloud, data disposal is much more difficult and risky.

First, a review of data disposal options in the legacy environment:

Physical Destruction of Media and Hardware   Any hardware or portable media contain-ing the data in question can be destroyed by burning, melting, impact (beating, drilling, grinding, and so forth), or industrial shredding. This is the preferred method of sanitiza-tion, since the data is physically unrecoverable.

Degaussing   This involves applying strong magnetic fields to the hardware and media where the data resides, effectively making them blank. It does not work with solid-state drives.

Overwriting   Multiple passes of random characters are written to the storage areas (par-ticular disk sectors) where the data resides, with a final pass of all zeroes or ones. This can be extremely time-consuming for large storage areas.

Cryptoshredding (AKA Cryptographic Erasure)   This involves encrypting the data with a strong encryption engine, and then taking the keys generated in that process, encrypting them with a different encryption engine, and destroying the keys.

WARNING   Hardware and media can never be sanitized by simply deleting the data. Deleting, as an operation, does not erase the data; it simply removes the logical pointers to the data for processing purposes.

In the cloud, many of these options are unavailable or not feasible. Because the cloud provider, not the data owner, owns the hardware, physical destruction is usually out of the question. Moreover, because of the difficulty of knowing the actual specific physical location(s) of the data at any given moment (or historically), it would be next to impossible to determine all the components and media that would need to be destroyed. Likewise, for that same reason, overwriting is not a practical means of sanitizing data in the cloud.

That leaves cryptoshredding as the sole pragmatic option for data disposal in the cloud.

As with the other data management functions, the organization needs to create a policy for data disposal. This policy should include detailed descriptions of the following:

- The process for data disposal
- Applicable regulations
- Clear direction of when data should be destroyed

Of course, we are also concerned with data remanence—that is, any data left over after sanitization and disposal methods have been attempted. If cryptoshredding is performed correctly, there should be no remanence; however, material that is somehow not included in the original encryption (say, a virtual instance that was offline during the encryption process, then added to the cloud environment) might be considered remanence. As in all cryptographic practices, proper implementation is essential for success.

NOTE   The data disposal policy addresses activities that take place in the Destroy phase of the data life cycle.

Summary

In Chapter 3, we have discussed data management functions within the data life cycle, including data retention, auditing, and disposal. We described the various roles, rights, and responsibilities associated with data ownership. We also reviewed intellectual property concepts and legal protections for intellectual property, as well as DRM solution objectives and functionality. This chapter discussed inventorying data assets, and the added value data discovery offers the organization. We touched on some jurisdictional concerns for data, which we will cover in more detail in Chapter 11. For all these topics, we also covered some of the challenges and risks cloud computing poses.

Exam Essentials

Know the different forms of data analytics.   Be familiar with the descriptions of datamining, real-time analytics, and agile business intelligence.

Understand the various roles, rights, and responsibilities related to data ownership.   Know who the data owner, controller, processor, and custodian are. Understand the rights and responsibilities associated with each.

Understand the purpose and method of data categorization/classification.   Know why and how data owners assign categories and classifications to specific datasets under their control.

Be familiar with data discovery methods.   Know how and when data is labeled, and by whom. Also be aware of content-based discovery and the use of metadata in discovery efforts.

Know the data life cycle.   Know all the phases of the data life cycle, in order. Know which phases include data labeling, content creation, DRM activities, data disposal, data retention, and data audits.

Be familiar with the various intellectual property protections.   Know the protections for copyrights, trademarks, patents, and trade secrets.

Know what should be included in policies for data retention, audit, and disposal. Understand essential aspects like terms of retention and disposal, retention formats, how regulations dictate these things, and how every policy needs to include details for maintenance, review, and enforcement.

Written Labs

1.   Read the NIST guidelines for cryptographic erasure (NIST SP 800-88 (rev. 1), Appendix D): http://nvlpubs.nist.gov/nistpubs/SpecialPublications/ NIST.SP.800-88r1.pdf.

2.   Select a sample device for lab purposes. Using the sample format shown in 800-88, D.1, answer the suitability questions regarding cryptoshredding for the device you have selected.

Review Questions

You can find the answers in Appendix A.

1. All of these are methods of data discovery, except:
   A. Content-based
   B. User-based
   C. Label-based
   D. Metadata-based

2. Data labels could include all the following, except:
   A. Date data was created
   B. Data owner
   C. Data value
   D. Data of scheduled destruction

3. Data labels could include all the following, except:
   A. Source
   B. Delivery vendor
   C. Handling restrictions
   D. Jurisdiction

4. Data labels could include all the following, except:
   A. Confidentiality level
   B. Distribution limitations
   C. Access restrictions
   D. Multifactor authentication

5. All the following are data analytics modes, except:
   A. Real-time analytics
   B. Datamining
   C. Agile business intelligence
   D. Refractory iterations

6. In the cloud motif, the data owner is usually:
   A. In another jurisdiction
   B. The cloud customer
   C. The cloud provider
   D. The cloud access security broker

7. In the cloud motif, the data processor is usually:

    A. The party that assigns access rights

    B. The cloud customer

    C. The cloud provider

    D. The cloud access security broker

8. Every security program and process should have which of the following?

    A. Foundational policy

    B. Severe penalties

    C. Multifactor authentication

    D. Homomorphic encryption

9. All policies within the organization should include a section that includes all of the following, except:

    A. Policy maintenance

    B. Policy review

    C. Policy enforcement

    D. Policy adjudication

10. The most pragmatic option for data disposal in the cloud is which of the following?

    A. Melting

    B. Cryptoshredding

    C. Cold fusion

    D. Overwriting

11. What is the intellectual property protection for the tangible expression of a creative idea?

    A. Copyright

    B. Patent

    C. Trademark

    D. Trade secret

12. What is the intellectual property protection for a useful manufacturing innovation?

    A. Copyright

    B. Patent

    C. Trademark

    D. Trade secret

13. What is the intellectual property protection for a very valuable set of sales leads?

    A. Copyright

    B. Patent

    C. Trademark

    D. Trade secret

14. What is the intellectual property protection for a confidential recipe for muffins?
    A. Copyright
    B. Patent
    C. Trademark
    D. Trade secret

15. What is the intellectual property protection for the logo of a new video game?
    A. Copyright
    B. Patent
    C. Trademark
    D. Trade secret

16. What is the aspect of the DMCA that has often been abused and places the burden of proof on the accused?
    A. Online service provider exemption
    B. Decryption program prohibition
    C. Takedown notice
    D. Puppet plasticity

17. What is the federal agency that accepts applications for new patents?
    A. USDA
    B. USPTO
    C. OSHA
    D. SEC

18. DRM tools use a variety of methods for enforcement of intellectual property rights. These include all the following, except:
    A. Support-based licensing
    B. Local agent enforcement
    C. Dip switch validity
    D. Media-present checks

19. All of the following regions have at least one country with an overarching, federal privacy law protecting personal data of its citizens, except:
    A. Asia
    B. Europe
    C. South America
    D. The United States

20. DRM solutions should generally include all the following functions, except:
    A. Persistency
    B. Automatic self-destruct
    C. Automatic expiration
    D. Dynamic policy control

Chapter

4

Cloud Data Security

THE OBJECTIVE OF THIS CHAPTER IS TO ACQUAINT THE READER WITH THE FOLLOWING CONCEPTS:

✓ **Domain 1: Architectural Concepts and Design Requirements**

- D. Understand Design Principles of Secure Cloud Computing
- D.1 Cloud Secure Data Lifecycle

✓ **Domain 2: Cloud Data Security**

- A. Understand Cloud Data Lifecycle
- A.1 Phases
- A.2 Relevant Data Security Technologies
- B. Design and Implement Cloud Data Storage Architectures
- B.1 Storage Types
- B.2 Threats to Storage Types
- B.3 Technologies Available to Address Threats
- C. Design and Apply Data Security Strategies
- C.1 Encryption
- C.2 Key Management
- C.3 Masking
- C.4 Tokenization
- C.5 Application of Technologies
- C.6 Emerging Technologies
- H. Design and Implement Auditability, Traceability, and Accountability of Data Events
- H2. Data Event Logging
- H.3 Storage and Analysis of Data Events
- H.4 Continuous Optimizations

✓ **Domain 3: Cloud Platform and Infrastructure Security**

- ▪ A. Comprehend Cloud Infrastructure Components
  - ▪ A.5 Storage

✓ **Domain 5: Operations**

- ▪ D. Manage Physical Infrastructure for Cloud Environment
  - ▪ D.8 Log Capture and Analysis
- ▪ G. Manage Logical Infrastructure for Cloud Environment
  - ▪ G.7 Log Capture and Analysis

As we migrate our data into the cloud, in addition to ensuring we're satisfying the functional requirements, we must carry with it the security aspects we already know from our legacy environments: the CIA Triad, data protection fundamentals, regulatory constraints, layered defense, and so forth. In this chapter, we will examine the particular security challenges and techniques necessary for making a cloud format both useful and trustworthy.

Cloud Data Life Cycle

Data in the cloud should be perceived, in the general case, to have the same needs and properties as data in the legacy environment. The data life cycle still has a purpose; only the implementation particulars will change. Figure 4.1 shows the common stages in the data life cycle.

FIGURE 4.1 Stages of the data life cycle

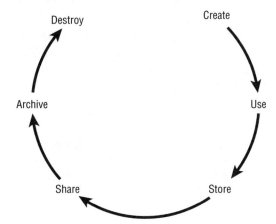

Data will still be created (Create phase)—in both the cloud and from remote users. It will be stored, in both the short term (Store phase) and long term (Archive phase), in the cloud. It will be manipulated and modified (Use phase) in the production environment hosted in the cloud. It will be transmitted to other users and made available for collaboration (Share phase) within the cloud; this is one of the significant benefits offered by cloud computing. In addition, we will still have a need to remove data from the production environment and sanitize the media afterward (Destroy phase).

Obviously, the particulars for performing these activities, and doing them in a secure fashion, will evolve to match any new environmental challenges.

In the cloud, each phase of the data life cycle will require particular protections. Let's review each of the phases in turn, and examine some specific control mechanisms we may want to apply in each.

Create

Data will most often be created by users accessing the cloud remotely. Depending on the use case, the data might be created locally, by users at their remote workstation, and then uploaded to the cloud, or in the cloud datacenter via remote manipulation of the data residing there.

Data Created Remotely   Data created by the user should be encrypted before uploading to the cloud. We want to protect against obvious vulnerabilities, including man-in-the-middle attacks and insider threat at the cloud datacenter. The cryptosystem used for this purpose should have a high work factor and be listed on the FIPS 140-2 list of approved crypto solutions. We should also implement good key management practices, which we'll cover later in this chapter.

The connection used to upload the data should also be secure, preferably with a IPSec VPN solution.

Data Created within the Cloud   Likewise, data created within the cloud via remote manipulation should be encrypted upon creation, to obviate unnecessary access or viewing by datacenter personnel. Again, key management should be performed according to best industry practices, as detailed later in this chapter.

Regardless of where, specifically, the data originates—in the cloud data-center via remote access or at the user's location—the Create phase necessitates all the activities described in Chapter 3, "Data Classification": categorization and classification; labeling, tagging, and marking; assigning metadata; and so forth.

Store

From the perspective of the life-cycle diagram, the Store phase takes place right after the Create phase, and before the Use and Share phases. This indicates that Store is usually meant to refer to near-term storage (as opposed to the Archive phase, which is obviously long-term storage).

For our purposes, we'll consider the activity in the Store phase to occur almost concurrently with the Create phase—that is, Store will happen as data is created. In that respect, we've already described the actions that should occur here: encryption for mitigating exposure to threats within the datacenter.

Use

We will need to utilize the same kinds of mechanisms when performing activity in the Use phase as well. Operations in the cloud environment will necessitate remote access, so those connections will all have to be secured, usually with an encrypted tunnel.

Data security in the Use phase will require considering other operational aspects as well. The platforms with which users connect to the cloud have to also be secured; in a BYOD environment, this will entail a holistic approach, since we can never be sure just what devices the users have. Users have to be trained to understand the new risks that go along with cloud computing, and how they will be expected to use the technology (such as VPN, DRM, and/or DLP agents assigned to them) in a safe manner. Data owners should also be careful to restrict permissions for modifying and processing their data; users should be limited to those functions that they absolutely require in order to perform their assigned tasks. And, as in many circumstances in both the cloud and legacy environments, logging and audit trails are important when data is being manipulated in any fashion.

On the provider side, secure use requires strong protections in the implementation of virtualization; the provider must ensure that data on a virtualized host can't be read or detected by other virtual hosts on that same device. Also, as has been stated several times (and will be repeated throughout the book), the provider will have to implement personnel and administrative controls, so that datacenter personnel can't access any raw customer data.

Share

Although global collaboration is a powerful capability afforded by the cloud, it comes with risks. If users can be anywhere on the planet, so can threats.

Many of the same security controls implemented in prior phases will be useful here: encrypted files and communications, DRM solutions, and so forth. We also have to craft sharing restrictions based on jurisdiction; we may need to limit or prevent data being sent to certain locations, in accordance with regulatory mandates. These restrictions can take the form of either export controls or import controls, so the security professional must be familiar with both, for all regions where the organization's data might be shared.

🌐 **Real World Scenario**

Export and Import Restrictions

Here are export restrictions you should be familiar with:

International Traffic in Arms Regulations (ITAR) (United States)   State Department prohibitions on defense-related exports; can include cryptography systems.

Export Administration Regulations (EAR) (United States)   Department of Commerce prohibitions on dual-use items (technologies that could be used for both commercial and military purposes).

Here are import restrictions you should be familiar with:

Cryptography (Various)   Many countries have restrictions on importing cryptosystems or material that has been encrypted. When doing business in or with a nation with crypto restrictions, it is the security professional's responsibility to know and understand these local mandates.

The Wassenaar Arrangement   A group of 41 member countries have agreed to mutually inform each other about conventional military shipments to non-member countries. Not a treaty, and therefore not legally binding, but may require your organization to notify your government in order to stay in compliance.

Cloud customers should also consider implementing some form of egress monitoring in the Share phase; this will be discussed in the "Egress Monitoring (DLP)" section, later in this chapter.

Archive

This is the phase for long-term storage, and we necessarily have to consider this longer timeframe when planning security controls for the data.

Cryptography will, as with most data-related controls, be an essential consideration. Key management is of utmost importance, because mismanaged keys can lead to additional exposure or to total loss of the data. If the keys are improperly stored (especially if they are stored alongside the data), there is an increased risk of loss; if keys are stored away from the data but not managed properly and lost, there will be no efficient means to recover the data.

The physical security of the data in long-term storage is also important. In choosing a storage location, we need to weigh risks and benefits for these facets of physical security:

Location   Where is the data being stored? What environmental factors will pose risks in that location (natural disasters, climate, etc.)? What jurisdictional aspects might bear consideration (local and national laws)? How distant is the archive location? Will it be feasible to access the data during contingency operations (for instance, during a natural disaster)? Is it far enough to be safe from events that impact the production environment, but close enough to reach that data during those events?

Format   Is the data being stored on some physical medium such as tape backup or magnetic storage? Is the media highly portable, and in need of additional security controls for theft? Will that medium be affected by environmental factors? How long do we expect to retain this data? Will it be in a format still accessible by production hardware when we need it?

 Think of all the archaic media formats used to store data in the past, the cost of those formats, and how complicated it would be to find hardware capable of accessing that data today: Jaz disks, zip disks, Colorado backup tape systems, and so on. Will today's format be outmoded soon, and will we have the hardware necessary to pull that data into a future format?

Staff   Are personnel at the storage location employed by our organization? If not, does the contractor implement a personnel control suite sufficient for our purposes (background checks, reliance checks, monitoring, and so on)?

Procedure   How is data recovered when needed? How is it ported to the archive on a regular basis? How often are we doing full backups (and the frequency of incremental or differential backups)?

Archive phase activities in the cloud will largely be driven by whether we are doing backups in the cloud, whether we are using the same cloud provider for backups and our production environment, or whether we are using a different cloud provider for each. We have to consider all the same factors we would use in the legacy environment (as described earlier), but then also determine whether we could impose those same decisions in the cloud environment, on the cloud provider, via contractual means. How will this be monitored? How will it be enforced?

 Real World Scenario

Eggs in One Basket

There was a recent case of a software repository company that was hacked and bankrupted almost overnight. Their case demonstrates a number of things that a cloud customer should never do. In this instance, the mistake was placing their cloud backups in the same cloud as their production data. When the bad guys got hold of the cloud instance through compromised credentials and were discovered, they not only wiped out all production data to cover their tracks, but they also deleted all of the backup data—bankrupting the company overnight due to the loss of all intangible assets as well as the complete revocation of any type of trust or reputation the company might have had prior to the breach.

Destroy

We discussed destruction options for the legacy and cloud environments in Chapter 3. As we determined, cryptographic erasure (cryptoshredding) is the only feasible and thorough means currently available for the purpose, in the cloud environment.

Cloud Storage Architectures

There are various ways to store data in the cloud, each with attendant benefits and costs.

Volume Storage: File-Based Storage and Block Storage

With volume storage, the customer is allocated a storage space within the cloud; this storage space is represented as an attached drive to the user's virtual machine. From the customer's perspective, the virtual drive performs very much in the same manner as would a physical drive attached to a tangible device; actual locations and memory addresses are transparent to the user.

Volume storage architecture can take different forms; there is a great deal of discussion among cloud professionals about what type of volume might be preferable: file storage or block storage.

File Storage (Also "File-Level Storage" or "File-Based Storage")   The data is stored and displayed just as with a file structure in the legacy environment, as files and folders, with all the same hierarchical and naming functions. File storage architectures have become more popular with cloud technology and big data analytical tools and processes.

Block Storage   Whereas file storage has a hierarchy of folders and files, block storage is a blank volume that the customer or user can put anything into. Block storage might allow more flexibility and higher performance, but it requires a greater amount of administration and might entail installation of an OS or other app to store, sort, and retrieve the data. Block storage might be better suited for a volume and purpose that includes data of multiple types and kinds, such as enterprise backup services.

Storage architecture for volumes can include erasure coding, which is basically a means of implementing a RAID array data protection solution in the cloud. Volume storage can be offered in any of the cloud service models but is often associated with Infrastructure as a Service (IaaS).

Object-Based Storage

Object storage is just like it sounds: data is stored as objects, not as files or blocks. Objects include not only the actual production content, but metadata describing the content and object, and a unique address identifier for locating that specific object across an entire storage space.

Object storage architectures allow for a significant level of description, including the marking, labels, and classification and categorization specification we've talked about earlier. This also enhances the opportunity for indexing capabilities, data policy enforcement (such as DRM, described in Chapter 3, and DLP, discussed later in this chapter in the "Egress Monitoring (DLP)" section), and centralization of some data management functions.

Again, any of the cloud service models can include object storage architectures, but object storage is usually associated with IaaS.

Databases

Like their legacy counterparts, databases in the cloud provide some sort of structure for stored data. Data will be arranged according to characteristics and elements in the data itself, including a specific trait required to file the data known as the primary key. In the cloud, the database is usually backend storage in the datacenter, accessed by users utilizing online apps or APIs through a browser.

Databases can be implemented in any cloud service model, but they are most often configured to work with PaaS and SaaS.

Content Delivery Network (CDN)

A content delivery network (CDN) is a form of data caching, usually near geophysical locations of high use demand, for copies of data commonly requested by users. Perhaps the best example of why an organization would want to use a CDN is online multimedia streaming services: instead of dragging data from a datacenter to users at variable distances across a continent, the streaming service provider can place copies of the most requested media near metropolitan areas where those requests are likely to be made, thus improving bandwidth and delivery quality.

Cloud Data Security Foundational Strategies

Just as certain technologies make cloud computing feasible as a whole, certain technologies and practices make data security possible in the cloud and therefore also make cloud computing pragmatic and sensible.

Encryption

It should come as no surprise that cloud computing has a massive dependency in the form of encryption; you have probably noticed how many times, and in how many ways, encryption has been mentioned throughout the book so far.

Encryption will be used to protect data at rest, in transit, and in use. Encryption will be used on the remote user end to create the secure communication connection, on the cloud customer's enterprise to protect their own data, and within the datacenter by the cloud provider to ensure various cloud customers don't accidentally access each other's data.

Realistically, without encryption it would be impossible to use the cloud in any secure fashion.

The book has included some details about encryption implementations already, and will continue to do so as we discuss various aspects of cloud computing. In this section, we will focus on only two particular topics of encryption in the cloud: key management and an experimental encryption implementation that might create a whole new level of security and trust in the cloud.

Key Management

As we have noted before, how and where encryption keys are stored can affect the overall risk of the data in severe ways. Here are some things to remember and consider regarding key management for cloud computing:

Level of Protection   Encryption keys must be secured at the same level of control, or *higher*, as the data they protect. The sensitivity of the data dictates this level of protection, according to the organization's data security policies. Always, we should remember that the strength of the cryptosystem is only valid if private keys are not disclosed.

Key Recovery   Although you don't want to make access to user keys easy, there may be circumstances where you need to recover a key for a particular user, without that user's cooperation. This might be because the user was fired from the organization, or died, or lost their key. You need to have the technology and process for getting that key to access that data. Usually, this entails a procedure that involves multiple people, each with access to only a portion of the key.

Key Distribution   Issuing keys for a cryptosystem can be difficult and fraught with risk. If the key management process requires a secure connection to initiate the key creation procedure, how do you establish that secure session without a key? Often, passing keys out of band is a preferable, yet cumbersome and expensive, solution. Moreover, keys should never be passed in the clear.

Key Revocation   As mentioned earlier, there are plenty of reasons why you'd want to end a user's access to the enterprise; you therefore need a process for doing so.

Key Escrow   In many cases, having copies of keys held by a trusted third party in a secure environment is highly desirable; this can aid in many of the other key management efforts listed in this section.

Outsourcing Key Management   Keys should not be stored with the data they're protecting, and we shouldn't make physical access to keys readily available to anyone who doesn't have authorization and need to know for that data; therefore, in cloud computing, it is preferable to have the keys stored somewhere other than the cloud provider's datacenter. One solution is to host the keys within the organization, but that requires an expensive and complicated set of infrastructure and skilled personnel. This would attenuate some of the benefit (in reduced costs) we get from offloading our enterprise to the cloud provider. Another option is using a cloud access security broker (CASB). CASBs are third-party providers that handle IAM and key management services for cloud customers; the cost of using a CASB should be much lower than trying to maintain keys within the organization, and the CASB will have core competencies most cloud customers won't.

 Whether or not a cloud customer chooses to use a CASB or other means of key management, the preferred solution is *not* to store the crypto keys with the cloud provider.

Homomorphic Encryption

Homomorphic encryption is a developing technology that is intended to allow for processing of encrypted material without decrypting it first. This would be a huge boon for the field of cloud computing, because material could be encrypted locally (by remote users), uploaded in encrypted form to the cloud, accessed remotely (while still encrypted), and manipulated and utilized while still encrypted. In this way, the provider (and all personnel in the cloud datacenter) and anyone trying to intercept communication between the user and the cloud would never have the opportunity to view the data in plain-text form.

Again, homomorphic encryption is still in the research stage and not readily available for production environments. However, it is a fascinating development for our field and worth knowing about.

Masking, Obfuscation, Anonymization, and Tokenization

For other uses in the cloud, we may find it necessary to obscure actual data and instead use a representation of that data. We use the terms titling this section to describe that effort.

Here are some examples of purposes for which you'd want to do this:

Test Environments   New software should be tested in sandboxed environments before being deployed to the production environment. When performing this type of testing, actual production data should *never* be used within the sandbox. However, in order to determine the actual functionality and performance of the system, it will be necessary to use data that approximates closely the same traits and characteristics of the production data.

Enforcing Least Privilege   We know that the concept of least privilege entails limiting users to permissions and access absolutely necessary to perform their duties. In some cases, that might mean allowing the user access to elements of a dataset without revealing its entirety. For instance, a customer service representative might need to access a customer's account information, and be shown a screen with that information, but that data might be an abridged version of the customer's total account specifics.

Secure Remote Access   When a customer logs onto a web service, the customer's account might have some data abridged in similar fashion to the least privilege example. The screen might display some of the customer's preferences, but you might not want to display certain elements of the customer's account data, such as payment or personal information, to avoid risks such as hijacked sessions, stolen credentials, or shoulder-surfing.

So how are these activities performed? These are some techniques that you can use to obscure data for use in the cloud context:

Randomization   The replacement of the data (or part of the data) with random characters. Usually, and as with most cases of obscuring data, you want to leave the other traits (aside from displaying the actual data) intact: length of the string, character set (whether it was alphabetic or numerical, whether it had special characters, whether there was upper/lower case, etc.), and so forth.

Hashing   Using a one-way cryptographic function to create a digest of the original data. Using a hash algorithm to obscure the data gives you the benefit of ensuring it is unrecoverable, and you can also use it as an integrity check later. However, because hashing converts variable-length messages into fixed-length digests, you lose many of the properties of the original data.

Shuffling   Using different entries from within the same data set to represent the data. This has the obvious drawback of using actual production data.

Masking   Hiding the data with useless characters; for example, showing only the last four digits of a Social Security number: XXX-XX-1234. Can be used in the examples mentioned earlier, where the customer service representative or the customer gets authorized access to the account, but you want to obscure a portion of the data for additional security.

Nulls   Deleting the raw data from the display before it is represented, or displaying null sets.

 Real World Scenario

Handling Social Security Numbers Beyond Masking

During a recent audit of a regulated company who had utilized most of the encryption techniques mentioned in this section as part of their PCI compliance efforts, a surprising finding was discovered. It was found that customer representatives, who could not see Social Security numbers due to masking, were in fact exposed to full Social Security numbers during phone call conversations with customers. The customers, even though never asked, would sometimes just blurt out their entire Social Security number. What no one was aware of was that the annoying message you get at the start of customer service calls that says, "This call may be recorded for training purposes" resulted in those blurted-out messages being recorded. What is significant about the story is that the messages that were being recorded were also being stored in the cloud *and* were not encrypted. PCI only has standards for encrypting cardholder data, and no one ever suspected the voice messages that were recorded might expose such data. The story had a happy ending, though; the solution was a simple matter of adding encryption to the storage for the messages.

Obscuring can be done in either static or dynamic configurations. With the static technique, a new (representational) dataset is created as a copy from the original data, and only the obscured copy is used. In the dynamic method, data is obscured as it is called, like with the examples we described: the customer service agent or the customer is granted authorized access, but the data is obscured as it is fed to them.

We may also want to add another layer of abstraction to the data, to attenuate the possibility that sensitive information may be gleaned from otherwise mundane elements. For instance, even if we're obscuring a person's name in a given dataset, if we allow other information, such as age, location, and employer, it may be possible to determine the name without having direct access to that field. We call this "anonymization." This can be difficult to enact, because the data must be marked for anonymization as it is created, and this data is often included in free-entry fields, where it is harder to identify and distinguish from data that won't reveal anything sensitive.

Tokenization is the practice of having two distinct databases: one with the live, actual sensitive data, and one with nonrepresentational tokens mapped to each piece of that data (see Figure 4.2). In this method, the user or program calling the data is authenticated by the token server, which pulls the appropriate token from the token database, and then calls the actual data that maps to that token from the real database of production data, and finally presents it to the user or program. Tokenization adds significant overhead to the process but creates an extra degree of security. For tokenization to function properly, the token server must have strong authentication protocols.

FIGURE 4.2 Basic tokenization architecture

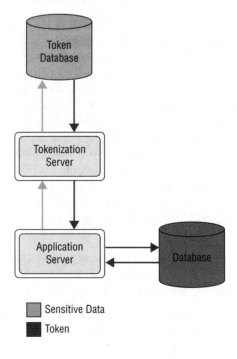

Security Information and Event Management

We use monitoring tools to know how well the systems and security controls in our IT environment are functioning, to detect anomalous activity, and to enforce policy. A large part of the monitoring effort comes in the form of logs: recording activity as it happens, sometimes from specialized devices that only conduct monitoring, and other times from operational systems themselves (with their integrated logging functions).

To better collect, manage, analyze, and display log data, a set of tools specifically for that purpose have become popular. These are known by a variety of terms, since there is no accepted standard: nomenclature includes security information management, security event management, security information and event management, and permutations of these (including acronyms such as SIM, SEM, and SIEM, pronounced in various ways).

Differentiating between what each purports to do is pointless; instead, we will discuss the general purpose of the family of tools, and refer to them all, inclusively, as "SIEM."

Goals of SIEM implementation include the following:

Centralize Collection of Log Data Because logs can be drawn from so many sources (workstations, OSs, servers, network devices, and so on), it can be useful to have a place to aggregate it all for additional processing. If nothing else, this simplifies the activity for the admins and analysts who will be tasked with monitoring the environment. This does create an additional risk, however: having all the log data in one location makes that location an attractive target for attackers, so any SIEM implementation will require additional layers of security controls.

Enhanced Analysis Capabilities Log analysis is a mundane, repetitive task that requires a special skillset and experience, and is not suited for full-time tasking (an analyst who stares at the same dataset and data feeds all day, day after day, will become inured to the activity, whereas an analyst who doesn't see the data from the environment often enough won't be as familiar with the baselines, and therefore won't recognize anomalous behavior). One way we can offset some the problems with log analysis is to automate some of the process. SIEM tools should have this capability, in addition to other functions such as advanced trend detection based on large datasets. One thing to remember, however, is that most automated tools will not recognize a particular set of attacks—the "low and slow" style of persistent threats, which may develop over weeks or months and that don't have dramatic indicators, and therefore may be confused with background attack noise and go undetected by automated analysis.

Dashboarding Management often doesn't understand IT functions, and even less about IT security. SIEMs often offer some graphical output display that is more intuitive and simple for managers to quickly grasp situations within the environment.

Automated Response Some SIEMs include automated alert and response capabilities that can be programmed to suit your policies and environment.

Like logging itself, SIEMs are only useful when someone is actually looking at what they produce; simply having the shiny box that performs security functions is nice, but unless the information it provides is being harvested by someone who knows what they're looking at, the SIEM can be just another bandage in a damaged environment, and won't really offer any benefit to the organization.

Egress Monitoring (DLP)

Another set of popular tools are for the purpose of egress monitoring—that is, examining data as it leaves the production environment. These are often called "DLP," which can stand for any combination of the terms data loss, leak prevention, and protection. We're just going to refer to them universally as DLP.

Like SIEM, DLP solutions generally have several major goals:

Additional Security   DLP can be used as another control in the layered defense strategy, one last mechanism designed for mitigating the possibility of inadvertent release or malicious disclosure.

Policy Enforcement   Users can be alerted by the DLP when they are attempting to perform an action that would violate the organization's policy (either accidentally or intentionally).

Enhanced Monitoring   The DLP tool can be set to provide one more log stream to the organization's monitoring suite.

Regulatory Compliance   Specific types and kinds of data can be identified by the DLP solution, and dissemination of that data can be controlled accordingly, in order to better adhere to regulatory mandates.

DLP solutions can often be linked to DRM tools, allowing extra functionality to the controls on intellectual property.

DLP tools can function in a variety of ways, but the general concept is that data is identified, activity is monitored, and policies are enforced.

The identification task can be automated, manual, or a combination of both. The tool might search the organization's entire storage volumes and production environment to match data against known templates; for instance, the DLP might search for numeric strings nine characters in length in order to detect Social Security numbers. The DLP also might use categorization and classification markings, labels, and metadata assigned by the data owner during the Create phase of the data life cycle. Or the DLP might use keyword searches for particular information known by the organization to be sensitive for its purposes.

The monitoring task can be implemented at the points of network egress (in legacy systems at the DMZ [demilitarized zone], but in the cloud this would be on all public-facing devices), or on all hosts that process data within the production environment. In the latter case, the DLP solution usually includes local agents installed on user workstations.

The enforcement mechanism can take many forms. The DLP might be set to alert management or security personnel when a user is conducting an activity that violates policy (say, sending an email attachment that contains data the organization has deemed sensitive). If what we're trying to prevent is more accidental disclosures (as opposed to malicious activity), the DLP might just warn users that the email they're sending contains sensitive data, and confirm that they really intended to do so. Or the DLP might be a bit more draconian, and prevent the user from sending the attachment, locking the user out of the account, and notifying management and security. The organization can tailor DLP action to its own needs.

DLP implementation in the cloud comes with related difficulties and costs, though. For one thing, the cloud provider may not allow the cloud customer sufficient access (in terms of both administrative permissions and installation of the requisite systems for implementation) to the datacenter environment, complicating successful configuration and usage. For another, DLP utilization incurs significant processing overhead; all that monitoring and functionality comes with a processing cost.

Summary

This chapter addressed the data life cycle within the cloud environment, as well as specific security challenges in each phase. We looked at different data storage architectures that might be implemented in the cloud, and which service model might be best suited for each. We discussed cryptography, including the importance and difficulty with key management, and the possibility of using homomorphic encryption in the future. There were several use cases describing why we might want to obscure raw data and only display selected portions during operations, and we talked about various methods for performing this task. We reviewed SIEM solutions, how and why they're implemented, and some risks associated with their use. Finally, we addressed the topic of egress monitoring, how DLP tools work, and specific problems that might be encountered when trying to deploy DLP solutions in the cloud.

Exam Essentials

Understand the risks and security controls associated with each phase of the cloud data life cycle.   Every phase has its own attendant risks, and those risks are usually associated with a particular set or type of security controls.

Understand how import/export restrictions affect the field of information security.   You should be familiar with the ITAR and the EAR, and know what the Wassenaar Arrangement is.

Understand the various cloud data storage architectures.   Be able to differentiate between file storage, block storage, databases, and CDN.

Understand how and why encryption is implemented in the cloud.   Know the essential elements of key management; in particular, know that encryption keys are not to be stored alongside the data they were used to encrypt. Know about the emerging technology known as homomorphic encryption, and how it might be used in the future to process encrypted data without having to decrypt it first.

Be familiar with the practice of obscuring data.   Know the different techniques of data masking, hiding, anonymization, and tokenization.

Be familiar with SIEM technology.   Understand the purposes of SIEM implementation, and the challenges associated with using those solutions.

Understand the importance of egress monitoring.   Be familiar with the goals of DLP solutions, how they are implemented, and what challenges a cloud customer might face trying to implement DLP within the cloud datacenter.

Written Labs

1.   Download and read the ISACA white paper on DLP at
     `www.isaca.org/Knowledge-Center/Research/ResearchDeliverables/Pages/Data-Leak-Prevention.aspx`.

2.   In no more than one page, summarize the operational risks listed in Figure 1 of that document.

Review Questions

You can find the answers in Appendix A.

1. All of the following are terms used to described the practice of obscuring original raw data so that only a portion is displayed for operational purposes, except:

    A. Tokenization

    B. Data discovery

    C. Obfuscation

    D. Masking

2. The goals of SIEM solution implementation include all of the following, except:

    A. Centralization of log streams

    B. Trend analysis

    C. Dashboarding

    D. Performance enhancement

3. The goals of DLP solution implementation include all of the following, except:

    A. Policy enforcement

    B. Elasticity

    C. Data discovery

    D. Loss of mitigation

4. DLP solutions can aid in deterring loss due to which of the following?

    A. Randomization

    B. Inadvertent disclosure

    C. Natural disaster

    D. Device failure

5. DLP solutions can aid in deterring loss due to which of the following?

    A. Malicious disclosure

    B. Performance issues

    C. Bad policy

    D. Power failure

6. What is the experimental technology that might lead to the possibility of processing encrypted data without having to decrypt it first?

    A. AES

    B. Link encryption

    C. Homomorphic encryption

    D. One-time pads

7. Proper implementation of DLP solutions for successful function requires which of the following?

A. Accurate data categorization

B. Physical access limitations

C. USB connectivity

D. Physical presence

8. Tokenization requires two distinct _____.

A. Authentication factors

B. Databases

C. Encryption keys

D. Personnel

9. Data masking can be used to provide all of the following functionality, except:

A. Secure remote access

B. Enforcing least privilege

C. Test data in sandboxed environments

D. Authentication of privileged users

10. DLP can be combined with what other security technology to enhance data controls?

A. DRM

B. SIEM

C. Kerberos

D. Hypervisors

11. What are the U.S. State Department controls on technology exports known as?

A. ITAR

B. EAR

C. EAL

D. DRM

12. What are the U.S. Commerce Department controls on technology exports known as?

A. ITAR

B. EAR

C. EAL

D. DRM

13. Cryptographic keys for encrypted data stored in the cloud should be _____.

A. At least 128 bits long

B. Not stored with the cloud provider

C. Split into groups

D. Generated with redundancy

14. Best practices for key management include all of the following, except:

    A. Have key recovery processes

    B. Maintain key security

    C. Pass keys out of band

    D. Ensure multifactor authentication

15. Cryptographic keys should be secured _____.

    A. To a level at least as high as the data they can decrypt

    B. In vaults

    C. By armed guards

    D. With two-person integrity

16. When crafting plans and policies for data archiving, we should consider all of the following, except:

    A. Archive location

    B. The backup process

    C. The format of the data

    D. Immediacy of the technology

17. What is the correct order of the phases of the data life cycle?

    A. Create, Store, Use, Archive, Share, Destroy

    B. Create, Store, Use, Share, Archive, Destroy

    C. Create, Use, Store, Share, Archive, Destroy

    D. Create, Archive, Store, Share, Use, Destroy

18. What are third-party providers of IAM functions for the cloud environment?

    A. DLPs

    B. CASBs

    C. SIEMs

    D. AESs

19. What is a cloud storage architecture that manages the data in a hierarchy of files?

    A. Object-based storage

    B. File-based storage

    C. Database

    D. CDN

20. What is a cloud storage architecture that manages the data in caches of copied content close to locations of high demand?

    A. Object-based storage

    B. File-based storage

    C. Database

    D. CDN

Chapter 5

Security in the Cloud

THE OBJECTIVE OF THIS CHAPTER IS TO ACQUAINT THE READER WITH THE FOLLOWING CONCEPTS:

✓ **Domain 1: Architectural Concepts and Design Requirements**

- B. Describe Cloud Reference Architecture

  - B.5 Cloud Cross-cutting Aspects

- C. Understand Security Concepts Relevant to Cloud Computing

  - C.7 Security Considerations for Different Cloud Categories

- D. Understand Design Principles of Secure Cloud Computing

  - D.2 Cloud Based Business Continuity/Disaster Recovery Planning

  - D.4 Functional Security Requirements

✓ **Domain 3: Cloud Platform and Infrastructure Security**

- A. Comprehend Cloud Infrastructure Components

  - A.4 Virtualization

- B. Analyze Risks to Cloud Infrastructure

  - B.2 Cloud Attack Vectors

  - B.3 Virtualization Risks

  - B.4 Counter-Measure Strategies

- C. Design and Plan Security Controls

  - C.3 Virtualization Systems Protection

- D. Plan Disaster Recovery and Business Continuity Management

  - D.4 Disaster Recovery/Business Continuity Strategy

  - D.5 Creation of the Plan

  - D.6 Implementation of the Plan

✓ **Domain 6: Legal and Compliance**

- D. Understand Implications of Cloud to Enterprise Risk Management

  - D.2 Difference Between Data Owner/Controller vs. Data Custodian/Processor

In this chapter, we will discuss the various rights and responsibilities involved in cloud computing, how those should be apportioned between the cloud provider and customer, specific risks posed by each cloud platform and service, and BC/DR strategies for use in the cloud.

Shared Cloud Platform Risks and Responsibilities

Because the cloud customer and provider will each be processing data that, at least in some part, belongs to the customer, they will share responsibilities and risks associated with that data. Simply put, these risks and responsibilities will be codified in the service contract between the parties. That contract, however, will be the result of a complex process of deliberation and negotiation.

Although the risks and responsibilities will be shared between the cloud provider and customer, the ultimate legal liability for unauthorized and illicit data disclosures will remain with the customer as the data owner. The cloud provider may be financially responsible, in whole or in part, depending on the terms of the contract, but the legal responsibility will be the customer's. This concept will be repeated throughout the book, as it's repeated throughout the CCSP CBK.

As an example of what this means and how it could affect the customer, let's say an unauthorized disclosure of PII that belongs to the customer occurs because of some failure on the part of the cloud provider. For the sake of argument, we'll also assume that the contract stipulates that the provider is financially liable for damages resulting from this failure.

Depending on the jurisdiction where the breach occurred and the jurisdiction of the subjects of the PII (that is, the state or country of citizenship/residence of the people whose PII was lost), statutes could dictate specific monetary damages owed by the cloud customer (again, the data owner) to either the government or the subjects or both. It is possible for the customer to eventually recover those damages from the provider (because of the contract and the fault), but the government will not seek them from the provider; the government will seek damages from the customer. It is the customer that the government will serve injunctions and orders to, not the provider. In addition, depending on the jurisdiction and the breach itself, it is the customer's officers who could face imprisonment, not the provider.

Moreover, even if the customer is protected by the provider's acceptance of financial responsibility, the legal repercussions are not the only negative impact the customer faces. The customer will likely be adversely affected by negative publicity, loss of faith among its clientele, perhaps decreased market share and a drop in share price (if the customer is publicly traded), and an increase in insurance premiums. It is therefore important for the customer to realize that the cash involved in damage awards and assignment of liability is only one aspect of the risk.

Of paramount importance is to understand that the customer's ultimate legal liability for data it owns remains true *even if the provider's failure was the result of negligence or malice*. That is a very considerable burden of risk, especially because it's a much higher standard than what we usually face in the security profession.

That said, the provider and customer still must come to terms regarding their particular responsibilities and obligations under the contract. To some degree, this will be driven by the nature of the service in question and what service and model the customer is purchasing. A graphical depiction of the general gradations of the various arrangements is shown in Figure 5.1.

FIGURE 5.1   Responsibilities according to service model

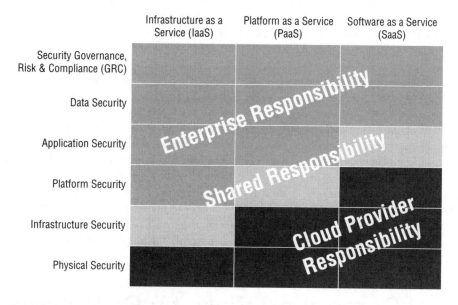

Again, this is not prescriptive, but a guide for possible contract negotiation.

There will be some dichotomy because of the two perspectives. The cloud provider and the customer are most concerned with two different things. The cloud customer is concerned about the data. The production environment on the cloud datacenter is the customer's lifeblood. Breaches, failures, and lack of availability are the things that most affect the customer. The provider, on the other hand, is mostly concerned with the security and operation of their datacenter, which is the provider's core competency and the way it survives and maintains profitability.

Therefore, the customer will be seeking maximal control over their data, with all the administrative power and insight into the datacenter operations it can acquire. The customer will want to impose policy, get logging data, and audit the performance and security of the datacenter.

The provider will be attempting to limit customer access as much as possible. The provider wants to refute control, deny insight, and refrain from disclosing any information that might be used for malicious purposes, which includes the list of security controls used for protecting the datacenter, procedures, and live monitoring equipment and data. In some cases, the provider might not even want to disclose the physical location of the datacenter, believing that secrecy can lead to security.

This creates an adversarial dynamic in the negotiation. Both parties must have a clear awareness of what outcomes they're seeking and the best means to get them. In many cases, the provider will have an advantage in this regard because the provider understands the function and design of the datacenter and therefore the known and expected outcomes of operation much better than most customers do. Organizations that are new to managed services in general and cloud computing specifically may not be aware of what, exactly, to ask for in the negotiation. It is therefore advisable that organizations without a core technical competency and familiarity with cloud operations seek external consultation when initially considering cloud migration and entering negotiations with providers.

Cloud Customers, Providers, and Similar Terms

In this chapter, we talk specifically about the cloud customer (the company, individual, or other entity that hires the cloud provider to take care of their data) and the cloud provider (the company that is hired to provide services, platforms, and/or applications that help with managing the cloud customer's data). In the real world, you might also see terms such as data customer, data owner, data controller, data provider, data custodian, and data processor. These terms are all attempts at describing who owns the data and who handles the data, which generally sifts out to being the cloud customer and the cloud provider, which are the terms we will use pretty consistently for our discussion.

Cloud Computing Risks by Deployment and Service Model

To prepare for cloud migration and the requisite contract negotiation (and for familiarization with CCSP CBK content), it is useful to review the risks particular to each of the cloud deployment models (private, community, public, and hybrid) and service models (IaaS, PaaS, and SaaS).

Private Cloud

A private cloud configuration is a legacy configuration of a datacenter, often with distributed computing and BYOD capabilities. The organization controls the entire infrastructure (hardware, software, facilities, administrative personnel, security controls, and so on). These components might be owned, leased, or some combination thereof.

Many of the potential operating risks are somewhat attenuated by maintaining this level of control. Policy promulgation and enforcement, network performance and security monitoring, personnel management, physical security and access, privileged account management, and auditing capability are all enhanced by ownership.

However, this entails a great deal of overhead expense and effort and does not attenuate all risks. Moreover, the organization may not be in the specific field of IT provisioning, operation, and security, so employing personnel with the necessary skillsets is a significant additional expense.

Risks that all private cloud operators face include the following:

Personnel Threats   This includes both inadvertent and malicious threats. In the private cloud, personnel controls remain at the behest of the organization, which can be reassuring.

Natural disasters   In the private cloud, the organization knows exactly how prepared they are to cope with this situation and how often, what kind, and where backups are done.

External Attacks   These attacks can take many forms, such as unauthorized access, eavesdropping, DOS/DDoS, and so on.

Regulatory Noncompliance   In private configurations, full control resides internally, and the organization can know its exact regulatory exposure and confidently ensure that it is complying with all relevant regulations.

Malware   This can be considered an external or internal threat, depending on the source of the infection.

None of these risks are unique to the private cloud, but handling them internally provides the organization with complete knowledge and control of how each of these threats is being managed.

Private cloud deployments are probably best suited to large organizations that have their own internal IT and security capabilities. While there will be a variety of risks to the enterprise, the organization retains autonomy and authority for all aspects of the production environment. This can be costly, but it is an excellent way to ensure all risks of concern to the organization are being addressed to the satisfaction of the organization.

Community Cloud

In a community cloud configuration, resources are shared and dispersed among an affinity group. Infrastructure can be owned and/or operated jointly, individually, centrally, across the community, or in any combination and mixture of these options.

The benefits of this deployment model each come with attendant risks:

Resiliency Through Shared Ownership   Because the network ownership and operation is scattered among users, the environment is more likely to survive the loss of a significant number of nodes without affecting the others. However, this introduces additional risks because each node is its own point of entry and a vulnerability in any one node can result in an intrusion on the others. This, of course, means that unity of configuration management and baselines is almost impossible (and very difficult to enforce). With distributed ownership comes distributed decision making in terms of policy and administration.

Shared Costs   Overhead and cost of the infrastructure is shared among the members of the community, but so is access and control.

No Need for Centralized Administration for Performance and Monitoring   Although this removes many burdens of centralized administration, it also removes the reliability of centralized and homogenized standards for performance and security monitoring.

Public Cloud

This is the deployment model that has the most focus in the CCSP CBK and the model most likely to provide the most benefit to the greatest number of cloud customers. In the public cloud, a company offers cloud services to any entity that wants to become a cloud customer, be it an individual, company, government agency, or other organization.

Many of the same risks exist in the public cloud as in the private cloud: personnel threats (inadvertent and malicious), external threats, natural disasters, and so forth. Some of them are obviated by the public cloud's similarity to the community cloud, such as distributed infrastructure, shared costs, and reduced need for administrative capability. However, it is these same benefits that entail the additional risks of the public cloud. The organization will lose control, oversight, audit, and enforcement capabilities—basically, all the assurance of maintaining a private cloud internal to the organization.

There are some additional risks that are unique to the public cloud that also must be considered. We'll discuss those in some detail in the following subsections.

Vendor Lock-In

In ceding control of the production environment and data to an external party, the organization creates a dependency on that provider. The expense and trouble of moving the data out of the provider's datacenter could be crippling to the organization, especially if the organization chose to do so before the end of the contract term. In a sense, this can make the organization a hostage of the provider and allow the provider to decrease service levels and/or increase prices as the provider sees fit. It's important to stress that this is *not* a commonplace occurrence. We do not mean to suggest that cloud providers are maliciously luring customers into unfavorable arrangements. However, the possibility exists for that dependency, and dependency is a risk.

Vendor lock-in (also known as provider lock-in) can be caused by other circumstances as well. For instance, if the provider uses a proprietary data format or medium to store information, the customer may not be able to move their data to another provider. The contract itself can be considered a form of lock-in, too, if it is punitive and puts an undue onus on the customer if the customer chooses to go to another provider. Alternatively, vendor lock-in can be caused by some sort of regulatory constraint, where finding another provider that will meet the specific regulatory needs of the organization could be difficult.

To avoid lock-in, the organization has to think in terms of *portability* when considering migration. We use the term "portability" to describe the general level of ease or difficulty when transferring data out of a provider's datacenter (regardless of whether it's being moved to another provider or to a private cloud).

There are several things an organization can do to enhance the portability of its data:

Ensure favorable contract terms for portability.   Make sure the organization considers an exit strategy, even while creating the initial agreement with the provider at the outset of migration. Is there a reduced-rate trial period in the provider environment? What is the penalty for early transfer (severing the contract)? At the end of the contract term, will there be any difficulty, contractually or in terms of performance, in moving the data to another provider? (See the real-world example "Ambiguity Is Scary.")

Avoid proprietary formats.   Don't sign with a provider unless the raw data can be recovered in a format that could be used at another provider's site. This might involve using some form of conversion before moving the data, and that conversion should be simple and inexpensive if the customer chooses to move.

Ensure there are no physical limitations to moving.   Make sure that the bandwidth leaving the old provider is sufficient for the purposes of moving your organization's entire data set and that the new provider can handle that size of importation.

Check for regulatory constraints.   There should be more than one cloud provider that can handle your organization's specific compliance needs. If your needs are bizarrely unique and restrictive (for instance, if your organization is a medical college that takes credit card payments, thus requiring you to simultaneously comply with FERPA, PCI, and HIPAA), that number of providers may be extremely limited.

 Real World Scenario

Ambiguity Is Scary

In the case of one public cloud provider, the contract stipulated a set of maximum monthly upload/download parameters, with additional fees assessed if these bounds were exceeded in any given month. This is commonplace, and the usual way cloud providers establish rates and provide for the appropriate level of resources to meet their customers' regular needs and still allow for cloud bursting.

Elsewhere in the contract, the terms for leaving at the end of any contract period were detailed to include a duration in which the customer could move their data away from the provider (it was 30 days).

What the contract *didn't* state was whether the same monthly limits (and fees for exceeding those limits) would be in effect during the month-long movement of data out of the provider's space in the event the customer chose to leave.

It seems obvious that the limits wouldn't be enforced during the transition period. Otherwise, how could a customer reasonably leave the provider? Assuming the customer was making maximal use of the service and uploading x bytes of data each month of a year-long contract term, there would be $12x$ bytes (12 times the established monthly limit) stored in the provider's datacenter at the end of the contract. If the limits were still in place, the customer would be facing considerable penalties in fees to move $12x$ bytes in that final month. Can the customer assume that this reasonable conclusion was the intention of the contract?

Of course not. We can never assume anything, especially when crafting contracts. Therefore, this is a question that would have to be resolved in writing and agreed to as an amendment or addition to the contract before both parties sign.

Vendor Lock-Out

Another problem associated with ceding control of the organization's data and production environment is referred to as vendor lock-out (also known as provider lock-out). Vendor lock-out can be caused when the cloud provider goes out of business, is acquired by another interest, or ceases operation for any reason. In these circumstances, the concern is whether the customer can still readily access and recover their data.

We cannot really plan for all the possible reasons vendor lock-out might occur. We can, however, be aware that the possibility exists and make decisions accordingly. Some of the factors we may want to consider when selecting a cloud provider include the following:

Provider Longevity How long has the provider been in business? Do they seem to be a market leader? This aspect may be more difficult than others to assess, because IT is an extremely volatile field and new entrants are constantly entering while stalwarts often leave with little warning. Cloud technology and services on a large scale, in particular, are a fairly recent development and may be more prone to significant and unexpected turbulence.

Core Competency Can this provider offer your organization what it needs? Are they capable of meeting all your service requirements? Do they have the staff, resources, and infrastructure to handle your organization's demands, as well as those of their other customers? One measure of the possible strength and suitability of a given provider is whether a cloud service is central to their offerings or is an additional function for their company.

Jurisdictional Suitability What country is the provider in, and which state? This question must be asked in terms of both where it is chartered and where it operates. Where is the datacenter? Where is its long-term storage and backup capability? Will your organization's data be crossing boundaries and borders? Can your organization use this provider and remain compliant with all applicable regulations?

Supply Chain Dependencies   Does the provider rely on any other entities for its critical functions, both upstream and downstream? Are there essential suppliers, vendors, and utilities without which the provider could not perform? This aspect will be very difficult to investigate without considerable disclosure on the part of the provider.

Legislative Environment   What pending statutes might affect your organization's ability to use that provider? This facet might carry the most potential impact for cloud customers and also be the most challenging to predict. For instance, almost nobody foresaw that Great Britain would leave the European Union in 2016, and the Brexit referendum entailed significant political and regulatory modifications for companies operating in both jurisdictions.

 Real World Scenario

Not If, But When

Some people might think that a provider's record of incidents should be used as a discriminator when considering vendor lock-out and that if a given vendor has proven susceptible to breaches or attacks or failures in the past, this should be a telling portent of their ability to survive in the future. This may not be the most useful method for measuring the suitability of a vendor. Instead, knowing that a vendor has suffered through incidents may indicate that this is a vendor you should strongly consider handling your business. Simply put: Everyone can and will be breached at some point, every system fails, and every organization experiences security issues. We should not be expecting a zero-fault environment. We should be looking for a fault-tolerant environment. How did the provider respond to the incidents? What did they do? What didn't they do? How did the market (and their customers) respond to the provider's handling of the matter? We can learn more from how a provider dealt with past security issues than a provider that claims to have never had any.

Multitenant Environments

Going into a public cloud means entering a multitenant environment. There will be no providers that will host your organization as their sole customer. (Indeed, you should be wary of any provider that would *want* to be in that position. It doesn't scale and wouldn't be profitable.) There are therefore specific risks in the public cloud configuration that do not exist in other models. These include the following:

Conflict of Interest   Provider personnel who administer your data and systems should not also be involved with any of your competitors who might also be that provider's customers. The provider should be careful to not create these situations or even the perception that they might exist. The CISSP CBK discusses an information flow model design for this express purpose: the Brewer-Nash model.

Escalation of Privilege   Authorized users may try to acquire unauthorized permissions. This might include users from organizations other than your own. A user who gains illicit administrative access may be able to gain control of devices that process other customers' data.

Information Bleed   With multiple customers processing and storing data over the same infrastructure, there is the possibility that data belonging to one customer will be read or received by another. Moreover, even if this does not happen with raw data, it might be possible for one customer to detect telltale information about another customer's activity, such as when the customer is processing data, how long the procedure takes, and so on.

Legal Activity   Data and devices within a datacenter may be subpoenaed or seized as evidence in a criminal investigation or as part of discovery for litigation purposes. This is of concern to any cloud customer because of the possibility that a particular asset might not only contain data that is the specific target of the investigation/litigation, but it might also include data belonging to other customers. (In other words, your data might be seized because it's on the same box as the data of another customer who is a target of law enforcement or plaintiffs.)

The Brewer-Nash Model

Although the Brewer-Nash Model is not included in the CCSP CBK (it is in the CISSP, though), it's useful to understand. Also known by the title of the paper in which it was proposed, "The Chinese Wall Security Policy" (https://www.cs.purdue.edu/homes/ninghui/readings/AccessControl/brewer_nash_89.pdf), it is the concept of aligning separation of duties and least privilege with dataflows to prevent conflicts of interest.

Brewer and Nash published their paper as a proposed way to resolve a shortcoming in the Bell-LaPadula (BLP) model—that a user who provides services to one set of customers in a commercial setting should not also be able to access data that belongs to a competing set of customers. BLP, designed for military and government purposes, did not take this into consideration. Instead of crafting rules that could isolate users based on which datasets they had previously accessed, BLP restricted user access to datasets based on classification of the data in each set and the user's own clearance level. Under Brewer-Nash, users are instead given permission to access datasets based on which datasets the user had previously seen, but it also takes into consideration the user's free will and ability to choose the initial sets to access.

Brewer-Nash is perhaps the most relevant model for cloud computing because of the nature of cloud administrators—inside a cloud datacenter, administrators working for the cloud provider could have physical (and perhaps logical) access to every cloud customer served by that facility. This might include customers in direct competition in the same industry. This creates a conflict of interest for the cloud administrator, as well as a potential avenue for corruption.

Proper use of the Brewer-Nash model might address these issues by reducing their likelihood and creating a policy that supports and enforces the model.

Hybrid Cloud

Hybrid cloud configurations, of course, include all the risks of the various models they combine. An organization considering migration into a hybrid cloud ought to be aware of all the risks discussed in each of the previous sections that are applicable to their particular choice of hybrid.

IaaS (Infrastructure as a Service)

In the IaaS (Infrastructure as a Service) model, the customer will have the most control over their resources, which might alleviate some concerns about trusting the provider or lacking insight into the environment. However, there are still risks that exist in the IaaS motif, although they are not usually unique to that configuration:

Personnel Threats   Again, a malicious or negligent insider (working for the provider) may cause significant negative impact to the customer, in large part because they have physical access to the resources within the datacenter where the customer's data resides.

External Threats   These include malware, hacking, DoS/DDoS, man-in-the-middle attacks, and so forth.

Lack of Specific Skillsets   Because so much of the environment will be administered by the customer, and all access will be via remote connections, there will be a significant burden on the customer's administrators and staff to provide both operational and security functions in IaaS. An organization that does not have sufficient personnel with the training and experience necessary for conducting these tasks in a cloud environment is introducing a sizable risk to its operations.

PaaS (Platform as a Service)

The PaaS (Platform as a Service) model will have other risks in addition to those included in the IaaS model. These include the following:

Interoperability Issues   Because the OS will be administered and updated by the provider, the customer's software may or may not function properly with each new adjustment to the environment.

Persistent Backdoors   PaaS is often used for software development and development operations (DevOps) efforts because the customer can install any software (production or testbed) over the infrastructure (hardware and OS) within the cloud environment. This model lends itself well to serving as a testbed for new applications. It can mimic the production environment with a structured sampling of all the systems from the live enterprise, and it also tests the interface with multiple various platforms through the remote access capability and opportunity to spread the test over multiple OSs. With all these benefits for DevOps, it is important to remember a significant risk that comes with that industry: backdoors left by developers after the final product ships. These are used for efficient editing and test cases so that the developer doesn't have to run the program all the way from the beginning to find the particular function that needs to be addressed. However, backdoors also serve as attack vectors if discovered and exploited by malicious parties. What was yesterday's development tool is tomorrow's zero-day exploit.

Virtualization   Because most PaaS offerings utilize virtualized OSs, the threats and risks associated with virtualization must be considered in this model. Please see the "Virtualization" section later in this chapter for more information about this.

Resource Sharing   Programs and instances run by the customer will operate on the same devices used by other customers, sometimes simultaneously. The possibility of information bleed and side-channel attacks exists and must be considered.

SaaS (Software as a Service)

All the risks inherent in the PaaS and IaaS models remain in the SaaS (Software as a Service) environment, along with these additional risks:

Proprietary Formats   The provider may be collecting, storing, and displaying data in a format owned by and unique to that provider. This can lead to vendor lock-in and decrease portability.

Virtualization   The risks from virtualization are enhanced in the SaaS environment because even more resource sharing and simultaneous multitenancy is going to occur. Again, refer to the next section, "Virtualization."

Web Application Security   Most SaaS offerings will rely on access through a browser, with some kind of application programming interface (API). Potential weaknesses within web apps pose a wide variety of risks and threats.

Virtualization

We have discussed the importance of virtualization throughout the book. In this section, we'll discuss the risks related to the use of virtualization in the cloud. Many of these possibilities require attenuation through use of controls that can only be implemented by the cloud provider, so the cloud customer must rely on contractual provisions for implementation and enforcement.

Attacks on the Hypervisor   Instead of attacking a virtualized instance, which might only result in successfully breaching the content of one (virtualized) workstation, malicious actors might attempt to penetrate the hypervisor, which is the system that acts as the interface and controller between the virtualized instances and the resources of the given host devices on which they reside.

There are two types of hypervisors, known as Type 1 and Type 2. Type 1 is also called a bare-metal or hardware hypervisor. It resides directly on the host machine, often as bootable software. Type 2 is a software hypervisor, and it runs on top of the OS that runs on a host device.

Attackers prefer Type 2 hypervisors because of the larger surface area. They can attack the hypervisor itself, the underlying OS, and the machine directly, whereas Type 1 attacks are restricted to the hypervisor and the machine. OSs are also more complex than hypervisors, creating the increased potential for included vulnerabilities.

Guest Escape   An improperly designed or poorly configured virtualized machine or hypervisor might allow for a user to leave the confines of their own virtualized instance. This is referred to as *guest escape* or *virtual machine (VM) escape*. A user who has successfully performed guest escape might be able to access other virtualized instances on the same host and view, copy, or modify data stored there. Worse, the user might be able to access the host itself and therefore be able to affect all the instances on the machine. And the worst potential situation is known as *host escape*, where a user can not only leave their own virtualized instance but can even leave the host machine, accessing other devices on the network. This may be unlikely, as it would only result from some rather egregious failures in hardware, software, policy, and personnel performance (or significant combinations thereof), but it is a risk and must be considered.

Information Bleed   This is another risk stemming from malfunctions or failures. The possibility exists that processing performed on one virtualized instance may be detected, in whole or in part, by other instances on the same host. In order for this risk to be detrimental, the loss does not even have to be the raw data itself. It might instead be only indicative of the processing occurring on the affected instance. For example, it might be possible to detect that a certain operation is happening on the affected instance and that the operation lasts for a specific duration. This kind of process-specific information can tell a malicious actor about the types of security controls on the instance or what kind of operations are being conducted. This can provide the attacker with an advantage because they might be able to narrow down a list of possible attack vectors to only those that will function in that circumstance, or they might gain an insight into what types of material might be acquired from a successful attack.

Data Seizure   Legal activity might result in a host machine being confiscated or inspected by law enforcement or plaintiffs' attorneys, and the host machine might include virtualized instances belonging to your organization, even though your organization was not the target.

Cloud Attack Surface

Cloud datacenters can be perceived as similar to DMZs in legacy enterprises. Because everything in the cloud can be accessed remotely, it can be considered exposed to the Internet, to a greater or lesser extent. Instead of the discrete perimeter of a private network, cloud configurations may be more porous or might be considered to have to no specific perimeter boundary at all.

In this section, we'll discuss threats to specific cloud platforms and countermeasures that may facilitate trust in cloud usage.

Threats by Deployment Model

Although many of the threats to cloud computing are the same as those we faced in legacy operations, they might manifest in novel ways or pose a greater risk. In this section, we'll examine the threats to the private, community, public, and hybrid cloud models.

Private Cloud

A private cloud is basically an internal network with remote access capabilities. This is basically what we thought of as an "enterprise" before the concept and term "cloud computing" was popularized. All the threats common to that motif pose a risk to private cloud architectures. These include but are not limited to the following:

Malware   Malicious software downloaded from the Internet or uploaded to the internal network can cause a wide variety of problems, including data loss, loss of control of devices, interruption of operations, and so forth.

Internal Threats   These can be the result of malicious or accidental activity on the part of employees or others who have been granted access (such as contractors and maintenance personnel).

External Attackers   Entities outside the organization may want to attack the network for any number of reasons, including financial gain, hacktivism, political goals, perceived grievances, and so on. These attacks can take many forms and manifest a variety of effects, including DoS/DDoS, data breach, legal repercussions, and more.

Man-in-the-Middle Attacks   This is the colloquial term for any attack where the attacker inserts themselves between the sender and receiver. This can take the form of simple eavesdropping to acquire data, or it can be a more advanced attack, such as the attacker posing as one of the participants in order to gain further control/access or modifying data traffic to introduce false or damaging information into the communication. The remote access capability of a private cloud enhances the exposure to this type of threat, compared to legacy configurations where all network access was limited to internal users.

Social Engineering   As in all operations, private clouds are susceptible to social engineering threats. Indeed, the private cloud may increase potential vectors for social engineering activities because of the nature of remote operations—the need for users to reset passwords with the assistance of administrators, the prodigious use of email for communications, distribution of access tokens and crypto keys, and so on.

Theft/Loss of Devices   Again, the convenience and enhanced operational capability of remote access also comes with additional threats. In a BYOD environment, especially, the loss or theft of a user's device can lead to unauthorized access and exploitation of the private cloud.

Regulatory Violations   Regulations affect almost all IT operations, but a private cloud adds greater risk that the organization will not be able to maintain compliance. The increased opportunity and efficiency for disseminating information also increases the likelihood of violating applicable regulations.

Natural Disasters   All operations are prone to disruption from natural disasters, and no geographical region is free of risk from this threat. They only differ in location. (Location and climate dictate the types and frequencies of disasters, such as hurricanes, floods, wildfires, tornadoes, earthquakes, volcanoes, mudslides, and so on.) The private cloud can be susceptible to disasters in at least two ways: a disaster could strike the organization's datacenter itself, or it could strike the utilities serving the datacenter (the ISP, electrical provider, and so on).

Community Cloud

Community cloud operations include all the same threats as private cloud implementations (see the previous section), with these additional concerns:

Loss of Policy Control   Because ownership is distributed in a community cloud, centralized policy promulgation and enforcement is not usually an option.

Loss of Physical Control   Again, distributed ownership means not only a decrease in expenses, but a decreased amount of control as well. Lack of physical control equates to a relative decrease in physical security.

Lack of Audit Access   Tied to the loss of physical control, it may be impractical or impossible to conduct audits in a distributed environment.

Public Cloud

Compounding the threats faced by the aforementioned architectures (private and community clouds), the public cloud not only includes all the threats those models faced, but these additional threats:

Rogue Administrator   This is an enhanced form of the insider threat. The public cloud incurs the possibility that an insider with more than just basic access may act in a malicious or irresponsible manner. Because public cloud providers will be managing your systems and data, a bad actor or careless employee could take the form of a network/system architect, engineer, or administrator, potentially causing far more damage than a user in the legacy environment could accomplish. Moreover, because the cloud provider's personnel are one degree removed from the control of the organization (as a cloud customer), there is little likelihood of finding a means to create and enforce requirements that can attenuate this threat.

Escalation of Privilege   This is another extension of the insider threat category. This type of threat is what happens when authorized users try to increase their level of access/permissions, for either malicious or operational reasons. (Not all attempts to escalate privilege are malicious in nature. Some users are willing to violate policy in order to increase their own ability to perform their tasks or to avoid annoying or cumbersome regulations.) The likelihood of this type of threat increases in the public cloud because users are faced with not one but at least two sets of governance—that of their own organization and that of the provider. This can cause delays in requests to modify or grant additional access/permission, which can in turn lead to user attempts to circumvent policy.

Contractual Failure   A poorly crafted contract can lead to vendor lock-in, unfavorable terms, lack of necessary services, and other risks, and it should be perceived as a threat.

> Although natural disasters can still affect the public cloud architecture, the public cloud can actually provide some protection and insulation from natural disasters as well. In fact, one of the advantages of migrating to a public cloud configuration is the security offered by fast replication, regular backups, and distributed, remote processing and storage of data offered by cloud providers.

Hybrid Cloud

All the threats posed to the other forms of cloud computing also exist in a hybrid design, with the additional risk of compounding those threats through the loss of uniformity and centralized control.

Countermeasure Methodology

The following is a discussion of some countermeasures that can be adopted in order to address each of the threats for each of the cloud models discussed in the preceding sections. This coverage is by no means exhaustive or prescriptive and should only be taken as a means to inform the reader and stimulate consideration of possible security activity.

Malware   Host-based and network-based antimalware applications and agents can be employed in actual host devices and virtualized instances. Specific training can be provided for all users regarding the methods used for introducing malware into a cloud environment and how to defeat them. Continual monitoring of network traffic and baseline configurations can be used to detect anomalous activity and performance degradation that may be indicative of infections. Regular updates and patches should be implemented, perhaps including automatic checks for virtual machines as they are instantiated at every boot.

Internal Threats   Prior to hiring, aggressive background checks, résumé/reference confirmation, and skills and knowledge testing should be conducted. For existing employees, personnel policies should be used that include comprehensive and recurring training, mandatory vacation and job rotation, and two-person integrity in those situations where it makes financial and operational sense. Solid workflow policies should include separation of duties and least privilege. Active surveillance and monitoring programs, both physical and electronic, can be used. Data should be masked and obfuscated for all personnel who don't need to work directly with raw data. Egress monitoring should include data loss, leak prevention, and protection technology.

External Attackers Countermeasures include hardened devices, hypervisors, and virtual machines, with a solid security baseline and thorough configuration and change management protocols, as well as strong access controls, possibly even outsourced to a third party such as a cloud access security broker (CASB). It's also important for the organization to understand how the organization is perceived by the subject; this kind of data can be used for threat assessment and identification, as well as offering some predictive capability, which could provide a much more timely response than a reactive way of handling threats. Threat intelligence services offer this functionality.

 Real World Scenario

Protection vs. Security

In 2011, Sony sued a man named George Hotz after Hotz published an exploit that allowed PlayStation 3 owners to subvert internal controls on the game console and take full control of the device. Sony's actions are understandable. The company intended to protect its brand by obviating opportunities for PlayStation users to breach DRM solutions and infringe on software copyrights. Hotz's position is likewise reasonable. Hotz asserted that the owner of a device should be allowed to utilize it in any manner they see fit and that preventing such capabilities on the pretense that this ability might be abused by malicious actors ought not restrict those who have no such intent.

Sony's legal right to defend its property notwithstanding, the action was seen by some as abusive. Sony, a multinational giant with vast resources, was pursuing what was obviously a punitive course against an individual with limited resources and supposedly no ill intent. The hacking group known as Anonymous considered Hotz a kindred spirit and took umbrage at Sony's actions. A hacker claiming to act on behalf of Anonymous launched a three-day attack against Sony's PlayStation Network (PSN), resulting in a breach that exposed account information of 77 million PSN users (arguably the largest known breach in history at that time) and an extended shutdown of the game service. The eventual cost of the attack, according to statements attributed to Sony in news reports, exceeded $171 million, including lost revenue, legal fees, and customer restitution.

It's difficult to imagine the loss of root control over PlayStation devices costing Sony more than the damages related to the hack. This in no way suggests that the illegal attack on PSN is justifiable or reasonable. However, Sony's failure to understand public perception of its position and action exposed Sony to a much greater threat than the one the company was trying to prevent. In handling security matters, even when your organization is legally and ethically in the right, an objective, holistic view can be useful to attenuate unintentional escalation of risk.

Sony and Hotz reached an out-of-court settlement, the full terms of which are not available.

Man-in-the-Middle Attacks   One way to mitigate these attacks is to encrypt data in transit, including authentication activity. You can also use secure session technology and enforcement.

Social Engineering   Training, training, training. Use incentive programs (perhaps including spot bonuses and accolades) to identify personnel who resist social engineering attempts and bring them to the attention of the security office.

Theft/Loss of Devices   Countermeasures include encryption of stored material to attenuate the efficacy of theft, strict physical access controls, limited or no USB functionality (up to and including physically destroying USB ports), detailed and comprehensive inventory control and monitoring, and remote wipe or kill capability for portable devices.

Regulatory Violations   Hire knowledgeable, trained personnel with applicable skillsets. Defer to general counsel in planning and managing your system. Implement DRM solutions. Use encryption and obfuscation and masking as necessary.

Natural Disasters   The cloud provider should ensure multiple redundancies for all systems and services for the datacenter, including ISPs and utilities. The cloud customer can arrange for a disaster backup with the same cloud provider, with another cloud provider, or offline. For further discussion of this topic, see the section "Disaster Recovery (DR) and Business Continuity Management (BCM)" later in this chapter.

Loss of Policy Control   Strong contractual terms should be employed that ensure the provider is adhering to a security program that is at least as effective and thorough as what the customer would institute in an enterprise the customer owned and controlled. Detailed and extensive audits should be conducted by the customer or a trusted third party.

Loss of Physical Control   You can use all of the protections listed in the internal threats, theft/loss of devices, and loss of policy control entries in this list.

Lack of Audit Access   If the provider refuses to allow the customer to directly audit the facility, the customer must rely on a trusted third party instead. If the provider limits access to full third-party reports, the customer must insist on contractual protections to transfer as much of the financial liability for security failures to the provider as possible, including additional punitive damages.

Rogue Administrator   Countermeasures include all the controls listed in the internal threats entry in this list, with additional physical, logical, and administrative controls for all privileged accounts and personnel, including thorough and secure logging of all administrative activities, locked racks, monitoring of physical access to devices in real time, implementation of video surveillance, and financial monitoring of privileged personnel.

Escalation of Privilege   Extensive access control and authentication tools and techniques should be implemented. Countermeasures also include analysis and review of all log data by trained, skilled personnel on a frequent basis, combined with automated tools such as SIEM, SIM, and SEM solutions.

Contractual Failure   To protect against vendor lock-in/lock-out, the customer might consider full offsite backups, secured and kept by the customer or a trusted third-party vendor, for reconstitution with another cloud provider in the event of severe contractual disagreement.

Legal Seizure   As has been mentioned in previous chapters, legal action (either for prosecutorial or litigatory purposes) might result in unannounced or unexpected loss or disclosure of the organization's data. The revised BIA should take this possibility into account, and we need to consider the use of encryption for data in the cloud.

Disaster Recovery (DR) and Business Continuity Management (BCM)

Entire books have been written about this topic. We're not going to be able to address it completely in this one. Instead, we'll focus on those areas of BC/DR most applicable to cloud computing, specifically with the CCSP CBK and exam in mind. In this section, we'll go over BIA concerns specific to cloud platforms and the establishment of shared BC/DR planning and responsibilities between the cloud provider and customer.

Cloud-Specific BIA Concerns

In migrating to a cloud service architecture, your organization will want to review its existing business impact analysis (BIA) and consider a new BIA, or at least a partial assessment, for cloud-specific concerns and the new risks and opportunities offered by the cloud. Some of the potential impacts are things you should have already included in your original BIA, but these may be more significant and take new forms in the cloud. For instance, the loss of an ISP would have affected your organization in its previous (non-cloud) configuration, but losing connectivity after migration might have a more detrimental effect. Unlike a legacy environment, an organization conducting operations in the cloud will not be able to conduct scaled-back, local computing without connectivity to the provider.

Potential emergent BIA concerns include, but are not limited to, the following:

New Dependencies   Your data and operations will be reliant on external parties in whole new ways after migration. Not only will you have to depend on the cloud provider to meet your organization's needs, but all the downstream and upstream dependencies associated with the provider as well, including the provider's vendors, suppliers, utilities, personnel, and so on. The BIA should take into account possibilities involving the provider's inability to meet service requirements, in addition to similar failings on the part of any of the provider's requisite entities.

Regulatory Failure   The efficiency and ease of data distribution in the cloud enhances potential violations of regulations, as users and administrators alike promulgate and disseminate data in new ways. The cloud provider presents another potential point of failure for regulatory compliance as well. Even if your organization is fully compliant internally, the provider might be unable or unwilling to adhere to your policies. Regulatory failures could include insufficient protection for PII/ePHI data to comply with statutory requirements such as GLBA, HIPAA, FERPA, or SOX, and they might also take the form of contractual inadequacies, such as copyright licensing violations. The BIA needs to include discussion of possible impacts from this situation.

Data Breach/Inadvertent Disclosure   Cloud computing magnifies the likelihood and impact of two existing risks: internal personnel and remote access. Moreover, because full legal liability for breaches of PII can't be transferred to the provider, the cloud customer must reassess the potential impact and effect of an unauthorized disclosure, especially in terms of costs resulting from data breach notification legislative mandates. Other potential adverse results from breaches that should be addressed in the revised BIA include, but aren't limited to, public disclosure of deleterious internal communication and reporting; loss of competitive advantage; negative effect on customer, supplier, and vendor goodwill; and contractual violations.

Vendor Lock-in/Lock-out   The BIA should take these risks into account for any operations migrated to the cloud. Much of the data for this part of the report should be readily available and won't have to be re-created for the BIA, as it should have been performed as part of the cost-benefit analysis when the organization first considered migration.

Customer/Provider Shared BC/DR Responsibilities

The negotiation between the customer and the provider will be extensive, addressing service needs, policy enforcement, audit capabilities, and so forth. One of the elements that definitely should be included in this discussion should be provisions for BC/DR, how and where it will be done, who is responsible for each part of the process, and so on. In this section, we'll describe aspects of cloud BC/DR that should be considered in these negotiations.

Logical Location of Backup Data/Systems

There are three general means of using cloud backups for BC/DR. For discussion purposes in this section, we'll be referring to both replicated data and systems as "backups." The basic ways of using cloud backups for BC/DR include the following:

Private Architecture, Cloud Service as Backup   If the organization maintains its own IT enterprise (whether it's in the form of a private cloud or a non-cloud network environment), BC/DR plans can include the use of a cloud provider as the backup. Negotiations with providers will have to include periodic upload bandwidth costs (which often include monthly caps as the limiting factor); frequency of backups; whether the organization will use a full, incremental, or differential motif; the security of the data and systems at the backup datacenter; and ISP costs. In this methodology, the customer should determine when failover will occur—that is, the customer can decide what constitutes an emergency situation and when normal (internal) operations will cease and the backup will be utilized as the operational network. This may involve a formal declaration to include notifying the provider and will almost certainly require additional cost for the duration of the crisis event. Failover might take the form of using the cloud service as a remote network (in an IaaS, PaaS, or SaaS arrangement), or it might require downloading the backup data from the cloud to another site for contingency operations. The negotiation between customer and provider should determine how and when that download occurs, how long it should take, and how and when data will be restored to the normal operations location at the end of the crisis event.

Cloud Operations, Cloud Provider as Backup   One of the attractive benefits of cloud operations is the resiliency and redundancy offered by cloud datacenters, especially from market leaders. Cloud providers might offer a backup solution as a feature of their service—a backup located at another datacenter owned by the provider in case of disaster-level events. In this motif, the provider will have all the responsibility for determining the location and configuration of the backup and most of the responsibility for assessing and declaring disaster events. The customer may have some minimal participation in the failover process, but that's the exception rather than the rule. BC/DR activity, including failover, should usually be transparent to the customer in this case. Moreover, if this feature is offered as part of the normal cloud operation, it will usually be at no or little additional cost.

Cloud Operations, Third-Party Cloud Backup Provider   In this situation, regular operations are hosted by the cloud provider, but contingency operations require failover to another cloud provider. The customer may opt for this selection in order to distribute risk, enhance redundancy, or preemptively attenuate the possibility of vendor lock-out/lock-in. This may be the most complicated BC/DR arrangement to negotiate because it will have to involve preparations and coordination between all three parties, and roles and responsibilities must be explicitly and thoroughly delineated. Under this motif, both the primary cloud provider and the cloud customer will take part in emergency assessment and declaration, and failover may require joint effort. This can impede the process, especially during crises when cooperation and clear communication is most difficult. The cloud customer will also have to negotiate all the terms in the first model in this list (private architecture, cloud service as a backup), with both the primary and backup cloud providers. Usually, this will also be a relatively expensive methodology—the backup provider will not be a cost bundled with other features offered by the primary provider, and both failover and contingency operations will entail additional expenses. (However, some of the increased costs might be offset by payments from the primary provider if conditions of SLAs are not met because of the crisis event.)

Declaration

The declaration of disaster events is a crucial step in the BC/DR process. The cloud customer and provider must decide, prior to the contingency, who specifically will be authorized to make this decision and the explicit process for communicating when it has been made.

Within the customer organization, this authority should be formally assigned to a specific office or person, and there should be a deputy or backup named in case the primary is unavailable. Both the primary and backups should receive detailed emergency operations training that should include extensive and thorough understanding of the organization's specific BC/DR plan. The persons selected for this authority should be empowered by senior management to have the full capability to declare the emergency and initiate failover procedures.

The organization should have a warning system in place to assess impending disaster situations. This is not always possible with certain kinds of contingencies, but some may be anticipated with at least slight notice. The organization should be prepared to fail over in advance of the actual crisis event in order to maintain continuity of operations. The customer and the provider must agree on what will constitute formal notice so that failover occurs, but they may set up a preliminary schedule of preparatory communications before formal declaration is finalized and announced.

If the cloud provider has to conduct some failover activity, the contract should stipulate the time in which this has to be done after notice has been received (for example, within 10 minutes of formal declaration). If failover is automated and fully controlled by the customer, that should also be expressly detailed in the contract.

Resumption of normal activities following a contingency event will likewise require formal notification. Early return to operations may cause an extension of the disaster or result in the loss of data or assets. As with emergency declaration, return to normal operations should be tasked to a specific entity within the customer's organization, and the person making that decision should be fully aware of the risks and implications inherent in it. The process for doing so should also be enumerated within the contract.

> As in all things related to security practices, but especially in disaster situations, health and human safety are the paramount concern of any plan or process.

Testing

Having backups is an admirable practice, fulfills statutory requirements, and satisfies some legal due care obligations. However, merely creating a backup is not sufficient. If you never try to use your backups until an actual crisis event, you have no assurance that they will function as planned.

Failover testing (and return to normal operations) must be performed in order to demonstrate the efficacy of the plan and procedures. It also hones the skills of the personnel involved and allows for additional training opportunities. Of course, the testing itself constitutes an interruption in normal service and ought not be taken lightly. There is risk and cost involved with performing the test.

Most industry guidance stipulates that such testing occur at least annually. This amount might be increased, depending on the nature of the organization and its operations.

BC/DR testing will have to be coordinated with the cloud provider. This should be planned well in advance of the scheduled testing. Care should be taken to determine and assign specific responsibilities to participants, and all liability for problems incurred during the failover or in returning to normal operations should be detailed in the contract.

Summary

In this chapter, we've discussed the shared and distinct responsibilities of the cloud customer and provider in terms of managing risk as well as BC/DR activities. We also explored the specific risks associated with each of the cloud computing platforms (private, community, public, hybrid, IaaS, PaaS, and SaaS), and detailed countermeasures for dealing with them.

Finally, we discussed some of the potential threats and vulnerabilities that constitute the cloud attack surface.

Exam Essentials

Know how responsibilities are shared between the customer and provider.   Understand the notional chart depicted in Figure 5.1 at the beginning of the chapter and how the level of responsibility for each party largely depends on the amount of service being provided.

Know the risks associated with each type of cloud platform.   Memorizing the list might not be necessary, but you should understand the material sufficiently to the point where you could determine which risks are relevant to which particular platform.

Have a thorough understanding of countermeasures used in cloud computing.   Again, rote memorization is probably not the best technique for familiarizing yourself with this important material, but you, as a practitioner as well as a student, should have a degree of comprehension of each potential risk and threat sufficient to match it to specific security controls for attenuation.

Understand BC/DR in the cloud.   Be aware of the similarities to BC/DR plans and activities in the legacy environment, but pay particular attention to the increased complexity of arrangements necessary between cloud customer and provider and the significant importance of the contract in this regard.

Written Labs

1. Locate two cloud providers online. Review their posted policies (preferably, boilerplate versions of their service contracts) regarding real-time or regular full backups, particularly in the context of BC/DR.

2. In less than one page, compare and contrast the two offerings, specifically discussing how each deals with bandwidth for backups, pricing structure, and their suitability for data portability to other cloud providers.

Review Questions

You can find the answers in Appendix A.

1. What is the term we use to describe the general ease and efficiency of moving data from one cloud provider either to another cloud provider or down from the cloud?

   A. Mobility

   B. Elasticity

   C. Obfuscation

   D. Portability

2. The various models generally available for cloud BC/DR activities include all of the following except:

   A. Private architecture, cloud backup

   B. Cloud provider, backup from same provider

   C. Cloud provider, backup from another cloud provider

   D. Cloud provider, backup from private provider

3. Countermeasures for protecting cloud operations against external attackers include all of the following except:

   A. Continual monitoring for anomalous activity

   B. Detailed and extensive background checks

   C. Hardened devices and systems, including servers, hosts, hypervisors, and virtual machines

   D. Regular and detailed configuration/change management activities

4. All of the following are techniques to enhance the portability of cloud data, in order to minimize the potential of vendor lock-in except:

   A. Avoid proprietary data formats

   B. Use DRM and DLP solutions widely throughout the cloud operation

   C. Ensure there are no physical limitations to moving

   D. Ensure favorable contract terms to support portability

5. Which of the following is a technique used to attenuate risks to the cloud environment, resulting in loss or theft of a device used for remote access?

   A. Remote kill switch

   B. Dual control

   C. Muddling

   D. Safe harbor

6. Each of the following are dependencies that must be considered when reviewing the BIA after cloud migration except:

    A. The cloud provider's suppliers

    B. The cloud provider's vendors

    C. The cloud provider's utilities

    D. The cloud provider's resellers

7. When reviewing the BIA after a cloud migration, the organization should take into account new factors related to data breach impacts. One of these new factors is:

    A. Legal liability can't be transferred to the cloud provider.

    B. Many states have data breach notification laws.

    C. Breaches can cause the loss of proprietary data.

    D. Breaches can cause the loss of intellectual property.

8. The cloud customer will have the most control of their data and systems, and the cloud provider will have the least amount of responsibility, in which cloud computing arrangement?

    A. IaaS

    B. PaaS

    C. SaaS

    D. Community cloud

9. After a cloud migration, the BIA should be updated to include a review of the new risks and impacts associated with cloud operations; this review should include an analysis of the possibility of vendor lock-in/lock-out. Analysis of this risk may not have to be performed as a new effort, because a lot of the material that would be included is already available from which of the following?

    A. NIST

    B. The cloud provider

    C. The cost-benefit analysis the organization conducted when deciding on cloud migration

    D. Open source providers

10. A poorly negotiated cloud service contract could result in all the following detrimental effects except:

    A. Vendor lock-in

    B. Malware

    C. Unfavorable terms

    D. Lack of necessary services

11. Because of multitenancy, specific risks in the public cloud that don't exist in the other cloud service models include all the following except:

    A.   Risk of loss/disclosure due to legal seizures

    B.   Information bleed

    C.   DoS/DDoS

    D.   Escalation of privilege

12. Countermeasures for protecting cloud operations against internal threats include all of the following except:

    A.   Aggressive background checks

    B.   Hardened perimeter devices

    C.   Skills and knowledge testing

    D.   Extensive and comprehensive training programs, including initial, recurring, and refresher sessions

13. Countermeasures for protecting cloud operations against internal threats include all of the following except:

    A.   Active physical surveillance and monitoring

    B.   Active electronic surveillance and monitoring

    C.   Redundant ISPs

    D.   Masking and obfuscation of data for all personnel without need to know for raw data

14. Countermeasures for protecting cloud operations against internal threats include all of the following except:

    A.   Broad contractual protections to ensure the provider is ensuring an extreme level of trust in its own personnel

    B.   Financial penalties for the cloud provider in the event of negligence or malice on the part of its own personnel

    C.   DLP solutions

    D.   Scalability

15. Countermeasures for protecting cloud operations against internal threats include all of the following except:

    A.   Separation of duties

    B.   Least privilege

    C.   Conflict of interest

    D.   Mandatory vacation

16. Benefits for addressing BC/DR offered by cloud operations include all of the following except:

    A.   Metered service

    B.   Distributed, remote processing, and storage of data

    C.   Fast replication

    D.   Regular backups offered by cloud providers

17. All of the following methods can be used to attenuate the harm caused by escalation of privilege except:

    A. Extensive access control and authentication tools and techniques

    B. Analysis and review of all log data by trained, skilled personnel on a frequent basis

    C. Periodic and effective use of cryptographic sanitization tools

    D. The use of automated analysis tools such as SIM, SIEM, and SEM solutions

18. What is the hypervisor malicious attackers would prefer to attack?

    A. Type 1

    B. Type 2

    C. Type 3

    D. Type 4

19. What is the term used to describe loss of access to data because the cloud provider has ceased operation?

    A. Closing

    B. Vendor lock-out

    C. Vendor lock-in

    D. Masking

20. Because PaaS implementations are so often used for software development, what is one of the vulnerabilities that should always be kept in mind?

    A. Malware

    B. Loss/theft of portable devices

    C. Backdoors

    D. DoS/DDoS

Chapter 6

Responsibilities in the Cloud

THE OBJECTIVE OF THIS CHAPTER IS TO ACQUAINT THE READER WITH THE FOLLOWING CONCEPTS:

✓ **Domain 1: Architectural Concepts and Design Requirements**

 ▪ C. Understand Security Concepts Relevant to Cloud Computing

  ▪ C.4 Network Security

✓ **Domain 2: Cloud Data Security**

 ▪ E. Design and Implement Relevant Jurisdictional Data Protections for Personally Identifiable Information (PII)

  ▪ E.4 Mapping and Definition of Controls

 ▪ H. Design and Implement Auditability, Traceability, and Accountability of Data Events

  ▪ H.1 Definition of Event Sources and Identity Attribution Requirement

✓ **Domain 3: Cloud Platform and Infrastructure Security**

 ▪ A. Comprehend Cloud Infrastructure Components

  ▪ A.2 Network and Communications

  ▪ A.3 Compute

  ▪ A.6 Management Plane

 ▪ C. Design and Plan Security Controls

  ▪ C.2 System and Communication Protection

✓ **Domain 4: Cloud Application Security**

 ▪ C. Use Verified Secure Software

  ▪ C.3 Community Knowledge

 ▪ D. Comprehend the Software Development Lifecycle

  ▪ D.3 Software Configuration Management and Versioning

✓ **Domain 5: Operations**

- A. Support the Planning Process for the Data Center Design
  - A.2 Physical Design
- B. Implement and Build Physical Infrastructure for Cloud Environment
  - B.1 Secure Configuration of Hardware Specific Requirements
  - B.2 Installation and Configuration of Virtualization Management Toolsets
- C. Run Physical Infrastructure for Cloud Environment
  - C.3 OS Hardening via Application of Baseline
  - C.4 Availability of Standalone Hosts
  - C.5 Availability of Clustered Hosts
- D. Manage Physical Infrastructure for Cloud Environment
  - D.1 Configuring Access Controls for Remote Access
  - D.2 OS Baseline Compliance Monitoring and Remediation
  - D.6 Backup and Restore of Host Configuration
  - D.7 Implementation of Network Security Controls
  - D.9 Management Plane
- E. Build Logical Infrastructure for Cloud Environment
  - E.1 Secure Configuration of Virtual Hardware Specific Requirements
  - E.2 Installation of Guest OS Virtualization Toolsets
- F. Run Logical Infrastructure for Cloud Environment
  - F.2 OS Hardening via Application of Baseline
  - F.3 Availability of the Guest OS
- G. Manage Logical Infrastructure for Cloud Environment
  - G.1 Access Control for Remote Access
  - G.5 Backup and Restore of Guest OS Configuration
  - G.6 Implementation of Network Security Controls
  - G.8 Management Plane

Contracted cloud computing is unlike other operational modes and also unlike other managed IT service arrangements. In the case of cloud computing, the data owner ostensibly owns the information being stored and processed but does not have control over how it is stored and processed or who specifically handles the information (in terms of administration). Perhaps most intriguing of all, the data owner does not actually have physical access to the places and devices where that information *is*. The customer has all the responsibility and liability for protecting the information according to legal standards and regulation but often cannot mandate the actual protections and security measures in order to accomplish this. This is a very strange, unnatural situation.

It's tough to think of an equivalent scenario. Perhaps one that comes close is brokered financial investment, where you give your money to someone else who manages it, invests it how they think best, and uses whatever security measures they determine are most beneficial to protect it. You don't have control over where the money goes or which particular security controls are implemented. You might shop around between investment brokers, trying to find one that offers better protections than all the rest, but it's probably unlikely you'll find much variety, much less be able to dictate the terms of the broker's operations. Depending on what kind of investment vehicle is being used, you might have no assurances that the money is protected from malfeasance and negligence on the part of the broker— many types of investments are not subject to insurance.

What about how the cloud customer is still liable for regulatory infractions and breaches that result in loss of PII, even if the root cause was the cloud vendor's wrongdoing? The financial-investment analogy is a bit stretched, but it still holds true: If someone gives you their money to invest for them, and you give it to a third party, and the third party loses it, you are still responsible for the loss of the money. In that respect, the cloud customer receives assets of value from their clientele (in the form of PII), then gives it to a third party (the cloud vendor), while still remaining responsible for negative outcomes associated with those assets.

Because of the novelty of this arrangement and because the field of cloud computing itself is so new, many of the aspects that protect and support the financial industry do not yet exist in the cloud environment and the details are still getting sorted out. Perhaps most importantly, the case law that has shaped the financial sector—those thousands of cases involving finance that have been tried and ruled on over the past few hundred years— simply have not yet occurred in the IT and InfoSec realm and won't for some time.

So the relationships between the cloud customer and the cloud vendor, the end client and the regulators, the government and the credit firm, are not at all yet solidified and codified in a manner readily understood by anyone, in terms of conclusive results in the event of unusual occurrences. In fact, it might be said that we don't know what to expect as usual or unusual in this field, quite yet.

In this chapter, we will explore some of the ways that these relationships are currently taking form and what to expect in terms of what each party wants and how they will prefer to operate. We're going to examine the roles involved in the arrangement, including third parties, and we'll also cover some of the contractual elements and technologies that make the relationship work, particularly application programming interfaces (APIs).

Foundations of Managed Services

Some element of adversarial relationship exists between the cloud customer and cloud vendor because they have somewhat different goals. The cloud customer wants to maximize their computing capabilities and security of information while minimizing their costs. The cloud vendor wants to maximize their profits while minimizing what they have to provide (which is expressed in terms of computing capabilities and security of information).

There is a great deal of obvious tension between these goals, which is why negotiation of the contract and the SLAs is vital. Luckily, there is also a great deal of overlap, which makes the relationship tenable and profitable for both parties. It is in the vendor's best interest not to allow security breaches. Repeated security failings would sour the market for their product/brand and expose them to continual lawsuits, which reduces profits. It is in the vendor's best interest to provide excellent service and more than the customer expects because doing so attracts clients and increases market share.

The gray areas are where the risks exist and where both parties must establish strong delineation of duties and responsibilities in order to protect themselves and their stakeholders (see Figure 6.1). As we've mentioned throughout this book, the type of service model/platform affects the nature and extent of each party's rights and tasks.

FIGURE 6.1   Responsibilities, by service model

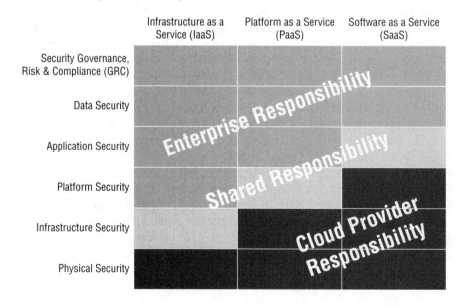

Business Requirements

The primary intent for the cloud customer should be to meet business requirements. This could involve increasing efficiency, meeting regulatory needs, and ensuring durability of capabilities during contingencies, but it should always involve reducing cost. Even if the cloud customer is a nonprofit entity and is not interested in maximizing profits, it is in the interest of all stakeholders to minimize expenses and maximize productivity.

Other business requirements will vary, depending on the industry and particular organization. Business drives all other considerations (including security) and is the primary focus of all decisions. In order to determine what is and is not a business requirement, senior management can make use of the artifacts created in various processes, including business impact analysis, risk analysis, asset inventory, and so on. To translate those requirements into cloud contract elements, SLAs, and operational functions, senior managers in a cloud customer organization can seek guidance and input from both internal and external sources.

When the business requirements have been converted into functional needs, they can be calibrated by contract terms and SLAs. These elements of legal agreement between the parties codify particular responsibilities and expectations of each, and related pricing.

Business Requirements: The Cloud Provider Perspective

What sort of business goals and operating requirements does the provider face, and how are those achieved? In a very simplistic way, that question can be answered with two short responses: be profitable and ensure all customer needs (in the form of contracts and SLAs) are being met. A more complex explanation should include a discussion of the physical establishment of the cloud provider's datacenter and equipment, the security aspects involved in that physical plant and architecture, and the logical design and security aspects of the datacenter.

Cloud Provider Responsibilities: The Physical Plant

The cloud provider needs a datacenter from which to provide services to its customers. The physical plant of the datacenter will include the campus on which the datacenter facility is located, the physical components inside that facility, and the services that support and connect them.

One of the first decisions a cloud provider will have to make is whether to build or buy a facility in which to situate the datacenter. As with all decisions, each option has benefits and risks.

In purchasing a piece of property and building an entirely new datacenter, the cloud provider gets to dictate every aspect of the facility, ensuring it is absolutely suited to the purpose. The provider will have much more control of how the facilities are designed, which can lead to better control over physical access to the property and buildings, as well as optimized performance of the systems within the datacenter. This, however, is often much more expensive than purchasing or leasing an existing facility. It also requires a long-term plan for continued growth and development of the business, which often involves purchasing a larger piece of land than is initially needed for the first datacenter, with the understanding that additional datacenters (or additional facilities) might be built on that same property in the future to increase capacity as the business grows.

The alternative, of course, is to purchase or lease an existing facility and retrofit it to the needs of the cloud provider. Although this may be less costly, especially in the short term, it may include limitations that ownership would not. For instance, if the property is being leased, the owner may not approve of all changes the provider (as a tenant) would like to make. Even if the property is owned by the provider, other external forces might limit the extent and type of changes the provider desires. This is particularly true in metropolitan settings, where zoning limitations and municipal building codes might be strict and very specific.

> One popular method of avoiding the restrictions that often come with locating a physical plant in an urban setting is to locate the datacenter in a remote, rural setting. There are often less controls on development in these areas, and the property itself is almost always much cheaper. A factor the provider must consider, however, is the additional costs that are quite likely in situating a business in remote areas, such as creating robust, redundant utility connections for connectivity and power services.

Whichever method the provider selects, other aspects of the location itself must be taken into consideration, such as proximity to customers, ability to attract suitable personnel to staff that location, and the location's propensity for natural disasters and civil unrest.

Regardless of the build or buy decision the provider has made, the provider has to fill the facility with the physical devices that constitute a datacenter. While the specific vendors and manufacturers of the devices inside a cloud datacenter may differ from provider to provider, there are some general characteristics that will be common to most. These include the following:

Secure Hardware Components   Because of the ubiquitous use of virtualization in the cloud environment, hardware devices will have to be configured properly to ensure secure implementation of hypervisors, virtual machines, and virtual OSs. This can and should include specific BIOS settings on each hardware component, following vendor and manufacturer guidance, installing centralized virtualization management toolsets on each device, and, if cryptoprocessing will be used, ensuring the hardware has the proper settings for utilization of the Trusted Platform Module (TPM) standard. BIOS is the firmware flashed into the processor of a computer, and the TPM standard dictates how processors can be used specifically for cryptographic functions.

> The notional perspective of cloud datacenter components usually divides the interior physical plant into three groups: compute, storage, and networking. Compute nodes are the hosts, where users will process operational data. Storage nodes are where the data is securely stored, either for near-term or long-term purposes. Networking is all the equipment used for connecting the other nodes—the hardware devices such as routers and switches, and the cables that connect them.

Manage hardware configuration.   As with OS baselining (which we'll discuss later in this chapter), a template for the secure configuration of each specific device should be constructed, and it should be replicated whenever a new device of that particular type is added to the environment. The baseline hardware configuration should be saved in a secure manner and kept current through the formal change management process (including any required patches and updates). This is true for each of the nodes, regardless of purpose, including the compute and storage nodes, networking devices, and anything used to connect and monitor each of the nodes.

Set hardware to log events and incidents.   While the granularity and specificity of which system events to capture might differ from device to device or customer to customer, the provider should ensure that sufficient data related to the activity on each machine is being saved for possible future use (including incident investigation and forensic purposes). This event data should be sufficient to determine exactly what occurred and the identity of the users involved in each event (which is also known as attribution).

Determine compute component composition by customer need.   Some cloud customers might not be suited to a multitenant environment and would prefer to only have their data processed and stored in and on devices specifically and exclusively assigned to them (the customer). While the use of stand-alone hosts is outside the norm for cloud datacenters, most cloud providers will offer the option, albeit at an increased service fee (the provider will have to deploy and administer those devices and datasets separately from other customers within the same datacenter, which increases the cost of provision). Unlike stand-alone hosts assigned to specific customers, clustered hosts will provide scalable management benefits, allowing customers who opt for the multitenant environment to realize significant cost savings. Both stand-alone and clustered hosts must be configured and supported in such a way as to maintain high availability. This includes ensuring redundancy of the components themselves and the services that support them.

Configure secure remote administrative access.   It is very likely that either the provider or the customer (or both) will have to access the hardware in order to perform some administrative function. This access will quite often be in the form of a remote connection and will therefore require particular security controls to ensure only authorized users are performing permitted actions. Security enhancements for remote access might include implementing session encryption for the access connection, strong authentication for remote users and administrators, and enhanced logging for accounts with administrative permissions.

Cloud Provider Responsibilities: Secure Logical Framework

In addition to securing the hardware components, the cloud provider must ensure that the logical elements are likewise protected. This includes the following:

Installation of Virtual OSs   The provider must ensure that the virtual OSs installed in the datacenter (on virtual or hardware hosts) are configured and installed in a secure manner. In addition, as virtual OSs are deployed in the environment, virtualization management tools should be installed concurrently, to ensure the provider's ability to monitor the virtual environment for both performance and security issues, and to enforce configuration policy. This is particularly important for creating and maintaining a secure hypervisor configuration—a weak hypervisor could allow malicious actors to access and attack many of the virtual assets and a great deal of the production data.

Secure Configuration of Various Virtualized Elements   In addition to the tangible hardware used in the datacenter, any virtual elements must also be configured in a secure fashion to attenuate potential risks such as data leakage and malicious aggregation. This is not limited to virtual hosts and OSs, but it should also include any virtualized networking or storage assets.

Cloud Provider Responsibilities: Secure Networking

Of course, in addition to securing the hardware and logical configurations, the provider will have to ensure that the networking architecture and components are secure. This will often involve many of the same tactics and methods used in the legacy (non-cloud) environment, as well as some cloud-specific permutations. A brief overview of both these areas follows.

Firewalls

Firewalls are tools that limit communications based on some criteria. They can be either hardware or software, or a combination of both. Firewalls can be stand-alone devices or integrated into other network nodes such as hosts and servers. The criteria for determining which traffic is allowed and which is not can take the form of rules (such as which services or protocols are allowed, which ports are to be used, from whom and when traffic should be allowed, and so forth), or behavior-sensing algorithms (the firewall is taught which behavior is "normal," for both the environment and the user, and deviations from the normal baseline are noted by the firewall), or stateful inspection (the firewall understands the expected pattern of conversation in a protocol, and recognizes deviations), or even inspection of content.

IDS/IPS

Intrusion-detection systems (IDSs) and intrusion prevention systems (IPSs) are very similar to firewalls in that they monitor network traffic. These can also use defined rule sets, behavior-based algorithms, content, or stateful inspection to detect anomalous activity. The explicit difference between an IDS and an IPS is that an IDS usually only reports suspicious activity, alerting responders (such as the security office), whereas the IPS can be set to take defensive action when suspicious activity is recognized (such as closing ports and services), in addition to sending alerts. In the modern environment, most of these solutions serve both purposes.

Honeypots

A honeypot is a tool used to detect, identify, isolate, and analyze attacks by attracting attackers. This is usually a dummy machine with useless data, partially secured and configured as if it was a realistic portion of the production environment. When attackers penetrate it and attempt nefarious activity (such as installing rootkits or other malware, escalating their privileges, or disabling functionality), the security team can monitor and record the attackers' behavior. This information can be used for defensive purposes in the actual production environment, or as evidence in litigation and prosecution actions.

Vulnerability Assessments

A vulnerability assessment is a scan of the network in order to detect known vulner-abilities. These can, of course, be automated so that they're scalable for networks of any appreciable size. The unfortunate flaw in vulnerability assessments is that they will only detect what they know to be looking for. That is, they only detect known vulnerabilities, and any extant vulnerabilities that are not part of the scan will go unnoticed. Vulnerability assessments can't prevent attackers from discovering previously unknown vulnerabilities in systems and attacking them. These forms of attacks are often referred to as zero-day exploits.

Communication Protection

The connections between the various nodes and between the datacenter and the rest of the world must also be secured. As has already been mentioned, data in transit can be protected in several ways:

Encryption   Data can be encrypted across the network, attenuating the possibility that someone who does not have unauthorized access (an external attacker, perhaps, or a mali-cious insider) would be able to acquire raw data in plaintext. If network traffic was encrypt-ed with a sufficient work factor, it would not reveal sensitive data even if someone captured it. Remote connections can also be encrypted, providing the same kind of protection for user access. Of course, encryption comes with a cost: the processing overhead increases with the volume of encrypted data, some other security controls (such as DRM, DLP, and IDS/IPS solutions) might not function in the same manner because they cannot recognize the content of the traffic, and key storage is always an issue.

Virtual Private Networks (VPNs)   Creating a secure tunnel across untrusted networks (such as the Internet) can aid in obviating man-in-the-middle attacks such as eavesdropping and interception of sensitive data, particularly when combined with encryption.

Strong Authentication   As with the other aspects of securing the cloud datacenter, authenti-cation schema such as the use of robust tokens and requiring multifactor authentication can reduce the likelihood of unauthorized users gaining access, and restricting authorized users to permitted activities.

Management Plane

With the wide use of virtualization, cloud-specific logical configurations, and software-defined networking (SDN), each of the cloud datacenter elements discussed in this sec-tion of the chapter (the hardware, the logical configuration, and the networking elements) will most likely be managed through a centralized management and control interface, often referred to as the "management plane" or the "control plane." This interface gives a great deal of control to the administrators, analysts, and architects who will design, oversee, manage, and troubleshoot the cloud datacenter. The management plane can be used in each of the physical, logical, and networking areas of the datacenter, for various tasks, such as:

- **Physical:** Applying, detecting, and enforcement of hardware baseline configurations

- **Logical:** Scheduling tasks, optimization resource allocation, maintaining and updating software and virtualized hardware

- **Networking:** All network management and administration tasks (except, of course, direct physical procedures, such as connecting cabling to boxes)

Of course, the management plane also poses a significant center of risk, as well as a potential single point of failure. The cloud provider must take great pains to ensure that the management plane is configured correctly and securely, that sufficient redundancy exists for every aspect of the management plane so that there is no interruption of service, and that extremely strong access control is implemented for the management plane to attenuate possible attempts to subvert or invade it.

Cloud Provider Responsibilities: Mapping and Selection of Controls

No matter what design and architecture options are employed in the cloud datacenter, the cloud provider (like any IT infrastructure owner or operator) must apply the proper security controls, according the relevant regulatory frameworks and the planned usage. This is especially true of, but not limited to, regulation concerning personally identifiable information (PII).

Published governance should guide the selection of appropriate controls for every aspect of datacenter operation (physical, logical, administrative, personnel, intangible, and tangible assets). All security policy should be based on this guidance, and all controls should be justified according to the particular regulations and standards applicable to the datacenter and its customers.

There are many types of regulation and appropriate standards, and they are discussed throughout this book. The cloud provider must understand which are applicable to the datacenter (in terms of both location and operation) and to the customers (in terms of both location and operations). For instance, each physical location will be subject to the jurisdiction of relevant laws. The "physical location" includes *both* where the datacenter is physically situated *and* the location of each cloud customer.

For example, a cloud datacenter in Park City, with customers in Omaha and Edina, would be subject to not only the data breach notification and privacy laws in Utah, but also those of Nebraska and Minnesota, *as well as* any municipal codes regarding privacy and data protection for those particular cities.

In addition to physical location, the type of operations taking place in the cloud datacenter will dictate which regulations are applicable (and therefore, which controls are required). A cloud customer processing, say, medical information would be subject to HIPAA, whereas those processing credit card transactions would be subject to PCI regulation (and a cloud customer doing both will require controls sufficient for fulfilling both).

There are guides and matrices of controls required by almost all relevant regulations available, usually for free. One of particular use in the cloud environment is the Cloud Security Alliance Cloud Controls Matrix (CSA CCM: `https://cloudsecurityalliance .org/group/cloud-controls-matrix/`), detailed elsewhere in this book. It maps requisite controls and control groups to specific contractual and legislated regulation, and it is extremely useful.

Shared Responsibilities by Service Type

Again, referring to Figure 6.1, we can review what portions of the cloud environment will be tasked to which party. This is, of course, a description of the general case, for many or most cloud customer–provider relationships, but it's not prescriptive by any means.

IaaS

Because the cloud provider is only hosting the hardware and utilities, their only sole responsibility will be for physical security of the facility and systems. Both parties will share the responsibility for securing the infrastructure. Admittedly, this will be to a lesser extent for the cloud customer because the cloud customer will be installing the OS, which can significantly affect the security of the underlying systems, and the customer will be responsible for this aspect of infrastructure security. The customer will have sole responsibility for all other security aspects.

PaaS

In a PaaS model, the cloud customer will be installing programs on top of operating systems loaded and managed by the cloud vendor. The vendor might offer a variety of OSs, allowing the customer to ensure interoperability on a number of platforms. This can be extremely useful if the customer anticipates end users in a heterogeneous environment (for instance, in a BYOD configuration, with users accessing systems through different web browsers on a multitude of devices).

Therefore, in PaaS, the cloud provider will still maintain physical security control of the facility and hardware but will now also be responsible for securing and maintaining the OS. The cloud customer will remain obligated to provide all other security.

SaaS

As you can expect, in SaaS modes, the cloud provider will have to maintain physical security for the underlying infrastructure and OS as in the previous models, but will have to secure the programs as well. In this case, the cloud customer will only be left with very specific aspects of security: access and administration of assign user permissions to the data.

Because the customer is the nominal data owner, the customer will always have ultimate control of who has authorization to view and manipulate the data (with the exception of those who have physical access to the hosts on which it resides, which always remains with the provider). In no circumstance will this fall to the purview of the cloud provider. Even if the task of provisioning access and accounts is contracted to the provider, the customer is still legally and ethically responsible for the security of the data itself.

Shared Administration of OS, Middleware, or Applications

In the PaaS and SaaS modes, both the cloud provider and customer will have to share some elements of control over the software elements to a greater or lesser extent. For instance, in PaaS, the customer will make updates and modifications to software they have installed (and sometimes designed) and administer on the hosted systems. The cloud provider might have some role to play in this process, as the hardware may need to be adjusted accordingly to allow for any new functionality, and that is the sole responsibility of the provider. Moreover, the provider may have to ensure security controls still function and provide the level of desired coverage upon adoption of the updates.

Operating System Baseline Configuration and Management

Perhaps one of the most useful practices for creating a secure cloud environment will be a carryover from the legacy motif—creating secure baseline configurations of the OS.

The operating system is, itself, a large attack surface, offering a great many potential avenues to malicious actors if not set correctly. As with the hosts themselves, the operating systems in a secure environment should be hardened—that is, configured in a secure manner. Hardening the operating system can include the following (and more):

- Removing unnecessary services and libraries
- Closing unused ports
- Installing antimalware agents
- Limiting administrator access
- Ensuring default accounts are removed
- Ensuring event/incident logging is enabled

It would be cumbersome to perform the activities necessary to reach this configuration on each OS, individually and manually, so instead it is preferable to create one template, the secure OS baseline, and replicate that baseline whenever a new machine is deployed (and, in the virtual environment, whenever a new user image is created). This can be done with automated tools. We can also use those tools (or similar ones) to continually check the environment to ensure all current images and machines have an OS that meets the baseline configuration. Any OS configuration that differs from the baseline and is detected by the monitoring tool should be addressed accordingly (this might include patching or a reinstallation/rollback of the entire OS configuration).

Deviations from the baseline might have legitimate purposes. However, some specialized uses and users may require adjustments to the baseline for their business tasks. In such cases, the deviation should be formally approved by the change/configuration management process and limited to situations, OS instances, and machines where that function is necessary. Configuration monitoring tools should be adjusted accordingly and the asset inventory updated, so that these particular cases are not constantly setting off alerts and so that administrators don't accidentally apply the baseline configuration.

In cloud environments, where virtualization and multiple disparate customers are so prevalent, it is also important to feature the capability for capturing (and restoring) the OS of any customer and virtual guest in order to ensure the customer's particular needs are being met. There are a number of methods for copying and backing up the guest OS, such as taking snapshots of the virtual image, using software tools that install agents on the virtual machine for that purpose, and centralized, agentless configuration management solutions. When a customer needs to replicate a specific OS, the saved configuration can be copied from the backup, on the same virtual machine or others. The cloud provider and cloud customer will have to negotiate and determine how often OS configuration backups are being made and on which systems.

Aside from maintaining the OS, baselining and configuration management is likewise important for other applications. The provider and the customer will have to determine who will be responsible for establishing the secure build of the configuration template, as well as perform version control activities.

Version control for applications includes following vendor recommendations, applying requisite patches and upgrades, ensuring interoperability with the rest of the environment, and documenting all changes and developments. Documentation is particularly important in support of efforts to provide consistency across the environment and to have sufficient tracking of the current software state for the business continuity and disaster recovery (BC/DR), and for any necessary forensic and discovery activities.

The Benefit of Many Eyeballs

When choosing applications and APIs for the cloud environment, cloud customers may be tempted to use software from vendors they've never done business with before and have no prior knowledge of, because it offers something of enhanced value, such as a particular functionality or very low price. There is obviously a risk to using software from unverified sources: unknown and untested software could contain vulnerabilities and attack vectors that would otherwise be controlled for in the formal secure development or acquisition process.

One possible method for attenuating this possibility is the use of crowdsourcing—determining from other users (current and past) what their experience with particular software offered in the form of results, good or bad. This can be taken a bit further, with a decision to trust open source programs over those with proprietary code. It is far more likely that open source software has been vetted by more people with more perspectives than even professionally developed software from known sources with rigorous testing methods. Leveraging the power of the community for evaluation purposes is a powerful tool.

Share Responsibilities: Data Access

Of course, in all models, the cloud customer (and their users) will need access and the ability to modify the data. This will require some degree of sharing administration capabilities, however minimal. For instance, the data may be processed in a database, and the database administrator may be in the employ of the cloud provider or the cloud customer, or there may be database administrators in both organizations, and they might have shared or overlapping duties.

The data owner (customer) will always retain fundamental liability for data protection, and will therefore be the end arbiter of granting access and permissions for that dataset. This may be implemented via a number of methods: direct administration of user identity and authorization processes; contracting the tasks to the cloud provider, under strict instructions and through a specified verification procedure; or perhaps contracting out the duties to a third party, such as a cloud access security broker (CASB), who will perform these administrative tasks on the customer's behalf.

Let's review some examples of processes that might facilitate each method.

Customer Directly Administers Access

If the cloud customer retains control of these duties, then the customer will provision, manage, and remove user accounts without input or cooperation with the cloud provider. This could be performed by administrators working within the customer's organization, remotely accessing the OS on the cloud host devices and manipulating the access control systems (say, updating the ACLs) manually. When a new user needs an account, the entire operation is initiated, executed, and completed within the cloud customer's organization.

In IaaS, this would always be the case, since the cloud provider has no oversight or control of the OS. With PaaS and SaaS, however, this will be a bit more complicated, because the cloud provider is obligated (and invested) to control the OS and software completely. Ceding administrative access to the customer will require a great deal of trust and additional controls and will almost certainly be limited to this very specific purpose.

The elements of this process must be spelled out, in great detail, in the contract and SLAs between the customer and provider.

Figure 6.2 shows a workflow example.

FIGURE 6.2   Customer Directly Administers Access

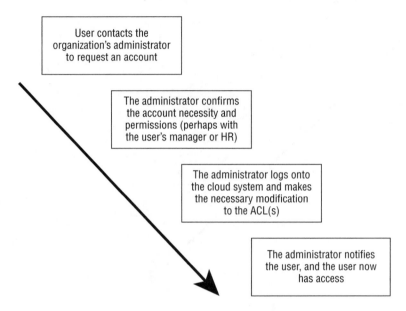

Provider Administers Access on Behalf of the Customer

In this type of setup, any new user must submit a request to the provider, either directly or through some point of contact within the customer organization. The provider will need to verify the request is legitimate and correct by contacting the customer through a predetermined process, and then create the account and assign the appropriate permissions. See Figure 6.3.

Third-Party (CASB) Administers Access on Behalf of the Customer

The CASB will have some of the duties and access relegated to the other parties in the previous examples. The user will make the request to the CASB or to a local administrator, and the CASB will verify the account and then assign the appropriate access and permissions. See Figure 6.4.

FIGURE 6.3   Provider Administers Access on Behalf of the Customer

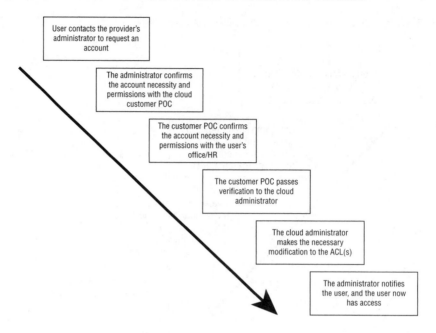

FIGURE 6.4   Third-Party (CASB) Administers Access on Behalf of the Customer

Lack of Physical Access

The cloud provider will not have any reason to allow the customer physical access to the facility and devices containing the customer's data. In fact, the provider will have every reason to prevent this. There will be a great many customers, with various levels of trust, and the more people who have knowledge of the physical location, security controls, and layout of the datacenter, the greater the risk to the data and operations.

From the customer's perspective, this is both beneficial and challenging. It is beneficial because it increases the customer's trust in the provider (the customer has limited access, but *all* customers have limited access). It is challenging because the customer is forced to rely on the provider's assertions of security without the customer having any means to reliably validate and verify those assertions for themselves.

Audits

Unfortunately, the cloud provider's unwillingness to allow physical access to the facility also applies to the customer's auditors, and in most cases auditors probably won't even have access to data streams and documentary artifacts necessary to perform a reasonable audit with a suitable level of veracity. This is especially troubling for those organizations that have regulatory requirements for performing and providing audits to their stakeholders (including regulators).

 The lack of physical access to the cloud provider's facility also means that the preferred means of attenuating data remanence risks and ensuring secure data disposal (such as physical destruction of the host devices, drives, and media) will not be available to the customer. We've discussed the current best alternatives in other chapters, so won't repeat it here.

For auditing purposes, then, what the customer is likely to get instead is audits performed on the vendor's behalf, by licensed and chartered auditors made known to the customers and public. It is, of course, in the provider's best interest to publish these audits, in the hope of increasing public perception of the reliability and trustworthiness of the provider's services, and thus increasing customer satisfaction and market share. However, the provider does not want to share a detailed audit of security controls for the very same reason they don't want to allow physical access: a security control audit that revealed specific aspects and configuration of controls would provide a roadmap of attack for malicious actors.

Instead, the provider is likely to publish an audit assurance statement: something from the auditor that states, in formal terms, that an audit was performed, and that the auditor finds the results suitable for the purposes of the provider's operations—a seal of approval, if you will.

Currently, this usually takes the form of an SOC 3 audit report. Let's delve into the SOC reports and their intended purpose, because this material is significant for both exam and practical purposes.

The SOC reports are part of the SSAE reporting format created by the American Institute of Certified Public Accountants (AICPA). These are uniformly recognized as being acceptable for regulatory purposes in many industries, although they were specifically designed as mechanisms for ensuring compliance with the Sarbanes-Oxley Act (colloquially referred to as "SOX"), which governs publicly traded corporations.

 Real World Scenario

Darning SOX

SOX was the Congressional response to some high-profile perfidy in several corporate cases, including WorldCom and Adelphia, that transpired in the late 1990s and early 2000s.

But perhaps the most well-known and direct progenitor of the SOX legislation was the Enron scandal, in which, among other things, executives of that corporation deceived creditors, regulators, and shareholders on a vast basis, with a number of brazen techniques and scams, such as burying losses due to foreign investment failures in numerous spin-off shell subsidiaries (one was even named "Chewco, LLP," after the Star Wars character Chewbacca, in a demonstration of blatant hubris).

Enron's underhandedness extended to its co-conspirators, including the entity that was supposed to be its auditor, Arthur Andersen, LLP. Among other wrongdoing, Arthur Andersen had created a conflict of interest for itself by selling Enron both auditing *and* business consulting services. But the singular act that became burned into the minds of the public (and regulators and legislators) as indicative of the Enron–Arthur Andersen debacle was Arthur Andersen's decision to undertake a massive document-shredding operation just as law enforcers and regulators were announcing their investigation into Enron's activities.

When later questioned about the choice to begin destroying what was obviously potential evidence, Arthur Andersen executives made the claim that it was their policy—and, indeed, their professional duty—to destroy all customer-specific documentation and files at the end of a contractual engagement and that Enron had just severed their contract with Arthur Andersen before the shredding began.

Prosecutors were not amused: sure, the policy did exist, and due diligence in ensuring customer privacy probably should entail destruction of material containing sensitive material, but in the Enron case, Arthur Andersen made some dramatic and rather blatant efforts to destroy everything related to Enron, massively and rapidly. The prosecutors asked Arthur Andersen executives if their standard destruction practices (and policy) required that they rent industrial shredders expressly for the purpose and run those shredders night and day over a weekend, at the end of every engagement. The executives admitted that, no, this was not the case.

In response to the Enron, WorldCom, and Adelphia cases, lawmakers created SOX, which, among its many provisions (the statute itself is 66 pages long, in PDF form: `https://www.sec.gov/about/laws/soa2002.pdf`), requires that auditors report on the trustworthiness of the financial reporting documents (to deter Enron-like efforts to defraud shareholders), and also the organization's own controls used to protect the organization's security, availability, processing integrity, confidentiality, and privacy. It also requires that any notification of pending investigation (criminal or litigatory) requires a suspension of all data-destruction activities within the organization, and that this notice supersedes all other subordinate laws and organizational policies.

Arthur Andersen was known as one of the Big 5 accounting firms in the United States for many years. After Enron, there is no more Arthur Andersen.

There are three SOC report categories: SOC 1, SOC 2, and SOC 3. Each of them is meant for a specific purpose, and there are further subclasses of reports as well.

SOC 1 reports are strictly for auditing the financial reporting instruments of a corporation, and therefore have nothing to do with our field and are no interest to us. It's worth knowing that they exist (SOC 1 is mentioned in the CBK, and it's important to know the distinction between them and SOC 2 and SOC 3 reports), and that there are two subclasses of SOC 1 reports: Type 1 and Type 2. Other than that, you should never have to deal with them in practice, because they are not germane to computer security or cloud computing.

SOC 2 reports are the ones that are particular to our field. They are specifically intended to report audits of any controls on an organization's security, availability, processing integrity, confidentiality, and privacy. Therefore, a cloud provider intending to prove its trustworthiness would look to an SOC 2 report as the artifact that demonstrated it.

SOC 2 reports also come in two subclasses: Type 1 and Type 2. The SOC 2 Type 1 is not extremely useful for determining the security and trust of an organization. The SOC 2 Type 1 only reviews the *design* of controls, not how they are implemented and maintained, or their function. The SOC 2 Type 2 report, however, does just that. This is why the SOC 2 Type 2 is the sort of report that is extremely useful for getting a true assessment of an organization's security posture.

However, cloud vendors will probably never share an SOC 2 Type 2 report with any customer or even release it outside the provider's organization. The SOC 2 Type 2 report is extremely detailed and provides exactly the kind of description and configuration that the cloud provider is trying to restrict from wide dissemination. It's basically a handbook for attacking that cloud provider.

So, instead, what we're more likely to see, as cloud customers, is an SOC 3 report. The SOC 3 is the "seal of approval" mentioned earlier in this chapter. It contains no actual data about the security controls of the audit target and is instead just an assertion that the audit was conducted and that the target organization passed. That's it.

This makes it of dubious use for verifying the trustworthiness of an organization. Instead of taking the word of a company that the company is trustworthy, with no evidence offered in support of their word, we are asked to take the word of an auditor hired by that company that the company is trustworthy, with no evidence offered to support the auditor's assertion.

Again, this is currently the practice accepted in the industry. We expect this to evolve in the near future.

We expect another form of audit to emerge, specific to the field of cloud computing, and become the new standard. Most likely, this will be the CSA Security, Trust, and Assurance Registry (STAR) program, which is still in nascent form (https://cloudsecurityalliance.org/star/).

Shared Policy

In addition to the (most likely SOC 3) audit reports, the cloud customer will have to rely on the contract and the SLAs to ensure that the provider is securing the data to an extent and with the controls sufficient for the customer's purposes, including compliance with regulatory structures. These tools (the contract and the SLAs) will not obviate the customer's legal responsibilities in the event of a breach, but they *will* help the customer seek financial restitution for damages caused to the customer and their end clients in a breach that occurred because of negligence or malfeasance on the part of the provider.

In pursuit of this effort, and as contractual elements, the customer and provider may agree to share doctrinal mechanisms in common, such as industry standards, guidelines, vendor documentation, and other policy and procedural artifacts. This could be true whether the service is IaaS, PaaS, or SaaS. If the parties choose this type of arrangement, both must agree to work from the same version of each artifact, and must involve the other in any change management process that affects the documents (even if that involvement is limited to notification). This process and any limitations must be codified in the contract from the outset of the relationship.

Shared Monitoring and Testing

Another area where providers and customers may find common ground in sharing responsibilities is security monitoring and testing. The provider may allow the customer access to data streams or administrative capabilities on devices in order for the customer to perform their own monitoring and testing activities, in conjunction with or (more likely) addition to the provider's own efforts.

Again, because of the provider's inherent requirements to ensure security throughout the cloud environment, this access is most probably going to be very limited. The customer will be granted access only to those specific aspects of the enterprise that will not affect or give any insight into any of the provider's other customers resident on the cloud. The provider's concern is twofold: not allowing any specific customer or user enough capability to cause significant harm to the enterprise through accident or malicious intent, and not disclosing any customer's data or operation to any other customer.

Even with this limited amount of transparency, though, it is possible for the customer to have a greater certainty and trust in the security controls and performance if the customer is allowed to monitor and test the data and behavior of the network, and to ensure that the general set of security controls and protective measures available to all customers are sufficient and not problematic for the customer's specific dataset.

For instance, the provider may allow the customer to either access audit and performance logs, or to even configure settings of these, on resources limited to that customer's use. Or the provider may deliver SIM, SEM, or SIEM log data to the customer so that the customer might perform their own analysis and internal reporting with it.

Also, the provider might act in concert with the customer to configure and deploy a DLP solution that could issue alerts or reports on any data egress activity—limited, of course, to the customer's own specific data. This may be more cumbersome and challenging because of the nature of shared resources in the cloud environment (shared between customers), and because of the wide use of virtualization (requiring DLP solutions expressly designed for the purpose).

For testing purposes, the provider may allow the customer access to a scaled-down, limited portion of the cloud environment that mimics the overall infrastructure, in order for the customer to perform small-scale testing of their data and usage in a sandboxed, isolated manner. This could improve the customer's confidence in the production environment, enhancing their trust in the provider's ability to protect the customer's data, and to administer the network in such a way that there is no untoward impact to the customer's critical functions.

Again, these capabilities would necessarily be limited and must be formally agreed to by both parties, in the contract and SLAs, prior to the commencement of the business arrangement.

Summary

In this chapter, we have explored how both parties will be able to act independently and in concert to assure for themselves and each other that the security of the network and the data on it will not be unduly affected. We discussed which responsibilities might be distinct to each party in different cloud models and which aspects might be shared.

Exam Essentials

Know the cloud provider's responsibilities for providing secure physical, logical, and networking elements in the datacenter.   Understand how the provider will use secure processes, methods, and controls to provide the customer with a trusted environment in which to conduct business. Know the various network security components and tools. Be familiar with the process of mapping specific security controls and control groups to applicable regulatory guidance.

Understand which party will most likely have which specific security responsibilities in each of the cloud service models.   Know what the provider and customer each are tasked with in IaaS, PaaS, and SaaS configurations.

Understand which responsibilities the cloud customer and cloud provider are likely to share.   Know that OS and application baselining and management responsibilities are likely to be shared, as are identity and access management, to some degree.

Know the different types of audit reports most likely to be used for cloud datacenters. Understand the difference between SOC 1, 2, and 3 reports, and Types 1 and 2 of SOC 2 and SOC 3. Know which is preferred for detailed analysis and which the cloud customer is most likely to have access to.

Written Labs

1. Visit the web page for the CSA's STAR program (https://cloudsecurityalliance .org/star/).

2. Download the Consensus Assessments Initiative Questionnaire: https:// cloudsecurityalliance.org/download/consensus-assessments-initiative -questionnaire-v3-0-1/.

3. Review the questionnaire. Understand the operational security aspects a cloud data service provider will be expected to verify and attest to. Think of these aspects in terms of what you've learned so far from this book.

4. Visit the actual Registry itself: https://cloudsecurityalliance.org/star/#_registry.

5. Select any registered provider, and download their (completed) questionnaire.

6. In one page or less, describe three security aspects of their responses that you find interesting or alarming, or that should be of concern to a cloud customer considering using that provider.

Review Questions

You can find the answers in Appendix A.

1. What is the cloud service model in which the customer is responsible for administration of the OS?

   A. IaaS

   B. PaaS

   C. SaaS

   D. QaaS

2. To address shared monitoring and testing responsibilities in a cloud configuration, the provider might offer all these to the cloud customer except:

   A. Access to audit logs and performance data

   B. SIM, SEIM, and SEM logs

   C. DLP solution results

   D. Security control administration

3. In addition to whatever audit results the provider shares with the customer, what other mechanism does the customer have to ensure trust in the provider's performance and duties?

   A. Statutes

   B. The contract

   C. Security control matrix

   D. HIPAA

4. Which kind of SSAE audit report is a cloud customer most likely to receive from a cloud provider?

   A. SOC 1 Type 1

   B. SOC 2 Type 2

   C. SOC 1 Type 2

   D. SOC 3

5. Which kind of SSAE audit report is most beneficial for a cloud customer, even though it's unlikely the cloud provider will share it?

   A. SOC 1 Type 1

   B. SOC 2 Type 2

   C. SOC 1 Type 2

   D. SOC 3

6. As a result of scandals involving publicly traded corporations such as Enron, WorldCom, and Adelphi, Congress passed legislation known as:

    A. FERPA

    B. GLBA

    C. SOX

    D. HIPAA

7. Hardening the operating system refers to all of the following except:

    A. Limiting administrator access

    B. Removing antimalware agents

    C. Closing unused ports

    D. Removing unnecessary services and libraries

8. The cloud customer's trust in the cloud provider can be enhanced by all of the following except:

    A. Audits

    B. Shared administration

    C. Real-time video surveillance

    D. SLAs

9. User access to the cloud environment can be administered in all of the following ways except:

    A. Customer directly administers access

    B. Customer provides administration on behalf of the provider

    C. Provider provides administration on behalf the customer

    D. Third party provides administration on behalf of the customer

10. Which kind of SSAE audit reviews controls dealing with the organization's controls for assuring the confidentiality, integrity, and availability of data?

    A. SOC 1

    B. SOC 2

    C. SOC 3

    D. SOC 4

11. Which kind of SSAE report comes with a seal of approval from a certified auditor?

    A. SOC 1

    B. SOC 2

    C. SOC 3

    D. SOC 4

12. Which of the following is a cloud provider likely to provide to its customers in order to enhance the customer's trust in the provider?

    A. Site visit access

    B. SOC 2 Type 2

    C. Audit and performance log data

    D. Backend administrative access

13. In all cloud models, the customer will be given access and ability to modify which of the following?

    A. Data

    B. Security controls

    C. User permissions

    D. OS

14. In all cloud models, security controls are driven by which of the following?

    A. Virtualization engine

    B. Hypervisor

    C. SLAs

    D. Business requirements

15. In all cloud models, the _____ will retain ultimate liability and responsibility for any data loss or disclosure.

    A. Vendor

    B. Customer

    C. State

    D. Administrator

16. Why will cloud providers be unlikely to allow physical access to their datacenters?

    A. They want to enhance security by keeping information about physical layout and controls confidential.

    B. They want to enhance exclusivity for their customers, so only an elite tier of higher-paying clientele will be allowed physical access.

    C. They want to minimize traffic in those areas, to maximize efficiency of operational personnel.

    D. Most datacenters are inhospitable to human life, so minimizing physical access also minimizes safety concerns.

17. Which type of software is most likely to be reviewed by the most personnel, with the most varied perspectives?

    A. Database management software

    B. Open source software

    C. Secure software

    D. Proprietary software

18. A firewall can use all of the following techniques for controlling traffic except:

   A. Rule sets

   B. Behavior analysis

   C. Content filtering

   D. Randomization

19. A honeypot should contain _____ data.

   A. Raw

   B. Production

   C. Useless

   D. Sensitive

20. Vulnerability assessments cannot detect which of the following?

   A. Malware

   B. Defined vulnerabilities

   C. Zero-day exploits

   D. Programming flaws

Chapter 7

Cloud Application Security

THE OBJECTIVE OF THIS CHAPTER IS TO ACQUAINT THE READER WITH THE FOLLOWING CONCEPTS:

✓ **Domain 1: Architectural Concepts and Design Requirements**

- C. Understand Security Concepts Relevant to Cloud Computing
  - C.1 Cryptography
  - C.2 Access Control
  - C.6 Common Threats

✓ **Domain 2: Cloud Data Security**

- C. Design and Apply Data Security Strategies
  - C.6 Emerging Technologies

✓ **Domain 3: Cloud Platform and Infrastructure Security**

- C. Design and Plan Security Controls
  - C.4 Management of Identification, Authentication, and Authorization in Cloud Infrastructure

✓ **Domain 4: Cloud Application Security**

- A. Recognize the Need For Training and Awareness in Application Security
  - A.1 Cloud Development Basics
  - A.2 Common Pitfalls
  - A.3 Common Vulnerabilities
- B. Understand Cloud Software Assurance and Validation
  - B.1 Cloud-based Functional Testing
  - B.2 Cloud Secure Development Lifecycle
  - B.3 Security Testing
- C. Use Verified Software
  - C.1 Approved API

In this chapter, we continue to explore cloud computing by learning about application design and architecture for the cloud as well as application testing and validation to ensure our cloud applications are safe and secure. In the cloud context, applications are the main focus of the Software-as-a-Service (SaaS) model. These web applications are the software that is consumed as part of the cloud offering. We will discuss and review their design, architecture, validation, processes, and life cycle, as well as the tools used to build and deploy successful cloud applications.

In this chapter, we will examine the importance of training and awareness and issues involved with moving to or building applications for the cloud environment. We will also take an in-depth look at the software development life cycle, identity and access management, cloud application architecture, and software assurance and validation.

Training and Awareness

We're going to cover security training programs thoroughly in Chapter 8, "Operations Elements." In this chapter, we'll look at awareness in terms of risk to the organization's assets and operations when considering cloud migration. Any migration effort must be viewed holistically so that all potential negative effects and security risks are addressed. This is best accomplished when all stakeholders involved in the organization's operations (whether they are in technical, functional, or support positions) are aware of the nature of the cloud and its attendant risks.

Because applications manipulate data, we must determine the sensitivity characteristics of our data or we may end up using it in such a way that we are exposed to unnecessary risks. For instance, does the data or the results of its manipulation and processing contain personally identifiable information (PII) such as name, address, Social Security numbers, or health information? If so, the application, along with the data to be stored and manipulated, may not be a good fit for a cloud application solution. Moving an application to the cloud may or may not reduce risks, which is why it is so important to evaluate your situation and application before moving into the cloud.

It is also important to consider the responsibilities associated with using cloud data. When we begin discussing cloud applications, data concerns must be adequately addressed, as it is vital that the data owner understand very clearly the responsibilities of each of the players in this endeavor. See Figure 7.1.

FIGURE 7.1   Customer/Provider Responsibilities, By Service Model

As you can see from Figure 7.1 there are differing responsibilities for each service and delivery model. However, the data owner is always ultimately responsible for all data. We cannot state this emphatically enough, and you will hear it throughout this book. Regardless of what SLAs say or what the cloud provider can show you or attest to, the ultimate responsibility always comes down to the data owner.

On the other hand, if the nature and sensitivity of the data is such that it changes constantly or is of little real value, then moving the associated applications and related data to the cloud may make good sense, both from a computing and storage perspective and more importantly from the business perspective. An example of this might be a wholesaler that uses images of products with SKUs so that customers can order items online. As long as the actual purchase occurs in a different application, the catalog of items would be of little value to anyone other than the customer placing the order. In addition, as prices change rapidly, any associated prices would also be worth very little. Therefore, the catalog application and its associated images and pricing could more than likely be easily moved to the cloud and secured with minimal effort and risk.

There are also instances where it makes more sense to move an application into the cloud because the security is *better*. For instance, many banking institutions host their primary, or what is called their "core banking" application, in the cloud specifically because they do not have the resources, experience, and tools to securely manage the applications themselves. The core application is generally what they use for day-to-day teller transactions, deposit, withdrawals, and so forth. Cloud providers of these core services generally have 24×7 staff who monitor everything and are highly trained and skilled in these areas, providing resources many companies simply cannot afford. For these specific providers, there are also regulatory incentives for them to ensure that data is secure and that applications work as designed. Even in instances where they may have code issues, it is usually a matter of the application *not* doing something as opposed to it performing a transaction that would cause problems. These applications are thoroughly tested before being allowed to touch a customer's account information.

An often-used term for moving an entire application to the cloud without any significant changes is *forklifting*. This refers to the idea of moving an existing legacy enterprise application to the cloud with little or no code changes. Although many times these are self-contained stand-alone applications that have operated successfully in the enterprise environment, dependency on certain infrastructure aspects of the legacy enterprise that might not be replicated in the cloud, and other issues such as the use of proprietary libraries that the cloud environment does not also have, can crop up and can cause serious problems in transition efforts. Not only are all apps not natively ready for the cloud, many cannot move to the cloud at all without some type of extensive code changes. Lastly, many applications, particularly office applications such as accounting and word processing applications, now have alternative cloud-based versions, minimizing or removing the need to move those applications as they exist in local systems to the cloud.

 Open source libraries can be potentially problematic in the cloud. The libraries, by virtue of being open source, are often more susceptible to tampering, which puts your enterprise application at greater risk.

Developers often face challenges when working in a new and unfamiliar environment. For instance, they may be used to working in a certain language or framework that may not be available to them on a particular platform. There is also a serious lack of documentation on cloud application development, architecture, and security due to its immature nature. Therefore, developers have more things to learn, which can slow down the process, or worse yet, they do not learn and plow ahead with disastrous results.

The Treacherous 12

The Cloud Security Alliance (CSA) publishes a report about every three years on Cloud Computing Top Threats. The 2016 report is titled, "The Treacherous 12, Cloud Computing Top Threats in 2016." This is a compilation by the CSA Top Threats Working Group, which consists of some of the most noted experts in all of cloud computing. These experts from around the world and many different backgrounds come together to conduct research into data breaches and malicious intrusions, publish surveys, and develop this list of top cloud computing threats. Although the format has changed somewhat from the 2013 report titled "The Notorious Nine," many of the same problems still exist three years later. This is similar to issues raised by the OWASP Top 10 that continue to baffle computer and information security experts. We know what the problems are, yet we continue to make the same mistakes repeatedly. For more information on the CSA Top Threats Working Group reports, visit https://cloudsecurityalliance.org/group/top-threats/#_downloads.

There are also a number of challenges that must be faced due to the complexities of the cloud-computing model. Some of the issues and characteristics that developers and administrators must deal with include the following:

Multitenancy   This is the concept of sharing resources with other cloud customers simultaneously.

Third-Party Admins   These are cloud providers who manage administration of your system and who are not under your control.

Deployment Models (Public, Private, Community, Hybrid)   Certain models such as the hybrid model remove or reduce the authority and execution of security controls in the environment.

Service Models (IaaS, PaaS, and SaaS)   Developers may or may not have control over the particular infrastructure, platform, or even application stack that they must work with.

Another area of complexity and concern for the CCSP is that of understanding the appropriate use and design of encryption technologies in the cloud and with cloud applications. Encryption is one of the more effective control mechanisms for securing digital data and, in many cases, is the only viable option for the cloud customer to have a sense of assurance regarding the security of their data, because the customer won't have administrative or physical control of the cloud resources and infrastructure.

All of these factors demonstrate why learning more about the cloud environment and the challenges of working in this setting is so important. Not all applications will run in the cloud. Some will work well, others not so much. They must be examined on a case-by-case basis with these factors and characteristics in mind.

Common Cloud Application Deployment Pitfalls

In the following sections, we will discuss some of the more common pitfalls that developers face when deploying cloud applications. Whether the same functionality will be available on-premise versus off-premise, poor documentation and training, tenancy separation, and the use of secure and validated APIs are all significant challenges developers face in deploying applications in the cloud environment. We discuss training in detail in Chapter 8. We'll examine these other issues in the following sections.

On-Premise Apps Do Not Always Transfer (and Vice Versa)

On-premise (or "on-prem" applications as they are often called) are usually designed to be run in a fast, local environment where data is accessed, processed, and stored locally. Moving these to the cloud is not always practical or even possible. Problems encountered can be as simple as making calls back to the enterprise and as complex as code that will not run effectively on certain cloud-based web platforms.

One issue that can arise from inexperience of cloud application development is the use of remote calls. These calls are made by the application, usually to some form of database. Moreover, they are typically designed to work rather quickly. When placed in a cloud environment, calls have to be made back to the enterprise where the data resides; performance can quickly degrade to the point where the application doesn't work at all. Enterprise application developers often do not have to contend with speed or bandwidth issues due to running on a local area network (LAN). A lack of routing involvement and high-speed switches make these very quick and responsive even if code is sometimes not well written. One example would be when the application makes numerous calls in order to assemble a single piece of data, as opposed to making a single call and collecting it all at once. These design issues can slow a cloud application down to the point that it simply does not function properly. These calls create numerous sessions and take up processor and memory resources, and eventually entire systems can slow to a crawl.

Lastly, the legacy on-prem applications are not typically asked to share resources such as CPU, RAM, and bandwidth, again allowing poorly designed code to run adequately on a faster local network but then failing to meet expectations when moved to the cloud.

Poor Documentation

The lack of proper documentation is not a new risk introduced by cloud computing, but it is instead a harsh reality in our field. Developers are constantly being goaded to rush applications into production, while documentation is a slow, methodical process that does not add to functionality or performance. Moreover, the skills necessary for software design don't often overlap into the skillset for technical documentation, so the two efforts are largely performed by different people, which adds another layer of complication and delay to the process.

Finally, if the on-prem legacy environment is not properly documented (as is often the case), this will further deter efforts to have adequate documentation when the environment is moved to the cloud.

Not All Apps Are Cloud Ready

Some applications, specifically database applications, might run even better in the cloud. Typically cloud storage is faster than older enterprise spinning disks, and the data usually has a much smaller distance to travel in order to reach compute and storage components since they are all stored in the same logical units.

However, they are not all ready for the cloud. Oftentimes, code must be reevaluated and altered in order to run effectively in the cloud. Encryption may be needed that had not been used in the past, and a host of other issues exist. Even though some apps will eventually run successfully in the cloud, they are not always immediately ready and may require code or configuration changes in order to work effectively.

Tenancy Separation

In the legacy enterprise, where all infrastructure and resources are owned and controlled by the organization, there is no risk of other tenants (including the organization's competitors!) accessing the organization's data through inadvertent "data bleed" between applications, OSs, guest images, and users. The exact opposite is true of the cloud environment: all those possibilities exist, so the risk of each must be addressed by significant use of countermeasures that ensure access control, process isolation, and denial of guest/host escape attempts…and all these countermeasures will be dependent on remote administration (and will most likely require significant negotiation and cooperation with the provider).

Use of Secure, Validated APIs

One feature that makes cloud-based operations so desirable is the flexibility to use current datasets in new and novel ways; this capability is offered and enhanced through the deployment of a wide variety of APIs, many of which can be chosen by the cloud customer, and even still more that can be selected by the user (on the user's own platform or device, in a BYOD environment). Although the variety of options is enticing, it brings an attendant risk: the APIs used to provide this capability might be of questionable origin.

It behooves the cloud customer to formalize a policy and process for vetting, selecting, and deploying only those APIs that can be validated in some fashion—a method for determining the trustworthiness of the source and the software itself. This process should be included in the organization's acquisition and development program, as well as the change management effort.

Cloud-Secure Software Development Life Cycle (SDLC)

The cloud-secure software development life cycle (SDLC) has the same foundational structure as the traditional SDLC, although there are some factors when dealing with the cloud that need to be taken into account. Just like data, software has a useful life cycle based on phases or stages of development and use (see Figure 7.2). Although the name and number of stages can be debated, they generally include at least the following core stages:

1. Defining
2. Designing
3. Development
4. Testing

FIGURE 7.2   The Cloud Secure Software Development Life Cycle (SDLC)

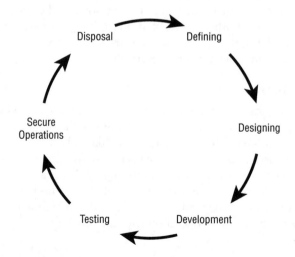

In the definition phase, we are focused on identifying the business needs of the application, such as accounting, database, or customer relationship management. Regardless of the application's purpose, it is vital that the definition phase ferret out all aspects of the business needs in relationship to it. We try to refrain from choosing any specific tools or technologies at this point; the temptation to do so creates a situation where we have a foregone conclusion ("We're going to use Tech X") instead of truly considering all possibilities that might best satisfy the business requirements.

In the design phase, we begin to develop user stories (what the user will want to accomplish and how to go about it), what the interface will look like, and whether it will require the use or development of any APIs. This is also where we would identify what programming language (Python, Visual Basic, and so on) and architecture (REST, SOAP, and so on) we will use.

The development phase is where the code is written. The code takes into account the previously established definition and design parameters. Some testing of code snippets may occur in this phase to determine whether the code is working as designed. However, major testing will occur later in the process.

In the testing phase of application development, activities such as penetration testing and vulnerability scanning against the application are performed. We will use techniques and tools for both dynamic and static testing or dynamic application security testing (DAST) and static application security testing (SAST). We will go into these testing methods later in the chapter.

Some models also include secure operations and disposal as important stages of the SDLC.

Once all the other stages are finished, the application would then enter into what some call the *secure operations phase*. This is after thorough testing has been successfully completed and the application and its environment are deemed secure.

The disposal phase is not included in the CCSP CBK but is worthy of mention here. Once the software has completed its job or has been replaced by a newer or different application, it must then be securely disposed of. Most software companies have a published software life cycle as part of their customer-facing information. It includes lifespans of the applications with specifics about things like how long and what kind of security patches will be available to the customer. Out-of-date and no longer supported software poses a risk to the enterprise in many ways, mostly due to vendors stopping the support or development of patches for any new vulnerabilities discovered beyond the published end of life (EOL). This is why EOL applications should be disposed of and replaced with whatever has taken over their functionality.

Most web and cloud applications are a bit different than traditional applications in that they can often be updated in place continually and may stay in service for a very long time. If anything, you may see them no longer supporting certain features, but rarely does development stop; as long as the vendor and application remain a viable solution, they will probably stay patched and up to date.

An exception to this is the case where a vendor creates an application that incorporates existing technologies or libraries and the vendor doesn't update the application as newer and safer versions of the technologies are released. The software gets older and harder to upgrade because of the significant jump usually encountered with the evolving technology. One example of this might be where a developer creates a web application that uses a specific database runtime engine. That runtime engine is then updated numerous times over the years, and it changes enough that the original code in the web application will not work with the newest release of the runtime engine. Now you are in a situation where either you get rid of your application and develop a new one or you continue using it and accept the risks associated with doing so. Many companies, rather than expending resources to keep their applications up to date, will run them until they actually cause problems before correcting them. That usually winds up being at least as expensive as if they had kept the original applications up to date. This is the folly of software engineering.

The real purpose of engaging in, learning about, and working with the cloud secure software development life cycle is so that we have some assurances that the cloud applications we are using are as safe as possible from vulnerabilities and any other risks that might result in data being compromised.

Several models of the cloud-secure software development life cycle have been put forth by a number of organizations. However, they are all quite similar in that they are a framework for the secure development of cloud applications, so they generally cover the same ideas but sometimes with different labels. One example is structured like this:

1. Application requirements
2. Application design
3. Implementation
4. Verification
5. Release to production

Another well-known model uses these phases:

1. Planning and analysis
2. Defining
3. Designing
4. Development
5. Testing
6. Maintenance

You can begin to see patterns emerge that have to do with planning, designing, testing, and releasing in some fashion or another. One area that is not very well covered in either of these models or in the CCSP CBK is the notion of *application disposal*. In a full life cycle, all applications will end or morph into their next iteration. For the reasons previously discussed in this section, disposal is an important part of the cloud-secure software development life cycle, even though it is not covered in the current CCSP CBK exam.

ISO/IEC 27034-1 Standards for Secure Application Development

In developing a more mature, well-rounded, and widely accepted practice, standards and guidelines needed to be created in order to more specifically outline requirements for best practices in application development. ISO/IEC 27034-1 solves that problem in many ways.

ISO/IEC 27034-1, "Information Technology – Security Techniques – Application Security," provides one of the most widely accepted set of standards and guidelines for secure application development. ISO/IEC 27034-1 is a comprehensive set of standards that cover many aspects of application development. A few of the key elements include the organizational normative framework (ONF), the application normative framework (ANF), and the application security management process (APSM).

Part of ISO/IEC 27034-1 lays out the ONF for all of the components of best practices with regard to application security. The standard is composed of the following categories:

- Business Context
- Regulatory Context
- Technical Context
- Specifications
- Roles, Responsibilities, and Qualifications
- Processes
- Application Security Control (ASC) Library

The application normative framework (ANF) is used together with the ONF in that it is created for a specific application. The ANF shares the applicable parts of the ONF needed to achieve an application's required level of security and the level of trust desired.

The ANF-to-ONF relationship is a one-to-one relationship; every application has an ANF that maps back to the ONF. However, the ONF-to-ANF relationship is one-to-many. The ONF has many ANFs, but the ANF has only one ONF. Make sure you understand this concept.

Identity and Access Management (IAM)

Identity and access management (IAM) is an area of great importance to the CCSP candidate. IAM is about the people, processes, and procedures used to create, manage, and destroy identities of all kinds. Whether you are dealing with system administrators or plain users of cloud services, the creation and management of identities is key in maintaining secure operations.

IAM systems consist of several components, as shown in Figure 7.3. First and foremost is that they are designed to verify or authenticate users to gain access to resources. Once authenticated, the users are then authorized and given subsequent access to resources. The user is generally managed through a central user repository. This is often accomplished with role-based access. This allows for a broader and more consistent set of controls for users. Rather than the administrator having to create, modify, delete, and otherwise manage a user, role-based access allows the administrator to modify the role a user has, thereby impacting the entire group in that role at once.

FIGURE 7.3 IAM Elements

IAM functionality is divided into identity management and access management:

Identity Management Identity management is the process whereby individuals are given access to system resources by associating user rights with a given identity. Provisioning is the first phase of identity management, where each subject is issued a unique identity assertion (something that serves as an identification, such as a user ID). During this process, the user is usually also issued a password for use in authenticating the identity assertion. The entity issuing the password and identity assertion will retain a record of each for use in recognizing the user later (when the user uses them to log in to resources). The generation, storage, and security controls of these passwords is known as *password management*. In a self-service identity management configuration (as opposed to a provider-managed configuration), the cloud customer is in charge of provisioning each user's identity/identity assertion.

Access Management Access management is the part of the process that deals with controlling access to resources once they have been granted. Access management is what tries to identify who a user is and what they are allowed to access each time they attempt to access a resource. This is accomplished through a combination of means:

Authentication Establishes identity by asking who you are and determining whether you are a legitimate user (often by combining the use of an identity assertion and an authentication factor; for example, a user ID and password).

Authorization Evaluates what you have access to after authentication occurs (in many cases, this means comparing the identity assertion against an access control list [ACL]).

Policy Management Serves as the enforcement arm of authentication and authorization and is established based on business needs and senior management decisions.

Federation An association of organizations that facilitate the exchange of information as appropriate about users and access to resources, allowing them to share resources across disparate organizations.

Identity Repositories The directory services for the administration of user accounts and their associated attributes.

These components are stored in what is called an identity repository directory. Think of it as the Active Directory on steroids. The schema used is much more detailed and has many more uses, and it is a valuable crown jewel that must be protected at all costs. A breach of this component would be devastating to the organization.

Besides identity repositories and their directory, other core facets of IAM include federated identity management, federation standards, federated identity providers, various types of single sign-on (SSO), multifactor authentication, and supplemental security devices. These concepts will be explored in the following sections.

Identity Repositories and Directory Services

Identity repositories are the store of information or attributes of identities. Directory services are how those identities and attributes are managed. They allow the administrator to customize user roles, identities, and so on. All of this becomes even more important when we deal with federation, as there must be a consistent means of accessing these identities and their associated attributes in order to work across disparate systems.

Here are some of the most widely used directory services:

- X.500 and LDAP
- Microsoft Active Directory
- Novell eDirectory
- Metadata replication and synchronization

Single Sign-On (SSO)

When an organization has a variety of resources that each require authentication, usage and utilization can become cumbersome for users, especially when they have to keep track of passwords and user IDs that have different requirements (length, complexity, and so forth). Single sign-on (SSO) is a way to address this and simplify the operational experience for the user.

While there are several ways to implement SSO, in general the term refers to a situation where the user signs in once, usually to an authentication server; then when the user wants to access the organization's resources (say, on different servers throughout the environment), each resource will query the authentication server to determine if the user is logged in and properly authenticated; the authentication server then approves the request and the resource server grants the user access. All of this should be transparent to the user, streamlining their use of the resources on the network. Theoretically, the user could log in just once per day, when they sit down at their desk to begin work, and never have to reenter any additional sign-on credentials.

Federated Identity Management

Federated identity management (or "federation," in general) is much the same as normal identity management except it is used to manage identities across disparate organizations. You can think of it as single sign-on (SSO) for multiple organizations.

Let's look at an example. A group of research universities want to share their research data. They can create a federation so that a scientist signing in at their own university, on their own system, can then access all the research resources of the other universities in the federation, without having to present other, new identity and authentication credentials.

There are two general types of federation: the web-of-trust model and use of a third-party identifier.

In the web of trust, each member of the federation (that is, each organization that wants to share resources and users) has to review and approve each other member for inclusion in the federation. While it's a good method to be sure that everyone else in the federation reaches your particular level of trust, this can become costly and unwieldy once the federation reaches a significant number of member organizations—it just doesn't scale well.

By using a third-party identifier, on the other hand, the member organizations outsource their responsibilities to review and approve each other to some external party (that each of them trust, of course) who will take on this responsibility on behalf of all the members. This is a popular model in the cloud environment, where the identifier role can often be combined with other functions (for instance, crypto key management) and outsourced to a cloud access security broker (CASB).

When discussing federation, we apply the terms *identity provider* and *relying parties*. The identity provider is the entity that provisions and authenticates identity assertions (validating users, provisioning user IDs and passwords, managing both, deprovisioning them, and so forth) and the relying party is any member of the federation that shares resources based on authenticated identities.

In the web-of-trust model, the identity provider is each member of the federation (provisioning identity assertions for each of their users, respectively) *and* they are also the relying parties (sharing resources with each other, based on those authenticated identities.

In the trusted third-party model of federation, the identity provider is the trusted third party, and the relying parties are each member organization within the federation.

Federation Standards

There are a number of federation standards, but the most widely used one is Security Assertion Markup Language (SAML). The latest version of SAML is SAML 2.0. It is XML based and consists of a framework for communicating authentication, authorization or entitlement information, and attribute information across organizations. In other words, it is a means for users from outside organizations to be verified and validated as authorized users inside or with another organization without the user having to create identities in both locations.

Some of the other standards that exist in this area are as follows:

WS-Federation This uses the term *realms* in explaining its capabilities to allow organizations to trust each other's identity information across organizations.

OAuth Often used in authorization with mobile apps, the OAuth framework provides third-party applications limited access to HTTP services.

OpenID Connect This is an interoperable authentication protocol based on the OAuth 2 specification. It allows developers to authenticate their users across websites and applications without having to manage usernames and passwords.

Multifactor Authentication

Multifactor authentication has become more popular and widespread in the last five years due to increased demand for better authorization security and dropping prices of the technology. Only a few years ago, multifactor mechanisms were far outside the financial reach of anyone except government facilities that required very high levels of security or other highly regulated industries such as banking. Many banks have used such technology since the early 2000s to facilitate secure wire transfers.

Multifactor authentication is composed of, at a minimum, two of the following aspects—something you know, something you are, or something you have. Something you know can be a password, passphrase, and so on. Something you have can be something like a number-generating key fob, a smartphone capable of receiving text messages, or even a phone that can receive a call and then transmit a number or key to the individual but that is only accessible from a very specific phone number. Something you are is a biometric trait of yourself, as a living creature. This could be as unique and specific as your DNA fingerprint, or as cursorily general as a photograph.

The authentication solutions featuring the "know" and "have" aspects are especially useful with remote access security where presenting a biometric factor would be awkward, because they help to prevent an unauthorized user from accessing an account or data without both pieces of the authentication mechanism. It is one thing to steal or guess a password on an account, but it is much harder for someone to obtain both a password and a key generated by a device to which only you have access.

You will usually see government employees who work in classified settings using solutions that leverage the "have" and "know" factors. They are typically tokens, or devices, that generate a number that is synchronized with a server in the home environment. This keeps any would-be malicious user from guessing the number and stealing a key. So again, even if your password or passphrase were compromised, the second factor used in authentication would be virtually impossible to re-create.

In addition, the numbers generated by these tokens change every 30–60 seconds. It would be virtually impossible for a malicious attacker to accidentally guess the second factor's number, and even if they did, it would change again within 30–60 seconds. This is exactly why high-security environments like law enforcement, high-level government agencies, and other highly regulated industries use them.

Supplemental Security Devices

There are a few additional security devices with which the CCSP candidate should be familiar. The first of these would be the generic firewall. The firewall is designed as the access point for traffic entering or leaving the perimeter of a network. Firewalls come in a variety of designs and capabilities. However, they are all created to provide some type of protection from unauthorized traffic entering or leaving a network. Early on, these devices were limited to simply port blocking with no ability to see inside the packets traversing the interface. Then *stateful packet inspection* came into the picture, which allowed firewalls to prevent inbound traffic from entering unless the connection had been initiated from inside the network.

Today's application-aware firewalls are far superior to their predecessors of even a few years ago. However, the battle rages on with attackers and their wily ways, which leads us to the web application firewall (WAF). See Figure 7.4.

FIGURE 7.4   Firewalls

The web application firewall (WAF) was first required under PCI regulations several years ago. These firewalls are deployed in addition to any network firewall and are designed to protect specific web-based applications. PCI requires them as a way of protecting credit card data egress from a web application that may be handling online transactions. These firewalls are specific enough that they know the way the application should be behaving and can detect even the smallest unusual activity and bring it to a stop. In addition, WAFs can also provide protection against such network-based attacks as DoS or DDoS attacks. WAFs function at Layer 7 of the OSI model.

Another form of protection is database activity monitoring (DAM). Again, as with the web application firewall, the idea is to have a piece of software or a dedicated appliance watching databases for any type of unusual requests or activity and then to be able to send alerts and even take actions to stop malicious activity. These DAMs can be either agent based or network based, meaning an agent resides on the machine or instance of the database or a network agent monitors traffic to and from the database.

One of the newest forms of security designed to work in conjunction with both WAFs and DAMs is something called *deception technology*. Deception technology works something like this. Let's say a DAM has picked up some actor poking around with SQL injection attacks to see if they can find a weakness in the database or if the WAF will stop them. Deception occurs by quietly rerouting what may be attack traffic to another network segment with databases populated with phony data and triggers that can capture the attack. Although this is often referred to as a honeypot, there are now companies that will set up and manage these deceptive networks for you and not only move the attack traffic away from targets but inform law enforcement and even trap the attacker with logs.

API gateways are also an important part of a layered security model. They can be used to impose such controls on API activity as

- Acting as an API proxy so as to not directly expose the API

- Implementing access control to the API

- Limiting connections so that bandwidth is available for all applications, which can also help in the event of an internal DoS or DDoS attack

- Allowing for API logging

- Allowing for metrics to be assembled from API access logs

- Providing for additional API security filtering

XML gateways work in much the same way, except they work around *how* sensitive data and services are exposed to APIs. They can be either software- or hardware-based and can implement some types of data loss prevention (DLP).

Cloud Application Architecture

It is important that we examine the mechanisms behind the scenes that make application security and software development for the cloud work, as well as the weaknesses and vulnerabilities associated with each. The CCSP candidate needs to understand how to evaluate and discover these for the customer.

Application programming interfaces (APIs) are the coding components that allow applications to speak to one another, generally through a web interface of some kind. We hope that this occurs in a safe and secure manner. However, that is not always the case, and the cloud security professional should know how to determine risks and threats associated with the use of APIs. To do so, we will now examine APIs in more detail.

Application Programming Interfaces

There are two common types of APIs in use with cloud-based applications today that the CCSP candidate must understand. The first is RESTful APIs. REST stands for Representational State Transfer. It is a software architecture designed to scale the abilities of web-based applications. It is based on guidelines and best practices for creating these scalable web applications. These standards, when followed, allow web applications to access other applications, databases, and so on in order to extend their functionality. Other characteristics of the REST model include the following:

- It's lightweight.
- It uses simple URLs.
- It is not reliant on XML.
- It's scalable.
- It outputs in many formats (CSV, JSON, and so on).
- It's efficient, which means it uses smaller messages than XML.

    Some examples of situations where REST works well are

- When bandwidth is limited
- When stateless operations are used
- When caching is needed

The other common type of APIs is SOAP APIs. Simple Object Access Protocol (SOAP) is a protocol specification providing for the exchange of structured information or data in web services. It also works over other protocols such as SMTP, FTP, and HTTP.

Some of the characteristics of SOAP include the following:

- Standards-based
- Reliant on XML
- Highly intolerant of errors
- Slower
- Built-in error handling

Some examples of where SOAP works or fits in better are

- Asynchronous processing
- Format contracts
- Stateful operations

Neither API format is necessarily better than the other. They each have their place and work in different ways depending on their use and the needs of the application. Later we will revisit APIs as they relate to the software development life cycle and supply chain management. However, for now it is important to understand that regardless of what type of API you use to offer web services, you are granting another application access to the primary application and any data it may have access to. This can present many security challenges for the consumer since they do not have the skillset to be able to evaluate the security of any specific API they might be accessing. In addition, there may be other APIs in play that a user is not aware of but that are used on the same system. This can then lead to data leakage or other problems if the APIs in question have not been sufficiently vetted and validated to ensure they provide adequate security.

Tenancy Separation

Multitenancy refers to the notion of hosting multiple cloud tenants on a single host while sharing resources. For instance, a typical host machine can support numerous virtual tenants based on the amount of CPU, RAM, and storage it has. These tenants, while running on the same host, are maintained separately in their virtual environments. This is known as *tenancy separation*. It is vitally important that configurations be made in such a way as to ensure absolute adherence to this principle. If not, such issues as data leakage and corruption could occur. Imagine an accounting program computing with someone else's data. The results could be disastrous. On the other hand, imagine that another company has gotten access to your personal information because of storage misconfigurations. The tenant could be exposed to regulatory, legal, or financial damages should such an instance occur. And, as we have stated repeatedly, it is the data owner who is ultimately responsible. If a misconfiguration were to occur, you might have recourse with your provider, but that does not preclude you from bearing legal responsibility for your users.

Mainframes used in the financial sector have long been used in a manner that requires tenant separation, so developers working in the financial industry have created strong methods for performing and enforcing tenant separation. While the use of mainframes does not exactly fit the usual cloud computing model (mainframes often do not work well with Web apps, and are usually single-purpose machines), both cloud providers and cloud customers may consider using mainframes in circumstances where tenancy separation is paramount and other solutions aren't suitable.

Cryptography

Although we will not be discussing the specifics of encryption here, the CCSP candidate must be familiar with the different types of encryption, the places where it is used, and the use case for each. This is just one more example of where the CCSP can add value to the customer since most customers do not understand the different types and use cases for encryption. What follows are descriptions of several of these and how they can be effectively used as part of the overall cloud application security scheme.

Encryption of Data at Rest   Data at rest, whether it be short-term or long-term storage, should be protected from multitenancy issues and similar problems. When working in the cloud, you are in a shared environment and must always be aware of possible data leakage. Therefore, encrypting data at rest is a great way to prevent anyone from seeing data that they are not authorized to see. Encryption involves the use of keys. Without access to the proper keys, the data is unreadable and unusable, which ensures its safety from prying eyes. This use of encryption also protects the consumer from what might ultimately be determined to be lawful but unwanted access to their data. There may be situations where, while your data is logically separated from someone else's data, both sets of data are physically stored together on a hard drive that is confiscated for legal reasons. You would not want the police or other prying eyes to have access to your data even though they have a valid warrant for other data on the same drive.

Encryption of Data in Transit   Encryption of data in transit is necessary for many of the same reasons, with the added threat that while data is being transmitted, unauthorized eyes might land on it or redirect it, causing data leakage. Encrypting data in transit also uses encryption keys, typically in the form of SSL certificates. The proper care of those certificates is paramount. If compromised, you have lost the keys to the kingdom. Cloud-based certificate providers spend millions of dollars on securing their operations for this very reason.

Encryption of Data While in Use   Another use case of encryption that is not anywhere close to widespread adoption is something called *homomorphic encryption*. The idea is that if we could keep a dataset encrypted while being manipulated in memory or shared with another application, we would then never have to decrypt it, making the data transaction safer on an order of magnitudes. Another way to look at this is that homomorphic encryption will produce the same result when operating on cipher text as would occur using the same data in clear text. One impediment to the implementation of this idea is that homomorphic encryption is very slow due to the heavy mathematical calculations that are needed. Therefore, it is not an effective solution today.

The single most effective way to combat multitenancy issues, data leakage, and similar problems is by using encryption. We call the field of dealing with encryption *cryptography*. It has to do with differing types, strengths, and uses of encryption to protect datasets from unauthorized access.

We have mentioned the notion of data at rest, data in transit, and data storage or archiving. Each of these uses a slightly different encryption technology to achieve the same result, which is to keep prying eyes from seeing what they should not be allowed to see and to provide for integrity or nonrepudiation. There are a number of encryption technologies that you will be expected to identify and describe in your CCSP exam:

Transport Layer Security (TLS)   TLS is a protocol designed to ensure privacy when communicating between applications. This can occur between two servers such as two SMTP servers passing mail, or between a client and a web server as in the case of an application that passes confidential or protected information of some type. In years gone by, this type of encryption put a burden on both the server and the client, but today's advanced application-specific integrated circuits (ASICs) solve that problem. These chips are designed specifically to handle cryptographic functions and are therefore much faster and efficient than having the main CPU in a machine handle the encryption. This is known as *crypto offloading*, but that term is not included in your test materials.

Secure Sockets Layer (SSL)   Invented and first adopted by Netscape back in the mid-1990s, SSL was originally meant to encrypt data transmissions between servers, much like its replacement TLS. SSL was deprecated in 2015 but is still used in many enterprises, since it was ubiquitous and upgrading or transitioning can be costly and time-consuming.

Virtual Private Networks (VPNs)   Virtual private networks were developed as we began to acquire more and more bandwidth to satisfy the needs of remote workers to securely access data on their company's internal networks. There are two types of VPNs: purely virtual and virtual with security. The first is what you still see in Multiprotocol Label Switching (MPLS) networks (somewhat similar to the older frame relay circuits used in the 1990s) whereby a shim is attached to each packet traversing the MPLS network. This is much like a Layer 2 VLAN shim, but it moves the data across a WAN. However, while the packet in theory cannot be seen to any other packets because of its distinguishing shim, it is *not* encrypted. It is a VPN but without the benefit of encryption.

An encrypted VPN should technically be referred to as an IPSec VPN, meaning it is a VPN of the IPSec (IP security) type. There are numerous ways these types of VPNs can be configured, but the one thing they all have in common is encryption from end to end. This then accomplishes the idea of having a worker remotely connect from their workstation or laptop to the corporate VPN or IPSec gateway so that they can transmit and receive data in a safe and secure manner without worrying about whether someone on an unsecured hotel Wi-Fi network is capturing their packets.

Whole-Instance Encryption   Better known as whole-disk encryption (WDE), this is the idea of encrypting all of a system's data at rest in one instance. Rather than having special folders, the entire storage medium is encrypted. In today's world of lightweight and super-fast smart devices and laptops, it is a good idea to encrypt your entire data storage. Again, consider the issue of the criminal who is sharing space with you in a cloud multitenant environment who gets arrested, and the police seize all the cloud hard drives, including the one with your data, even if you are not part of the problem. Without some form of encryption, your entire dataset is at risk of being exposed. In addition, in a virtualized environment such as cloud computing, *snapshots* are made of the virtual machines for recovery purposes. These, too, can be seized or accessed if not properly encrypted. And lastly, as mentioned previously, in years past this type of encryption would generally destroy the performance of anything but the most powerful machines. But with the advent of stronger and faster processors, even a small smart device can be totally encrypted without harming performance.

Volume Encryption   Much like encrypting an entire device, volume encryption refers to only encrypting a partition on a hard drive as opposed to the entire disk. This is useful when the entire disk does not need to be encrypted as only the protected sections have data of any value. For example, you may have a cloud-based accounting application that stores and manipulates financial data. You certainly want the data of your finances encrypted to protect them, but it may not be necessary to also have the part of the volume or disk with the software encrypted since it contains no data of any value.

Sometimes customer or users will add an additional layer of protection by encrypting files or folders. This way, they hold the keys to unencrypt the data, should the disk or volume be breached in some manner.

Keep in mind that the key (no pun intended) to securing any encryption scheme is the safe storage and management of the keys used to encrypt and decrypt. It is not essential to go into details in the CCSP exam about these issues because they are covered in other (ISC)[2] CBKs such as the CISSP. What is important is that the CCSP candidate be aware of each of these uses of encryption and their application with regard to cloud computing.

Sandboxing

Sandboxing can mean many things today, but in the realm of cloud computing, sandboxing refers to the concept of a protected area being utilized for testing untested or untrusted code or to better understand if an application is working the way it was intended to work. These sandboxes are usually protected areas in memory that will not allow processes of any kind to run outside the environment or allow access inside from any other application or process. Many developers today will rent such cloud platforms specifically for testing. Because the model is based on metered usage, the developer only has to pay for it as long as they are using it. Once the application development has completed, they can turn the service down and stop paying for it.

Application Virtualization

Application virtualization is a somewhat misunderstood term. The idea of application virtualization has to do with running applications in a trusted virtual environment. It is a little like sandboxing, but instead of sandboxing a process, application virtualization allows you to run full applications in a protected space. In addition, because you are doing this virtually, you can run applications that would otherwise not run on the host system. The best example of this is the Linux application WINE. WINE is itself an application virtualization platform that then provides a Linux machine with the ability to run Windows-based applications. This also provides for a space where new apps can be tested, for instance with Windows, without allowing the app to touch what would normally be the external Windows machine.

Microsoft App-V and XenApp also allow users to perform application virtualization.

All of these mechanisms are designed to allow testing applications for such things as whether they will work appropriately in the cloud. However, there are other considerations as well that need be accounted for. These include processes to define and assert some type of software assurance and validation. We must be able to articulate the processes involved in ensuring that our applications function as needed and required, while also mitigating the risks of any vulnerabilities, defects, and malicious code. We will examine these in more detail in the following sections.

Cloud Application Assurance and Validation

To effectively test our web applications, we need to be familiar with a number of application security testing methods and tools. In this section we will explore the most important and most used of these and attempt to give the CCSP candidate a solid understanding of how and when each of these methods and tools should be used.

Threat Modeling

There are several threat modeling tools such as Trike, AS/NZS 4360 and CVSS. However, for the purposes of the CCSP exam, we will cover only the STRIDE model.

Created by Microsoft some time ago, the STRIDE threat model has been widely adopted. The model provides a standardized way of describing threats by their attributes. Then by looking at your application and applying these threat types, you can cover almost all categories to see whether your application has a vulnerability and what type it is. The STRIDE acronym stands for the following:

Spoofing   Any impersonation such as IP or user spoofing

Tampering   With data output, data input, or data that is stored

Repudiation   When the inability to deny one's action has been compromised

Information Disclosure   Data leakage or an outright breach

Denial of Service   Any type of attack that could cause the application to be unavailable, thereby voiding the CIA triangle of security

Elevation of Privilege   The ability to elevate a user account privilege above the authorized level

STRIDE is particularly useful as part of the SDLC in attempting to identify vulnerabilities throughout the build process. The STRIDE model enables us to do this. When evaluating cloud application security, these six concepts help in identifying and classifying threats or vulnerabilities and help form a common language used to describe them. That way, we can systematically address them through better coding techniques or other control mechanisms.

Threat modeling helps prepare for some of the more common application vulnerabilities that developers will encounter when working with cloud applications, which include the following:

Injection   This is when a malicious user attempts to inject a string of some type into a field in order to manipulate the application's actions or reveal unauthorized data. Examples include such things as SQL, LDAP, and OS injections. If the injection is successful, either unauthorized data is seen or other manipulative actions are taken.

Broken Authentication   This occurs when a malicious user is able to break a session and steal items like tokens, passwords, or keys. This then allows the malicious user to hijack the system.

Cross-Site Scripting (XSS)   XSS is one of the most widely seen application flaws, next to injections. XSS occurs when an application allows untrusted data to be sent to a web browser without proper validation or escaping. This then allows the malicious user to execute code or hijack sessions in the user's browser.

Insecure Direct Object Access   This refers to an occurrence that involves a reference to an internal object, like a file, without access control checks or other controls in place to ensure attackers cannot manipulate data.

Security Misconfigurations   Security misconfigurations are a large area of concern because they usually involve humans—and humans make mistakes. It is vital, when exposing any application to the Internet or cloud users, that the security configuration involve double and triple checking, routine auditing, and whenever possible automated processes to harden systems and applications to keep them up to date.

Sensitive Data Exposure   Here we are referring to the disclosure of information such as PII, healthcare, credit cards, and so on. Without proper controls in place such as those we have previously discussed (encryption, data masking, tokenization, and so on), sensitive data can leak by an application or system. Therefore, it is paramount that penetration testing and audit measures be in place that routinely check for misconfigurations or new code that might have slipped in that could possibly expose sensitive data.

Missing Function-Level Access Control   An application should always verify function-level access privileges before granting access of that functionality to the user interface (UI). If this is not implemented properly, malicious users may be able to forge requests that will allow them functionality without authorization.

Cross-Site Request Forgery (CSRF)   A CSRF manipulates a logged-on user's browser to send a forged HTTP request along with cookies and other authentication information in an effort to force the victim's browser to generate a request that a vulnerable application thinks is a legitimate request form the user.

Using Components with Known Vulnerabilities   This is becoming more of a problem as developers use more open source (read *free*) libraries and frameworks that very often run with elevated privileges. These elevated privileges give an attacker a way, once on a system, to gain those same privileges and then take control of whatever they want.

Invalidated Redirects and Forwards   Oftentimes developers will use redirects without validation, which may expose applications to untrusted data or other applications. Without this validation, malicious users can alter the redirects to point the user to malicious sites such as phishing sites.

Some of the risks associated with these vulnerabilities can be very high and include such things as the list that the CSA came up with in 2013 titled "The Notorious Nine":

1. Data loss: Data can be lost through poor application or database design, corruption, or hardware failures.

2. Data breaches: Breaches are due usually to poor database security design or configuration whereby data is exposed without proper authorization.

3. Account takeover or hijacking: This happens when attacks are designed to steal or wedge themselves into the middle of a conversation in order to gain control.

4. Insecure APIs: APIs are the connective tissue of cloud-based web applications and if not properly designed and implemented can cause gaping holes in the security fabric.

5. Denial-of-service (DoS): Both denial-of-service and the even more dreaded distributed denial-of-service attacks are designed to make an application or service unavailable so that a service interruption occurs.

6. Insider threats: Disgruntled employees can wreak havoc on a system.

7. Abuse of cloud services: Consumers sometimes misuse their cloud services for illegal or immoral activities.

8. Insufficient due diligence: Cloud consumers can get into big trouble if they do not follow good due diligence practices.

9. Shared technology issues: While the underlying infrastructure items themselves often were never designed for a multitenancy situation, they respond pretty well to modern virtualization software. However, the consumer must always be wary of the dangers presented in the cloud environment when someone makes a configuration error or has a disgruntled employee. These threats can negate even the most sophisticated control mechanisms.

 Real World Scenario

Real-World Insider Threats

Several years ago, a disgruntled IT employee of a major U.S. city was fired. That employee had access to numerous administrative-level accounts across network equipment and servers on the city's private cloud. He retaliated by locking city employees out of these systems, crippling their ability to conduct key activities. One of the affected systems was the payroll system. Once he locked the accounts, city employees could not be paid.

After discovering the intrusion, police were able to identify the former employee and took him into custody. He sat in jail for almost seven days before caving in to law enforcement's questioning and gave up the passwords.

Try to imagine what would happen if someone were to do this to a cloud services provider such as Google or Amazon. The outcome could be disastrous. In the case of the city, emergency services were affected, too. What if it had been a hospital? All of the potential repercussions must be considered when attempting to move into the cloud environment in any way.

 Real World Scenario

DDoS Attacks on DNS Providers

Recently a large DNS provider on the East Coast of the United States experienced a DDoS attack launched from thousands of Internet of Things (IoT) devices from around the world. These devices consisted of things like wireless routers infected with botnet malware and other items such as closed-caption TV or CCTB cameras. When combined, these devices attacked not just an IP but web or cloud services. In this particular instance the service attacked was a DNS provider. As a result, some of the largest online retailers in the country were offline for several hours, not because their site was down, but because the DNS servers, which direct traffic all over the Internet, were down and therefore could not direct traffic to these sites. This went on for almost a day and cost estimates were well into millions of dollars in lost sales.

DDoS attacks are just one of the Achilles heels of cloud computing. Trying to take down a Google or Microsoft or Amazon would be extremely difficult due to the mitigation mechanisms they have in place. However, these are no help when the DNS system itself fails. In addition, these systems are much less secure, since they have never had to face attacks of this type and magnitude. And unless they develop more sophisticated ways of dealing with these threats, cloud providers could be in for a bumpy ride over the next few years.

Quality of Service

One item that is easy to overlook in designing and securely deploying cloud applications is that of quality of service (QoS) assurance. In the cloud model, QoS refers to the idea of ensuring that you do not over-control your environment with security measures that degrade your application's performance.

Encryption is the first example that comes to mind. Turning on encryption in most databases causes a slowdown in performance due to the processing power required for the encryption and decryption process to occur. Applications such as SQL are much better at that today because of improved technology and faster equipment, but it still needs to be factored into the equation.

Another example might be running host-based intrusion detection systems (HIDs) on a server. Usually this is agent based, and because it requires the viewing of all connections and data coming into and leaving the device, it can have a significant impact on performance.

The point of all this is to be careful in your application deployment design models and only use security controls that are needed and adequate to reduce risk to acceptable levels.

Software Security Testing

Testing the security aspects of software requires a specialized skillset. In this section we will look at some of the methodologies, testing concepts, and tools used to verify and validate that we have the appropriate controls in place to satisfy our security needs.

We begin by examining penetration testing and vulnerability scanning. Although both are quite useful and have their place in the realm of application testing, they serve very different purposes and are used in different ways.

Vulnerability scanning involves looking at an application from the outside to see if there are any vulnerabilities that might be taken advantage of. Vulnerability scanning does not necessarily identify configuration errors (although some may be encountered and discovered) but is more of an inventory of known vulnerabilities parsed against the application or network being scanned. These types of scanners are often employed by hackers as part of ongoing reconnaissance for vulnerabilities to be used later in attacks. However, when we perform vulnerability scanning to test our own system, no exploitation occurs and, as long as the scans are performed properly, no damage occurs to the systems. Sometimes errors occur, but usually at worst the system will need a reboot.

The downside, of course, to vulnerability scanning is that it can only detect the vulnerabilities for which it has definitions—that is, known vulnerabilities. Any vulnerabilities not currently known and included in the scanning tool will remain in place and can later become zero-day exploits when attackers figure out how to use them.

 Real World Scenario

Vulnerability Scanning in the Real World

Once while performing a rather innocuous internal reconnaissance scan, this author was told the IP range in question was clear to scan. I was assured that there were no devices that could possibly be disrupted or damaged. So off I went and launched my scan. Only minutes later one of the staff came racing into the area where I was working with a somewhat terrified look on his face and asked me to stop what I was doing immediately.

Of course I complied and assured him that I had not gone anywhere other than the specified IPs in question and that my scan was extremely lightweight and could not possibly damage even an aging web server. However, what he had not anticipated was that there was a large mainframe in the same subnet. When you scan something for recon purposes, especially when it is an internal scan and you are not trying to hide your activity, you scan all 65,000+ ports available in the TCP/IP stack.

Well, it seems that mainframes log each and every connection to any port on their systems. And mainframes typically have multiple IPs assigned to them for different purposes. So, the mainframe in question was logging each and every one of the 65,000+ connection attempts that the scanning software was making on each and every interface. Needless to say, it created a short-term DoS attack.

All ended well as the mainframe was forevermore relegated to a DO NOT SCAN UNDER ANY CIRCUMSTANCE moratorium and has not produced a problem since.

The moral of the story is: Don't rely on staff as your only source of information. Make sure you check, double-check, and triple-check each and every detail of your scans and be prepared to stop them immediately if need be. Never leave a scan unattended, even if things are quiet and going smoothly. You never know when that next IP will take a hit and cause you problems.

Penetration testing is designed to find vulnerabilities and to then exploit them to the point of actually gaining unauthorized access to systems or data. These tests usually begin with a reconnaissance and/or vulnerability scan to identify system weaknesses and then move on to the penetration phase. Penetration testing might be distinguished from vulnerability scanning in that it includes an active component (the penetration of the environment), whereas vulnerability scanning is almost exclusively passive.

It is extremely important to mention again that under no circumstances should you ever attempt any type of vulnerability scanning or penetration testing against an application or system without full authorization to do so. You could be violating several laws and get into some very deep trouble. In addition, you might even jeopardize your ISP account if they do not allow such activity in your end-user license agreement (EULA). Even though it is done almost every day, each time you step across the line you are taking a huge chance. Get permission first.

The OWASP Top 10

The Open Web Application Security Project (OWASP) is a collective effort of web developers sharing and analyzing information about web applications and security features and risks. While OWASP offers a variety of resources such as development guides, white papers, and security tools, all at no cost, the organization is best known for publishing the Top 10, a list of web app security risks developed from surveys conducted every three years.

The Top 10 is based on self-reported data about actual breaches. A notable aspect of the Top 10 list is that it pretty much contains the same ten vulnerabilities each time. They may change in rank on the list, but the list itself almost always has the same items listed year after year. See the following graphic:

OWASP Top 10 – 2010 (Previous)	OWASP Top 10 – 2013 (New)
A1 – Injection	A1 – Injection
A3 – Broken Authentication and Session Management	A2 – Broken Authentication and Session Management
A2 – Cross-Site Scripting (XSS)	A3 – Cross-Site Scripting (XSS)
A4 – Insecure Direct Object References	A4 – Insecure Direct Object References
A6 – Security Misconfiguration	A5 – Security Misconfiguration
A7 – Insecure Cryptographic Storage – Merged with A9 →	A6 – Sensitive Data Exposure
A8 – Failure to Restrict URL Access – Broadened into →	A7 – Missing Function Level Access Control
A5 – Cross-Site Request Forgery (CSRF)	A8 – Cross-Site Request Forgery (CSRF)
<buried in A6: Security Misconfiguration>	A9 – Using Known Vulnerable Components
A10 – Unvalidated Redirects and Forwards	A10 – Unvalidated Redirects and Forwards
A9 – Insufficient Transport Layer Protection	Merged with 2010-A7 into new 2013-A6

The other thing worth recognizing about the Top 10 is that almost every entry on the list, no matter what year the list is from, can be addressed by one security control: disciplined programming habits. Just about every vulnerability that makes the list is caused by not including a basic countermeasure in the program itself (for instance, field checking to prevent SQL injection). All of these problems have been known as basic elements required in secure programming for decades; none of them are new or novel or kept as proprietary secrets by software vendors.

Why, then, do we continue to see these vulnerabilities, year after year and report after report? Why do programmers not include the necessary controls and ensure breaches of that nature never occur again? Are programmers just lazy and ignorant?

Of course not. However, like any other industry, programming vendors are driven by business requirements, and there is one requirement that can cause the inclusion of these common, known vulnerabilities: planned release dates. In the effort to bring the software product to market on time, as well as complete necessary testing and include up-to-the-minute functionality, developers and programmers are often rushed and don't have the chance to include all the requisite controls to address these vulnerabilities.

This is understandable, if lamentable. If there were no hard-and-fast deadlines for shipping products, software development might be an unending activity with nonstop testing and limitless scope creep. Therefore, developers must find a happy medium that balances both business needs and security needs if we are to ever overcome our self-created obstacles.

The OWASP Top 10 project has not been updated since 2013. In 2016 OWASP began data collection for an update to be released in 2017 so check www.owasp.org to see if their latest list shows significant changes.

In addition to testing the environment as a suitably secure place for the application to function, we need to test the application itself to determine whether it has inherent security weaknesses and flaws. There are two general approaches:

White-Box Testing   Reviewing the source code. This requires a testing team with two kinds of skills and knowledge: how to read the code the program was written with and a deep understanding of security. Personnel with both capabilities are rare (and expensive). We also have to be careful not to use the same developers who wrote the code in performing the test; the testing team needs to be composed of people with entirely "fresh" eyes and no inherent conflict of interest.

Black-Box Testing   Testing the program as it functions, in runtime. In black-box testing, the source code is not reviewed; instead, the testing team uses inputs and results from the application itself, as it's running.

Because white-box and black-box testing can reveal different security issues, it's usually best to employ both in the testing regimen.

Next you'll look at SAST and DAST, two ways of testing the security of applications. See Figure 7.5.

FIGURE 7.5   Testing Issues

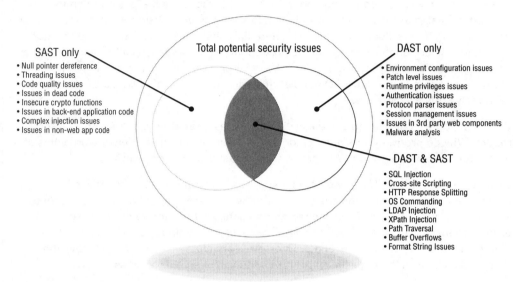

Static application security testing (SAST) is a useful method of security application testing. *Static* means that the source code, byte code, and binaries are all tested without executing the application. These sources of code are examined for known security flaws and vulnerabilities to attempt to catch them prior to going into production. This type of testing is often used in the early stages of application development as the full application is not testable in any other way at that time.

SAST testing is useful in finding such security problems as cross-site scripting (XSS) errors, SQL injection vulnerabilities, buffer overflows, unhandled error conditions, and backdoors. This type of test usually delivers more results and more accuracy than its counterpart dynamic application security testing (DAST).

Unlike SAST, DAST is considered a black-box test since the code is not revealed and the test must look for problems and vulnerabilities while the application is running. It is most effective when used against standard HTTP and other HTML web application interfaces.

 Although SAST and DAST are completely different types of testing methodology, they are often used in conjunction so as to observe or test the applications from more than one vantage point. They are also generally used in conjunction with routine code reviews.

One way to address application security issues is by having in place not only best coding practices, including code reviews and testing, but also a solid approach to risk mitigation. One of the more widely used models in the United States is NIST's Framework for Improving Critical Infrastructure Cybersecurity. While intended for use in utilities and national projects (e.g., the power grid and rail and roadway controls), the same concepts can be applied to smaller-scale uses.

This framework consists of three major components:

- Framework Core Components
  - Identify
  - Protect
  - Detect
  - Respond
  - Recover
- Framework Profile: Used to assist the organization in aligning activities with business requirements
- Framework Implementation Tiers: Used to identify where the organization is with regard to their particular approach

Approved APIs

As we have mentioned earlier, APIs are a large part of cloud application development because they allow other applications to consume web services from the application, thereby expanding its capabilities. In addition, they provide for automation and integration with third-party tools, again aimed at extending the functionality of the application. However, this does not come without risk. There are both consumers and providers of web services provided by APIs, and they each present special considerations.

When consuming APIs, the developer is relying on the API developer to have built in appropriate security controls and conducted testing and validation to ensure the integrity and security of the application. However, there is no way to ascertain this in advance. For instance, there are no certifications of APIs. You are reliant on the vendor's promise that data exchanges have been tested and validated.

One of the most significant problems with using APIs is that not everyone who creates them uses the same level of scrutiny. APIs are sometimes coded with little or no validation or security testing. Consumption of these APIs without any type of validation can lead to data leakage, poor authentication, and authorization and application failure. In addition, manipulating an unsecured API could at the worst lead to a data breach. What's more, when an application is updated or changed, the API may expose items that were not exposed before.

One way to overcome these issues is to ensure that processes are in place that allow for constant testing and review of APIs.

Software Supply Chain (API) Management

Another issue that is becoming more pronounced is that of software supply chain management. More and more, developers are finding ways to leverage APIs with third-party applications. This is what APIs are designed to do. The problem lies in third-party developers who build applications, leveraging upstream APIs and then adding their own to be consumed by yet another application, and so on. This chain of APIs can quickly spin out of control to the point that the end consumer has almost no way of knowing what other applications they may or may not be sending data upstream, and vice versa. This can create a nightmare for a company. Oftentimes, the consumer will overlook these deficiencies if the functionality offered by the application is appealing enough.

Securing Open Source Software

There is a philosophical disagreement in the InfoSec community about whether proprietary software (where the source code is hidden from everyone except the vendor) is preferable and more secure than the open source variety (where the source code is published, and anyone can review it, make modifications, and publish derivative versions).

Both offer some value. However, it is generally agreed that open source programs are more flexible, provide largely the same protections, and have a greater range of functionality than their proprietary counterparts (think Mozilla Firefox versus Microsoft Internet Explorer).

Perhaps one of the main points in favor of proprietary options is the possibility that liability will map back to the vendor—that breaches or other impact due to failures in the program can be blamed on the vendor, who may be held accountable (although it's difficult to think of examples where this has occurred). Another benefit might be the active and constant efforts of vendors to update and secure their proprietary applications.

Conversely, the benefit of choosing open source programs often includes a reduced price (or, indeed, having it free of charge), and the opportunity to review, for yourself, the code to test it for security vulnerabilities. Open source code also allows the user to make whatever modifications they choose in order to add or enhance functionality.

Agility

More and more development shops are implementing something called *Agile development*. This framework is designed to greatly speed up the development of software so that it can be delivered in a more timely manner to the customer. In these instances, open source libraries are sometimes considered the most expedient and cost-effective way to accomplish this in the short run. The customer gets the software quicker and cheaper and with all the functionality they have requested. The problem is that Agile focuses on timely delivery and not longevity or security of the application. They do not necessarily overlook them, but they are not a core part of their development process. This can easily lead to the situation where vulnerabilities are later discovered with no means to correct the issues short of redesigning or rebuilding the application.

Runtime Application Self-Protection (RASP)

RASP assists in the prevention of successful attack by protecting itself through the ability to reconfigure itself without human intervention. This typically occurs in response to certain types of threats or faults. It is called *runtime* protection because it comes into play by launching itself as the application is executed in memory.

Secure Code Reviews

Secure code review is the process for identifying and mitigating pieces of code in an application that has exposed a potential vulnerability. This audit of code is also designed to ensure that proper controls are in place that are appropriate for the functions within the application.

After many years of security professionals screaming about insecure code and coding practices, secure coding classes are beginning to crop up at major colleges and universities. However, this is to some degree still a self-taught area of expertise, so resources tend to be few and far between. One place that is having a huge impact is Carnegie Mellon University. Its Software Engineering Institute (SEI) specializes in training and providing best practice guidance in the practices surrounding secure coding. For more information, visit https://sei.cmu.edu.

OWASP Top 9 Coding Flaws

The following list, referred to as the OWASP 9 secure coding recommendations, warns against these practices in order to develop a secure coding environment. They reference these as the nine most common flaws in code development that lead to security issues.

- Input validation
- Source code design
- Info leakage and improper error handling
- Direct object reference
- Resource usage
- API usage
- Best practice violations
- Weak session management
- Use of HTTP Get query strings

OWASP believes that, if application developers avoided these nine simple design flaws, the vast majority of security breaches would not occur.

 Don't confuse the OWASP Top 9 Coding Flaws with the OWASP Top 10, which is a list of a list of web app security risks, or CSA's Treacherous 12, which deals with cloud computing top threats. The OWASP Top 10 and CSA's Treacherous 12 are discussed earlier in this chapter.

Summary

In this chapter we have discussed awareness of application-portability issues, the application software development life cycle, how to verify software through testing, how to select trusted software, how to design and use identity and access management systems, appropriate cloud application architecture, and cloud software assurance and validation.

Exam Essentials

Understand the differences between ANF and ONF.   ONF stands for the framework of so-called containers for all subcomponents of application security best practices catalogued and leveraged by an organization. It is composed of ANFs.

ANF stands for any subset of the ONF of the organization surrounding a specific business application to reach the targeted level of trust.

Be able to articulate the components of the STRIDE threat model.   The STRIDE threat model stands for the six threat categories:

- Spoofing
- Tampering
- Repudiation
- Information disclosure
- Denial of service
- Elevation of privilege

Be able to describe the stages of the SDLC.   Be sure to understand the stages in the SDLC model. The SDLC consists of the following stages:

- Defining
- Designing
- Developing
- Testing
- Secure Operations
- Disposal

Understand identity and access management and how it fits into the cloud environment.   IAM plays a critical role in managing users with the advent of role-based access. Understand the importance of this and federated identities.

Comprehend the specifics of cloud application architecture.   Not all applications are designed to run in the cloud. Be sure to understand the differences in architecture when designing or attempting to move applications.

Written Labs

1. Identify one cloud application that you use and identify any and all APIs in use. Be sure to include third-party APIs that may be used that cannot be identified or validated.

2. Describe the similarities and differences between the cloud software development life cycle and other models.

3. Identify and describe at least two components of the cloud application architecture.

4. Describe the functions of an identity management solution in the cloud environment.

Review Questions

You can find the answers in Appendix A.

1. Which of the following best represents the definition of REST?
   A. Built on protocol standards
   B. Lightweight and scalable
   C. Relies heavily on XML
   D. Only supports XML output

2. Which of the following is not one of the SDLC phases?
   A. Define
   B. Reject
   C. Design
   D. Test

3. Which of the following is *not* a component of the of the STRIDE model?
   A. Spoofing
   B. Repudiation
   C. Information disclosure
   D. External pen testing

4. Which of the following best describes SAST?
   A. A set of technologies that analyze application source code, and bit code for coding and design problems that would indicate a security problem or vulnerability
   B. A set of technologies that analyze application bit code, and binaries for coding and design problems that would indicate a security problem or vulnerability
   C. A set of technologies that analyze application source code, byte code, and binaries for coding and design problems that would indicate a security problem or vulnerability
   D. A set of technologies that analyze application source code for coding and design problems that would indicate a security problem or vulnerability

5. Which of the following best describes data masking?
   A. A method where the last few numbers in a dataset are not obscured. These are often used for authentication.
   B. A method for creating similar but inauthentic datasets used for software testing and user training.
   C. A method used to protect prying eyes from data such as social security numbers and credit card data.
   D. Data masking involves stripping out all similar digits in a string of numbers so as to obscure the original number.

6. Which of the following best describes a sandbox?

A. An isolated space where transactions are protected from malicious software

B. A space where you can safely execute malicious code to see what it does

C. An isolated space where untested code and experimentation can safely occur separate from the production environment

D. An isolated space where untested code and experimentation can safely occur within the production environment

7. Identity and access management (IAM) is a security discipline that ensures which of the following?

A. That all users are properly authorized

B. That the right individual gets access to the right resources at the right time for the right reasons

C. That all users are properly authenticated

D. That unauthorized users will get access to the right resources at the right time for the right reasons

8. In a federated identity arrangement using a trusted third-party model, who is the identity provider and who is the relying party?

A. A contracted third party/the various member organizations of the federation

B. The users of the various organizations within the federation/a CASB

C. Each member organization/a trusted third party

D. Each member organization/each member organization

9. Which of the following best describes the Organizational Normative Framework (ONF)?

A. A container for components of an application's security, best practices, catalogued and leveraged by the organization

B. A framework of containers for all components of application security, best practices, catalogued and leveraged by the organization

C. A set of application security, and best practices, catalogued and leveraged by the organization

D. A framework of containers for some of the components of application security, best practices, catalogued and leveraged by the organization

10. APIs are defined as which of the following?

A. A set of protocols, and tools for building software applications to access a web-based software application or tool

B. A set of standards for building software applications to access a web-based software application or tool

C. A set of routines, standards, protocols, and tools for building software applications to access a web-based software application or tool

D. A set of routines and tools for building software applications to access web-based software applications

11. The application normative framework is best described as which of the following?

   A.   A stand-alone framework for storing security practices for the ONF

   B.   A subset of the ONF

   C.   A superset of the ONF

   D.   The complete ONF

12. Which of the following best describes SAML?

   A.   A standard for developing secure application management logistics

   B.   A standard for exchanging authentication and authorization data between security domains

   C.   A standard for exchanging usernames and passwords across devices

   D.   A standard used for directory synchronization

13. Which of the following best describes the purpose and scope of ISO/IEC 27034-1?

   A.   Describes international privacy standards for cloud computing

   B.   Provides an overview of application security that introduces definitive concepts, principles, and processes involved in application security

   C.   Serves as a newer replacement for NIST 800-53 r4

   D.   Provides an overview of network and infrastructure security designed to secure cloud applications

14. Which of the following best describes data masking?

   A.   Data masking is used in place of encryption for better performance.

   B.   Data masking is used to hide PII.

   C.   Data masking is used to create a similar, inauthentic dataset used for training and software testing.

   D.   Data masking is used in place of production data.

15. Database activity monitoring (DAM) can be:

   A.   Host-based or network-based

   B.   Server-based or client-based

   C.   Used in the place of encryption

   D.   Used in place of data masking

16. Web application firewalls (WAFs) are designed primarily to protect applications from common attacks like:

   A.   Syn floods

   B.   Ransomware

   C.   XSS and SQL injection

   D.   Password cracking

17. Multifactor authentication consists of at least two items. Which of the following best represents this concept?

   A. A complex password and a secret code

   B. Complex passwords and an HSM

   C. A hardware token and a magnetic strip card

   D. Something you know and something you have

18. SOAP is a protocol specification providing for the exchange of structured information or data in web services. Which of the following is *not* true of SOAP?

   A. Standards-based

   B. Reliant on XML

   C. Extremely fast

   D. Works over numerous protocols

19. Dynamic application security testing (DAST) is best described as which of the following?

   A. Test performed on an application or software product while it is using real data in production

   B. Test performed on an application or software product while it is being executed in memory in an operating system.

   C. Test performed on an application or software product while being consumed by cloud customers

   D. Masking

20. Sandboxing provides which of the following?

   A. A test environment that isolates untrusted code changes for testing in a production environment

   B. A test environment that isolates untrusted code changes for testing in a nonproduction environment

   C. A testing environment where new and experimental code can be tested in a production environment

   D. A testing environment that prevents isolated code from running in a nonproduction environment

Chapter

8

Operations Elements

THE OBJECTIVE OF THIS CHAPTER IS TO ACQUAINT THE READER WITH THE FOLLOWING CONCEPTS:

✓ **Domain 1: Architectural Concepts and Design Requirements**

- C. Understand Security Concepts Relevant to Cloud Computing
  - C.5 Virtualization Security
- E. Identify Trusted Cloud Services
  - E.1 Certification Against Criteria

✓ **Domain 2: Cloud Data Security**

- B. Design and Implement Cloud Data Storage Architectures
  - B1 Storage Types
- C. Design and Apply Data Security Strategies
  - C.6 Emerging Technologies

✓ **Domain 3: Cloud Platform and Infrastructure Security**

- A. Comprehend Cloud Infrastructure Components
  - A.1 Physical Environment
  - A.5 Storage

✓ **Domain 4: Cloud Application Security**

- A. Recognize the Need for Training and Awareness in Application Security
  - A.1 Cloud Development Basics
- B. Understand Cloud Software Assurance and Validation
  - B.1 Cloud-based Functional Testing
  - B.3 Security Testing

✓ Domain 5: Operations

- ▪ A. Support the Planning Process for the Data Center Design
  - ▪ A.1 Logical Design
  - ▪ A.3 Environmental Design
- ▪ C. Run Physical Infrastructure for Cloud Environment
  - ▪ C.1 Configuration of Access Control for Local Access
  - ▪ C.5 Availability of Clustered Hosts
- ▪ I. Conduct Risk Assessment to Logical and Physical Infra-structure

Although most IT and InfoSec practitioners will probably spend the majority of their time providing professional services to cloud customers, the CCSP CBK and exam also require the ability to understand the perspective of the cloud provider to some extent. In this chapter, we'll continue our review of the internal working of a cloud provider (and the provider's datacenter) in a bit more detail.

Physical/Logical Operations

The cloud datacenter has to be robust and resilient to all types of threats, from natural disasters to hacking attacks to simple component failure. This strength and capability has to be comprehensive and exhaustive enough to provide close to continuous system operation and data access (referred to as "uptime") for multiple customers with a wide spectrum of service needs.

Currently, the industry standard for uptime in cloud service provision is "five nines," which means 99.999% uptime (in some cases, uptime offered by providers exceeds this boundary, to 99.9999%). That's a vast difference in the level of service expected just as recently as a decade ago. At that time, managed services were often not based in the cloud and instead took the form of contractors leasing and maintaining IT devices and networking capability to customers, often inside the customers' own facilities. Back then, expected outages for regular maintenance, upgrades, and routine component loss likely incurred scheduled downtime of up to three days each month. Five nines, over a calendar year, on the other hand, equates to less than six minutes *per year*.

In this section, we'll review standards and methods created for the purpose of achieving an uptime of five nines.

Uptime and Availability

The CSSP CBK expressly differentiates between uptime and availability. In the most literal of senses, this is true. A datacenter could be providing continuous uptime, but the cloud customer may encounter availability problems. For instance, the customer's ability to connect to the datacenter may be limited by a failure within the customer's ISP. This would be a lack of availability from the customer's perspective but not a lack of uptime on the part of the provider. The datacenter is up, but the customer can't reach it.

This may seem like splitting hairs because, realistically, most professionals (or, for that matter, courts or regulators) already would not expect an entity to be responsible for agencies and externalities outside its control. Nobody would consider the cloud provider to be liable for the failure of the customer's ISP in the first place. Certainly, the cloud provider could not be held liable for not meeting the terms of the SLA in such a circumstance.

That aside, for practical purposes, the terms *uptime* and *availability* are usually meant to communicate the same notion: the cloud provider's ability to offer service within the parameters specified in the SLA, without undue interruption, with the implicit understanding that the provider is not responsible for the customer's inability to access the datacenter for reasons outside the provider's purview.

However, for academic and testing purposes, in the strictest sense, they are not synonymous.

Facilities and Redundancy

A vast majority of the effort to ensure continuous uptime will be spent providing redundancy of physical components and infrastructure. With sufficient replication of hardware and media, elements can be lost without impact to operations.

When designing a datacenter, consider redundancy not only for the IT systems and infrastructure, but for all aspects of functionality that support the operation of the datacenter. These include utilities (electrical power receipt/distribution, water, communications connectivity), staff, emergency capabilities (mostly power generation and fuel for same, as well as egress paths for personnel), HVAC, and security controls.

Power Redundancy

IT systems cannot operate without electricity. The datacenter will require a power source of sufficient level to operate all the core processing and storage systems for all customers, as well as those support systems necessary to run the datacenter (such as HVAC and lighting). The cloud provider will want to consider two major aspects of redundancy for primary power needs: energy utility providers and the actual physical connections from the providers to the datacenter's campus.

Power Provider Redundancy

Finding multiple power utilities for a single physical plant might prove challenging. Most municipalities are not served by more than one power provider, by legal construct. Power companies are usually granted some form of local monopoly, based on the premise that competing providers would harm the community's ability to receive power on a cost-effective basis. This is because of the costs of creating and maintaining multiple sets of infrastructure to generate and deliver power. Theoretically, every power provider would have to have its own generation plant, electrical grid, and all that entails, to include lines running to each building for all its customers. This could lead to an overabundance of cables and wires in the service area and decrease the opportunity to create economies of scale by limiting infrastructure to one set. Regardless of whether this theory is true (and it is questionable; telephone service provision was once limited, based on the same reasoning, and that market not only survived the breakup of the telephone service monopoly, but flourished and expanded, while consumer costs dropped considerably, without an overabundance of telephone infrastructure affecting neighborhoods), most metropolitan areas will not have more than one power provider.

Moreover, the geographic locations often deemed most desirable for datacenters are even less likely to have multiple power providers for other reasons. Because datacenters are costly to erect, require a large footprint, and need very little in terms of external services (other than power and communications connectivity), remote rural areas are often seen to be optimal for building datacenters: land is cheap, zoning limitations are greatly reduced or nonexistent, and there is less chance of impact from certain types of external threats (civil unrest, fire from neighboring buildings, basic crimes/vandalism, and so on). However, rural areas are also often served by only one power provider, not because of statutory fiat, but because it is not profitable for more than one vendor to offer services in areas with low population density. This could, in turn, make it difficult for cloud providers to find multiple power utilities to serve their datacenter.

Power Line Redundancy

There is a form of attack that almost everyone who has worked in the IT field for any length of time has suffered: having your entire IT enterprise being DOSed by a backhoe. For some reason, backhoes (and bulldozers, and steam shovels) seem to magically be able to locate and slice power and communication lines that lead to buildings, even if the lines are buried sufficiently underground or raised far enough into the air, and even if these locations are clearly marked by utility inspectors before construction activity begins. It's like a natural law: if you, as a security professional, see construction equipment in the parking lot of your campus, prepare to lose power and communications.

 Also, squirrels. Squirrels. The authors have known of more than one organization that has been DOSed by squirrels dining on the power and communication lines. In one case, it happened the same organization more than once. This is not a joke. But it is kind of funny.

So it behooves the cloud provider to ensure that all power and communication lines that connect to each of the buildings on the campus are not only replicated, but that the connections are replicated *on opposite sides of each building*. We want to avoid the backhoe taking out both lines simultaneously, and the likelihood of construction scheduled on both sides of a facility at the same time is somewhat less than on just one side at a time.

Power Conditioning and Distribution Redundancy

Another aspect of power provisioning for the datacenter is the ancillary necessary infrastructure, including power conditioning apparatus and distribution mechanisms.

Raw power from most power mains is not suitable for commercial IT systems. The electricity must be adjusted so as to optimize its suitability for system performance. We call this *conditioning*. Conditioning usually involves adjusting the voltage on the line. It also includes surge protectors, which attenuate the effects of power spikes that might occur as the result of natural forces (such as storms) or uncontrolled activity elsewhere in the grid.

When designing a datacenter, it is a good practice to also plan for redundancy in these power conditioners as well as the other aspects of the electrical system. Likewise, other aspects of the power system within the datacenter that should be similarly replicated include any distribution node, such as transformers or substations, as well as the conduit that actually carries power to each facility.

When discussing electrical power and resilient design, it's important to also address backup power systems, such as batteries and generators. We will cover that aspect in Chapter 9, "Operations Management," in the "Business Continuity and Disaster Recovery (BC/DR)" section.

Communications Redundancy

Many of the same challenges associated with finding multiple power providers will affect plans for redundant communication providers. In geographically isolated areas, finding even one broadband ISP might be difficult, let alone two or more. However, cloud datacenters bring enough demand and need for service that ISPs may build out their current infrastructure specifically to serve those datacenters.

Personnel Redundancy

When considering redundancy and resiliency design for datacenters, remember the personnel who administer and support the IT components. Some of the techniques we can adopt to provide this increased level of robustness among personnel resources are as follows:

Cross-Training   Whenever possible, have personnel trained not only in their primary duties, but in another employee's duties as well (and vice versa). That way, they can serve as relief or backups for each other for crisis purposes or for ease of scheduling (this is particularly useful in datacenters, where constant uptime often means shiftwork, which entails scheduling challenges). This technique, however, is very expensive. Having all personnel trained in multiple disciplines requires not only a significant training budget, but high salaries reflecting investment in top-flight personnel. Only high-quality employees will have the discipline and ability to fulfill a range of functional tasks in areas other than their main duties. If this methodology is utilized to create personnel redundancy, it's important to ensure that all staffers are engaged in tasks that exercise each of their skillsets on a recurring basis so that they maintain currency in each area and the training does not atrophy.

Water   As was mentioned in the preceding section regarding power service, utility redundancy is an important consideration for cloud datacenters. Another utility that may be overlooked in contingency planning is water and water providers. Water supports both personnel and systems for drinking, cooling, and fire suppression. Like electricity, finding multiple water providers in a given area might be difficult. Unlike electricity, however, water is not as difficult or dangerous to generate, transport, and store. In addition to subscribing to the local water district, datacenter owners can acquire potable water from wells on their own property, or they can contract with hauling companies who can bring water tanks in by rail or truck. Water can be stored on site for a fairly long time, in cisterns or cooling towers (and a well serves the dual purpose of provision and storage). When designing redundancy for water supply, it is also important to remember to include multiple pumping facilities to ensure sufficient pressure, and the power to run those pumps.

Egress   Recall the paramount concern for all security efforts: health and human safety. The datacenter buildings—all of them—should have multiple points of escape in case of emergency. This does not have to make your physical defenses porous; emergency exits can be one-way portals (such as doors with interior-facing push-bars, and no means to open them from the outside), and ingress can still be severely limited and tightly controlled. Remember to design deluge fire suppression systems over paths of egress.

Lighting   In terms of continuous uptime, lights may not seem like an essential element of operations. However, consider a datacenter without interior lighting or a lighting system without power. Because most datacenters don't have windows (windows are both a safety and a security risk and are largely unnecessary in datacenters), a lighting system failure would result in a facility that was both uncomfortable and hazardous for people to occupy, much less get work done. Emergency lights, particularly along egress routes, are important (and often required by building codes), as is ensuring that the lighting is connected to any backup power supply.

Security Redundancy

In designing security for the physical plant and site layout, it is essential to bear in mind one of the most fundamental concepts in our field: defense in depth. As has been mentioned previously throughout this book, defense in depth (or "layered defense") entails multiple differing security controls protecting the same assets, often with a variety of technological levels, and an assortment of the three categories of controls (physical, administrative, and logical/technical).

For a cloud datacenter to meet sufficient due diligence requirements (and attenuate the likelihood of potential threats and risks) pertaining to physical security, all the basic protective measures must be included, and the redundancy should come in the form of layering, as opposed to repetition. For instance, layered physical defense does not mean having two or three concentric fence lines at the perimeter; it instead might mean including a guard patrol who monitors the fence line, a video surveillance capability, and electronic monitoring of tampering attempts on the fence. This offers redundancy of protection (in the sense of the single control that is "perimeter security"; other physical security measures are also necessary, of course) as well as resiliency. This particularly challenges human attackers, who will need a variety of tools and techniques to breach the defenses, as opposed to just one (in the listed example, a wire cutter). Our goal is to make breaching complicated.

In addition to the perimeter, some other physical security aspects that ought to be included in design include the following:

- Vehicular approach/access, to include driveways that wind and curve and/or include speed bumps as well as bollards

- Guest/visitor access through a controlled entry point, involving formal reception (perhaps a sign-in log, video surveillance, and specific staff tasked with that duty)

- Proper placement of hazardous or vital resources (such as electrical supply, storage, and distribution components, particularly generators and fuel) such that it is not directly located near personnel or in the path of vehicles

- Interior physical access controls, such as badging, keys, combinations, turnstiles, and so on

- Specific physical protections for highly sensitive assets, such as safes and inventory tracking mechanisms (perhaps RFIDs)

- Fire detection and suppression systems

- Sufficient power for all these functions, in the event of a primary power disruption

⊕ Real World Scenario

Rate the Design

Let's review the notional design of a facility, in context of the practices listed in the "Security Redundancy" section. Review this diagram of a cloud datacenter campus and determine if it has sufficient resiliency, redundancy, and security. Consider what you think are both good and bad points.

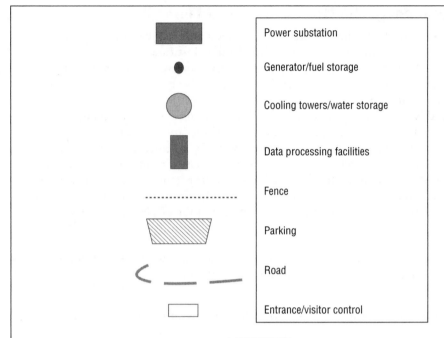

	Power substation
	Generator/fuel storage
	Cooling towers/water storage
	Data processing facilities
	Fence
	Parking
	Road
	Entrance/visitor control

LEGEND

What do you think of this facility? Does it feature the proper aspects described earlier?

Here are some of the positive attributes you may have noticed:

- The roadway approach curves disallow a straight path at the facility.

- There is a centralized entrance for staff and visitors, controlling ingress.

- There seems to be adequate replication of all necessary facilities, including power, water, and data processing.

And here are some questionable aspects:

- One set of generators and fuel storage (the lower set) seems to be too close to some of the other buildings, posing a fire and health hazard.

- We can't explicitly tell from the diagram, but it seems as if there is only one layer of perimeter security—the fence. If possible, it should be augmented with additional, varied layers of security, such as surveillance cameras and security patrols.

- It would be preferable to have the power facilities on opposite sides of the campus.

Holistic Redundancy: The Uptime Institute Tiers

Currently, (ISC)^2 looks to the Uptime Institute (UI) for standards related to datacenter redundancy in pursuit of continuous operations. The Uptime Institute (https://uptimeinstitute.com) is an advisory organization for matters related to IT service. UI publishes a standard for datacenter design, and it also certifies datacenters for compliance with this standard.

The UI standard is split into four tiers, in ascending durability of the datacenter. The standard itself is available for download from the UI's website, free of charge. The tier descriptions themselves are also included, verbatim, in the CCSP CBK (Domain 5). We won't reproduce the whole text in this work, but we highly recommend you review it, in detail, from either of those sources. Instead, we'll discuss the pertinent specifics in this section. (All emphasis in the descriptions of the tiers is added by the authors for the purpose of demonstrating the differences between them, and not part of the original document.)

Tier 1

Tier 1 is a simplistic datacenter, with little or no redundancy and is labeled Basic Site Infrastructure. It lists the minimum requirements for a datacenter, which must include the following:

- Dedicated space for IT systems

- An uninterruptible power supply (UPS) system for line conditioning and backup purposes

- Sufficient cooling systems to serve all critical equipment

- A power generator for extended electrical outages, with at least 12 hours of fuel to run the generator at sufficient load to power the IT systems

 Twelve hours is the standard fuel requirement for all four tiers.

Tier 1 datacenters also have these features:

- Scheduled maintenance will require systems (including critical systems) to be taken offline.

- Both planned and unplanned maintenance and response activity may take systems (including critical systems) offline.

- Untoward personnel activity (both inadvertent and malicious) will result in downtime.

- Annual maintenance is necessary to safely operate the datacenter and requires full shutdown (including critical systems). Without this maintenance, the datacenter is likely to suffer increased outages and disruptions.

If the datacenter described in Tier 1 is so sensitive to such a wide array of risks, why is it even considered suitable for operation? Who would want to be a customer of such a service? Well, obviously, the cost of running a facility of this type is going to be much less expensive, and that cost savings is most likely reflected in the price the customer will be asked to pay. Also, this type of facility may be appealing to an organization that is only using the cloud service as a backup for its own enterprise and data (perhaps even the organization's own private cloud), and it only needs to be available occasionally and very temporarily. From this perspective, a Tier 1 datacenter might be suitable as a hot/warm site for the organization, with data uploaded on an infrequent basis (perhaps weekly or monthly), or it might even serve as a cold site, where data is only uploaded at those times when the organization is experiencing an emergency situation and needs to enact contingency operations.

So a Tier 1 datacenter might be the least expensive (if also the least functional) option for an organization that does not require constant uptime and access to resources and data.

Tier 2

A Tier 2 datacenter is slightly more robust than Tier 1, and it is named for its defining characteristics: Redundant Site Infrastructure Capacity Components. It features all the attributes of the Tier 1 design, with these additional elements:

- Critical operations do not have to be interrupted for scheduled replacement and maintenance of any of the redundant components; however, there may be downtime for any disconnection of power distribution systems and lines.

- Contrary to Tier 1, where untoward personnel activity *will* cause downtime, in Tier 2 it *may* cause downtime.

- Unplanned failures of components or systems might result in downtime.

With the benefit of rudimentary redundancy, the Tier 2 datacenter is obviously more suited to cloud operations and is more appealing for that purpose. It may still be more affordable than the higher-tier offerings, but it is now viable as a dependable alternative for continuous use. This may be a good option for small organizations looking to operate in the public cloud environment while still maintaining a relatively low overhead.

Tier 3

The Tier 3 design is known as a Concurrently Maintainable Site Infrastructure. As the name indicates, the facility features both the redundant capacity components of a Tier 2 build and the added benefit of multiple distribution paths (where only a sole path is needed to serve critical operations at any given time). Other characteristics that differentiate Tier 3 from the prior levels include the following:

- There are dual power supplies for all IT systems.

- Critical operations can continue even if any single component or power element is out of service for scheduled maintenance or replacement.

- Unplanned loss of a *component may* cause downtime; the loss of a single *system*, on the other hand, *will* cause downtime. (The implied distinction is that a component is one node in a multinode system; while each system will have redundant components, not all systems are redundant.)

- Planned maintenance (to include scheduled holistic annual maintenance of the facility) will not necessarily result in downtime; however, the risk of downtime may be increased during this activity. This temporary elevated risk does not make the datacenter lose its Tier 3 rating for the duration.

Obviously, a cloud provider offering a Tier 3 datacenter is a viable candidate for organizations looking to migrate to the public cloud. Most organizations with regular operational needs might consider a Tier 3 option. Those organizations with specialized needs (perhaps organizations with highly sensitive material, such as governmental agencies or entities that utilize a great deal of intellectual property, or large-scale organizations with absolute constant uptime requirements) might instead consider a Tier 4 option, but the Tier 3 should serve the purpose for all others.

Tier 4

The Fault-Tolerant Site Infrastructure is the premium datacenter offering. As the Uptime Institute repeats in the description of this tier, *each and every* element and system of the facility (whether for IT processing, the physical plant, power distribution, or anything else) has integral redundancy such that critical operations can survive both planned and unplanned downtime at the loss of any component or system. Does this mean a Tier 4 datacenter is indestructible, with permanent uptime? Of course not. Anyone marketing such an offering should be viewed with suspicion. However, it is the most robust, resilient option available.

In addition to all Tier 3 features, the Tier 4 datacenter will include these characteristics:

- There is redundancy of both IT and electrical components, where the various multiple components are independent and physically separate from each other.
- Even after the loss of any facility infrastructure element, there will be sufficient power and cooling for critical operations.
- The loss of any single system, component, or distribution element *will not* affect critical operations.
- The facility will feature automatic response capabilities for infrastructure control systems such that the critical operations will not be affected by infrastructure failures.
- Any single loss, event, or personnel activity will not cause downtime of critical operations.
- Scheduled maintenance can be performed without affecting critical operations. However, while one set of assets is in the maintenance state, the datacenter may be at increased risk of failure due to an event affecting the alternate assets. During this temporary maintenance state, the facility does not lose its Tier 4 rating.

Obviously, a Tier 4 datacenter should be fit to serve any organization considering cloud migration, regardless of the sensitivity of their information assets or uptime needs. It will likewise be the most expensive selection and will probably be therefore limited to those organizations that have the wherewithal to afford it.

🌐 Real World Scenario

Trusting Redundancy

One particular cloud customer has created a paradigm of utmost trust in the redundancy and resiliency of their network: Netflix.

In 2011, Netflix revealed, via its tech blog (`http://techblog.netflix.com`), the Simian Army: a set of testing and monitoring applications the company uses to constantly assess its capability to continue service during contingency situations. The use of these tools demonstrates the willingness and foresight of Netflix to actually create hazards in order to refine and improve their service.

The Simian Army is not just a suite of automated alert and response software, although it does include the Doctor Monkey, which performs both functions after searching all of Netflix's resources to find any degradation in performance. The Simian Army includes several programs that confounded computer security professionals because of the bravery required to wield them: the Chaos Monkey and the Chaos Gorilla, specifically. These two programs are not responsive: they are aggressive. They purposefully and randomly shut down elements of the Netflix resource network. Netflix largely runs on the Amazon Web Services public cloud. The Chaos Monkey disables specific production instances, and the Chaos Gorilla shuts down entire Amazon availability zones. The intention is to ensure that all the load-balancing capabilities built into the entire network can weather the failure and continue providing service in a manner that is transparent to customers.

That is beyond bold. It's a move some security professionals might call foolhardy, and management at many organizations would deem crazy. Basically, the company is DOSing itself. But it's also brilliant, gutsy, and ultimately necessary: it is quite likely the only way to be absolutely certain that all the planning and design of redundant systems and the automated response controls that manage them are fully functional in real time.

We don't recommend this approach for every organization, but those organizations that want total assurance that their cloud resources are wholly fault-tolerant might want to consider it. And Netflix has made that capability available to the world: not only did they announce the existence of the Simian Army on a public website, but in 2014, the company made the Chaos Monkey open source and free for download: `https://github.com/Netflix/security_monkey`.

It's one level of brave to create a methodology as far outside the box as to attack your own resources. It's another to announce to the world that you're using this methodology. What if it goes awry? Wouldn't the failure be compounded by the shame of being caught in your evident hubris?

But it's a champion level of courageousness to publish the toolset of that methodology and let the world play with it, knowing that there will be a subset of users who might try to...well...*monkey* with it, in order to eventually attack you. It's a heroic gamble, that the benefits of a million Chaos Monkeys banging away at systems will be tweaked and refined by the open source community, and that the goodwill (and improved software) will come back to Netflix like interest on a loan.

This is a very laudable, admirable, and forward-thinking attitude. And we recommend the Netflix Tech Blog for even more, similar content. The blog is written in an approachable, relaxed manner, with a nice blend of technical and managerial information. For readers of this book, especially, the Netflix blog will hold a great deal of interest for their discussion of the company's decision to move into the public cloud, what their approach was, and the pitfalls they faced.

Virtualization Operations

From a cloud provider perspective, virtualization is an absolute necessity. It's the only way to properly manage the cost of hosting multiple customers in a scalable manner and still provide them with near-constant uptime.

Virtualization poses specific risks, many of which have been described in previous chapters. In the next few subsections, we'll discuss what a cloud provider should be considering when planning virtualization operations.

Personnel Isolation

Because administrators working for the cloud provider will have physical access to devices that may run instances belonging to several customers in the same field (that is, the cloud customers on the same host may be competitors), the cloud provider has to ensure that any impropriety, conflict of interest, or even perception of conflict of interest doesn't affect the level of service the customers receive. For example, if competing customers are resident on a single host and some contingency forces the administrators to halt one instance or the other in order to maintain the functionality of the device, the administrator should not favor one over the other; preferably, the administrator should make the choice solely on the basis of overall datacenter performance and operation.

In theory, it is best to mask the nature and details of a customer's business from the administrators. In practice, that might be less than ideal, and it may be impossible to achieve if such knowledge enhances the administrators' ability to meet customers' needs. The Brewer-Nash model, also known as the Chinese Wall model, seeks to ensure that goal. The concept, first posited in a 1989 IEEE paper on the subject, distinguishes access and permissions of administrators based on policy. (You can read the paper at https:// www.cs.purdue.edu/homes/ninghui/readings/AccessControl/brewer_nash_89.pdf.) A cloud provider pursuing this end might want to enact such a policy and test it for functionality.

Hypervisor Hardening

Because the hypervisor is a prime target for attackers (controlling the hypervisor might allow access to the data in every instance), the hypervisor should receive all the security attention that would have been shown for a bastion host in the DMZ of a legacy network. The hypervisor should be updated and patched to vendor standards, there should be no default accounts on it, and it should be monitored by automatic sensors as well as logs and log review analysis. If the cloud provider has to choose between types of hypervisors, the bare-metal (Type 1) hypervisor is preferable to the hypervisor that runs off the OS (Type 2), because it will offer less attack surface.

Instance Isolation

Each virtual machine (that is, each instance or guest) should be logically isolated from the others with strict logical controls. (They can't be physically isolated, by nature of virtualization and automatic load balancing.) Not only should raw data be prevented from leaking from one instance to another, but all metadata as well. No instance should be able to tell if another instance is even present on the same host, much less what that instance is doing or how long it takes to do it.

Whatever controls are put in place to ensure this isolation should be tested and monitored, both in the sandbox testbed and in the live environment, on a continual basis.

Furthermore, the possibility of guest escape (a user escalating a privilege such that the user can leave the virtual instance and access the host machine itself) should be attenuated as much as possible.

Host Isolation

As with guest escape, the cloud provider should be intrinsically concerned about the possibility of a user on a virtual instance elevating themselves to the point where they can leave the virtual machine, access the host, and reach the network the host is connected to, eventually reaching other host devices or assets on the network.

All hosts must be both physically and logically isolated from one another as much as possible. They will obviously still be connected to the network and so will, in some fashion, all "touch" each other, so those connections should be minimized and secured as much as possible. Moreover, network monitoring should be thorough and detailed, such that any host escape activity would be immediately recognized and response would result.

Storage Operations

In addition to hosts used to run virtualized instances for customer operations, the cloud datacenter will also include devices used for near-term and long-term storage of both data and instance images.

Clustered Storage and Coupling

Most often, storage devices will be clustered in groups, providing increased performance, flexibility, and reliability. Clustered storage architectures can take one of two types: tightly coupled or loosely coupled.

In the tightly coupled architecture, all the storage devices are directly connected to a shared physical backplane, thus connecting all of them directly (the "tightly" aspect). Each component of the cluster is aware of the others and subscribes to the same policies and rule sets. A tightly coupled cluster is usually confined to more restrictive design parameters, often because the devices might need to be from the same vendor in order to function properly. Although this may be a limiting factor, a tightly coupled architecture will also enhance performance as it scales: the performance of each element is added to the overall performance of the cluster, allowing greater and greater power as it increases in size.

A loosely coupled cluster, on the other hand, will allow for greater flexibility. Each node of the cluster is independent of the others, and new nodes can be added for any purpose or use as needed. They are only logically connected and don't share the same proximate physical framework, so they are only distantly physically connected through communication media (the "loosely" aspect). Performance does not necessarily scale, however, because the nodes don't build on one another. But this might not be an important facet of the storage architecture, since storage commands and performance requirements are fairly simple.

Volume vs. Object

Another way of viewing storage options is how the data is stored. Typically, two modes could be used: volume storage and object storage. In volume storage, disk space is apportioned to the customer and is allocated to each of the guest instances the customer uses. The virtualized OS of the guest then imposes a filesystem on the volume as necessary. This is sometimes referred to as "block storage." In object storage, all data is stored in a filesystem, and customers are given access to the parts of the hierarchy to which they're assigned.

Resiliency

There are also two general ways for creating data protection in a cloud storage cluster: RAID (redundant array of independent disks, although originally termed as redundant array of inexpensive disks) and data dispersion. These two ways of creating data protection are very similar and provide a level of resiliency—that is, a reasonable amount of assurance that the physical and/or logical environment might be partially affected by detrimental occurrences (outages, attacks, and so on), but the overall bulk of data will not be lost permanently.

In most RAID configurations, all data is stored across the various disks in a method known as *striping*. This allows data to be recovered in a more efficient manner because if one of the drives fails, the missing data can be filled in by the other drives. In some RAID schemes (there are many, known as RAID 0–10, with different levels of performance, redundancy, and integrity, depending on the owner's needs), parity bits are added to the raw data to aid in recovery after a drive failure.

Data dispersion is a similar technique, where data is sliced into "chunks" that are encrypted along with parity bits and then written to various drives in the cloud cluster. Data dispersion can be seen as equivalent to creating a RAID array in a cloud environment. This technique is also often referred to as *bit splitting*.

SAN vs. NAS

Yet another decision to be made in storage architecture is whether to use network attached storage (NAS) or a storage area network (SAN).

A NAS is a network file server with a drive or group of drives, portions of which are assigned to users on that network. The user will see a NAS as a file server and can share files to it. NAS commonly uses TCP/IP.

A SAN is a group of devices connected to the network that provide storage space to users. Typically, the storage apportioned to the user is mounted to that user's machine, like an empty drive. The user can then format and implement a filesystem in that space according to their own preference. SANs usually use iSCSI or Fibre Channel protocols.

Both the NAS and the SAN should be fairly transparent to the user. The storage space should be available and apparent to the user regardless of the actual location of the user's device or the storage components.

Physical and Logical Isolation

In this chapter, we've already discussed the need for both physical and logical isolation of personnel, the various virtualized instances, and storage devices in a cluster. The same principles should be applied throughout the cloud datacenter to include other isolation techniques and technologies. These include restricted physical access to devices, secure interface devices, and restricted logical access to devices.

Restricted Physical Access to Devices

Access to racks in the datacenter should be limited to those administrators and maintainers who absolutely need to reach the devices in order to perform their job functions. Entry and egress should be controlled, monitored, and logged. Racks should be locked, and keys for each respective rack should have to be checked out only for the duration of use. Likewise, KVMs should have to be checked out by the administrator needing to use them for a specific task and checked in at their return.

Secure KVMs

The human interface devices such as keyboards, video displays, and mice (KVMs) used to access production devices—both processing and storage—should be hardened for security purposes. Secure KVMs differ from their mundane counterparts in that they are designed to deter and detect tampering. They are also, as might be expected, usually quite a bit more expensive.

Secure KVMs should have the following traits:

Secure Data Ports   These reduce the likelihood of data leaking between computers that are connected through the KVM.

Tamper Labels   These provide clear indication if the unit housing has been breached. They might also be supported by warning lights that alert you when the unit is opened.

Fixed Firmware   This cannot be flashed or reprogrammed.

Soldered Circuit Board   Soldering is used instead of adhesive so that the board itself or its components cannot be removed and replaced.

Reduced Buffer   Data is not stored beyond the immediate needs of the device.

Air-Gapped Pushbuttons   When switching between multiple devices connected to the unit, the current connection is physically broken before a new one is made.

Restricted Logical Access to Devices

Where possible, devices should be located on secure subnets, limiting the ability of malicious intruders. (This may be difficult in a cloud environment, where resources are apportioned automatically and across the entirety of the cloud space.) Use of USB ports should be severely controlled and eliminated wherever possible. (Physically, permanently disabling unused ports is not a bad option.) Restrict the potential for any portable media to be carried into or out of the datacenter undetected.

Security Training and Awareness

It's a cliché, but everyone in the environment is involved in security. It is therefore important that everyone have at least a modicum of security training and awareness. Even if their area of specialty does not involve implementing security controls or practices, all personnel must at least know how to perform their job functions in a secure manner.

In a cloud datacenter facility, this effort will be at least somewhat easier than other environments, insofar as almost everyone already employed in this field will have a modicum of technical skill and training, which heavily implies that they have already been exposed to a great deal of information about secure IT practices. This does *not,* however, obviate the requirement for formal internal training in accordance with local policy and associated regulation. It is also absolutely essential to present and document formal training and relevant awareness programs in order to demonstrate due diligence.

There is no industry standard definition for the terms *training*, *education*, and *awareness*. There is as much disagreement on the specifics of these concepts as with any other amorphous topic in the IT and security professions. For our purposes, we'll use these explanations:

Training   The formal presentation of material, often delivered by internal subject matter experts. It addresses and explains matters of the organization's policies, content mandated by regulation, and industry best practices for the organization's field.

Education   The formal presentation of material in an academic setting, often for credit toward a degree.

Awareness   The additional, informal, often voluntary presentation of material for the purpose of reminding and raising attention among staff.

Another cliché of our industry: Awareness programs use posters to convey security messages in a passive, unobtrusive way. As far as these authors know, there has not been any conclusive research to determine the efficacy of posters as a medium for conveying security-related information. Bearing that in mind, if you see "posters" on the exam, the question is about awareness.

With this perspective in mind, we're going to discuss security training, education, and awareness in depth.

Training Program Categories

This section on training will be a lot more comprehensive than what is included in the CCSP CBK and what you will likely see on the exam. It is included here, however, because you may find it valuable from an operational and professional standpoint. If you are solely interested in the material that cleaves to the CBK (and probably the exam), feel free to limit your review to the first few paragraphs of each subsection.

Security training programs are often split into three delivery categories: initial, recurring, and refresher training. Let's examine each in turn.

Initial Training

Initial training is delivered to personnel when they first enter the employ of the organization. Often thorough and comprehensive, this should be mandatory for all personnel, regardless of their position or role. The content should be broad enough to address the security policies and procedures all staff will be expected to understand and comply with, but it should have sufficient specificity so that everyone knows how to perform basic security functions.

Topics that might be covered could include the following:

- Password policy, including how passwords are issued, what form passwords will take, duration until expiration, how to request password reset, and stressing the need for keeping passwords secret.

- Physical security, including access to the facility, what to do if staff encounters people inside the facility they don't recognize, and emergency egress.

- The use of any security credentials or tokens.

- How to report security concerns, such as anomalous behavior, lost credentials, and so forth. This should include means to contact the security office.

- The acceptable use policy (AUP), in detail, including enforcement mechanisms. Of course, all personnel must sign the AUP before having access to organizational facilities and assets.

The initial training session will often be the first opportunity for all employees to meet representatives from the security office. This is a very good reason for security team members to present the material, instead of trainers from other departments (such as HR). You can accomplish many crucial things during initial training, things that will heighten the organization's security and reduce risk.

For instance, you can change any preconceived notions employees might have of the security office and personnel. Historically, the security office has been operated and utilized in an adversarial manner to operational staff. This all too often causes a lack of coordination and cooperation between the security office and the rest of the organization. As mentioned elsewhere throughout this book, such conflict creates a distrust and sometimes even fear among users and managers, when considering the security office as a participant in operations. That kind of poisoned relationship can adversely impact the organization as a whole, in two major ways:

▪ If employees make a mistake with security implications (say, losing a valuable organizational asset or inadvertently installing malware on the organization's environment), they are far less likely to report the matter promptly and fully and are more likely to try to hide it. The sooner security teams can respond to perceived problems, the greater the chance for ameliorating the negative effects, so we want to have users think of the security office as approachable and understanding, not Draconian.

▪ The security office is already at odds with the operational environment, by nature of the inherent trade-off in the two fields. The security office will constantly be telling operations managers and personnel why something can't be done (for instance, at the Change Management Board, as department and project heads request new functionality and systems and the security representative explains additional costs of controls and increased responsibility for risk). If efforts are not made to alleviate the stress of dealing with the security office, line-of-business managers and users might attempt workarounds in order to create additional functionality for performing their tasks more efficiently, instead of following proper, formal channels and requesting permission. These rogue elements can add unplanned (and even unknown) vulnerabilities to the environment, and they greatly increase the overall risk.

For these reasons, it greatly behooves the security team to create a positive first impression with the initial training session. It helps to be approachable and deliver the training in such a way as to stress that the security office exists to aid and support all users and operations, not to prevent them from doing their jobs or punish them. This takes finesse, as a significant part of the material will be explaining negative outcomes of failure to properly perform security-related tasks.

Some ways to deliver the content in a manner that may be more acceptable and appreciated by attendees include the following:

Explain the reasons for security measures.   Everyone likes being treated as a professional and understanding the rationale behind the rules. Security can even be an interesting topic, and attendees will feel informed if they are taught some of the causes and methods of breaches and attacks.

Demonstrate extreme openness to questions and concerns.   Involve participants in conversation, instead of reading a prepared list of rules to them. Let them solicit your expertise to resolve any lack of understanding they might have or to learn more about specific subjects.

This accomplishes several beneficial things: it makes the security office seem less frightening and negative; it enhances their understanding of security procedures, which can in turn lead to greater likelihood they will comply; and it may address something you had forgotten to include in the presentation or something you might want to add to future training sessions.

 If you are going to use Microsoft PowerPoint to deliver a training session, *do not read the content on the slides to the audience.* Your audience members can read. They are professionals. The subject matter on the slide is a guide to following the content you are delivering in your presentation. It is not a verbatim text of your speech. PowerPoint is not a teleprompter—or it shouldn't be, anyway.

Use as many real-world examples and anecdotes as possible.   People are fascinated by crime and wrongdoing. Use this to your advantage, and share stories of the types of malicious activities that are the cause for the policies you're discussing.

Hand out premiums.   Give out pens, notepads, drinking mugs, water bottles, or any other kind of trinkets you can think of, with the contact information for the security office clearly emblazoned on them all.

Serve food.   If you want personnel to think fondly of the security office, feed them. This does wonders for staff morale, team building, and your image.

Recurring Training

Recurring training is for continual updating of security knowledge that builds on the fundamentals taught in the initial training session. This should be done on a regular basis, on a schedule according to the needs of the organization, regulatory environment, and industry fluctuations. At the very least, each employee should receive recurring training annually.

Material comprising recurring sessions should include any updates and modifications to security practices and procedures within the organization, changes to regulations and policies, and the introduction of any new elements in the infrastructure.

Recurring training can also be blended with awareness efforts and used to compound the beneficial relationship fostered in the initial training session (mentioned in the previous section). All too often, security failings are used as the nominal reason for punitive measures in the workplace—transfers, demotions, firings, and so on. Instead, it is extremely helpful to laud any user efforts to report potential security concerns. Highlight and congratulate the employees, specifically and by name, who have contacted the security office to report security issues throughout the period since the last refresher training. This can take the rudimentary form of organization-wide emails or being a feature on the organization's website or internal announcements page. If your organization wants to demonstrate support for defense in depth that includes all personnel, it is even better to offer these congratulations at a live session, in front of all attendees, with a senior manager or executive presenting a letter of commendation or some other form of thanks on behalf of the organization.

If recurring training sessions are to include in-person attendance, it is preferable to encourage voluntary attendance instead of imposing a mandate. People are more willing to come with an open mind if they weren't ordered to be there. Here are some of the things you might consider in order to escalate the likelihood of a good turnout:

Serve food.   This was already mentioned in the section on initial training but bears repeating. Nothing brings bodies like free food.

Make it entertaining.   Because security is such a serious subject, we often present it in a somber, sacred tone. This shuts down listeners and is just plain boring. Introduce an aspect of enjoyment to the proceedings, and personnel will be both more likely to attend and to truly listen to what you have to tell them.

Create a competition.   Pit department against department in some kind of friendly rivalry. Attendance can be one measure of scoring; another might be a trivia competition between representatives of each department, with some sort of tangible reward for the winning department. Make the reward something actually appealing to the participants: an extra day of paid vacation, cash bonuses, or—need we repeat it?—food.

Another way to increase participation and interest in recurring training is to offer courses that staff are actually enthused about attending. This might be vendor training offered at appealing offsite locations or accredited courses that can be used by employees seeking continuing education credits. Do *not* just hire some outside consultant to come deliver a mandatory lecture to all staff of material they probably already know. That is *boring*, and attendees will only be thinking two things: how they could better spend the time performing their own tasks in a productive manner instead of sitting through the session and how much the consultant is getting paid instead of the organization offering bonuses to employees.

Document, document, document *all* recurring training sessions, including annotating content and the names of all recipients. This is incredibly important for demonstrating due diligence efforts if the matter should ever come up.

Refresher Training

Refresher training sessions are offered to those personnel who have demonstrated a need for additional lessons. This might include those personnel who have had an extended absence from the workplace (for instance, a month or more) or who have missed a recurring training session.

This might also be offered to those personnel who have failed some element of security practice, such as those who have created a breach, inadvertently installed malware, or were named in an audit for not knowing or demonstrating proper security practices. It is important to remember that you're trying to foster an amenable relationship between operations and security, so these sessions should not be punitive in nature or recriminatory. Be sure to bear in mind—and tell your audience—that a security failure is not a grievous shortcoming, but an opportunity to learn how to improve.

As in all training matters, document every refresher training session to include the subject matter and the participants.

Additional Training Insights

All training can be offered as live presentations or online courseware. There are benefits and drawbacks to both methods.

Live Training   Having the participants interact with the subject matter expert can be extremely valuable, both because attendees can better understand the material and because they'll be a lot more likely to recall the information if it is presented in a manner they appreciate and comprehend. Tracking and documenting live sessions poses some difficulty, though, as it often requires some form of taking attendance, which gets complicated as the employee population scales.

Online Courseware   Computer-based training is an incredibly powerful tool that can streamline a lot of the hassle of scheduling live class sessions. It allows every employee to access the material when it is at their convenience, from the comfort of their own workplace (or, depending on your delivery mechanism, their own home), and to study it at their own pace. However, these traits also make online training prone to external distraction, and many employees just see it as a chore to be endured; instead of paying attention to the content, they just mash buttons until it's over and they can get back to whatever they wanted to be doing. However, online courseware tools usually offer excellent tracking functionality and provide granular documentation capabilities even with large user groups.

Another fundamental aspect of security training is policy. If the organization is truly in favor of making security a priority, then this should be reflected in governance. Carrying forward an idea included in the previous subsections: reducing the adversarial nature of the user and security team relationship can be supported by appropriate policy. Include and formalize a reward program for employees that provide security insight (by, say, reporting security issues they discover), with adequate funding. Don't take punitive measures against personnel who inadvertently cause a security problem. Dramatic enforcement should only be used in the case of malicious or criminal behavior.

Senior management can exhibit another way of endorsing the importance of security, too. If initial training sessions are presented to live audiences, then a member of senior management should be in attendance at each one, in order to stress how crucially they take the subject matter. A recorded message from some executive is *not* a sufficient replacement for this personal involvement in the process. We've all seen recorded messages from important people, and they often come across as facile and silly. Not everyone looks good on camera, and very, very few executives look or sound sincere when taping a video. It becomes a farce and usually detracts from the lesson instead of accentuating it. Moreover, if new managers, directors, and executives attend the same initial and recurring security training sessions as other employees, then all personnel will be more likely to appreciate the material.

Basic Operational Application Security

At this point, we want to include some basic security methods that can be used to reduce the risk to applications hosted in a cloud datacenter and aid in the selection of controls to protect them. The use of these techniques can be undertaken by either the cloud vendor (in

SaaS motifs) or the customer (in IaaS and PaaS). We include them here, in the coverage of operational considerations, because almost all production environments in the cloud will rely heavily on the use of applications (see Chapter 5, and the discussion of APIs), making proper application security a chief concern. If you already have other InfoSec certifications (such as the CISSP), you may be familiar with these methods, since they are often included in discussion of the SDLC and secure SDLC. The areas included here are threat modeling and application security testing techniques.

Threat Modeling

Threat modeling is the practice of viewing the application from the perspective of a potential attacker. (Specifically, for application security; this method can also be abstracted out to view the entire environment or operation from the attacker's perspective.) In this way, threat modeling can be seen as an application-specific form of penetration testing, although, realistically, it involves more than just causing a breach or gaining access (the "penetration"), as you'll see.

There are many ways to perform threat modeling. For instance, a vulnerability scan could be perceived as a low-level sort of threat model—attackers will be looking for the same (known) vulnerabilities that a vulnerability scan looks for.

There are several formal constructs that exist to aid threat modeling efforts. One of the more popular is the STRIDE model, developed by Microsoft. STRIDE is an acronym used to parse the various types of attacks and malicious techniques that might be used against software:

S (Spoofing)   These are attempts by attackers to obfuscate their origin or nature by misrepresenting identification elements such as login credentials, IP address, email address, MAC address, and so forth.

T (Tampering)   These are attacks that either use or intend to make unauthorized modifications to actual data, affecting the integrity of information or communications.

R (Repudiation)   These threats are associated with users who deny performing an action without other parties having any way to prove otherwise—for example, a user performs an illegal operation in a system that lacks the ability to trace the prohibited operations.

I (Information Disclosure)   This is just as it sounds—unauthorized access to information.

D (Denial of Service)   This is any attack that results in loss of availability to authorized entities.

E (Escalation of Privilege)   This is the ability of any user to gain permissions above their authorized level. While this seems as if it would be limited to internal threats only, consider environments where members of the public can view material, even in a passive manner, such as a public web page; a malicious visitor who can take some control or increased access to the environment can still be said to be escalating privilege.

Each of these categories of attack could be launched internally or externally, inadvertently or with malicious intent. It is the responsibility of the system owner to determine if possibilities are likely and to impose rigorous controls to protect against each mode of security failure.

STRIDE Resources

Microsoft has made the STRIDE model and suggestions for its implementation freely available on their website: `https://msdn.microsoft.com/en-us/library/ee823878(v=cs.20).aspx`.

An example of how STRIDE might be used to evaluate the potential attacks on a web commerce server is provided as well: `https://msdn.microsoft.com/en-us/library/ee798544(v=cs.20).aspx`.

Microsoft also offers an automated tool designed to aid in applying the STRIDE model to any software. It is available, free of charge, from their website: `https://www.microsoft.com/en-us/download/details.aspx?id=49168`.

While STRIDE is widely used in the software development community, other models exist as well. For instance, the Trike model (and its associated tool) is an open source alternative offered by Octotrike (`http://octotrike.org`) and cited by OWASP (`https://www.owasp.org/index.php/Threat_Risk_Modeling#Trike`). It is also possible to apply risk models for the purpose of threat modeling, because these usually take into account the nature of potential attacks, their likelihood, and their potential impact.

Whatever method is used to determine possible avenues of attack, the system owner's ultimate task is to develop a redundant, overlapping set of security controls that can attenuate these threats.

Application Testing Methods

It is also important for any system owner or developer to inspect their applications for vulnerabilities and defects that may lead to vulnerabilities before putting their application into production. In this section, we'll briefly describe some of the methods used for this purpose from a rather high-level perspective. Again, readers familiar with the SDLC and its secure implementation should already have some knowledge of this material.

Static application security testing (SAST) is a direct review of the actual source code comprising an application. It is often to referred to as "white-box testing." Benefits include direct and early assessment of potential flaws, long before the application is even considered for the production environment. Unfortunately, effective SAST requires a great deal of specific knowledge of the particular code, as well as expert comprehension of potential negative outcomes. This kind of skillset is usually found in personnel already involved in programming; it's rare that an organization would have this sort of person available for the limited task of software testing. So SAST might often be performed by contract personnel on a finite basis. This introduces an additional potential detriment to the development process: The number of iterations for which they can be tasked might be extremely limited, and certainly expensive. However, application owners want to be sure that applications are *not* being tested by the developers who wrote them. There is too much chance that the developers will miss errors they've made (or else they would not have made them), or that they will be understandably inherently biased toward their own creation. This would pose a conflict of interest and violate the principle of separation of duties.

Dynamic application security testing (DAST), on the other hand, does not pertain to source code. Instead, it reviews outcomes of the application as it is executed in runtime. It is often referred to as "black-box testing." In comparison to SAST, DAST should require less expertise to perform and therefore have less associated expense and more possible iterations that are easily scheduled. However, DAST is not nearly as granular as SAST, and something that might have been revealed by expert SAST might be missed in DAST.

Of course, it is possible—and desirable—to perform both kinds of testing on a particular application.

Summary

In this chapter, we've discussed the use of redundancy in the design of cloud datacenters and made the reader aware of the Uptime Institute's four tiers for describing and certifying that quality. We also discussed training motifs and requirements, how training is related to due diligence efforts, and suggestions for properly utilizing training to reduce the risk within your organization. Finally, we described basic application security methods, including threat modeling and software testing.

Exam Essentials

Understand how redundancy is implemented in the design of the cloud datacenter. Be sure to remember that all infrastructure, systems, and components require redundancy, including utilities (power, water, and connectivity), processing capabilities, data storage, personnel, and emergency and contingency services (including paths of egress, power, light, and fuel).

Know the four tiers of datacenter redundancy published by the Uptime Institute. While memorizing the aspects of each would be difficult, it is possible to understand the escalation in sophistication of design from Tier 1 to Tier 4 and the basic differences between each.

Know the significant aspects of training and awareness. Understand how training impacts the risk of the organization, and know which elements best support training efforts (specifically, senior management endorsement, adequate funding, and applicability to job tasks).

Understand the differences between SAST and DAST. Know which is white-box testing, which is black-box testing, which involves review of source code, and which is performed in runtime.

Written Labs

1. Imagine an application that might be used by an organization hosted in a cloud environment. In one paragraph, describe the purpose and use of this application, including the user base, types of data it processes, and the interface.

2. Using the STRIDE model, analyze potential points of security failure in the application from the first lab. According to Microsoft, it's possible to identify up to 40 points of failure in a two-hour analysis; in 30 minutes, come up with three.

3. Use one paragraph to describe each potential threat; use an additional paragraph to describe possible security controls that might be applied to attenuate that threat. The controls may be repeated (that is, you can use the same control for more than one threat), but the explanation paragraph of each should apply to each specific threat and therefore cannot just be copied.

Review Questions

You can find the answers in Appendix A.

1. What is the lowest tier of datacenter redundancy, according to the Uptime Institute?
    A. 1
    B. V
    C. C
    D. 4

2. What is the amount of fuel that should be on hand to power generators for backup datacenter power, in all tiers, according to the Uptime Institute?
    A. 1
    B. 1,000 gallons
    C. 12 hours
    D. As much as needed to ensure all systems may be gracefully shut down and data securely stored

3. Which of the following is *not* one of the three types of training?
    A. Integral
    B. Initial
    C. Recurring
    D. Refresher

4. Which of the following is part of the STRIDE model?
    A. Repudiation
    B. Redundancy
    C. Resiliency
    D. Rijndael

5. Which of the following is *not* part of the STRIDE model?
    A. Spoofing
    B. Tampering
    C. Resiliency
    D. Information disclosure

6. Which of the following is *not* a feature of SAST?
    A. Source code review
    B. Team-building efforts
    C. "White-box" testing
    D. Highly skilled, often expensive outside consultants

7. Which of the following is *not* a feature of DAST?

    A. Testing in runtime

    B. User teams performing executable testing

    C. "Black-box" testing

    D. Binary inspection

8. Which of the following is *not* a feature of a secure KVM component?

    A. Keystroke logging

    B. Sealed exterior case

    C. Welded chipsets

    D. Push-button selectors

9. What type of redundancy can we expect to find in a datacenter of any tier?

    A. All operational components

    B. All infrastructure

    C. Emergency egress

    D. Full power capabilities

10. What should be the primary focus of datacenter redundancy and contingency planning?

    A. Critical path/operations

    B. Health and human safety

    C. Infrastructure supporting the production environment

    D. Power and HVAC

11. Which of the following techniques for ensuring cloud datacenter storage resiliency uses parity bits and disk striping?

    A. Cloud-bursting

    B. RAID

    C. Data dispersion

    D. SAN

12. Which resiliency technique attenuates the possible loss of functional capabilities during contingency operations?

    A. Cross-training

    B. Metered usage

    C. Proper placement of HVAC temperature measurements tools

    D. Raised floors

13. Which of the following has *not* been attributed as the cause of lost capabilities due to DoS?

   A. Hackers

   B. Construction equipment

   C. Changing regulatory motif

   D. Squirrels

14. Which of the following aids in the ability to demonstrate due diligence efforts?

   A. Redundant power lines

   B. HVAC placement

   C. Security training documentation

   D. Bollards

15. What is often a major challenge to getting both redundant power and communications utility connections?

   A. Expense

   B. Carrying medium

   C. Personnel deployment

   D. Location of many datacenters

16. Which of the following is *not* an aspect of physical security that ought to be considered in the planning and design of a cloud datacenter facility?

   A. Perimeter

   B. Vehicular approach/traffic

   C. Fire suppression

   D. Elevation of dropped ceilings

17. The Brewer-Nash security model is also known as which of the following?

   A. MAC

   B. The Chinese Wall model

   C. Preventive measures

   D. RBAC

18. Which kind of hypervisor would malicious actors prefer to attack, ostensibly because it offers a greater attack surface?

   A. Cat IV

   B. Type II

   C. Bare metal

   D. Converged

19. Which of the following techniques for ensuring cloud datacenter storage resiliency uses encrypted chunks of data?

    A. Cloud-bursting

    B. RAID

    C. Data dispersion

    D. SAN

20. Security training should *not* be:

    A. Documented

    B. Internal

    C. A means to foster a non-adversarial relationship between the security office and operations personnel

    D. Boring

Chapter

9

Operations Management

THE OBJECTIVE OF THIS CHAPTER IS TO ACQUAINT THE READER WITH THE FOLLOWING CONCEPTS:

✓ **Domain 1: Architectural Concepts and Design Requirements**

- A. Understand Cloud Computing Concepts
  - A.2. Cloud Computing Roles
- D. Understand Design Principles of Secure Cloud Computing
  - D.2. Cloud Based Business Continuity/Disaster Recovery Planning

✓ **Domain 3: Cloud Platform and Infrastructure Security**

- C. Design and Plan Security Controls
  - C.1. Physical and Environmental Protection
- D. Plan Disaster Recovery and Business Continuity Management
  - D.1. Understanding of the Cloud Environment
  - D.2. Understanding of the Business Requirements
  - D.3. Understanding of the Risks
  - D.4. Disaster Recovery/Business Continuity Strategy
  - D.5. Creation of the Plan
  - D.6. Implementation of the Plan

✓ **Domain 5: Operations**

- D. Manage Physical Infrastructure for Cloud Environment
  - D.2 Baseline Compliance Monitoring and Remediation
  - D.3. Patch Management
  - D.4. Performance Monitoring
  - D.5. Hardware Monitoring

- G. Manage Logical Infrastructure for Cloud Environment
  - G.2. OS Baseline Compliance Monitoring and Remediation
  - G.3. Patch Management
  - G.4. Performance Monitoring
- H. Ensure Compliance with Regulations and Controls
  - H.1. Change Management
  - H.2. Continuity Management
  - H.4. Continual Service Improvement Management
  - H.7. Release Management
  - H.8. Deployment Management
  - H.9. Configuration Management
  - H.12. Capacity Management

This chapter covers the essential aspects of operations monitoring, capacity, and maintenance, change and configuration management, and BC/DR for cloud datacenters.

In other chapters, we often refer to the cloud customer as "your organization" or make other related associations (using "your" or "we" to indicate the cloud customer's perspective in many matters). In this chapter, the focus is almost exclusively on the cloud provider, specifically the provider's datacenter. We may refer to actions associated with the provider with the same pronouns used for the customer elsewhere ("you," "your," or "we"); hopefully, context will prevent any misunderstanding.

In this chapter, we'll discuss the various practices cloud datacenter operators should use to optimize performance and enhance durability of their infrastructure and systems. This will include coverage of systems monitoring, the configuration and change management program, and BC/DR from a vendor perspective.

Monitoring, Capacity, and Maintenance

It's important for datacenter operators to know how their hardware, software, and network are being utilized and what demand is being placed on all the relevant resources. This information helps datacenter operators know how to better apportion and allocate all those items in order to fulfill customer needs (and maintain compliance with SLAs).

Monitoring

Software, hardware, and network components need to be evaluated in real time so as to understand which systems may be nearing capacity use and so that the organization can respond as quickly as possible when problems arise. This can and should be done with several of the possible tools at the operator's disposal:

OS Logging   Most operating systems have integral toolsets for monitoring performance and events. Aside from the security uses mentioned elsewhere in the book, the cloud vendor can set OS logs to alert administrators when usage approaches a level of capacity utilization or performance degradation that may affect SLA parameters. These can include CPU usage, memory usage, disk space (virtual or tangible), and disk I/O timing (an indicator of slow writing/reading to/from the disk).

Hardware Monitoring   As with the OS, many vendors include performance-monitoring tools in common device builds. These can be used to measure such performance indicators as CPU temperature, fan speed, voltages (consumption and throughput), CPU load and clock speed, and drive temperature. Commercial products are also available to collect and supply this data and provide alerts, if this functionality is not integral to the devices from the manufacturer.

Network Monitoring   In addition to the OS and the devices themselves, the various network elements (including not only the hardware and the software, but the distribution facets such as cabling and software-defined networking [SDN] control planes) need to be monitored. The provider should ensure that current capacity meets customer needs (and increased customer demand, to assure that the flexibility and scalability traits of cloud computing are still provided) and that the network is not overburdened or subjected to unacceptable latency.

> As with all log data, the performance monitoring information can be fed into a SEIM, SEM, or SIM system for centralized analysis and review.

In addition to the hardware and software, it is important to monitor ambient conditions within the datacenter. In particular, temperature and humidity are essential data points for optimizing operations and performance. It's important to capture a realistic portrayal of the temperature within the datacenter, perhaps by averaging measurements across several thermometric devices located throughout the airflow process. For performance monitoring purposes, our target metrics will be the standards created by Technical Committee 9.9 of the American Society of Heating, Refrigerating and Air-Conditioning Engineers (ASHRAE), published in 2016. ASHRAE offers extremely detailed recommendations for a wide variety of aspects of the datacenter, including the IT equipment, power supply, and battery backups, all of which can be quite useful to a datacenter operator or security practitioner. These are available free of charge from the ASHRAE website: https://tc0909.ashraetcs.org/documents/ASHRAE_TC0909_Power_White_Paper_22_June_2016_REVISED.pdf. It's also a generally good read and worth investing some of your time reviewing.

While there are many specific and detailed recommendations, the general ASHRAE recommended ranges for a datacenter are

- Temperature: 64 to 81° F (18 to 27° C)

- Humidity: Dew point of 42 to 59° F (5.5 to 15° C), relative humidity of 60%

While these ranges give a general notion of the condition of the ambient environment within a datacenter, the ASHRAE guidance is a lot more detailed regarding specific ranges, based on the type, age, and location of the equipment. The operator should determine which guidance is most applicable to their facility. Moreover, ASHRAE offers this advice solely from a platform-agnostic perspective. Datacenter operators must also take into account any guidance and recommendations from device manufacturers regarding ambient ranges affecting performance parameters for their specific products.

Effects of Ambient Temperature and Ambient Humidity

What roles do temperature and humidity play, in terms of affecting equipment performance?

An ambient temperature that is too high may allow equipment to overheat. High-capacity electrical components generate a great deal of waste heat, and the devices can be sensitive to conditions that exceed their operating parameters. An ambient temperature that is too low can be a risk to health and human safety; touching bare metal at the freezing point can burn or remove skin; moreover, people working in such conditions would simply be uncomfortable and unhappy, conditions that lead to dissatisfaction, which in turn lead to security risks.

An ambient humidity that is too high can promote corrosion of metallic components, as well as mold and other organisms. An ambient temperature that is too low can enhance the possibility of static discharge, which might affect both personnel and equipment, as well as increase the potential for fires.

Maintenance

Continual uptime requires maintaining the overall environment constantly. This also includes maintaining individual components both on a scheduled basis and at unscheduled times as necessary. In this section, we'll discuss general maintenance matters, updates, upgrades, and patch management.

General Maintenance Concepts

The operational modes of datacenters can be perceived as two categories: normal and maintenance mode. Realistically, the datacenter, taken holistically, will constantly be in maintenance mode, as ongoing maintenance of specific systems and components is necessary for continuous uptime. Therefore, a cloud datacenter can be expected to be considered in constant normal mode, with various individual systems and devices continually in maintenance mode to ensure constant operations. This is especially true for Tier 3 and 4 datacenters, where redundant components, lines, and systems allow for maintenance to occur simultaneously with uninterrupted critical operations.

Let's instead look at systems and devices in terms of the normal and maintenance modes. When a system or device is put into maintenance mode, the datacenter operator must ensure the following tasks are successful:

All operational instances are removed from the system/device before entering maintenance mode.   We don't want to affect any transactions in a customer's production environment. We therefore must migrate any virtualized instances off the specific systems and devices where they might be hosted before we begin maintenance activities.

Prevent all new logins.   For the same reason as the previous task, we don't want customers logging into the affected systems and devices.

Ensure logging is continued, and begin enhanced logging.   Administrator activities are much more powerful, and therefore rife with risk, than the actions of common users. It is therefore recommended that you log administrator actions at a greater rate and level of detail than that of users. Maintenance mode is an administrative function, so the increased logging is necessary.

 Before moving a system or device from maintenance mode back to normal operation, it is important to test that it has all the original functionality necessary for customer purposes, that the maintenance was successful, and that proper documentation of all activity is complete.

Updates

Industry best practice includes ensuring we comply with all vendor guidance regarding specific products. In fact, failing to adhere to vendor specifications can be a sign that the operator has failed in providing necessary due care, whereas documented adherence to vendor instructions can demonstrate due diligence.

In addition to configuration prior to deployment (discussed as part of the "Change and Configuration Management (CM)" section later in this chapter), vendors will issue ongoing maintenance instructions, often in the form of updates. (This can be both in the form of application packages for software and firmware installs for hardware. The former can also be in the form of patches, which we'll discuss specifically later in this section.)

The update process should be formalized in the operator's governance (as should *all* processes, and they should all spawn from policy). It should include the following elements, at a minimum:

Document how, when, and why the update was initiated.   If promulgated by the vendor, annotate the details of the communication (date, update code or number, explanation and justification; some of this may be included by reference, such as with a URL to the vendor's page announcing the update instructions).

Move the update through the change management (CM) process.   All modifications to the facility should be through the CM methodology and documented as such. Details on the CM process are included later in this chapter, but it should be stressed that sandbox testing be included as part of CM before the update is applied.

1. Put the systems and devices into maintenance mode. Observe the recommendations in the previous section of this chapter.

2. Apply the update to the necessary systems and devices. Annotate the asset inventory to reflect the changes.

3. Verify the update. Run tests on the production environment to ensure all necessary systems and devices have received the update. If any were missed, repeat the installation until it is complete.

4. Validate the modifications. Ensure that the intended results of the update have taken effect and that the updated systems and devices interact appropriately with the rest of the production environment.

5. Return to normal operations. Resume regular business.

Upgrades

In this context, we distinguish updates from upgrades with this purpose: updates are applied to existing systems and components, whereas upgrades are the replacement of older elements for new ones. The upgrade process should largely map to the one for updates, including formalization in governance, CM methodology, testing, and so forth. Particular attention in upgrading needs to be placed on documenting the changes in the asset inventory, not only adding the new elements but annotating the removal and secure disposal of the old ones. This, of course, means that secure disposal is one element of the upgrade process that is not included in updates.

Patch Management

Patches are a variety of updates most commonly associated with software. We distinguish them here by their frequency: software vendors commonly issue patches for both immediate response to a given need (such as a newfound vulnerability) and for routine purposes (fixing, adding, or enhancing functionality) on a regular basis.

The patch management process must be formalized in much the same manner as updates and upgrades, with its inclusion in policy and so forth. However, patches incur additional risks and challenges, so this section is set aside to deal with those specifically. The following subsections relate suggestions and considerations to take into account when managing patches for a cloud datacenter.

Timing

When a vendor issues a patch, there is a binary risk faced by all those affected: if they fail to apply the patch, they may be seen to be failing in providing due care for those customers utilizing the unpatched products; if the patch is applied in haste, it may adversely affect the production environment, harming the customer's ability to operate. The latter case is especially true when patches are issued in response to a newfound vulnerability and the vendor was rushed to identify the flaw, find and create a solution, publish the fix, and issue the patch. In the rush to deal with the problem (even more especially when the vulnerability is well publicized and garners public attention), the patch may cause other vulnerabilities or affect other systems by attenuating some interoperability or interface capability.

It is therefore difficult to know exactly when to apply patches relative to how soon after they were issued. It is contingent upon the operator to make this decision only after weighing the merits of either choice.

A datacenter operator may be tempted to allow others in the field to apply the patch first, in order to determine its effect and outcome based on the experiences of competitors. The risk in that option is that in the meantime loss or harm might be caused by or occur via the vulnerability the patch was meant to attenuate. This might lend strong support in a lawsuit to recover damages because those customers harmed by the loss can rightly claim that the provider knew of the risk, did not take the steps of due diligence made by others in the field, and allowed harm to come through negligence. This might even support claims for additional or punitive damages. Again, while the tactic may be sound, it carries this additional risk.

Implementation: Automated or Manual

Patches can be applied with mechanized tools or by personnel. There are obvious benefits and risks for both methods. The operator will have to decide which to use on both a general basis (by policy) and for each case when a patch is issued if the circumstances demand. The risks and benefits for each include the following:

Automated   A mechanized approach will allow for much faster delivery to far more targets than a manual approach. Patch tools might also include a reporting function that annotates which targets have received the patch, cross-referenced against the asset inventory, and have an alerting function to inform administrators which targets have been missed. Without a capable human observer, however, the tool might not function thoroughly or properly, the patches might be misapplied, or the reports might be inaccurate or portray an inaccurate picture of completeness.

Manual   Trained and experienced personnel may be more trustworthy than a mechanized tool and might understand when anomalous activity occurs. However, with the vast number of elements that will need to be patched in a cloud datacenter, the repetitiveness and boredom of the patch process may lead even a seasoned administrator to miss a number of targets. Moreover, the process will be much, much slower than the automated option and may not be as thorough.

Dates

As the patch is pushed throughout the environment, the actual date/time stamp may become an important—and misleading—matter in acquiring and acknowledging receipt. For example, say that an automated tool requires an agent that is installed locally on each target. If certain targets are not running when the patch happens and won't be operating until the next calendar day (according to the internal clock on the target), the local agent may not receive the patch because it may check against the central controller for patches *for the current day.*

This problem can be compounded when patch agents are set to check for patches according to a time specified by the internal clock, and different targets have internal clocks set to differing time zones (in the case, say, of customers who are geographically dispersed).

This problem is not limited to automated tools, either. If a manual method is used, the administrators may be applying a patch at a given time/date when not all customers and users have their targets operating, so those targets might not receive the patch, and the administrators might not realize that targets that don't currently appear in scans may need to be patched at some later time/date. Moreover, if patches are being done manually, the process will necessarily be extended so that administrators can be sure to reach all potential targets as they come online.

All these possibilities are escalated in a cloud motif because of the wide use of virtualization. All virtualized instances saved as images and not currently instantiated during patch delivery will be receiving the patch only after they are next booted. This means that the process will endure until all virtual machines have been made live, which could represent a significant amount of time after the decision to implement the patch. The result is a relatively long delay between the time the operator decides to implement the patch and the time of 100 percent completion. This reflects poorly on the process and the operator, especially in the eyes of regulators and courts.

Perhaps the optimum technique is to combine the benefits of each method, using both manual and automated approaches. Manual oversight is valuable in determining applicability of patches and testing patches for suitability in the environment, while automated tools can be used to propagate patches and ensure uniform application.

Change and Configuration Management (CM)

Datacenter operators, like anyone who owns an IT network, need to develop and maintain a realistic concept of what assets they control, the state of those assets, and explicit information about each asset. This goes beyond (but includes) the asset inventory—the hardware, software, and media they own. It also includes documented record of configuration for all these elements, versioning, deviations, exceptions, and the rationale for each, as well as a formal process for determining how, when, and why modifications need to be made.

There are primarily two processes used by the industry to accomplish this effort: change management and configuration management. Change management usually deals with modifications to the network, such as the acquisition and deployment of new systems and components and the disposal of those taken out of service. Configuration management usually concerns modifications to a known set of parameters regarding each element of the network, including what settings each has, how the controls are implemented, and so forth.

Realistically, in many organizations both sets of functions are accomplished by a single process and body. For the purposes of our discussion of operational functions, we're going to aggregate them and put them under one label: CM. We'll do this to simplify the information, even though a cloud vendor should probably have the wherewithal and functional and personnel specialization sufficient to provide both as separate activities. The purposes of both are so similar in intent and procedure as to be understood as one concept.

Baselines

CM, regardless of the flavor, begins with baselining, which is a way of taking an accurate account of the desired standard state. For change management, that's a depiction of the network and systems, based on a comprehensive, detailed asset inventory. For configuration management, it's a standard build for all systems, from the settings in the OS to the setup of each application.

The baseline is a general-purpose map of the network and systems, based on the required functionality as well as security. Security controls should be incorporated in the baseline, with a thorough description of each one's purpose, dependencies, and supporting rationale (that is, a statement explaining what we hope to accomplish with each control). It is absolutely essential to include the controls so that we are fully informed about risk management as we consider modifications to the environment through the CM process. If we're changing the control set in any way or adding new systems and functionality to the environment, we need to know if there will be any resultant increased risk and, therefore, if we need to add any compensatory controls to manage the new risk levels.

While creating the baseline, it's helpful to get input from all stakeholders: the IT department, the security office, management, and even users. The baseline should be an excellent reflection of the risk appetite of the organization and provide the optimum balance of security and operational functionality.

Preferably, the baseline should suit the largest population of systems in the organization. If it's going to be used as a template (particularly in configuration management), we'll get the most value from it if it applies to the greatest number of covered systems. However, it may be useful or pragmatic to have a number of baselines that are based on each department's, office's, or project's needs. If you opt for having multiple baselines, you *must* ensure that each distinct build is interoperable with the others and that the control coverage of each one is equitable. It would be inopportune to have an entire department fail a regulatory compliance audit because that department's baseline lost a category of security coverage.

Deviations and Exceptions

It is important to continually test the baselines to determine that all assets are accounted for and to detect anything that differs from the baseline. Any such deviations, intentional or unintentional, authorized or unauthorized, must be documented and reviewed. These deviations might be the result of faulty patch management processes, a rogue device set up by a particular office or user, an intrusion by an external attackers, or poor versioning and administrative practices. It is the duty of those personnel who are assigned CM roles to determine the cause and any necessary follow-up activity. CM roles are discussed in the next section.

While the baseline serves as the standard against which to compare and validate all systems in the organization, it is best not to use it as an absolute. There will be a significant number of requests for exceptions for particular users, offices, and projects that need functionality not accorded by the general baseline.

Make sure that the baseline is flexible and practical and that the exception request process is timely and responsive to the needs of the organization and its users. A cumbersome, slow exception process will lead to frustrated users and managers, which can, in turn, lead to unauthorized workarounds implemented without the permission of the CM authority.

An adversarial, unresponsive exception process will undermine security efforts of the organization. Everyone will find a way to perform their job functions, regardless of whether their workarounds are approved or are the most secure means of performing those functions. Uninformed personnel, acting out of desperation, are more likely to make rogue modifications that lack the proper security countermeasures than would the trained, skilled professionals whose job it is to secure the environment. It is much better to compromise the sanctity of the baseline with full cooperation than to mandate that no exceptions will be allowed or to make the process burdensome and complicated for users and offices. Remember: It is the job of security practitioners to support operations, not to hinder those engaged in productivity.

Tracking exceptions and deviations is useful for another essential purpose in addition to ensuring regulatory compliance and security control coverage: if enough exception requests are being made that all ask for the same or similar functionality that deviates from the baseline, *change the baseline*. The baseline is not serving the purpose if it continually needs routine modification for repeated, equivalent requests. Moreover, addressing exception requests takes more time and effort than modifying the baseline to incorporate new, additional security controls to allow for the excepted functionality.

Roles and Process

The CM process (as with all processes) should be formalized in the organization's governance. This policy should include provisions for the following:

- Composition of the CM board (CMB)
- The process, in detail
- Documentation requirements
- Instructions for requesting exceptions
- Assignment of CM tasks, such as validation scanning, analysis, and deviation notification
- Procedures for addressing deviations, upon detection
- Enforcement measures and responsibility

The CMB should be composed of representatives from all stakeholders within the organization. Recommended representatives include personnel from IT, security, legal, management, the user group, finance and acquisition, and HR. Any other participants that the organization deems useful can certainly be included in the CMB.

The CMB will be responsible for reviewing change and exception requests. The board will determine if the change will enhance functionality and productivity, whether the change is funded, what potential security impacts the change will incur, and what additional measures (in terms of funding, training, security controls, or staffing) might be necessary to make the change successful and reasonable.

The CMB should meet often enough that changes and exception requests are not delayed unduly so that users and departments are not frustrated by the process. However, it should not meet so often that the time set aside for the CMB becomes work; the personnel involved in the CMB all have other primary duties, and participation in the CMB will impact their productivity. In some cases, depending on the organization, the CMB meets on an ad hoc basis, responding only when change and exception requests meet a certain threshold. This can entail some risk, however, as CMB members might lose some familiarity with the process in the interim, and scheduling a meeting of the CMB with so many disparate offices might be awkward if the CMB is not a regular, prioritized occurrence. As with much of the material addressed in this book, this is a trade-off of risk and benefit, and the organization should decide accordingly.

The process has two forms: one that will occur once and the other, which is repetitious. The former is the initial baseline effort; the latter is the normal operational mode.

The initial process should look something like this (amended as necessary for each organization's individual circumstances):

1. Full asset inventory: In order to know what is being managed, it's crucial to know what you have. This effort need not be independent of all other similar efforts and may in fact be aided by information pulled from other sources (such as the business impact assessment [BIA]).

2. Codification of the baseline: This should be a formal action, including all members of the CMB (and perhaps more, for the initial effort; each department and project may want to contribute and participate, as the baseline will affect all their future work). The baseline should be negotiated in terms of cost–benefit and risk analyses. Again, it is quite reasonable to use existing sources to inform this negotiation, including the organization's risk management framework, enterprise and security architecture, and so on.

3. Secure baseline build: A version of the baseline, as codified by the CMB, is constructed and stored for later use.

4. Deployment of new assets: This step is for configuration management, typically. When a new asset is acquired (for instance, a new host purchased for use by a new employee), the baseline configuration needs to be installed on that asset, in accordance with CM policy and procedures, and CMB guidance.

In the normal operational mode of the organization, the CM process is slightly different:

1. CMB meetings: The CMB meets to review and analyze change and exception requests. The CMB can authorize or disallow requests, and it can require additional effort before authorization. (For instance, the CMB can task the security office to perform additional detailed security analysis of the potential impact resulting if the request were authorized, or the CMB might require the requestor to budget additional funding for the request if the CMB determines the request would require supplemental training, administration, and security controls compared to what the requestor initially expected.)

2. CM testing: If the CMB authorizes a request, the new modification must be tested before deployment. Usually, such testing should take place in an isolated sandbox network that mimics all the systems, components, infrastructure, traffic, and processing of the production network, without ever touching the production network. Testing should determine whether there is any undue impact on security, interoperability, or functionality expected as a result of the modification.

3. Deployment: The modification is made in accordance with appropriate guidance and is reported to the CMB upon completion.

4. Documentation: All modifications to the environment are documented and reflected in the asset inventory (and, as necessary, in the baseline).

 Secure disposal of an asset is also a modification to the IT environment and therefore needs to be reflected in the asset inventory and reported to the CMB.

Taxing Taxonomy

In the CBK and CIB, Domain 5 (Operations), section H ("Ensure Compliance with Regulations and Controls") were largely based on ISO 17788. That standard, published in 2014 and drafted even earlier, was created long before the current form and understanding of cloud computing. It contains a lot of information that in current thinking are misleading or potentially erroneous. ISO 17788 is not an operational standard but merely definitions for a conversation that has long since moved on to another taxonomy. The good news is that it won't be on the exam. To avoid confusing the reader, we are only discussing Domain 5, section H topics to the extent that they are relevant and reflect contemporary real-world usage.

Business Continuity and Disaster Recovery (BC/DR)

Business continuity and disaster recovery (BC/DR) has been addressed in other sections of this book, relative to specific topics. Here, we cover some of the general aspects and approaches, with some additional focus on facility continuity.

There is no total agreement within our industry on the exact definitions of the terms *business continuity*, *disaster recovery*, *event*, or even simply *disaster* for that matter. For the purposes of this discussion and to create awareness of the (ISC)² perspective on the matter, we'll use the following explanations:

- *Business continuity efforts* are concerned with maintaining critical operations during any interruption in service, whereas *disaster recovery* efforts are focused on the resumption of operations after an interruption due to disaster. The two are related and in many organizations are rolled into one effort.

- An *event* is any unscheduled adverse impact to the operating environment. An event is distinguished from a *disaster* by the duration of impact. We consider an event's impact to last three days or less; a disaster's impact lasts longer. An event can become a disaster. Causes of either/both can be anthropogenic, natural forces, internal or external, malicious or accidental.

Because they can be so similar, we'll discuss BC/DR efforts together for most of the coverage of the topic and only make distinctions when needed.

Primary Focus

The paramount importance in BC/DR planning and efforts should be health and human safety, as in all security matters. There is no justification for prioritizing any asset to any degree higher than personnel, except in very, very limited cases. These are limited to organizations dealing with national security, and, even in those cases, are likewise limited to situations where human harm and loss of life might only be necessary to prevent greater losses (such as in the protection of assets that might result in vast devastation, such as nuclear, biological, or chemical products).

With that in mind, any BC/DR efforts should prioritize notification and evacuation as well as protection and egress.

Notification should take several redundant and differing forms, to ensure widest and most thorough dissemination. Suggestions for possible notification avenues include telephone call tree rosters, website postings, and SMS blasts. Notification should include the organization's personnel, the public, and regulatory and response agencies, depending on who might be affected by the circumstance.

 Real World Scenario

Notification on Notice

Notification strategies can be adversely affected by both the event and disaster and the tendency for complacency.

For instance, the authors have some personal experience with the September 11, 2001 attacks and serving in a DoD agency near the Pentagon that day. The agency's notification plan included a telephone call tree, a traditional notification method long used by the military for both warning and mustering efforts. Unfortunately, because the attacks were so dramatic and the public response was so comprehensive, the telephone networks were largely overwhelmed with communication traffic; some landlines worked, but most cell coverage was blocked. Notification and contact were only possible after some workarounds had been arranged, including using rarer devices (such as Blackberrys) and SMS, as well as email and physically relaying messages in person.

Likewise, complacency can play a part in the effectiveness of notification efforts. The failure of personnel to voluntarily update their emergency contact information in a timely manner following a change is commonplace. How many of your personnel are informing HR when their cell number or home address changes? Is HR informing the security office (or whoever manages your BC/DR plan)? Is the contact list being updated in the BC/DR plan and kit?

Evacuation, protection, and egress methods will depend on the particular physical layout of the campus and facility. Some aspects that are generally included in addressing these needs include the following:

Getting the People Out   There should be no obstruction or delay of personnel leaving the facility. All doors along the emergency path should open instantly for exit (even if they were locked for entry). Sufficient lighting should be considered.

Getting the People Out Safely   Sprinkler systems along the egress route should be set to inundate the area, and not be restricted due to other considerations (such as property damage). Non-water fire-suppression systems (such as gas) cannot risk human life and must have additional controls (last-out switch, and so on). Communicate the emergency plans to all personnel, and train them in execution of the plan.

Designing for Protection   Other architectural, engineering, and coding concerns must meet local needs, such as facilities that are built to withstand and resist environment hazards (tornadoes in the Midwestern United States, flooding along the coasts, and so on).

Continuity of Operations

After we've seen to health and human safety concerns, our primary *business* focus should be continuity of critical operations.

To begin with, we have to determine what the organization's critical operations *are*. In a cloud datacenter, that will usually be dictated by the customer contracts and SLAs. This simplifies delineation of those elements necessary to support critical needs. Other extant sources can be extremely useful in this portion of the effort, most particularly the BIA, which informs us which assets would cause the greatest adverse impact if lost or interrupted. For instance, in a cloud datacenter, our main focus should be on connectivity, utilities, and processing capacity ("ping, power, pipe"). These are, therefore, our critical operations. Other ancillary business functions, such as marketing, sales, finance, HR, and so on, might be wholly dismissed or greatly attenuated without lasting impact to the organization and can be considered noncritical.

In formulating this inventory of critical assets, it is important to consider all elements that support critical functions, not limited to the hardware and tangible assets, but also specific personnel, software libraries, documentation, fundamental data, and so forth, without which we could not continue critical operations.

The BC/DR Plan

As with all plans, the BC/DR plan should be formalized in and derive from the organization's governance. Policy should dictate roles, terms of the plan, enforcement, and execution.

The plan should include both a general, exhaustive, detailed description of all aspects of BC/DR efforts and also limited, simple, straightforward procedures for enacting the plan and all response activities. Because the two categories of documentation differ so widely in content and purpose, they can often be included in the plan as appendices or attachments and referenced for the purpose of describing how and when each will be used (the detailed content for planning and after-action purposes; the simple procedures for use during the reaction to the event and disaster itself).

For BC/DR procedures, the authors are big fans of checklists. Checklists serve several purposes. They describe the specific actions necessary, they can be aligned in order of execution, and they can constitute a record, after the activity is complete, of actions taken, by whom, and when (if each checklist step is annotated with the time and initials of the person completing the action as it occurs). Checklists also serve another fundamental requirement of BC/DR plans used during a response action: they allow for someone to conduct the appropriate actions, even if that person has not had specific training or experience with that plan in that organization. Of course, it is always preferable to have the personnel assigned to BC/DR roles trained and practiced in the specific plan, but, especially in disasters but also during events, the assigned personnel are not always available.

The plan should include the following:

A List of the Items from the Asset Inventory Deemed Critical   This should include necessary hardware, software, and media, including versioning data and applicable patches.

The Circumstances Under Which an Event or Disaster Is Declared   Response comes with a cost. It is important to distinguish normal administration functions from event or disaster response because the formal response will obligate resources and affect productivity. Careful attention and explanation should be made for balancing the risks and benefits of overreaction and underreaction in terms of response: too frequently, and productivity will needlessly be adversely affected; too rarely, and response activities may be hindered by delays for the sake of caution.

Who Is Authorized to Make the Declaration   An authority needs to be named (an individual, role, or office) for the purpose of formal declaration of an event or disaster. We want to avoid the possibility of overreaction by allowing just anyone to initiate a formal response (like an emergency brake line in public transit), and we want to ensure that initiation is instigated by someone who is informed, qualified, trained, and responsible for making such a determination.

An authorized party must also formally declare a cessation of BC/DR activity and resumption of normal operations. This should only be done when there is a high degree of assurance that all safety and health hazards have been attenuated and operating conditions and risks have returned to normal. Resuming standard operations too soon can exacerbate the existing event or disaster or cause a new one.

Essential Points of Contact   This should include the contact information of offices responsible for BC/DR activity and tasks, as well as any external entities that may be involved (regulators, law enforcement, corporate authorities, press, vendors, customers, and so on). These should be as specific as possible to reduce difficulty in locating appropriate contacts during an actual response.

Detailed Actions, Tasks, and Activities   The aforementioned checklists.

All these elements can be included by reference. That is, each piece can be split out as an attachment or appendix to the BC/DR policy proper. The basic elements of all policies (explanation and rationale for the policy, enforcement activities, relevant regulations, and so on) can compose the body of the policy, as it will be less subject to continual changing and updating.

Updating the BC/DR policy will be a continual process. Many of the listed elements, as you can see, will be in almost constant flux (the points of contact information, specific personnel assigned particular tasks, the list of the current state of critical assets), so the relevant parts of the plan (the specific appendices and attachments) need to receive updates from the offices that have the pertinent data. For instance, the current state of critical assets might be updated by the CMB, as part of the CM process. The CMB will be in the best position to know all the current versions of systems and components.

The BC/DR Kit

There should be a container that holds all the necessary documentation and tools to conduct a proper BC/DR response action. This kit should be secure, durable, and compact. The container may be tangible or virtual. The contents might contain hard-copy versions of the appropriate documentation or electronic copies.

We recommend that the BC/DR kit exist in both tangible hard-copy and virtual electronic versions, because we are paranoid by habit, nature, and trade.

The kit should have a replication in at least one other location, depending on the plan. If the plan calls for reconstitution of critical operations at an offsite location, there should be a mirrored kit in that location. Otherwise, having at least two identical kits onsite, in different locations, aids in attenuating the consequences of one being unreachable and destroyed.

The kit should contain the following:

- A current copy of the plan, with all appendices and addenda.
- Emergency and backup communication equipment. These can take whatever form suits the purpose, location, and nature of the organization: cell phones, handheld radios, laptop with satellite modem, and so on.

- Copies of all appropriate network and infrastructure diagrams and architecture.

- Copies of all requisite software for creating a clean build of the critical systems, if necessary, with media containing appropriate updates and patches for current versioning.

- Emergency contact information (not already included in the plan). This might include a full notification list (as described earlier in this chapter).

- Documentation tools and equipment. Again, these can take many forms: pens and paper, laptop and portable printer, voice recorder, and so on.

- A small amount of emergency essentials (flashlight, water, rations, and so on).

- Fresh batteries sufficient for operating all powered equipment in the kit for at least 24 hours.

Obviously, keeping the kit stocked and current requires a level of effort similar to that of maintaining the plan itself (and includes the plan itself, as it is updated).

Relocation

Depending on the nature of the event and disaster and the specifics of the plan, the organization may choose to evacuate and relocate those personnel involved in critical operations to a specified alternate operating location. Prior to the existence of cloud capabilities for the purpose of backing up and restoring data at a secure, offsite location, hot and warm and cold sites were used for this purpose, and a skeleton crew of critical personnel were assigned to travel to the recovery site for the duration of the contingency operations and recovery.

With the advent of ubiquitous availability of cloud backup resources, the relocation site can be anywhere not affected by the event and disaster, as long as it has sufficient facilities for housing the personnel involved and bandwidth sufficient for the purpose. For instance, a hotel outside the area of effect could serve the purpose if it offers broadband capabilities and is additionally useful in that it also fulfills the function of safe lodging for the critical personnel.

If the organization considers relocation for BC/DR purposes, the plan might include these aspects:

- Tasking and activities should include representatives from the HR and finance department, as travel arrangements and payments will be necessary for all personnel involved in the relocation.

- Sufficient support should be provided for relocating dependents and family members of the personnel involved in critical operations for the duration of the response. When a disaster affects a locality, everyone involved will rightfully be concerned with their loved ones first and foremost. If this concern is not alleviated, their morale and focus on the tasks at hand will be diminished. It is better to assume the additional costs related to this option so as to gain the full attention of the personnel involved in the response.

- The distance of the relocation is, like all things related to the practice of security, a balance. You want the relocation site to be far enough away that it is not affected by whatever caused the interruption to standard operations, but not so far that the delay and expense of travel makes its utility unappealing.

- Joint operating agreements and memoranda of understanding can be used to establish cost-effective relocation sites at facilities belonging to other operations in the local area if the event or disaster only affects your organization's campus (in the event of highly localized events and disasters, such as a building fire).

Essential BC/DR Terminology

There are several BC/DR concepts that you need to understand:

MAD (Maximum Allowable Downtime)   How long it would take for an interruption in service to kill an organization, measured in time. For instance, if a company would fail because it had to halt operations for a week, then its MAD is one week.

RTO (Recovery Time Objective)   The BC/DR goal for recovery of operational capability after an interruption in service, measured in time. This does not have to include full operations (recovery); the capability can be limited to critical functions for the duration of the contingency event. The RTO *must* be less than the MAD. For example, a company might have an MAD of one week, while the company's BC/DR plan includes and supports an RTO of six days.

RPO (Recovery Point Objective)   The BC/DR goal for limiting the loss of data from an unplanned event. Confusingly, this is often measured in time. For instance, if an organization is doing full backups every day and is affected by some sort of disaster, that organization's BC/DR plan might include a goal of resuming critical operations at an alternate operating site with the last full backup, which would be an RPO of 24 hours. The recovery point objective for that organization would be the loss of no more than one day's worth of data.

Power

Interruptions to the normal power supply often result from events or disasters (or are themselves a reason to declare an event or disaster), so BC/DR plans and activities must take emergency power supply into account.

Near-term emergency power usually takes the form of battery backups, often as uninterruptible power supply (UPS) systems. These can be small units, feeding only particular individual devices or racks, or they can be large, supplying power to entire systems. Failover for these should be close to immediate, with appropriate line conditioning so that transitioning from utility power to UPS does not adversely affect the powered devices in any way. The line conditioner function in UPS often serves as an additional component of normal operations, dampening surges and dips in utility power automatically.

If you ever see an exam question about the expected duration of UPS power, the answer will be, "UPS should last long enough for graceful shutdown of affected systems." Battery backup should only be relied on to provide immediate and near-term power supply. Any power interruption for a longer period should be provided by other systems.

Short-term contingency power can be provided by generators. For the cloud datacenter, sufficient generator power is necessary for all critical systems and infrastructure, including HVAC and emergency lighting as well as fire suppression systems. For the higher-tier centers, redundant power is necessary, duplicating the minimum power required to ensure uninterrupted critical operations.

Generators that supply close to immediate power when utility electricity is interrupted have automatic transfer switches. Transfer switches sense when the utility provision fails, break the connection to the utility, start the generator, and provide generator power to the facility. An automatic transfer switch is *not* a viable replacement for a UPS, and the two should be used in conjunction, not in lieu of each other. Ideally, the generator and transfer switch should be rated to successfully provide sufficient power well within the duration of expected battery life of the UPS. Realistically, generators with transfer switches can be expected to provide power in less than a minute from loss of utility power, some in as little as 10 seconds.

Generators need fuel; this is usually gasoline, diesel, natural gas, or propane. Appropriate storage and supply of fuel should also be described and included in the BC/DR plan. As fuel is flammable, health and human safety concerns must be addressed in the storage and supply designs. For all datacenters, a minimum of at least 12 hours of fuel for all generators, powering all critical functions, must be available. Resupply of additional fuel should be scheduled and performed within those 12 hours. Supply contracts and appropriate notification information for the supplier should be included in the BC/DR plan and procedure checklists. For BC/DR purposes, the plan should anticipate at least 72 hours of generator operation before other alternatives are available.

Gasoline and diesel spoil. If your generators use these types of fuel, the plan must also include tasking and contracts for regular resupply and refresh within the spoilage period.

All fuel storage should be in secure containers and locations. Fuel and generators should be far removed from the path of vehicles, ideally outside normal traffic areas (with a provision made for secure vehicle access for resupply purposes).

Testing

Much like having backups without trying to restore, or having logs without doing log review and analysis, having a BC/DR plan is close to useless unless it is tested on a regular basis. Because testing the BC/DR will necessarily cause interruption to production, different forms of testing can be utilized for different purposes, adjusting the operational impact while achieving specific goals. Testing methods you should be familiar with include these:

Tabletop Testing   The essential participants (those who will take part in actual BC/DR activities and are formally tasked with such responsibilities) work together at a scheduled time (either together in a single room or remotely via some communication capability) to describe how they would perform their tasks in a given BC/DR scenario. This is the InfoSec equivalent of role-playing games, and it has the least impact on production of the testing alternatives.

Dry Run   The organization as a whole takes part in a scenario at a scheduled time, describing their responses during the test and performing some minimal actions (for instance, perhaps running the notification call tree to ensure all contact information is current), but without performing all the actual tasks. This has more impact on productivity than tabletop testing.

Full Test   The entire organization takes part in an unscheduled, unannounced practice scenario, performing their full BC/DR activities. As this could include system failover and facility evacuation, this test is the most useful for detecting shortcomings in the plan, but it has the greatest impact (to the extent it can cause a full, genuine interruption of service) on productivity.

In all forms of testing, it behooves the organization to use moderators. These personnel will act as guides and monitors of the response activity, provide scenario inputs to heighten realism and introduce some element of chaos (to simulate unplanned deviations from the procedures due to potential effects of the event and disaster), and document performance and any plan shortcomings. The moderators should not be tasked with BC/DR response activities for actual situations. Anyone with formal tasking should be a participant in the test. It might be useful to employ external consultants to serve as moderators so that all organizational personnel can take part in the exercise.

Summary

In this chapter, we've reviewed several essential elements of operations management for cloud datacenters. We discussed the importance of monitoring system and component performance, performing routine maintenance (to include patching), and certain risks and benefits associated with each. Issues related to environmental conditions such as temperature, humidity, and backup power supply were included. We also detailed specific approaches and methods for BC/DR planning and testing.

Exam Essentials

Understand systems and component monitoring.   Make sure you are familiar with the importance and purpose of monitoring aspects of all infrastructure, hardware, software, and media in the datacenter, including:

- Temperature
- Humidity
- Event logging

Have a thorough understanding of maintenance strategies and procedures. These strategies and procedures include maintenance mode versus normal operations, the process for conducting updates and upgrades, and the risks and benefits of manual versus automated patch management.

Know the purpose and general method of change management. Know the purpose and general method of CM. Understand the composition of the CMB and how it functions.

Understand all aspects of BC/DR strategy, planning, and testing. Focus on the BC/DR strategy, planning, and testing especially as it pertains to a cloud datacenter. Know about backup power considerations and methods for testing BC/DR plan efficacy.

Written Labs

1. Do a web search for power generators suitable for commercial use. Find at least three.

2. Using the ASHRAE standards, determine the suitability of each generator for a cloud datacenter operating modern IT equipment. The specific load and capacity of the datacenter can be of your own choosing. Be sure to state any assumptions and simulated input.

3. In a short paper (less than one page), compare and contrast the three generators that you found in your first lab. Include in your rationale (as a minimum) load capacity, price, and fuel consumption.

Review Questions

You can find the answers in Appendix A.

1. Which form of BC/DR testing has the most impact on operations?
   A. Tabletop
   B. Dry run
   C. Full test
   D. Structured test

2. Which form of BC/DR testing has the least impact on operations?
   A. Tabletop
   B. Dry run
   C. Full test
   D. Structured test

3. Which characteristic of liquid propane increases its desirability as a fuel for backup generators?
   A. Burn rate
   B. Price
   C. Does not spoil
   D. Flavor

4. How often should the CMB meet?
   A. Whenever regulations dictate
   B. Often enough to address organizational needs and attenuate frustration with delay
   C. Every week
   D. Annually

5. Adhering to ASHRAE standards for humidity can reduce the possibility of _____.
   A. Breach
   B. Static discharge
   C. Theft
   D. Inversion

6. A UPS should have enough power to last how long?
   A. 12 hours
   B. 10 minutes
   C. One day
   D. Long enough for graceful shutdown

7. A generator transfer switch should bring backup power online within what time frame?

  A. 10 seconds

  B. Before the recovery point objective is reached

  C. Before the UPS duration is exceeded

  D. Three days

8. Which characteristic of automated patching makes it attractive?

  A. Cost

  B. Speed

  C. Noise reduction

  D. Capability to recognize problems quickly

9. Which tool can reduce confusion and misunderstanding during a BC/DR response?

  A. Flashlight

  B. Controls matrix

  C. Checklist

  D. Call tree

10. When deciding whether to apply specific updates, it is best to follow _____, in order to demonstrate due care.

  A. Regulations

  B. Vendor guidance

  C. Internal policy

  D. Competitors' actions

11. The CMB should include representations from all of the following offices except:

  A. Regulators

  B. IT department

  C. Security office

  D. Management

12. For performance purposes, OS monitoring should include all of the following except:

  A. Disk space

  B. Disk I/O usage

  C. CPU usage

  D. Print spooling

13. Maintenance mode requires all of these actions except:

  A. Remove all active production instances

  B. Initiate enhanced security controls

  C. Prevent new logins

  D. Ensure logging continues

14. What is one of the reasons a baseline might be changed?

   A. Numerous change requests

   B. Power fluctuation

   C. To reduce redundancy

   D. Natural disaster

15. In addition to battery backup, a UPS can offer which capability?

   A. Communication redundancy

   B. Line conditioning

   C. Breach alert

   D. Confidentiality

16. Deviations from the baseline should be investigated and _____.

   A. Documented

   B. Enforced

   C. Revealed

   D. Encouraged

17. The baseline should cover which of the following?

   A. As many systems throughout the organization as possible

   B. Data breach alerting and reporting

   C. A process for version control

   D. All regulatory compliance requirements

18. A localized incident or disaster can be addressed in a cost-effective manner by using which of the following?

   A. UPS

   B. Generators

   C. Joint operating agreements

   D. Strict adherence to applicable regulations

19. Generator fuel storage for a cloud datacenter should last for how long, at a minimum?

   A. 10 minutes

   B. Three days

   C. Indefinitely

   D. 12 hours

20. The BC/DR kit should include all of the following except:

   A. Flashlight

   B. Documentation equipment

   C. Hard drives

   D. Annotated asset inventory

Chapter

10

Legal and Compliance
Part 1

THE OBJECTIVE OF THIS CHAPTER IS TO ACQUAINT THE READER WITH THE FOLLOWING CONCEPTS:

✓ **Domain 2: Cloud Data Security**

  ▪ E. Design and Implement Relevant Jurisdictional Data Protections for Personally Identifiable Information (PII)

    ▪ E.1 Data Privacy Acts

    ▪ E.5 Application of Defined Controls for PII

  ▪ H. Design and Implement Auditability, Traceability and Accountability of Data Events

    ▪ H.5. Chain of Custody and Non-repudiation

✓ **Domain 5: Operations**

  ▪ J. Understand the Collection, Acquisition and Preservation of Digital Evidence

    ▪ J.1. Proper Methodologies for Forensic Collection of Data

    ▪ J.2. Evidence Management

✓ **Domain 6: Legal and Compliance**

  ▪ A. Understand Legal Requirements and Unique Risks within the Cloud Environment

    ▪ A.1. International Legislation Conflicts

    ▪ A.2. Appraisal of Legal Risks Specific to Cloud Computing

    ▪ A.4. eDiscovery

    ▪ A.5. Forensics Requirements

  ▪ B. Understand Privacy Issues, Including Jurisdictional Variation

    ▪ B.1. Difference between Contractual and Regulated PII

    ▪ B.2. Country-Specific Legislation Related to PII/Data Privacy

The Legal and Compliance domain can be every bit as confusing and difficult to understand as some of the technology discussed throughout this book. International courts and tribunals weigh in on laws and regulations concerning what a global network operating behind the scenes is. There is also no shortage of laws, regulations, and standards that need to be complied with. The combination of all these factors provides a rich arena for our discussion.

It is important to remember that the nature of cloud computing lends itself to resource sharing based on demand as opposed to location. Therefore, datacenters located around the world store cloud data and run applications from multiple sources simultaneously. This presents challenges with security and privacy issues due to the complexity of local and international laws, regulations, and guidelines. In this chapter, we will attempt to provide a background and review of the important concepts, laws, regulations, and standards so that the CCSP candidate can provide sound advice and guidance when navigating these complex waters.

Legal Requirements and Unique Risks in the Cloud Environment

As one might imagine, the list of U.S. and international laws, regulations, and standards is quite lengthy and complex. The global economy spans multiple continents, many nation-states, and government entities. From the Asia Pacific region to Australia and New Zealand, the European Union (EU), Eastern bloc countries, and South America, a wide range of laws, regulations, and rules govern both data privacy and security safeguards. In this section, we will begin by exploring some fundamental legal concepts to help the CCSP candidate prepare for working in this complex global environment. To make matters even more concerning, there is no shortage of change and uncertainty. With the recent exit of Britain from the EU and the latest in case law changing Safe Harbor statues for U.S. companies, the years ahead will be full of challenges in this ever-expanding global economy.

Legal Concepts

Let's begin our discussion with some basic legal concepts that can be applied both in the United States and internationally. These terms form the foundation of knowledge that allows us to operate cloud activities across international borders with some semblance of consistency and fairness. We like to compare it to the way we use electricity. The only reason you can buy a $12 toaster in the United States, travel to China (most of China), plug it in, and it works, is because of standards or consistent rules for operating. These same principles, while just as complex, are what allow us to provide IaaS, PaaS, and SaaS across international boundaries, and it is important for the CCSP candidate to understand and assimilate them.

What follows in this section is a discussion of legal terms that are generally appropriate in both the United States and abroad. Legal scholars all over the world, with the exception of some third-world and Asiatic countries, subscribe to these ideas and principles even though they may be interpreted somewhat differently in their respective jurisdictions. As a result, the CCSP candidate should be aware and have a fundamental understanding of each in order to provide sage counsel to customers and to comprehend the risks of doing business in the global world of cloud computing.

There are three general bodies of law in the United States: criminal law, civil law, and administrative law (see Figure 10.1). There is another specific specialized body of law, unique to the military, known as the Uniform Code of Military Justice (UCMJ). If your organization is not involved directly in military work, the UCMJ does not usually affect you, so we won't dwell on that topic, but we'll address the other three. We're also going to examine the concept of intellectual property and the legal protections available for owners of this type of asset. In addition, we'll discuss the concepts of Doctrine of the Proper Law and Restatement (Second) Conflict of Law, which are common concepts used around the world.

FIGURE 10.1   Legal Foundations

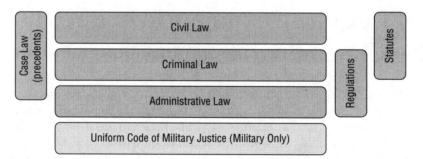

Criminal Law

Criminal law involves all legal matters where the government is in conflict with any person, group, or organization that violates statutes. Statutes (state and federal) are legislated by lawmakers. They are rules that define conduct prohibited by the government and are designed to provide for the safety and well-being of the public. One example is traffic laws, which when broken result in court appearances, fines, and so on. Other more obvious examples are robbery, theft, and murder.

Criminal law includes the federal court system and the various state courts. Under criminal law, punishments can include monetary fines, imprisonment, and even death. Enforcement of criminal law is called prosecution. Only the government can conduct law enforcement activity and prosecutions.

For the security practitioner, it is important to keep in mind that privacy violations around the world are in some cases seen as criminal violations. For instance, if certain privacy standards and procedures are not adequately followed—say, in the EU—you can be prosecuted for criminal violations, in addition to whatever damages result from the data breach.

State Laws

State laws are those that we typically think of on a day-to-day basis. Speed limits, state tax laws, the criminal code, and so on are all examples of laws enacted by a state legislature as opposed to those enacted at the national or federal level. Federal laws, however, often supersede state laws, particularly regarding the nature of interstate commerce. For instance, while many states have laws outlining how electronic medical records should be handled, federal legislation is usually more comprehensive and therefore followed. In some cases, such as California, the state law may in fact be more stringent, in which case it is followed. The general rule is that the most stringent of the laws apply to any situation unless there are other compelling reasons such as strict jurisdiction.

The United States is divided into 50 member entities that are referred to as *states*. Outside of the United States, most other countries use the word *state* as a synonym for *country*, and their member entities are known as *counties*, *jurisdictions*, *zones*, or a variety of other terms. It is important to keep this distinction in mind regarding the meaning of the word *state* when dealing with multiple nations.

Federal Laws

Unlike state laws, whose jurisdictions stop at the state line, federal laws govern the entire country. Examples are those against kidnapping and bank robbery. If a person were to rob a bank, which is a federally licensed institution, they would in fact be committing a federal crime and therefore be subject to federal pursuit, prosecution, and punishment. Often, states will handle these types of cases, as there are usually existing state laws in place as well. Generally, the issues of jurisdiction and subsequent prosecution are worked out in advance between law enforcement and court jurisdictional bodies.

As of 2005, the U.S. Department of Justice clarified that anyone who "knowingly" violates HIPAA regulations can face fines but also up to one year in jail. Although not a testing requirement, it may be interesting for you to know that the Final Omnibus Rule of March 2013 states that a Tier 3 criminal violation carries a potential 10-year imprisonment penalty. Specifically, it states "if the offense is committed with intent to sell, transfer, or use individually identifiable health information for commercial advantage, personal gain, or malicious harm, be fined not more than $250,000, imprisoned not more than 10 years, or both." See https://www.law.cornell.edu/uscode/text/42/1320d-6.

Civil Law

Civil law is the body of law, statutes, and so on that deals with personal and community-based law such as marriage and divorce as opposed to criminal or military law. It is the set of rules that govern private citizens and their disputes. As opposed to criminal law, the parties involved in civil law matters are strictly private entities, including individuals, groups, and organizations.

Typical examples of civil law cases are disputes (in the United States) over property boundaries, mineral rights, and marital divorce. Civil cases are called lawsuits or litigation. Punitive measures for civil cases can include restitution of monetary damages or requirement to perform actions (usually in response to a breach-of-contract case, which we'll address later in this section), but not imprisonment or death.

Contracts

A contract is an agreement between parties to engage in some specified activity, usually for mutual benefit. The contract between the cloud customer and cloud provider is a perfect example: in that contract, the cloud customer agrees to give the cloud provider money, and, in exchange, the cloud provider agrees to give the cloud customer some services. The contract often includes a finite duration for which the contract is in effect, a list of parties involved, the means for dispute resolution, and the jurisdiction's laws under which the contract will be subject (a physical place or government, such as "the state of Wisconsin," or "the city of Milwaukee, in the state of Wisconsin, in the United States").

Disputes arise from failure to perform according to activity specified in the contract, which is called a *breach*. In the event of a breach, a party to the contract can sue the others in order to get court-ordered relief in the form of money or other considerations (such as property, or the court forcing the breaching party to perform the activity that both parties agreed to in the first place).

Contract law applies to contractual items the CCSP candidate should be familiar with such as

- Service-level agreements (SLAs)
- Privacy-level agreements (PLAs)
- Operational-level agreement (OLAs)
- Payment Card Industry Data Security Standards (PCI DSS) contracts

A CCSP should be prepared to deal with exposure to these types of contracts in a cloud environment and/or with cloud customers. Furthermore, it is important to understand the distinctions regarding consequences and ramifications for violations of such contracts. Contract disputes are generally handled in civil court and involve reparative restitution in the event of a loss suffered by one party or the other, such as in the case of a provider failing to adequately meet the service levels in a cloud agreement.

Tort Law

Tort law refers to the body of rights, obligations, and remedies that set out reliefs for persons who have been harmed as a result of wrongful acts by others. Tort law and case precedence is what guides the courts in the handling of these civil cases whereby relief of some sort is sought. Tort law seeks to provide for the compensation of victims for injuries suffered at the hand of others by shifting the costs related to those injuries to the person who caused them. In addition, it acts as a deterrent to careless and risky behavior and provides for a legal remedy to rights that have been violated.

 Common law is the existing set of rulings and decisions made by courts, informed by cultural mores and legislation. These create *precedents*, which each party will cite in court as a means to sway the court to their own side of a case.

Administrative Law

The other body of law that affects most people is administrative law—laws not created by legislatures, but by executive decision and function. Many federal agencies can create, monitor, and enforce their own administrative law. These agencies have their own lawmaking departments, law enforcement personnel, courts, and judges that belong exclusively to those specific agencies. For instance, federal tax law is administered by the IRS, which creates those laws; investigates and enforces them with IRS agents; and decides outcomes in cases tried by lawyers and adjudicated by judges both in the employ of the IRS.

Intellectual Property

Intellectual property is a term describing intangible assets that are the property of the mind, also known as ideas. In the United States, courts recognize intellectual property rights, and there are a great many ways to protect these assets. We'll address four in this book: copyrights, trademarks, patents, and trade secrets.

Copyrights

Copyrights protect expressions of ideas. Ideas can be expressed through artistic works, such as books, plays, movies, songs, video games, and so on. They can also be expressed in commercial endeavors. For instance, software is protected by copyright.

In the United States, someone who creates an expression of an idea is automatically granted the copyright for that work. The creator of the asset does not have to do anything to earn or achieve a copyright. However, there are some elements that can affect the creator's ability to enforce their rights to that work. For instance, if the creator works for a person or company that hired them specifically to create that work, the intellectual property belongs to the employer. This is called "work for hire." An example would be a software programmer working for a video game company; all work product created by the programmer while in the company's employ belongs to the company, not to the programmer.

Also, while no action is required by the creator of a copyrighted work in order to gain a copyright, the creator may want to take some action to ensure their rights to that work will be recognized and not subject to dispute. For instance, it is possible to register this form of intellectual property with the U.S. Copyright Office (https://www.copyright.gov/) in order to have an official record of the date the work was created and who created it. That way, if anyone else tries to lay claim to that work or use it without permission, it will be easy for the original creator to prove their ownership in court.

In the United States, copyrights last for a period of 70–125 years after the death of the original creator, depending on the nature of how the intellectual property was created (that is, whether it was a work for hire, a group or individual effort, and so forth).

Trademarks

Trademark protection is for intellectual property used to immediately identify a brand. This usually includes logos or short audio tones (think of the three-note NBC chime). Trademarks can be issued by a state government or the U.S. Patent and Trademark Office (https://www.uspto.gov/). Trademarks last for as long as the property they protect is still being used commercially. This means they can sometimes be considered perpetual.

Patents

Patents protect formulas, processes, patterns, inventions, and plants.

For clarification, the term *plants* means the leafy, green things that grow out of the ground, not manufacturing facilities. Yes, you can patent a plant.

Here are examples of things that might be patented:

- The formula for a new pharmaceutical drug
- A smelting process for a new metallic alloy
- A fabric or textile pattern
- A new spice that can be grown in the soil, spliced together from cuttings of other vegetative growths
- A better mousetrap

To get patent protection for intellectual property, the prospective owner must submit an application to the U.S. Patent and Trademark Office, including enough detail to demonstrate the property is unique, novel, and useful. Patents last for 20 years from the date the application was submitted, with a few exceptions. Owning a patent for a specific intellectual property asset prevents anyone else from using that asset without the owner's permission.

Trade Secrets

The court acknowledges the ownership of private business material, such as client lists, processes, recipes, and so forth. This kind of intellectual property is known as a "trade secret." Perhaps the most glamorized trade secret in the popular culture is the formula for Coca-Cola. Intellectual property retains trade secret protection for as long as the business continues efforts to use it in commercial enterprise and maintains efforts to prevent its disclosure. In this regard, it can be viewed as a perpetual ownership right.

Enforcement of Intellectual Property Rights

While the courts (and the government) acknowledge ownership of property rights, it is often up to the owners to enforce these rights. For instance, if a company owns a patent on, say, a drug formula and someone else infringes on that patent by producing and selling a drug with the same formula, it is up to the aggrieved party, the original patent owner, to bring a civil suit against the copycat.

There are some exceptions, and the way these situations play out can often involve criminal actions as well. For instance, someone who steals intellectual property can be prosecuted—not for infringing on the property rights, but for theft (this has happened with the formula for Coca-Cola a number of times over the years). Similar results can occur when someone infringes on copyrighted material: the copyright holder can enforce their rights in civil court, but the government might prosecute the crimes of theft, piracy, or illegal trade.

Doctrine of the Proper Law

The *Doctrine of the Proper Law* is a term used to describe the processes associated with determining what legal jurisdiction will hear a dispute when one occurs. An example would be when multiple jurisdictions are involved and courts must decide where a case must be heard and decided.

Let's explore such a case for cloud computing. Say that a cloud provider with datacenters located in the United States, Ireland, and South America has had an extended outage that impacted customers' e-commerce sites, and those customers are suing for damages. Data for customers was stored in Ireland, the payment processing occurred in the United States, and the products were delivered from a warehouse in South America. While the company is based in Brussels, customers in three different countries are suing them. The Doctrine of the Proper Law is used to guide courts in deciding which of the jurisdictions involved is closest to the actual damages and to determine where the proper jurisdiction in the case lies. As a result, these cases can be quite complex when dealing with global cloud service providers.

Restatement (Second) Conflict of Law

The *Restatement (Second) Conflict of Law* refers to a collation of developments in common law that help the courts stay up with changes. Many states have conflicting laws, and judges use these *restatements* to assist them in determining which laws should apply when conflicts occur. Whichever state's laws fit the situation the best or are the most restrictive are what ultimately influence the decisions. Additionally, these court decisions are influenced by common law, which evolves over time as new precedents are set, and they, in turn, influence the evolution of the restatement.

U.S. Laws

In this section, we describe and discuss U.S. laws with the largest impact on cloud computing and with which the CCSP should be familiar. While there are emerging state laws that may or may not supersede these, we will focus on U.S. federal laws as they apply to cloud computing. Table 10.1 gives an overview of the most prominent U.S. laws and regulations.

TABLE 10.1   Important U.S. laws and regulations

Name	Purpose	Administrators	Enforcers
The Electronic Communication Privacy Act (ECPA)	Enhance laws restricting the government from putting wire taps on phone calls, updating them to include electronic communication in the form of data.	*	*
The Stored Communications Act (SCA, Title II of the Electronic Communications Privacy Act)	Restrict government from forcing ISPs to disclose customer data the ISP might possess.	*	*
Graham-Leach-Bliley Act (GLBA)	Allow banks to merge with and own insurance companies. Included in the law were stipulations that customer account information be kept secure and private, and that customers be allowed to opt out of any information-sharing arrangements the bank or insurer might engage in.	FDIC, FFIEC	FDIC and DFI
Sarbanes-Oxley Act (SOX)	Increase transparency into publicly traded corporations' financial activities. Includes provisions for securing data and expressly names the traits of confidentiality, integrity, and availability.	SEC	SEC
Health Insurance Portability and Accountability Act (HIPAA)	Protect patient records and data, known as electronic protected health information (ePHI).	DHHS	OCR
Family Educational Rights and Privacy Act (FERPA)	Prevent academic institutions from sharing student data with anyone other than parents of students (up to age 18) or the students (after age 18).	Department of Education	Department of Education (Family Policy Compliance Office)
The Digital Millennium Copyright Act (DMCA)	Update copyright provisions to protect owned data in an Internet-enabled world. Makes cracking of access controls on copyrighted media a crime, and enables copyright holders to require any site on the Internet to remove content that may belong to the copyright holder.	**	**

* The ECPA (and its subordinate parts, including the SCA) prevents the government from surveilling civilians. Ostensibly, the government would also be the entity enforcing and administering this law, and government law enforcement agencies would be the entities most likely to violate the law in the course of their activities. The reader can readily see the issues that might arise from this circular construct.

** The DMCA allows for aggrieved parties to bring civil suits to protect their interests, but it also has a provision that criminalizes a successful breach of access controls on copyrighted material.

You may not have to have a detailed knowledge of each of these laws and regulations, but you should be able to easily identify them and give a brief explanation of what they are about and where they fit into the realm of cloud computing. This chapter will not explore ECPA, FERPA, and DMCA in more detail, but the following sections will take a closer look at SCA, HIPAA, GLBA, and SOX.

Stored Communication Act (18 U.S.C. Chapter 121 §§ 2701–2712 [SCA])

Enacted as part of Title II of the Electronic Communications Privacy Act of 1986 (ECPA), the SCA addresses both voluntary and compelled disclosure of *stored wire and electronic communications and transactional records* held by third parties. It further provides for privacy protection regarding certain electronic communications and computing services from unauthorized access or interception by government entities. The ECPA was designed as an extension of the protections previously offered by the Computer Fraud and Abuse Act (CFAA) of 1986, and as a means to enhance and update earlier "wire tap" statutes.

New Net

The Internet as we know it today is completely different from the Internet of 1986, when the SCA was enacted. In 1986, most people had not even heard of the Internet. In addition, those who had were using 110- and 300-baud modems on dial-up connections mostly at colleges and universities or military installations. AOL had not been invented yet, and some modems still used the old acoustic handset coupler to make connections. TCP/IP, the protocol of the Internet itself, had yet to be fully embraced and was still in its infancy.

Because the Internet is nothing like it was in 1986, the way we interact and use services on the network today is very different. We have ubiquitous broadband access and have even begun shifting our video watching habits to that of streaming services. As a result, many security organizations have been working for years to amend the legislation to meet not only our current needs, but also those of the future.

Health Insurance Portability and Accountability Act of 1996 (HIPAA)

The federal Health Insurance Portability and Accountability Act (HIPAA), enacted in 1996, is a set of federal laws governing the handling of personal health information (PHI). The primary purpose of the law when it was enacted was to make it easier for people to keep health insurance policies, protect the confidentiality and security of their healthcare information, and help the healthcare industry control administrative costs. However, after a decade of changes, it is more about the adoption of national standards for electronic healthcare transactions and national identifiers for providers, health plans, and employers. PHI, or more accurately electronic protected health information (ePHI), can be stored via cloud computing but must have adequate security and privacy protections in place.

The Office for Civil Rights (OCR) is the federal enforcement arm of the Department of Health and Human Services (DHHS). They conduct audits, or subcontract to other third-party companies to perform such audits, and are responsible for reporting to DHHS any audit findings, policy violations, unreported breaches, and so on. DHHS then has the authority to impose fines, restrictions, or remedial requirements based on findings.

For many years, HIPAA was thought to be a *paper tiger*; a law with no teeth. However, after the passage of the HITECH act in 2010, DHHS, through its enforcement arm, the OCR and through their subcontractors, has been increasing the number of audits performed each year and most recently flattened the standards so that all rules that apply to *covered entities* now apply to subcontractors known as *business associates*. This means almost everyone involved with the provision of healthcare-related services must comply with the same set of rules.

The OCR audit results are pushed up to DHHS, who then makes a determination of whether action should be taken. Audit results stemming from *willful neglect* can even result in treble fines in certain circumstances. The fines are now being used to fund more audits in the future, thereby putting some very sharp teeth into the paper tiger's mouth.

There is nothing in the HIPAA regulations that specifically addresses cloud computing, but if cloud services are used they must meet the same criteria as any other systems.

HIPAA, the Privacy Rule, and the Security Rule

When HIPAA first passed in the 1990s (or back before the turn of the century, as I like to say), privacy of patient information was the primary concern. The Internet was still in its infancy and no one had even thought of a data breach of PHI, because it had never happened. The first primary regulation promulgated by the Department of Health and Human Services (DHHS) was the Privacy Rule. It contained language specific to maintaining the privacy of patient information as it was traditionally stored and used, on paper. It was also one of the first regulations in the United States to specifically address privacy.

With the explosion of networking, digital storage and the Internet came the Security Rule, followed by the Health Information Technology for Economic and Clinical Health (HITECH) Act of 2009, which provided financial incentives for medical practices and hospitals to convert paper record-keeping systems to digital. Because data breaches began to happen more and more often, this was an attempt to address issues surrounding this explosion in electronic digital storage of medical information while cloud computing was still in its infancy.

The Security Rule has attempted to address the problems encountered with this explosion of digital patient and medical records information processing and storage. As a result, there are now both a Privacy Rule and a Security Rule. While these most recent changes have been long in coming and have finally woken the sleeping giant of healthcare, it is again one more example of how people in the United States seem to see security and privacy as separate, whereas most of the EU and the rest of the world see them as the same. For a free copy of the documents discussed here, go to www.hhs.gov/hipaa/for-professionals.

Gramm-Leach-Bliley Act (GLBA)

The Gramm-Leach-Bliley Act (GLBA), also known as the Financial Services Modernization Act of 1999, was created to allow banks and financial institutions to merge. Lawmakers were wary of customer concerns that this type of consolidation might detract from individual privacy, so GLBA also includes a great many provisions specifying the kinds of protections and controls that financial institutions are required to use for securing customers' account information. For example, it requires all financial institutions to have a written information security plan (ISP), and later revisions of FDIC guidance require that an information security officer (ISO) be named and given adequate resources in order to implement the ISP.

 In conjunction with the Federal Deposit Insurance Corporation (FDIC), most states call their Department of Financial Institutions "the DFI" (although some states have other names for them).

For more information on GLBA, visit `https://www.fdic.gov/regulations/compliance/manual/8/VIII-1.1.pdf`.

Sarbanes-Oxley Act (SOX)

At the latter part of the last century, a number of large companies experienced total and unexpected financial collapse because of fraudulent accounting practices, poor audit practices, inadequate financial controls, and poor oversight by governing boards of directors. Some of the companies involved are now a distant memory (Enron, WorldCom, and Peregrine Systems, for example). As a result, in 2002 the Sarbanes-Oxley Act (SOX) was enacted as an attempt to prevent these kinds of poor practices and fraudulent activities from occurring in the future. Originally called the Public Company Accounting Reform and Investor Protection Act, it is commonly referred to as Sarbanes-Oxley, in honor of the two men who authored the legislation, Sen. Paul Sarbanes (D-MD) and Rep. Michael Oxley (R-OH), and it applies to all publicly traded corporations.

An important concept we will discuss later in this chapter and the next is the issue of auditor independence. Part of the problem with these failed companies was that the internal employees were encouraged and in fact rewarded for hiding accounting problems from the organization, regulators, and investors. As a result, the boards of directors of these companies pleaded ignorance of issues that resulted in their companies failing. This resulted in several executives' prosecution for negligence, and the legislative outcome was increased oversight and responsibility for board members. In addition, to prevent cover-ups in the future, the idea of external and independent auditors became a standard practice for publicly traded companies. Executives can no longer hide behind an excuse of ignorance. They have become culpable for any financial wrongdoings perpetrated by their companies.

The Securities and Exchange Commission (SEC) is the organization responsible for establishing standards and guidelines and conducting audits and imposing subsequent fines should any be required.

Testing of SOX controls has become a very lucrative business for accounting firms in recent years. Accounting controls designed to meet the requirements of SOX must be conducted on a strict schedule, and having a control fail or a SOX audit fail is a very bad thing—it could not only result in fines but could potentially have an impact on the stock price of the company in question. Therefore, publicly traded companies take this work very seriously and go to great lengths to ensure compliance.

If you are interested in learning more about the Sarbanes-Oxley Act, visit https://www.sec.gov/about/laws/soa2002.pdf.

International Laws

International laws determine how to settle disputes and manage relationships between countries. These include the following:

- Conventions establishing rules expressly recognized by member countries (like the Geneva Convention regarding the treatment of prisoners of war)

- Customs as they are practiced in a country and accepted as law

- General principles of law recognized by civilized nations (such as the right to a trial of some kind if accused)

- Judicial decisions or precedent as it has developed over time in a particular instance

- Trade regulations, including import agreements, tariff structures, and so forth

- Treaties, which can be created to solve a dispute (such as a war) or to create alliances

Laws, Frameworks, and Standards Around the World

Sovereign countries also have their own laws, applicable to their own jurisdictions. The *jurisdiction* is the land and people belonging to that country. The effects of a country's law does not cease at its borders, though. If a citizen from another country, or even one of the country's citizens operating outside that country, breaks that country's law, they can still be subject to prosecution and punishment by that country. For instance, a hacker that uses the Internet to attack a target in another country could be subject to that country's computer security laws. The hacker might be extradited (forcibly apprehended in their own country and transported to the country where the law was broken) to face trial.

🌐 Real World Scenario

Breaking the Law Is Always a Gamble

Sometimes, what is against the law in one jurisdiction is not against the law in another. In those circumstances, extradition can be difficult. If the person's actions are not illegal in their home nation and another nation wants to arrest them and bring them to trial, the home nation might refuse any such requests.

This was the case for David Carruthers, the CEO of a British-based online gambling company. In 2006, Carruthers was arrested by federal agents in the United States while he was changing planes in Dallas, between a flight from the UK and a flight to Costa Rica. The U.S. government charged Carruthers with "racketeering," stemming from the use of his company's services by U.S. citizens engaging in online gambling.

Online gambling, while illegal in the United States, is not illegal in the UK or Costa Rica, nor in many other parts of the world. It would have been difficult for the United States to extradite Carruthers from either the UK or Costa Rica because of this difference in the laws of the various countries, so federal agents waited until he was in the jurisdiction of the United States—the moment his plane touched down.

Carruthers served 33 months in prison.

It's important to understand the distinctions of laws and principles of various nations because cloud providers and customers might be operating in many different jurisdictions. The cloud is not limited to the borders of any given country.

While many of the legal definitions and principles in the United States apply to other parts of the world, there are some significant differences. The European Union (EU) has for many years taken a much stronger stance on privacy than the United States. In fact, the EU treats personal privacy protections for data in electronic form as a human right, while the United States has no formal, unified personal privacy law. Instead, the United States has certain laws (discussed in the previous sections) that deal with personal privacy for people who engage in activities in specific industries and sectors, such as financial services, medical care, education, and so forth. The EU, on the other hand, is well known for its "opt-in" policies versus the "opt-out" motif in the United States. This means that in the EU, generally speaking, in order for someone to access or use an individual's personal data or private information, that individual must first grant their permission, effectively opting in to that specific instance of sharing information. In the United States, the usual statutory model is just the opposite, wherein individuals must notify any party that the individual has shared information with that the data cannot thereafter be shared outside the limits of that initial agreement.

To clarify, let's use the example of a bank account. When a person goes to the bank and opens an account, the bank asks for a set of personal information, such as the person's name, Social Security number, home address, and so on. The person is granting the bank access to that information voluntarily, sharing it with the bank in order to get a bank account. In the United States, the bank is then required (by GLBA) to ask the person if they want to opt out of any additional information-sharing activity. If the person doesn't want the bank to share that data with any other entity (for instance, the bank might sell that information to the marketing department of other businesses), the person must give the bank a written statement declaring that the person is opting out. If the person does not opt out, then the bank is free to share that information however they see fit. GLBA requires that the bank ask the person, in writing, in hard copy, if the person wants to opt out of any data-sharing activity, at least once a year for every year that bank account stays open. In the EU, on the other hand, if a person was to open a bank account, the bank must ask the person if the person would allow the bank to share the person's personal data with any other entity. The bank would not be allowed, by law, to share any of that person's data until and unless the person grants explicit permission to the bank to do so.

Another important concept to consider in dealing with various countries is their approaches to PII. Information that can be used to identify an individual is often referred to in the industry as *personally identifiable information (PII)*. It can include the name and address of the individual. In the EU, PII also includes a person's cell phone number. The EU passed the EU Data Directive and the more recent Privacy Regulation to regulate PII. Many countries use these as a basic model for their own laws. Table 10.2 provides an overview of various countries and how their laws relate to the Data Directive and Privacy Regulation. The Data Directive and Privacy Regulation and the specific approaches different countries have to PII will be explored in more detail in the sections that follow.

TABLE 10.2 Countries and their laws relating to the EU Data Directive and Privacy Regulation

Nation	Federal PII Law that complies with the EU Data Directive and Privacy Regulation	Notes
The EU	Yes	28 member states (countries) comprise the EU, with that number dropping to 27 in 2017–2018 when the UK formalizes leaving the union. The EU treats PII as a human right, with severely stringent protections for individuals.
United States	No	Personal privacy rights are often delineated in industry-specific laws (such as GLBA for financial services and HIPAA for medicine), but there is no overarching federal law ensuring individual personal privacy.

TABLE 10.2 Countries and their laws relating to the EU Data Directive and Privacy Regulation *(continued)*

Nation	Federal PII Law that complies with the EU Data Directive and Privacy Regulation	Notes
Australia and New Zealand	Yes	Laws in these countries conform to the EU policies.
Argentina	Yes	Local law is specifically based on the EU guidance.
EFTA	Yes	A four-member body that includes Switzerland, Norway, Iceland, and Lichtenstein. Swiss law, in particular, provides stringent privacy protections, particularly for banking information.
Israel	Yes	
Japan	Yes	
Canada	Yes	The Personal Information Protection and Electronic Documents Act (PIPEDA) conforms to the EU Data Directive and Privacy Regulation.

  Israel and Japan won't be discussed in more detail in this chapter, but for exam purposes it is important to remember that they also have personal privacy laws that are accepted by the EU for purposes of compliance with the Data Directive and Privacy Regulation.

The following sections sample some laws in other nations that have developed in response to privacy and data security concerns over the past 30 years. This should give the CCSP candidate a broader view of how the world perceives privacy and in particular some of the legal, regulatory, and operational challenges that come with working in a global environment.

EU Data Protection Directive 95/46 EC

The EU Data Protection Directive of 1995 (usually referred to as the "Data Directive") was the first major EU data privacy law. This overarching regulation describes the appropriate handling of personal and private information of all EU citizens. Any entity (be it a government agency, private company, or individual) gathering the PII of any citizen of the EU is subject to the Data Directive.

The Data Directive addresses individual personal privacy by codifying these seven principles:

Notice   The individual must be informed that personal information about them is being gathered or created.

Choice   Every individual can choose whether to disclose their personal information. No entity can gather or create personal information about an individual without that individual's explicit agreement.

Purpose   The individual must be told the specific use the information will be put to. This includes whether the data will be shared with any other entity.

Access   The individual is allowed to get copies of any of their own information held by any entity.

Integrity   The individual must be allowed to correct any of their own information if it is inaccurate.

Security   Any entity holding an individual's personal information is responsible for protecting that information and is ultimately liable for any unauthorized disclosure of that data.

Enforcement   All entities that have any personal data of any EU citizen understand that they are subject to enforcement actions by EU authorities.

This list largely conforms to a set of principles created by the Organisation for Economic Cooperation and Development (OECD). The OECD is a standards organization made up of representatives from many countries, and it publishes policy suggestions. Its standards are *not* legally binding and do not have the effect of a treaty or other law.

> This is an important distinction to be made: although the OECD's principles are not legally binding, the EU's Data Directive, which largely conforms to the OECD's principles, *is* legally binding.

In addition to these principles, the Data Directive also resulted in a principle unique to the EU: the "right to be forgotten." Under this principle, any individual can notify any entity that has PII for that individual and instruct that entity to delete and destroy all of that individual's PII in that entity's control. This is a very serious and powerful individual right, and compliance can be extremely difficult. Google disputed this principle when it was first proposed, claiming that the company would find it almost impossible to comply. The European Union High Court decided in favor of the right to be forgotten and against Google, and Google had to choose to accept compliance in order to operate in the EU.

Another major provision of the Data Directive was to prohibit any entity from collecting the PII of any EU citizen if that entity existed within the jurisdiction of a country that did not have a national law that explicitly supported all the provisions of the Data Directive. This meant, for instance, that any company in the United States would not be allowed to do business with EU citizens. The United States does not have a federal law that directly maps to the Data Directive.

The Europeans have a dim view of the ability of the United States to ensure the privacy of individuals. The Data Directive is a direct reflection of this attitude. And, in all fairness, the Europeans seem quite justified in their opinion, as the U.S. government has proven over a considerable period of time to be willing to collect information on all individuals (including citizens of the United States) without warrants or other legal justification. So the Data Directive can be seen as a law that expressly limits U.S. companies.

To allow some U.S.-based companies to operate legitimately inside the EU, the Data Directive included a set of *safe harbor* privacy rules designed to outline what American companies must do in order to comply with EU laws. These rules outlined the proper handling of storage and transmission of private information belonging to EU citizens.

The Safe Harbor provisions were as follows:

- Any U.S. company that wanted to collect EU citizen data must voluntarily agree to comply with the Data Directive.

- These companies had to sign up with a federal enforcement entity in the United States that would administer the program. For most companies, the Safe Harbor program was administered by the Department of Commerce (DoC). For the specific industries of airlines and shipping companies, the program was administered by the Department of Transportation (DoT).

- The companies had to agree to allow auditing and enforcement by the program administrators. For the DoC, the enforcement arm was the Federal Trade Commission (FTC), and the DoT enforced its program. Enforcement could include fines assessed for violations.

In May 2018, an update to the Data Directive will take effect; the new law is usually referred to as the "Privacy Regulation" or "Regulation," in context. The Privacy Regulation supersedes the Data Directive and ends the Safe Harbor program, replacing it with a new program known as Privacy Shield. As a result, the United States and the EU have been working on finalizing the new Privacy Shield Principles and framework. The Privacy Shield program will be much more stringent than Safe Harbor and includes some new provisions, including annual meetings of intelligence agency and law enforcement officials from the United States and EU to discuss policy and controls.

There is one final method that American companies can use if they want to have EU citizen PII and if they don't want to subscribe to Privacy Shield. They can create internal policies called "binding corporate rules" and "standard contractual clauses" that explicitly state full compliance with the Data Directive and Privacy Regulation. In this way, the company that chooses to use this method is basically stating their full agreement to be governed by the applicable EU laws. If a company chooses to use this method, however, it must first approach every individual EU country where the company wants to operate and have the government office responsible for oversight and enforcement of the Data Directive and Privacy Regulation accept and approve the company's policy.

A Brief History of the European Union (EU)

Commonly referred to as the EU, the European Union was initially formed in the early 1950s as part of the post–World War II recovery process. Until recently, it consisted of 28 nation-states, including the United Kingdom. Financial efforts eventually led to the creation and use of the euro as a common currency, even though several countries such as Britain continued to accept both local currency (the British pound) and the euro as legitimate forms of exchange.

In 2016, due to terror-related activities, immigration issues, and problems over fiscal management differences, Britain left the EU. This exit, known as Brexit (for British Exit), will no doubt have an evolving impact on the economies and data privacy rights, but the effects are still being determined. This is a situation worth watching closely, as any similar changes in the EU and the resultant changes in privacy and protection rules outlined in the rest of the chapter could easily result in radical changes for cloud providers and end users.

Both the Data Directive and the Privacy Regulation define roles for entities involved in the collection and creation of PII. It is important for the CCSP candidate to be familiar with these roles and how they apply to the relationship between cloud customers and providers.

Data Subject   The individual whom the PII refers to. A specific human being.

Data Controller   Any entity collecting or creating PII. In the cloud motif, the data controller is the cloud customer.

Data Processor   Any entity acting on behalf or at the behest of the data controller, performing any manipulation, storage, or transmission of the PII. In the cloud motif, the data processor is the cloud service provider.

Under the Data Directive and the Privacy Regulation, the data controller is ultimately responsible for *any* unauthorized disclosure of PII. That includes any malicious or negligent act on the part of the data processor. This is an extremely important point to understand. Legally, the data controller is responsible for all breaches, regardless of fault. To put this in perspective, let's say a cloud provider knowingly and willingly sold a cloud customer's data to another cloud customer. For purposes of liability, the cloud customer whose data was stolen would *still* be responsible for the breach, under the law, even though the customer did nothing wrong. The cloud customer might eventually be able to recover damages from the cloud provider in a civil suit, but the legal liability, including any initial legal costs for settling the breach, would be the customer's.

    Under the Data Directive and Privacy Regulation, PII is not limited to electronic data. It also covers any data stored in hard-copy form.

Australian Privacy Act of 1988

The Australian Privacy Act regulates the handling of personal information. It includes details regarding the collection, use, storage, disclosure, access to, and correction of personal information. It consists of fundamental privacy principles covering such issues as

- Transparency in the handling of personal information
- The rules on collecting information from solicitation
- Correctness and integrity of collected data

As you can see from the enactment date, Australia has been very proactive in the area of personal privacy rights for decades. They have also become host to a number of global cloud providers, making this law even more important.

Because the Australian Privacy Act meets all the requirements of the EU Data Directive and Privacy Regulation, Australian entities are allowed to collect and create PII for EU citizens and operate as if Australia belonged to the EU.

Canada's Personal Information Protection and Electronic Documents Act (PIPEDA)

This Canadian law provides for the protection of personal information collected, used, or disclosed in certain circumstances by providing for the use of electronic means to communicate or record information or transactions. It includes such specifics on filing complaints as how and with whom they are filed, and the remedies and enforcements available to the government for redress of such grievances. As you might imagine, Canada has a view of personal privacy more like that of the EU and unlike the United States.

The EU acknowledges PIPEDA as satisfactorily addressing the principles of the Data Directive and the Privacy Regulation. Therefore, entities in Canada (like those in Australia) can operate as if they were in the EU.

Argentina's Personal Data Protection Act

In 2000, Argentina passed the Data Protection Act with the explicit intent of ensuring adherence and compliance with the EU Data Directive. Because of this, the EU treats entities in Argentina as if they were in the EU and allows them to collect and create PII for EU citizens. Many datacenters in Argentina exist that manage services for EU customers.

The EFTA and Switzerland

Switzerland is not technically a member of the EU. Instead, it is a member of a four-nation smaller body known as the European Free Trade Association (EFTA). Swiss law has long been famous for protecting client privacy, specifically to support Switzerland's international banking industry. The EU recognizes EFTA regulation as stringent enough to protect EU citizen data under the Data Directive/Privacy Regulation, so Switzerland is ostensibly considered part of the EU in regard to being allowed to process privacy information.

Asia-Pacific Economic Cooperation (APEC) Privacy Framework

The Asia-Pacific Economic Cooperation (APEC) is a regional organization meant to work toward economic growth and cooperation of its member nations. APEC agreements are not legally binding and are followed only with voluntary compliance by those entities (usually private companies) that choose to participate.

Where the laws of some other jurisdictions (such as the EU) are meant to provide governmental protections to individual citizens, the APEC intent is to enhance the function of free markets through common adherence to PII protection principles. APEC members understand that consumers will not trust markets if their PII is not protected during participation in those markets. Therefore, APEC principles offer reassurance to consumers as an effort to increase faith in trading practices and thereby ensure mutual benefit for all involved.

APEC framework privacy principles rest on the following core ideas:

- Individuals know when their data is used, transmitted, or stored.

- Limitations on usage are based on what is known to the individuals.

- The entity collecting or creating PII has responsibilities toward maintaining data accuracy and integrity.

ISO/IEC 27017:2015

The International Organization for Standardization (ISO) and International Electrotechnical Commission (IEC) created ISO/IEC 27017:2015, a set of standards regarding the guidelines for information security controls applicable to the provision and use of cloud services and cloud service customers. In other words, it provides a set of standards for not only providing cloud services, but how cloud customer information and privacy should be controlled. Although ISO standards are recognized internationally, they are not law, and they do not reflect regulation by governmental bodies such as the EU.

However, the EU and other governments look closely at these types of internationally vetted standards when creating new laws and regulations. Their influence is seen in many of the EU and other international laws and standards. You may also see their influence in other regions such as Hong Kong, South America, Asia, and so on.

 ISO documents are not free! They can range in price from a hundred or so dollars to several hundred, depending on the specific document, size, age, and so on. And there are literally hundreds of them. This is one of the ways in which the ISO organization generates revenue to continue developing their standards. They are developed primarily by subject matter experts from around the world, who are all volunteers with the exception of the ISO staff. So get out your credit card if you want to see more than just a few teaser pages of any specific standard. For more information, go to www.iso.org/iso/home.htm.

The Difference Between Laws, Regulations and Standards

So what is the difference between all of these laws, regulations, standards, and frameworks? Laws are legal rules that are created by government entities such as a congress or parliament. Regulations are rules that are created by either other departments of government or external entities empowered by government. Failure to properly follow laws and regulations can result in punitive procedures that can include fines and imprisonment. Standards are created by other, nongovernmental organizations that provide frameworks and guidelines for businesses to follow. These are generally embraced by industries to provide a recognized, respectable standard for responsible, professional behavior. On occasion, some standards are strong enough and respected enough that laws or regulations are passed that establish them as the de facto standard of legal expectations as well.

Moreover, regulators (agents of government bodies or entities tasked by a government to enforce regulations) can find fault in an organization that fails to provide due care to its customers if that organization does not adopt the best practices and standards recognized within that organization's industry. This can create some ambiguity, because the government does not always dictate which standards are acceptable, so there may be some risk in an organization's choice of the wrong standard. FTC actions in the realm of IT security have had just such an effect. FTC regulators have demanded that organizations should follow industry standards for IT security practices, but they fail to state which industry standards are acceptable for that purpose—and every practitioner knows that there are many different standards to choose from in this industry, often with significantly differing levels of complexity and cost.

It's also important to note that there is an area of regulation that does not derive authority from the government: contractual regulation. For instance, Payment Card Industry (PCI) compliance is wholly voluntary but is also a regulated requirement for those who choose to participate in credit card processing (namely, merchants who accept credit card payments). Those participants agree to submit to PCI regulation, including audits and review of the participants' adoption and implementation of standards and applicable controls. It's not a law, but it is a regulatory framework, complete with regulators. For more information about the PCI council and the PCI Data Security Standards, go to https://www.pcisecuritystandards.org/.

Regardless of whether you're dealing with laws, regulations, or standards, everyone expects a reasonable degree of transparency—in other words, making things clear for all types of regulators and interested parties, at least to the degree that is expected and possible.

Potential Personal and Data Privacy Issues in the Cloud Environment

Due to the decentralized nature of cloud computing, geographic disparities come into play that make personal privacy and data privacy critical issues. In this section, we will discuss some of the challenges to protecting and managing personal privacy and data privacy in such a decentralized, dispersed, and global environment.

eDiscovery

Electronic discovery (eDiscovery) refers to the process of identifying and obtaining electronic evidence for either prosecutorial or litigation purposes. Determining which data in a set is pertinent can be difficult. Regardless of whether it is databases, records, email, or just simple files, identifying and locating applicable records can be quite challenging in the cloud due to the decentralized nature of the configuration. In addition, eDiscovery is a term used for several types of services such as SaaS-based and host-based solutions. These services range from eDiscovery tasks such as collection and preservation of evidence to hosted services with the ability to reach across cloud environments to provide eDiscovery on disparate and geographically dispersed datasets.

Moreover, because cloud computing so often takes the form of a multitenant environment, there is added complication in finding data owned by a specific customer while not intruding on other customers' data that might be located in the same storage volumes, the same drives, or the same machines. Trained professionals certified in the practice of eDiscovery are few, and most organizations don't have these people in their employ. When faced with eDiscovery activity, an organization would probably best be served by hiring a consultant who is expert and licensed for the purpose.

It is important for the cloud customer to be familiar with laws, SLAs, and other contractual agreements that can impact the user's ability to conduct eDiscovery should the need arise. This is especially important if international boundaries are crossed in the process.

Because of these complexities, eDiscovery in the cloud environment is an expanding and changing science and industry. It will continue to mature and develop in the years to come and will be impacted by the changing landscape of changing international laws and regulations such as the new EU Privacy Regulation and the exit of Britain from the EU.

Chain of Custody

All evidence needs to be tracked and monitored from the time it is recognized as evidence and acquired for that purpose. Clear documentation must record which people had access to the evidence, where the evidence was stored, what access controls were placed on the evidence, and what modifications or analysis was performed on the evidence from the moment it was collected until the time it reaches the court. We call this record and the principles for creating it the *chain of custody*.

Being able to demonstrate a strong chain of custody, where only specific, trusted personnel had access to the material, with no gaps in the timeline or loss of control, is very important for making an argument in court using that evidence. Any discrepancy in the chain of custody introduces doubt as to the disposition and content of the evidence. Although this does not make the evidence inadmissible, it does allow an opportunity for opposing counsel to reduce the power of your narrative. Any doubt regarding a particular piece or set of evidence will make that evidence much weaker.

When creating policies for maintaining a chain of custody or conducting activities requiring the preservation and monitoring of evidence, it is best to get input and guidance from counsel and perhaps even to use specialized consultants who are trained and experienced in this practice area.

Forensic Requirements

Conducting forensic activity in a cloud environment is a challenge no matter how you look at it. The nature of decentralized, off-premise data and its movement, storage, and processing across geopolitical boundaries all lead to a complex and perplexing environment when attempting to gather and analyze forensic data.

In addition, the international nature of cloud forensics has created the demand for an international standard applicable to everyone, regardless of their location. This helps standardize procedures across borders in an effort to limit the challenges to scientific findings.

The ISO developed a set of standards to meet this international challenge that resulted in the following standards for digital forensics:

ISO/IEC 27037:2012.   Guide for collecting, identifying, and preserving electronic evidence

ISO/IEC 27041:2015   Guide for incident investigations

ISO/IEC 27042: 2015   Guide for digital evidence analysis

ISO/IEC 27043:2015   Incident investigation principles and processes

ISO/IEC 27050-1:2016   Overview and principles for eDiscovery

The latest and most successful so far is ISO/IEC 27050-1:2016, which is fast becoming the de facto worldwide standard for eDiscovery. However, even with a standard like this, it takes a concerted effort on the part of each party involved to obtain accurate and useful forensic information.

International Conflict Resolution

As companies continue to build datacenters around the world to provide cloud computing services, the issues regarding where and in whose jurisdiction disputes will be resolved and the laws that apply will continue to become more and more complex. As cases erupt, international courts will arrive at decisions that contradict each other, precedents will be established, broken, and again reestablished and new laws will emerge, all complicating these geopolitical issues. These elements, combined with the shifting political leaderships and even the destruction of old geopolitical boundaries and the emergence of new ones, all tend to complicate the problems.

Cloud Forensic Challenges

The distributed model of cloud computing presents a number of challenges in the area of forensics. Data location, collection mechanisms, and international laws are all factors when dealing with situations that call for forensic work to be completed.

Do you know where your data is to start with? Are some parts of it on premise or off premise, and in either case where is the data located? Is it distributed across multiple data-centers, and if so, are those datacenters across international boundaries? If so, do international laws hinder your abilities to collect forensic information?

Do you have a working relationship with your cloud computing vendors? Are forensic issues spelled out in your SLA or other contract elements regarding your and their rights and responsibilities for data collection and maintenance?

Contractual and Regulated PII

Data that impacts personal privacy can take many forms. NIST Special Publication (SP) 800-122 talks about personally identifiable information (PII) as information about a person that can include such things as name, date of birth, and Social Security number. HIPAA calls this type of data "electronic protected health information" (ePHI), and it also includes any patient information, including medical records, and facial photos. GLBA includes customer account information such as account numbers and balances. The EU Data Directive and Privacy Regulation include the subject's cell phone number.

One particular consideration about privacy and protected private information is whether governance rules apply due to regulations or contractual circumstances.

Contractually regulated PII is that which must be protected as part of a contractual obligation. As with PCI DSS, certain rules must be followed as part of a contract between the payment processor and the vendor. There is no government regulation or enforcement in place to ensure compliance. If privacy is not adequately protected, it is a contractual matter to be settled between the parties to that contract.

Government-regulated PII, on the other hand, is that data that is governed by either statutory law or administrative regulation. Generally speaking, the location where PII is stored, processed, or transmitted determines what rules and regulations apply because that determines jurisdictions. The cloud entity must therefore abide by whatever protection mechanisms are in place with regard to these geographical locations. This can become quite complicated when the storage, processing, and transmission of data occur across multiple geopolitical boundaries. For example, if your PII is stored and processed in Germany but then transmitted to the United States, then both countries' jurisdictional legal and regulatory guidelines would apply. This is one more example of why the legal concepts mentioned earlier in the chapter become so important. When there is a dispute of some kind, sorting out jurisdictional disputes can be confusing and difficult to determine.

Direct and Indirect Identifiers

Privacy information can take many forms. The legally defined PII elements we described in the preceding section of this chapter are sometimes referred to as *direct identifiers*. Direct identifiers are those data elements that immediately reveal a specific individual (the person's name, Social Security or credit card number, and so on).

There are also *indirect identifiers*, which should also be protected. Indirect identifiers are the characteristics and traits of an individual that when aggregated could reveal the identity of that person. Each indirect identifier by itself is usually not sensitive, but if enough are collected they may provide sensitive information. For example, if we take a list of indirect identifiers that are not sensitive, such as a man, born in Wisconsin, currently living in New Orleans, who owns a dog, and performs work in the information security field, we might reveal the identity of one of the authors of this book and thus derive sensitive information (an identity) from information elements that are not sensitive (location, birthplace, pets, industry, and so on).

Audit Processes, Methodologies, and Cloud Adaptations

Like any other environment where security is a concern, audits provide a backstop to ensure that operations are not missing elements that pose undue risks to the organization. The audit process in cloud computing, while very much like any other environment, does have some unique challenges, which we will explore in more detail.

Virtualization

One of the first challenges that auditors must deal with in these complex and geopolitically diverse cloud environments is that of virtualization. You are no longer looking at physical devices but software instances or abstractions of devices. Even at the network layer, software-based virtual switches and routers are responsible for moving traffic around the cloud environment. That makes it hard for the auditor to identify all machines in the scope as you cannot go into a room and look to identify your targets. At best, you will have access to a management console with which to view the environment. This can at the very least be confusing and difficult for those unaccustomed to cloud computing.

There is also the need to understand the control mechanisms in play in a virtualized cloud environment. Virtualization brings with it a knowledge base that auditors unfamiliar with cloud technology will find confusing. One example would be that of auditing access to the hypervisor. You can see the accounts of the admins, but you may not be able to speak to them as they could reside in a different country. Alternatively, the provider may not even know who they are as they lay hidden behind the abstraction layer of the virtualized environment.

Scope

Defining the scope of an audit in a cloud-computing environment can also present challenges. Are you conducting an audit on the infrastructure of the cloud provider, the platform, or the applications involved? Depending on the service model you are using, audit scope can take many different forms. For instance, if you are simply using the provider as a Software as a Service (SaaS) vendor, should your audit scope involve the underlying infrastructure? Many vendors even provide third-party audits of those services to satisfy this need so that other auditors can focus on their particular area. This lends itself to some levels of trust as outlined in the discussion on SOC reports.

Additionally, the scope of the audit may or may not be confined to geographical or geopolitical boundaries. The auditor may only be auditing Infrastructure as a Service (IaaS) within the confines of a certain country. Anything outside these boundaries may be out of scope depending on the engagement.

Gap Analysis

Gap analysis is where most audit activities begin. To create an accurate frame of reference, a gap analysis is conducted, which is like a lightweight audit in that there are generally findings of weaknesses or vulnerabilities, but the purpose is to identify those weaknesses so they can be remediated prior to any further actual audit work. In addition, it provides the organization with a static point of reference from which to begin work in defining their strategic goals and objectives regarding risk remediation and control implementation. It also provides a starting point for those organizations in the early stages of an information system program development, providing them with a clear starting point.

Information Security Management Systems (ISMSs)

The idea of an information security management system (ISMS), sometimes also known as an internal information security controls system, was born as part of the ISO information security standards. When aligned with the ISO/IEC 27001 standards, an information security management system can be said to have all the components necessary to be successful.

The ISMS is intended to provide a standardized international model for the development and implementation of policies, procedures, and standards that take into account stakeholder identification and involvement in a top-down approach to addressing and managing risk in an organization. It is built on the premise that information should be adequately secured and to do so involves people, processes, and technology and the application of a risk management methodology and process managed by such an ISMS.

For more information, see www.iso.org/iso/iso27001.

Just a bit of nomenclature clarification: ISO derives from British beginnings, so the word *system* in the ISMS is the English, not American, use. In the United States, the word *program* might be used instead; what the ISMS covers is not a single system, but an entire, holistic, organizational approach to security. So an American company should have an internal security program, including all the policies and procedures related to security, the security controls within that organization, security personnel and specific roles and tasks they are assigned, and so forth.

The Right to Audit in Managed Services

The *right to audit* is a term that has caused some confusion in the past. In the world of auditing, it has historically meant that when dealing with outsourced vendors (in this case cloud computing vendors), the purchaser of the service could literally demand to audit a vendor at any given time and place of their choosing. In U.S. financial services auditing, it was quite common to even follow through with these audits as part of an organization's due diligence.

As you can imagine, this is a little difficult to do in a cloud-computing world. In banking, my vendor may be in Minneapolis and I can travel to and audit things like the racks in the datacenters. That does not scale well, however, when your provider is Microsoft and you have datacenters all over the world and no idea on which servers customer data may be on at any given time. Therefore, even if you wanted to audit your provider, where would you begin? And even if my cloud provider does in fact exist in the United States, the likelihood of them actually letting me audit them is slim to none. Just imagine what would happen with an organization the size of Microsoft if even a tiny fraction of its millions of customers demanded to let them to conduct audits. Not only would it never be allowed, the scale of the logistics involved would prevent it from ever happening.

Today, what *right to audit* has come to mean is that at any given time, I may ask you for any and all audit reports you may have prepared for customers in order to satisfy our need for due diligence. Keep in mind that these audits and reports can cost hundreds of thousands of dollars for providers to prepare and contain sensitive information so vendors do not just give them away.

Audit Scope Statements

Audit scope statements are the documented description of the information necessary for a client organization to fully understand the scope focus and other characteristics of the audit to be performed. They help to guide audit activities and provide clear boundaries of what is and what is not to be evaluated. For instance, if an audit scope is designed to evaluate the effectiveness of controls in an IaaS environment, then anything from the hypervisor up is not open for investigation or debate.

The scope statement also identifies what the audit results mean and how they are to be interpreted. To use the example of an IaaS model again: auditors reviewing the cloud provider are not likely to examine anything that appears in the logical stack above the physical layer, and maybe perhaps the hypervisor (if it's a Type 1 hypervisor), simply because all the other elements (the OS, the programs, the data) do not belong to the cloud provider—they belong to the cloud customers and therefore shouldn't fall into the auditors' purview.

Policies

Policies come in many sizes and varieties. They provide a voice and expression to the strategic goals and objectives of management and play an integral role in forming the security posture of an organization.

Organizational policies take the form of those intended to reduce exposure and minimize risk of financial and data losses, as well as other types of damages such as loss of reputation. Some of the other typical policies you will see in enterprise environments include things like an information security policy (as you'll recall from the GLBA law section), data classification and usage policies, acceptable use, and a host of other polices related to software, malware, and so on. In addition, you will usually see disaster recovery and business continuity policies, vendor management or outsourcing policies, and incident response or IR and forensic policies. As mentioned previously, all these policies are an expression of management's strategic goals and objectives with regard to managing and maintaining the risk profile of the organization.

In cloud computing we see much more emphasis on policies regarding things like access controls, data storage and recovery, and so on. Examples that are more specific would include remote access, password management, encryption, and how duties and responsibilities are separated and managed, especially for admins.

Different Types of Audit Reports

Internal audits are those performed by employees of an organization. Banks will often have an internal audit department and conduct periodic internal reviews in order to assess operational risks and such things as whether employees are following policies. They may also conduct ongoing audits into such activities as to whether Red Flag rules and cases are being handled properly, and they may conduct GLBA audits to ensure that they are meeting all FDIC regulations concerning their information security program.

Several of the reasons internal audits are weaker than external audits are as follows:

- They tend to get put off should other issues arise.
- The people doing the audits may lack experience.
- There may be pressure to not disclose security issues for fear of retribution.

External audits are performed almost as an audit of internal audits. External audits tend to be more independent because there is greater separation between the auditor and the organization. They also tend to be more thorough since they typically encompass the entire audit universe as opposed to internal audits of individual sectors of the business such as finance or IT.

 Real World Scenario

CAE Responsibilities and SOX

While working with a medium-sized, publicly traded corporation, I learned that the security staff were concerned about sharing any information with the audit department because the chief audit executive (CAE) thought it his responsibility to report *all* security matters to the board of directors as part of his fiduciary responsibilities under SOX. However, the effect of such a constrained view was that it actually stifled reporting of issues until they reached a point that they could no longer be overlooked. The security department was afraid to report findings to the audit department for fear of overreaction and thus began to treat internal audit activities with distrust rather than seeing them as useful adjuncts to their work.

This was certainly not what the SOX regulations were intended to result in, but it was the effect nevertheless. The idea of SOX was to push information up to the board of directors but not to the level of minutiae that wound up preventing revelations as in this case. The moral of the story is that cloud security professionals should work closely with internal auditors to ensure there is a clear expectation of privacy and assurance with regard to whistleblowing and that filter mechanisms are in place so that you reach the right balance of transparency while meeting regulatory requirements.

Auditor Independence

The idea of auditor independence goes back further than the passage of SOX, but the underlying reasons for the passage of SOX make the point clearly. A lack of auditor independence caused internal auditors to try to hide findings that were unflattering to the organization. This was primarily due to fear of losing one's job. Over time, a culture of nondisclosure became commonplace to the point that glaring and dangerous accounting errors occurred, having devastating effects on the organizations involved.

The lack of independence of the internal audit teams started the ball rolling in this dangerous game of corporate secret keeping and distancing of the board of directors from their responsibilities. Today, the board of directors is not only directly responsible to regulatory authorities, but is answerable to other parties, as demonstrated in the recent case of the

Target breach. The breach, caused by poor network segmentation, poor admin access, and poor vendor management of third-party service providers, has resulted in the shareholders getting into the game by launching civil lawsuits against board of director members for not performing adequate fiduciary oversight to prevent the occurrence from happening in the first place.

AICPA Reports and Standards

The American Institute of Certified Professional Accountants (AICPA) represents the CPA profession in the United States. They are a large and powerful organization that is responsible for most accounting and information security audit practices. They set the standards, create the guidelines and frameworks, and set the bar when it comes to what we call service organization audit and reporting practices. The AICPA creates and promulgates the Generally Accepted Accounting Practices (GAAP), which auditors and accountants adhere to in their professions.

Prior to SOX, the AICPA audit standard for reviewing publicly traded corporations was called the SAS 70. SOX mandated a great many new aspects for audits, so the AICPA created a new standard that superseded the SAS 70, and that standard is SSAE 16. The SSAE 16 standard outlines three families of audit reports: SOC 1, SOC 2, and SOC 3.

These standards, guidelines, and reports serve as the foundation for evaluating the safety and soundness of an organization's control framework and help to determine risk levels of doing business with the organization. They are used for instance to report on the effectiveness of controls in place in a cloud service environment, such as whether data backup and restore policies and procedures are working properly. They report on the effectiveness of proper separation and segmentation.

It is clear why these reports and activities are so important for the cloud provider. The results are a form of attestation to customers demonstrating that the controls in place used to protect data privacy and security are effective and function as designed. These assurances allow the cloud service consumer or customer to know that the services they are purchasing are providing adequate safety and privacy at the level the service organization provides.

The first of these reports is called the SOC 1. It is an audit engagement consisting solely of an examination of organizational financial reporting controls. For the purposes of a cloud customer trying to determine the suitability of a cloud provider, the SOC 1 is useless. It doesn't tell us anything about data protections, configuration resiliency, or any other element the customer needs to know. The SOC 1 is instead designed to serve the needs of investors and regulators, the two sets of people interested in the financial well-being of the target. To restate and reinforce: The SOC 1 does not serve an information security or IT security purpose.

SOC 2 reports review controls relevant to security, availability, processing integrity, confidentiality, or privacy. This is the report of most use to cloud customers (to determine the suitability of cloud providers) and IT security practitioners. SOC 2 reports come in Type I and Type II flavors. The SOC 2 Type I report only reviews controls as designed. That is, the audit examines the controls chosen by the target, but not how those controls are implemented or how well those controls actually work. For a cloud customer, the SOC 2 Type I is interesting but again not too useful.

The SOC 2 Type II, on the other hand, is a truly thorough review of the target's controls, including how they have been implemented and their efficacy. The SOC 2 Type II is a goldmine for the cloud customer. It gives the customer a realistic view of the provider's security posture and overall program.

Unfortunately, while the cloud customer will want to see the provider's SOC 2 Type II audit report, the provider may be reluctant to share it, and rightly so. The SOC 2 Type II is so detailed and contains so much information about the actual security controls implemented within the provider's environment that it would be a perfect attack map for a hostile actor. It is quite understandable that the cloud provider would not want to disseminate the SOC 2 Type II.

However, current trends in the industry have created a happy middle ground for the provider and the customer. Many cloud providers are offering the SOC 2 Type II reports to their customers with the stipulation that the customer signs a nondisclosure agreement and that the customer is vetted by the provider for trustworthiness before the provider will release the report. This gives assurances to the customer that the provider's security posture is adequate, and it gives assurances to the provider that their security methods and techniques are not being made available to someone who would want to use that information for malicious ends.

The SOC 3 report, on the other hand, is purely for public consumption and serves only as a seal of approval of sorts for public display without sharing any specific information regarding audit activity, control effectiveness, findings, and so on. It is literally just an attestation from the auditor that the audit has been conducted and that the target has successfully passed the audit. It contains no details and no substance. More cloud providers will be willing to disclose the SOC 3 report than either of the SOC 2 reports because that is what an SOC 3 is designed for.

Summary

As you have seen, the nature of international laws, standards, and regulation make the world of cloud computing complex and at times difficult to comprehend. The International Organization for Standardization (ISO) and the International Electrotechnical Commission

(IEC) have promulgated what have become the de facto standards for information security and privacy for the vast majority of the international community outside the United States. Inside the United States, auditors still work primarily with standards and regulations such as GLBA, PCI, and HIPAA. Agencies and governmental bodies generate these standards and regulations, making a consistent standard difficult to obtain. However, it is the CCSP's responsibility to understand all the challenges these present in order to provide sound advice when working with customers' and vendors' architectural, policy, and management efforts.

Exam Essentials

Have a fundamental understanding of the relevant ISO and ISO/IEC standards such as ISO 27001.   ISO standards are not laws, but are derived from experts all over the world who have come together to develop standards from which to operate. Many countries and coalitions such as the EU base many of their policies on ISO-related standards.

Be familiar with and have a fundamental grasp of U.S. security and privacy standards, regulations, and laws.   This includes contractual and legal compliance regulations, standards, and frameworks such as PCI, HIPAA, SOX, and GLBA. You should know the differences. PCI, for instance, is a contractual standard and not a law. HIPAA, on the other hand, like GLBA, is a federal law, and if audits turn up findings, it can result in fines and cease orders.

Have a clear understanding of issues surrounding and relating to eDiscovery.   This includes forensic evidence, chain of custody, and the challenges facing forensic collection in a cloud environment. Attempting eDiscovery in a cloud environment can be very challenging due to such things as geographical and geopolitical dispersion.

Understand audit processes.   Understand basic audit concepts such as internal versus external audits, as well as the differences and the importance of independence in conducting audits. Less reliable internal audits assist internal operations whereas external audits, being more independent, ferret out more thoroughly sensitive issues that might cause risk to the organization.

Be familiar with the basic definitions of personally identifiable information (PII).   Be familiar with the basic definitions of PII, contractual versus regulated, country-specific regulations, and differences. Also, understand the difference between sensitive and nonsensitive PII (using direct and indirect identifiers). In addition, be aware that even though PII may be nonsensitive, when combined with other nonsensitive information it can become sensitive.

Written Labs

1. Describe the primary differences between regulations, laws, and standards.
2. What are the HIPAA rules and why are they different?
3. Describe the primary differences between an SOC 1, an SOC 2, and an SOC 3 report.

Review Questions

You can find the answers in Appendix A.

1. Which of the following is the least challenging with regard to eDiscovery in the cloud?

   A. Decentralization of data storage

   B. Complexities of International law

   C. Identifying roles such as data owner, controller, and processor

   D. Forensic analysis

2. Legal controls refer to which of the following?

   A. Controls designed to comply with laws and regulations related to the cloud environment

   B. PCI DSS

   C. ISO 27001

   D. NIST 800-53r4

3. Which of the following terms is *not* associated with cloud forensics?

   A. Analysis

   B. eDiscovery

   C. Chain of custody

   D. Plausibility

4. Which of the following is *not* a component of contractual PII?

   A. Scope of processing

   B. Use of subcontractors

   C. Location of data

   D. Value of data

5. Which of the following is the best example of a key component of regulated PII?

   A. Items that *should* be implemented

   B. Mandatory breach reporting

   C. Audit rights of subcontractors

   D. PCI DSS

6. Which of the following is not associated with security?

   A. Confidentiality

   B. Availability

   C. Integrity

   D. Quality

7. Which of the following is the best advantage of external audits?

    A. Independence

    B. Oversight

    C. Cheaper

    D. Better results

8. Which of the following laws resulted from a lack of independence in audit practices?

    A. HIPAA

    B. GLBA

    C. SOX

    D. ISO 27064

9. Which of the following reports is no longer used?

    A. SAS 70

    B. SSAE 16

    C. SOC 1

    D. SOC 3

10. Which of the following report is most aligned with financial control audits?

    A. SOC 1

    B. SOC 2

    C. SOC 3

    D. SSAE 16

11. Which of the following is the primary purpose of an SOC 3 report?

    A. Absolute assurances

    B. Compliance with PCI/DSS

    C. HIPAA compliance

    D. Seal of approval

12. Gap analysis is performed for what reason?

    A. To begin the benchmarking process

    B. To provide assurances to cloud customers

    C. To assure proper accounting practices are being used

    D. To ensure all controls are in place and working properly

13. GAAPs are created and maintained by which organization?

    A. ISO

    B. ISO/IEC

    C. PCI Council

    D. AICPA

14. Which statute addresses security and privacy matters in the financial industry?

   A. GLBA

   B. FERPA

   C. SOX

   D. HIPAA

15. Which of the following is *not* an example of a highly regulated environment?

   A. Healthcare

   B. Financial services

   C. Wholesale or distribution

   D. Public companies

16. Which of the following SOC report subtypes represents a point in time?

   A. SOC 2

   B. Type I

   C. Type II

   D. SOC 3

17. Which of the following SOC report subtypes spans a period of time?

   A. SOC 2

   B. SOC 3

   C. SOC 1

   D. Type II

18. The right to be forgotten refers to which of the following?

   A. The right to no longer pay taxes

   B. Erasing criminal history

   C. The right to have all of a data owner's data erased

   D. Masking

19. The right to audit should be a part of what documents?

   A. SLA

   B. PLA

   C. All cloud providers

   D. Masking

20. SOX was enacted because of which of the following?

   A. Poor BOD oversight

   B. Lack of independent audits

   C. Poor financial controls

   D. All of the above

21. What is a key component of GLBA?

   A. The right to be forgotten

   B. EU Data Directives

   C. The information security program

   D. The right to audit

22. Which of the following are not associated with HIPAA controls?

   A. Administrative controls

   B. Technical controls

   C. Physical controls

   D. Financial controls

23. What does the doctrine of the proper law refer to?

   A. How jurisdictional disputes are settled

   B. The law that is applied after the first law is applied

   C. The determination of what law will apply to a case

   D. The proper handling of eDiscovery materials

24. The Restatement (Second) Conflict of Law refers to which of the following?

   A. The basis for deciding which laws are most appropriate in a situation where conflicting laws exist

   B. When judges restate the law in an opinion

   C. How jurisdictional disputes are settled

   D. Whether local or federal laws apply in a situation

25. Which of the following applies to the Stored Communications Act (SCA)?

   A. It's old.

   B. It's in bad need of updating.

   C. It's unclear with regard to current technologies.

   D. All of the above

Chapter 11

Legal and Compliance Part 2

THE OBJECTIVE OF THIS CHAPTER IS TO ACQUAINT THE READER WITH THE FOLLOWING CONCEPTS:

✓ **Domain 1: Architectural Concepts and Design Requirements**

- B. Described Cloud Reference Architecture
  - B.5. Cloud Cross-Cutting Aspects
- D. Understand Design Principles of Secure Cloud Computing
  - D.3. Cost Benefit Analysis
- E. Identify Trusted Cloud Services
  - E.1. Certification Against Criteria
  - E.2. System/Subsystem Product Certifications

✓ **Domain 3: Cloud Platform and Infrastructure Security**

- B. Analyze Risks Associated to Cloud Infrastructure
  - B.1. Risk Assessment/Analysis

✓ **Domain 5: Operations**

- K. Manage Communications with Relevant Parties
  - K.1. Vendors
  - K.2. Customers
  - K.3. Partners
  - K.4. Regulators
  - K.5. Other Stakeholders

✓ **Domain 6: Legal and Compliance**

- C. Understand Audit Process, Methodologies, and Required Adaptations for a Cloud Environment
  - C.8. Standards Requirements
  - C.11. Policies

In this chapter, we continue our discussion of the legal and compliance challenges in cloud computing. The global, decentralized nature of cloud computing presents numerous issues that we are just now grappling with in our endeavors to protect privacy rights, meet compliance demands, and maintain a secure computing environment.

This chapter will cover effective risk management, risk metrics, and strategies for an effective risk management program. We will round it out with a discussion of outsourcing, contract management, and the all-important service-level agreement (SLA).

The Impact of Diverse Geographical Locations and Legal Jurisdictions

As discussed in Chapter 10, "Legal and Compliance Part 1," the impact of the decentralized, geographically, and geopolitically dispersed model of cloud computing presents numerous challenges, including these:

- Data processing, storage, and computing, each occurring in different geopolitical realms
- Difficulties in assessing data actors
- Difficulties in locating data

A great deal of the difficulty in managing the legal ramifications of cloud computing stems from the design of cloud assets. They are necessarily dispersed, often across county, state, and even international borders. Resources are constantly being allocated and reallocated on a moment-to-moment basis. Also, specific control and administration of particular assets can be hard to ascertain and establish.

It is that transborder aspect that is most troublesome, in terms of allowing the cloud customer to maintain compliance with legal and regulatory mandates. As we discussed in the previous chapter, each jurisdiction can have its own governance, which can vary wildly from jurisdiction to jurisdiction, and jurisdictions can overlap. A city is in a county is in a state, which is in a country, and they might all have conflicting guidance and interests. Moreover, legislation and guidance is always in flux, especially in our industry. Lawmakers and standards bodies are constantly trying to catch up to the requirements and questions posed by new technologies and how those technologies are used. And these vagaries of law affect not only the cloud customer, in terms of how the customer must behave and respond to legal action, but also how the cloud provider must perform in response to these same stimuli.

The governance used by both entities—the cloud customer and the cloud provider—must take all of this into account in order to operate reasonably with acknowledgment of legal risks and liabilities in the cloud.

Policies

Policies are one of the foundational elements of a governance and risk management program. They guide the organization, based on standards and guidelines. Policies ensure that the organization is operating within its risk profile. Policies actually define, or are the expression of, the organization's risk tolerance.

Risk Appetite and Risk Tolerance

There are two aspects of every decision involving risk. The first is the potential benefit a decision offers, and the other is the opportunity associated with it. Banks loan money to people with good credit because the opportunity to make a profit from the interest on the loan outweighs the risk of the person defaulting on the loan. As the risk of default goes up, so does the interest rate until a point is reached where the risk is so high that a loan cannot even be obtained.

In the financial world, risk appetite and risk tolerance are very well understood. These are the drivers of Wall Street and every company in the world. Each day, businesses make decisions about risks they are either willing or not willing to take. People and businesses weigh the benefits of the opportunities against the risk of the same action. These activities are the expression of their willingness or not to take risk, generally called their *risk tolerance*. When engaging in risk tolerance, people and businesses consider how far they will go in taking risk before the potential risk outweighs the opportunity.

A more personal example of a risk decision based on risk versus opportunity might be the decision to climb up on the roof of your house to clean out the gutters. At age 35, this may seem like a simple task and you are very willing to take the risk of falling as you are pretty sure of yourself and your ability to maintain your balance. The benefit is that your gutters will be clean and not become clogged when it rains, as well as the cost savings you realize for not having to hire someone else to perform the task for you. However, at age 60, would you be willing to take the same risk? If you fell, you might lose the ability to do your job, costing you a great deal of money, and your balance is not what it once was. The cost of lost work is probably a lot less than the cost of hiring someone to clean the gutters in your stead (assuming that, by age 60, you make more money, per hour, than someone who is younger and earns money cleaning gutters).In other words, the benefit of having clean gutters may not be outweighed any longer by your willingness to risk falling. If, not, then your risk appetite (or conversely risk tolerance) has changed over time.

Working with businesses in the cloud is much the same in that they each have their own particular risk appetite and tolerance based on their individual situations. Some may be willing to have data spread across the world, whereas others may not. Some may be tightly regulated, disallowing them from taking certain risks, and others may be willing to skimp on security in the belief that it makes them more nimble. What is important to remember is that everyone is different and has different tolerances for risk and that tolerance can change over time or very quickly depending on circumstances.

Before the organization begins creating its policies, we start by identifying the stakeholders. This ensures that we have the right individuals involved in creating the expression of risk tolerance. These can include:

- Business unit leaders
- The board of directors
- Investors
- Regulators

The views, perceptions, and choices of these groups will influence the organization's willingness and ability to accept risk, but most of these stakeholders will not be directly involved in crafting organizational policy. For instance, the regulators won't (or shouldn't) help draft policy, but the regulations and regulators' enforcement of them establish how an organization can take risks and what risks it is allowed to take. The regulators, ostensibly acting on behalf of lawmakers and in turn working on behalf of the public (because they chose those lawmakers), are expressing the view of the public, vis-à-vis risk, on organizations. Say the organization offered a new product, but the risk of creating that product might result in an employee dying once per month; the organization might be willing to take on that risk if the potential profits were high enough, and the employees might be willing to take on that risk if the pay was high enough, but the regulators might take a dim view of offering such a product at the possible cost of human life, so the risk appetite of the organization would necessarily be limited by regulation.

The decision to risk human life is not necessarily unethical or immoral. Deep sea fishing has been one of the most fatal professions in the United States for more than one hundred years, and consumers have not stopped buying seafood en masse out of protest and loathing at the potential human cost of acquiring their meals. People engaged in commercial fishing choose to risk their lives to make very good money and seem to enjoy their work, regulators mandate reasonable safety requirements for the industry, and consumers enjoy seafood.

Once the stakeholder inputs have been adequately identified, the organization can begin building the policies needed in order to operate safely.

Interestingly, the FDIC and many state banking regulators use the term *safety and soundness exams* when they perform a certain type of IT general controls audit. It refers to the idea that the financial institution should be operating with policies in place that ensure the safety and soundness of all transactions and data storage. These can be some of the most rigorous of their exams, as they look at every operational unit involved in the transacting of business. They will even look at cleaning policies and contracts to ensure that things like background checks are performed on cleaning staff because they have direct physical access to offices without supervision.

Until recently, most bank examiners would have had a stroke had they come into a bank and discovered them using popular cloud services for things like email and file sharing. Today, however, that attitude has changed, and just like any business, financial services are looking for ways to save money and make their staff more productive. These are the same business drivers we have been discussing throughout the book.

Identifying and engaging relevant stakeholders is vital to the success of any cloud computing discussions or projects. But there are also challenges that may need to be overcome in order to effectively engage them.

For instance, policies must be malleable enough to reflect changing business opportunities, requirements, and operations. This may have never been truer than in the example of an organization migrating from a legacy environment to the cloud. Almost assuredly, the organization had policies in place that acknowledged the risks and opportunities of that environment (the legacy operation) and dealt with them accordingly. However, the risks and benefits in the cloud are much different, so the policies must be revisited, the guidance and stakeholder input reexamined, and new policies generated, amended, or appended to the old policies.

The variety and vagaries of multijurisdictional law make the regulatory stakeholders and their input especially complicated for cloud services and management. Instead of one regulatory framework to consider when drafting policy, the organization now must take into account every jurisdiction where the cloud provider might be storing, transmitting, and processing the organization's data, as well as every jurisdiction where any of the organization's end customers might reside. This latter part is especially troublesome, because when an organization operates on the cloud, it is assumed that the potential customer base is the web, meaning that the jurisdiction of the organization's customer is the entire planet.

It would be impossible to craft pertinent policy that met the needs and requirements of every jurisdiction in the world. Too many of them inherently conflict with others. So a significant portion of the effort that goes into promulgating policy is determining which jurisdictional mandates are most likely to bear on the organization's operations, where most of the end clientele will reside, where most of the cloud functions will take place, and so forth. It's a cost–benefit analysis of a lesser scale: instead of determining whether the organization has the risk appetite to perform a given function, this part of the effort will be used to determine which laws and regulators will be most likely to impact the organization and which ones should therefore have the most bearing on the organization's policy.

It should go without saying that while subject matter experts (such as the CCSP practitioner) will be called on to draft policies related to the organization's operations in the cloud, general counsel will provide an invaluable input when creating all the organization's policies. Attorneys will be the most versed in identifying, understanding, and tailoring documentation to address the multitude of jurisdictional regulation the organization might face.

As mentioned in the preceding paragraphs, subject matter experts will be called on to create particular policies for the organization. These experts might be internal employees and staff of the organization. They might be external consultants hired for the purpose. The policies might be purchased from an existing set that were designed and drafted by experts in that particular area of expertise and then tailored by the organization to meet its own needs. In this regard, the CCSP should expect to be called on to offer input and advice when the organization is formalizing cloud policy.

After the experts have drafted the policy, the policy must be presented to the decision makers: senior management and the board of directors. The subject matter experts may be called on to explain specific aspects of the policy, expound on particular threats and tangible benefits, and explain how these risks are being addressed by the policy. Senior management must understand these draft policies in order to make an informed decision in accepting them (and the risks and benefits they entail), or modifying the policies as they see fit. Ultimately, policy acceptance will come down to a senior manager signing the policy document and the board acknowledging their approval of the policy.

Once the policy has been formally accepted, it must be published and disseminated among those affected by the policy. Communication in an enterprise environment is challenging in and of itself. Cloud computing makes this communication even more complicated because of things like the IT administration staff not being local, time zone differences between the provider and customer, and the fact that providers could have literally thousands of other customers.

Communication to other business units or departments is vitally important as well. All of the internal and external stakeholders should be kept abreast of any changes or other issues related to policies and operations. Here are some common departments that include internal stakeholders:

- IT
- HR
- Vendor management
- Compliance
- Risk management
- Finance
- Operations

Some things that complicate communication are

- Disparate administrative workforce
- Time zone differences
- Ignorance of cloud computing models and concepts
- Poor understanding of business drivers
- Poor understanding of the organization's risk appetite

When discussing these matters with stakeholders, remember that in all likelihood they will not have a grasp of the cloud computing concepts held by the CCSP. Therefore, it is in everyone's best interest to take things slowly and to ensure that questions get answered adequately so that everyone is on the same page. It is also the CCSP's job to educate stakeholders about cloud computing risks and benefits so that they are better able to make fact-based decisions as opposed to relying on hearsay and gossip.

 How many times have you seen the joke on the Internet or a t-shirt that says "There is no cloud. Just other people's computers"? Many people still believe this, and tend to dumb down the conversations due to their understanding of the complexities of cloud computing. It is important that you, as the cloud-aware professional, acknowledge this and can communicate effectively to ensure an appropriate understanding of the issues surrounding cloud computing and the challenges it brings along with the business drivers and opportunities that have made it such a success.

Some of the policies that the organization will need to appropriately reflect the cloud computing paradigm are as follows:

- Information security policy (ISP)
- Acceptable use policy
- Data classification policy
- Network and Internet security
- Passwords
- Antimalware policy
- Software security
- Disaster recovery and data backup
- Remote and third-party access
- Segregation of duties
- Incident response plan
- Personnel security
- Identity and Access Management (IAM) policy
- Legal compliance
- Encryption

There will be times when a cloud provider will be unable to meet an organization's internal policy requirements. When that occurs, it is imperative that these deficiencies be taken into account and managed as part of any internal governance process. This will ensure that any contract elements or SLAs agreed on will not violate the organizational policies or place the organization at undue risk outside its risk tolerance levels.

Implications of the Cloud for Enterprise Risk Management

Cloud computing as it exists today has commoditized compute, storage, and networking services. Enterprise risk management has shifted in response to this change. It is vitally important that both the customer and the provider focus on risk management and the challenges presented with cloud computing. The cloud customer (in the role of data owner) is ultimately responsible for ensuring control effectiveness, but stored data, security, and risk management require a partnership between the customer and provider. See Figure 11.1.

FIGURE 11.1   Governance Takes Usage Into Account

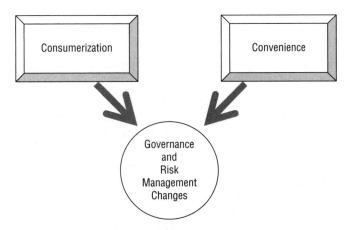

Before you explore the detailed discussion of risk management, you need to be familiar with some risk-related terms.

Key Risk Indicators (KRI)   Key risk indicators are those items that will be the first things that let you know something is amiss. In the financial industry, a KRI might be the stock market cycling wildly over the course of a single day. In cloud computing, it might be the announcement of the discovery of a new vulnerability that could impact your cloud provider. The idea is that you need to identify and closely monitor the things that will most quickly alert you to a change in the risk environment.

Risk Appetite/Tolerance   Risk tolerance and appetite are similar descriptors of how the organization views risk. As their appetite or tolerance increases, so does their willingness to take greater and greater risks. As it decreases, so does the associated willingness to take risk.

Risk Profiles   The risk profile of the organization is a comprehensive analysis of the possible risks the organization is exposed to. The risk profile should include a survey of the various operations the organization is engaged in, public perception of the organization, pending legislation that might affect the organization, the stability of countries where the organization operates, and so forth.

Risk Owners and Players   These are the individuals in the organization who together determine the organization's overall risk profile. For example, while one department may be willing to take moderately high risks in engaging cloud activities, another may have a lower risk tolerance. It is the aggregate of these individual tolerances that determines the organization's overall risk appetite.

Choices Involved in Managing Risk

Part of managing risk includes knowing what you want to do about it. An organization always has four choices when faced with risk:

- Risk avoidance
- Risk acceptance
- Risk transference
- Risk mitigation

The following sections will explore each of these options further.

Risk Avoidance

Risk avoidance is not a method for handling risk, but a response to the cost-benefit analysis when posed with a specific risk. If an organization is faced with a risk where the potential costs far outweigh the likely benefits, the organization may choose not to engage in the activity that would incur the risk *at all*. This is the only surefire method for eliminating a specific risk: don't conduct the risky activity.

For instance, if the activity is, say, taking a package across the ocean, and the risk includes such potential costs as drowning, soaking the package in seawater and rendering it worthless, losing both the package and the ship, and so on, and the potential benefit is being paid $5 to transport the package, the organization might (rightly) deem the risk not to be worth the reward and choose instead to stay out of the transoceanic delivery business. The organization can then be said to have engaged in risk avoidance.

Risk Acceptance

The direct opposite of risk avoidance is risk acceptance. In examining the potential benefits and risks of a certain activity, if the organization determines that the risks are minimal and the reward is substantial, the organization might choose to accept the risks involved in the endeavor and press on with the activity without any additional consideration.

To use the prior example, if the organization determines that the risks of transporting a package across the ocean are so low as to be negligible (say, if there is a sufficient historical record to indicate that nobody has drowned or lost a ship or package on similar journeys in the past 10 years), and the reward is estimable (if the organization is offered $5,000 instead of $5), then the organization make take the job of moving the package without any other consideration. This is risk acceptance.

To use some of the concepts of the prior discussion in this chapter, if the risk of the activity is estimated to be within the organization's *risk appetite*, then the organization might choose risk acceptance.

Risk Transference

Risk transference is a way to handle risk associated with an activity without accepting *all* the risk. With risk transference, the organization finds someone else to incur the potential risk of an endeavor at a fraction of the potential cost the organization would incur if the risk was realized.

Basically, when you think of risk transference, think one word: insurance. The organization is going to pay a portion of what the worst outcome would be in order to insulate against the cost of that worst outcome.

Back to the example from the previous sections: if the organization can buy shipping insurance for the task of delivering the package, then the worst-case scenario (someone drowning, losing the ship, and losing the package, and therefore losing the payment for transporting it) can be offset by a proportional payout from the underwriter. If the organization gets paid $5,000 to ship the package, then buys an insurance policy for $500 with terms such that failure to deliver or loss of the package results in a payout significant enough to mollify the client (the sender of the package) as well as recoup the costs the organization faces in performance (the expenses incurred in performing the activity, such as renting a boat, hiring someone to carry the package, and so on), and perhaps even an extraordinary payout in the event of an extraordinary risk being realized (the boat is attacked by sharks and everyone on board is eaten along with the package), then the reduced profit (reflecting the cost of the policy) might still be acceptable to the organization, with the additional assurance that the risks are being addressed.

Risk Mitigation

The final option in managing risk is risk mitigation, and this is the option that comprises the daily workload of most security practitioners. Risk mitigation is the practice of reducing risk to an acceptable level through the use of controls and countermeasures. That is to say that the organization implements controls in order to bring known risks to within that organization's risk appetite.

Using the same example as in the previous sections, controls that might be implemented to reduce the risk involved with shipping a package across the sea might include putting the package in a watertight container, affixing a tracking device to the package, equipping the ship conveying the package with anticollision sensors, and so on. When the organization has determined that the significant risks have been attenuated sufficiently with the proper controls, then the organization may decide that the business activity—shipping the package—has a sufficient chance of success.

There are two important things to note about risk mitigation:

- It is impossible to remove risk. Never believe anyone who says that something has "zero risk" or that a control offers "100 percent security." Even with all possible controls placed on a business function, there will still remain some level of risk; we call this "residual risk." If the residual risk that remains *after* controls have been implemented falls within the organization's risk appetite, then the organization might choose to perform that function. If the remaining residual risk exceeds the risk appetite of the organization, the controls are insufficient or the business is just too risky to perform.

- The cost of the controls must be less than the potential benefit of the business process, or the process is not profitable or worthwhile. You should never put a $10 lock on a $5 bicycle.

The organization can (and should) should consider and use differing types of controls when choosing to mitigate risk. In the security field, we usually group controls into three general types: physical, technical, and administrative.

Physical controls are controls that limit physical access to assets or that operate in a manner that reduces the impact of a physical event. Examples of physical controls include locks on doors, fire suppression equipment in datacenters, fences, and guards.

Technical controls, also referred to as logical controls, are those controls that enhance some facets of the CIA triad, usually operating within a system, often in electronic fashion. Possible technical controls include encryption mechanisms, access control lists to limit user permissions, and audit trails and logs of system activity.

Administrative controls are those processes and activities (necessarily not physical or technical) that provide some aspect of security. Examples: personnel background checks, scheduled routine log reviews, mandatory vacations, robust and comprehensive security policies and procedures, and designing business processes so that there are no single points of failure and so that proper separation of duties exists.

Combining the types of controls is a good way to provide the organization with some defense in depth (also known as a layered defense); that is, require any malicious actor to overcome not just multiple controls, but multiple *kinds* of controls, so that more than one skillset would be necessary to access or acquire protected assets. Think of it this way: if we only used locks to protect material, and we put locks on external entrances, internal doors, and on a safe containing sensitive assets, then an intruder would still only need one skillset (lock picking) to acquire that material. Instead, if we combined the use of locks with guard patrols, intrusion sensors, and encryption, then someone who wanted unauthorized access or ownership of sensitive material would not only have to know lock picking, but use subterfuge and stealth as well as decryption to get those assets.

There is no reason you can't combine some of the various risk management methods, and it's actually a good practice to do so. For instance, an organization can implement risk controls to perform risk mitigation *and* buy insurance to transfer risk *and then* will still have to do risk acceptance when allowing for the residual risk. The only risk management option that can't be combined with the others is risk avoidance, because avoiding the risk means not engaging in that business function, so there is nothing left to mitigate, transfer, or accept.

Risk Management Frameworks

Numerous risk management frameworks exist that are designed to assist the enterprise in developing sound risk management practices and management. However, for the purposes of the CCSP exam, we will only be discussing ISO 31000:2009, NIST 800-37, and the European Union Agency for Network and Information Security (ENISA) frameworks.

The Numbers Used in the Names of the Frameworks

Lots of numbers are used when describing some these standards, models, and frameworks, so let's take a little closer look.

You may be confused to sometimes see ISO/IEC as opposed to just ISO. ISO/IEC is a joint technical committee of the International Organization for Standardization (ISO) and the International Electrotechnical Commission (IEC). When you see standards with both sets of letters, it means that they were jointly created by both organizations. When looking at an ISO standard or model, the first number, such as 31000, represents the number in the series, and the number after the colon, such as :2009, represents the last year the standard was revised. Additionally, ISO documents are not free. Some are more expensive than others, but they are sold as a means of supporting the organization and can be quite expensive. For more information, go to www.iso.org/iso/home.html.

In the case of NIST standards, they tend to use a *revision* number such as 800-53 r4. This means that it is the fourth revision of the document since it was originally written. Sometimes they include *SP* in their name, which stands for *Special Publication*. NIST documents are paid for by U.S. tax dollars and provided for free to the world. For more information, go to https://www.nist.gov/publications.

COBIT (Control Objectives for Information Technology) 5 means that it is the fifth version of COBIT to be released since it was created. The first edition of COBIT was created in 1996. COBIT is published by ISACA, and they charge for the documents. However, if you are an ISACA member, you are entitled to one free set; additional sets must be purchased. For more information, go to www.isaca.org.

ISO 31000:2009

ISO 31000:2009 is an international standard that focuses on designing, implementing, and reviewing risk management processes and practices. The standard explains that proper implementation of a risk management process can be used to

- Create and protect value
- Integrate organizational procedures
- Be part of the decision-making process
- Explicitly address uncertainty

- Be a systematic, structured, and timely risk management program
- Ensure the risk management program is based on the best available information
- Be tailored to the organization's business requirements and actual risks
- Take human and cultural factors into account
- Ensure the risk management program is transparent and inclusive
- Create a risk management program that is dynamic, iterative, and responsive to change
- Facilitate continual improvement and enhancement of the organization

For more information please visit www.iso.org/iso/home/standards/iso31000.htm.

NIST SP 800-37 (Guide for Implementing the Risk Management Framework)

NIST SP 800-37 is the Guide for Implementing the Risk Management Framework (RMF). This particular risk management framework is a methodology for handling all organizational risk in a holistic, comprehensive, and continual manner. This RMF supersedes the old "Certification and Accreditation" model of cyclical inspections that have a specific duration (used widely in the military, intelligence, and federal communities). This RMF relies heavily on the use of automated solutions, risk analysis and assessment, and implementing controls based on those assessments, with continuous monitoring and improvement.

NIST SP 800-37 is a guide organizations can use to implement the RMF. Although NIST standards are developed for use by the federal government, they have begun to be accepted in many circles as best practices. For instance, companies in the United States may use the NIST model and publications in developing not only their information security program, but also their risk management program and practices. NIST publications and standards have the dual benefit of being widely acknowledged as expert and sensible, but also free of charge (all NIST documents are in the public domain). It takes little effort to adopt and adapt the NIST materials from their intended use in the federal space into use in a private sector or nonprofit endeavor.

Keep in mind that these documents are not as accepted in international markets as are ISO/IEC standards. Therefore, if you conduct business outside the United States, you may want to investigate the other standards in more detail. Some overseas companies will not even do business with U.S. companies unless they subscribe to and are certified under ISO standards.

For a free copy of SP 800-37, as well as many other NIST documents, visit http://csrc.nist.gov/publications/nistpubs/800-37-rev1/sp800-37-rev1-final.pdf.

European Union Agency for Network and Information Security (ENISA)

You could think of European Union Agency for Network and Information Security (ENISA) as a European counterpart to NIST. It is a standard and model developed in Europe. While it is international in nature within the confines of Europe, it is not as globally accepted in the way ISO standards are.

ENISA is responsible for producing *Cloud Computing: Benefits, Risks, and Recommendations for Information Security*. It identifies 35 types of risks organizations should consider but goes further by identifying the top eight security risks based on likelihood and impact:

- Loss of governance
- Lock-in
- Isolation failure
- Compliance risk
- Management interface failure
- Data protection
- Malicious insider
- Insecure or incomplete data deletion

For more information about ENISA, please visit https://www.enisa.europa.eu.

NOTE   If you are studying CCSP in a group environment, a useful exercise is to break up into three groups. Each group can take one of the three frameworks discussed, spend some time studying it, and then review the key points of each. When completed, join the other two groups and compare notes. Pay particular attention to how they differ in the United States as compared to Europe and the rest of the world.

Risk Management Metrics

To understand whether control mechanisms and policies are effective, it is important to identify risk management metrics that will reflect the effectiveness of your program. To do this, you can use what is referred to as a risk scorecard. These cards help you derive some relative value for risk of the activities for which you are engaged. They might, for instance, look something like this:

5. Critical
4. High
4. Moderate
2. Low
1. Minimal

Each of these levels would need to be defined so that risks could be adequately described. For instance, something that is critical (No. 5) might cause irrevocable reputational and financial damage, whereas something that is moderate (No. 4) might only cause some recoverable reputational and financial damage. Some companies even quantify these so there are actual dollar amounts attached to each. For example:

- Critical => $100,000 in damages
- High => $50,000 but < $100,000

In addition, metrics may be attached to specific types of risk or damage, as shown in Figure 11.2.

FIGURE 11.2 Assigning Numerical Value to Risk

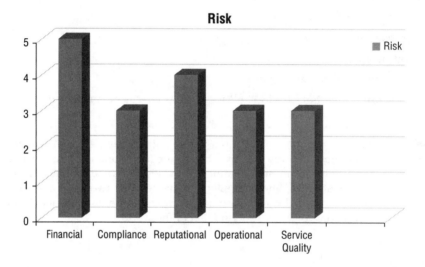

Contracts and Service-Level Agreements (SLAs)

The most important documents establishing, defining, and enforcing the relationship between the cloud provider and cloud customer are the contract and the service-level agreement (SLA). The contract describes in detail exactly what both parties' responsibilities are, what services are being contracted, and what provisions are in place for the safety, security, integrity, and availability of those same services. The SLA is the list of defined, specific, numerical metrics that will used to determine whether the provider is sufficiently meeting the contract terms during each period of performance.

Perhaps the most important relationship between the two documents is that the contract stipulates the penalty imposed on the cloud provider if any metric of the SLA is not met during a certain performance period. For instance, if the period of performance is one month, and the SLA contains a metric that states, "Downtime will not exceed five (5) seconds per calendar month," and the cloud provider has six seconds of downtime in December, then the contract should allow the cloud customer to withhold payment for the cost that would otherwise be paid for that month, without any interruption of the continued service that is scheduled for January. This is a penalty imposed on the provider for failing to meet the needs of the customer, a sort of guarantee built into the contract and enforced on a periodic basis.

Let's begin by examining some of the essential components and activities that might be expressed in the contract between a provider and customer:

- Availability
- Performance
- Security and privacy of data
- Logging and reporting
- Data location
- Data format and structure
- Portability
- Identification and problem resolution
- Change management
- Dispute mediation
- Exit strategy options
- Components activity
- Uptime guarantees (the five 9s principle)
- Penalties (for both consumer and provider)
- Penalty exclusions (instances where penalties are not invoked)
- Suspension of service
- Provider liability
- Data protection requirements
- Disaster recovery
- Security recommendations

As you can see, this assortment of details about services can be quite comprehensive. And if the CCSP or the cloud customer does not complete their due diligence by carefully scrutinizing the details of the contract, you could find yourself in quite a pickle. There are many considerations for what should be in the contract, depending on the needs of the organization.

The SLA, on the other hand, will assign specific numerical values to the performance objectives outlined in the contract. Using a sampling from the list of possible contract elements, the related SLA might include details like this:

- The cloud customer will have full, constant access to the customer's accounts and data at all times, with an allowed exception of service interruption no greater than 24 hours per calendar quarter (where service interruption is the fault of the provider).

- Data moved to or from the provider's resources and control at the defined price will not exceed 40 gigabytes per hour; data movement exceeding this rate will incur additional costs as defined in the standard rate sheet included in the contract.

- Customer service inquiries from the customer to the provider will be addressed via direct email or telephone contact within three hours of transmission.

While both the contract and the SLA may contain numerical values, the SLA will expressly include numerical metrics used to determine that recurring performance goals are met.

It's very important that the customer consider all possible situations and risks associated with the customer's business requirements when crafting and negotiating the contract and SLA. Suppose that the provider promises availability that amounts to no more than 24 hours of downtime in any given quarter. That seems pretty fair on the surface. But what if the customer is an online retailer who does 30 percent of their annual business the day after Thanksgiving, and that is the 24-hour period of an outage? It could devastate the customer's business and yet still be within the confines of the SLA.

The written labs at the end of the chapter mention looking at a video of the CSA CTP protocol. In that video, you can see how customers can pick and choose the parameters of their individual SLA needs. The person who shuts down his or her business the day after Thanksgiving may not care at all about a day's outage. But the protocol will show you how to make better decisions about what you want in your SLA as opposed to just signing it without understanding what you are getting into.

It is also important to look at the quality of the items delivered as part of your SLA. For instance, being connected and available is one thing, but if the servers at the other end are sluggish, customer experience may lag. If bandwidth is sluggish or there is jitter, again, consumer experience suffers. So in your SLA you must also adequately address these quality of service (QoS) issues. Here are some more examples:

- Availability
- Outage duration
- Capacity metrics
- Performance metrics
- Storage device metrics
- Server capacity metrics
- Instance startup time metric
- Response time metric
- Completion time metric
- Mean time to switchover
- Storage capability
- Server scalability

 The Cloud Security Alliance (CSA) has created an annual report on threats and has given them somewhat funny names. In 2013 the report was called *The Notorious Nine* and in 2016 it was named *The Treacherous 12*. Both names were due to the number of cloud computing threats or groups of threats that were identified that year. It is intended to let people know the nature of prevalent cloud threats, much like the OWASP (Open Web Application Security Project) Top Ten, which is a list of the top ten threats found or exposed in applications across the Internet.

Business Requirements

Before entering into any type of contract for cloud computing services, the organization should evaluate a number of things. First, there should be some compelling reason for engaging the cloud provider. Decisions should be made that assist the business in reaching its long-term goals. They should never be made because they seem attractive or your competitors are doing it. You should have sound business reasons for deciding to use a cloud provider and for determining which one to choose.

As part of the due diligence in looking at cloud computing as a viable solution for the business, a few more items should be examined. Perhaps not all business units need to be involved in decision making. Perhaps some changes will have little or no impact on them, in which case they do not need to be involved. This is called *scoping*, which is used to refer to including only departments or business units impacted by any cloud engagement.

Another important aspect of evaluating cloud computing solution is that of regulatory compliance. It is vital that you investigate what regulators' expectations are with regard to cloud computing solutions and the additional or differing risks that engaging in the cloud solution will bring to the organization.

Lastly, you must look closely at the costs associated with any types of disaster recovery or outage situations and what you are able to withstand. Measurements such as recovery time objective (RTO), recovery point objective (RPO), and maximum allowable downtime (MAD) are critical in making decisions about choosing cloud computing solutions. You must be able to withstand certain amounts of outages based on your risk profile as they are bound to occur at some time. Knowing how to handle them and how your cloud provider will handle them is imperative.

Cloud Contract Design and Management for Outsourcing

It is important that things like appropriate governance be involved in contract design and management of outsourcing. An in-depth understanding of contracts and contract management is important and in large enterprises is often managed by a separate department. It is the CCSP's responsibility to ensure that these contract managers understand the details of what they are managing so that the organization does not incur undue risk.

One example of adequate governance is how often contracts are renewed. This can and should be on at least an annual basis (if not sooner should there be problems). Items such as how conflicts will be resolved are also an important factor. In other words, what happens when the relationship between the customer and consumer hits a bump?

Two other vitally important aspects of contracts have to do with the notion of data portability and vendor lock-in. *Vendor lock-in* is getting stuck with a certain provider, generally either as a result of detrimental contract terms or technical limitations. Data portability is the trait customers seek in order to avoid lock-in. *Data portability* is the term used to describe the ease of moving data from one cloud provider to another (or away from the cloud provider and back to a legacy enterprise environment). The greater the portability of the data, the less chance of vendor lock-in.

If you choose to stop doing business with your cloud vendor, what happens to your data? Is it transportable? Can you move it to another provider? Will the data be in some type of universal format so it usable? Will you have a reasonable amount of time to move your data should conflicts go unresolved? And what will happen to your data once you leave the provider? Have you or they made arrangements for adequate data deletion using such techniques as crypto-shredding? These questions are all important things to consider when managing outsourcing contracts.

Identifying Appropriate Supply Chain and Vendor Management Processes

When discussing supply chain and vendor management in the realm of cloud computing, we are talking about things that bring risk into the equation. For instance, while relying on legacy internal servers to deliver application to end users, outages can be handled very quickly as there is usually staff standing by to correct problems. In a cloud scenario, the cloud vendor may only be providing IaaS, and as a result, when you have application problems, getting to the cloud environment to correct them could be more problematic.

In addition, other factors such as availability come into play in a cloud. In looking at a supply chain, several parties may be involved in delivering your cloud service:

- Cloud carriers (the ISPs between the cloud customer and the cloud provider)
- Platform provider (the vendors supplying the operating systems used in the cloud service)
- Application provider (the vendors supplying the software used in the cloud service)

These can all be different entities making up the supply chain. Should any one of these become unavailable for some reason or cause problems in accessing resources, you have a problem. These are risks associated with supply chain management and must be handled accordingly.

To adequately understand your risk exposure, you must first and foremost understand your SLAs and your provider's abilities to make good on them.

In addition to the items listed earlier, the service-level agreement should further contain these elements:

- Performance
- Security and privacy protections
- Logging and reporting

- Disaster recovery metrics
  - Recovery time objectives (RTOs)
  - Maximum period of tolerable disruption (MPTD)
- Location of data
- Data format and structure
- Data portability
- Problem identification and resolution procedures
- Change management process
- Dispute mediation process
- Exit expectations

Common Criteria Assurance Framework (ISO/IEC 15408-1:2009)

Common Criteria Assurance Framework (ISO/IEC 15408-1:2009) is yet another international standard designed to provide assurances for security claims by vendors. It establishes a common criterion for evaluating those items.

The primary goal is to ensure customers that security products they purchase have been thoroughly tested by independent third-party testers and meet the requirements the customer has specified.

One thing to keep in mind is that the certification of the product only certifies its capabilities. If misconfigured or mismanaged, it is no more secure than anything else the customer might use.

For more information visit about the Common Criteria and ISO/IEC 15408-1:2009, go to www.iso.org/iso/catalogue_detail.htm?csnumber=50341.

Cloud Computing Certification

The Cloud Certification Schemes List (CCSL) provides an overview of different existing certification schemes. It describes the main characteristics relevant to cloud computing and cloud computing customers. It also attempts to answer questions such as the following in an effort to provide the customer with adequate knowledge in order to make a well-informed decision about a cloud provider:

- Which are the underlying standards?
- Who issues the cert?
- Is the CSP audited?
- Who conducts the audits (internal vs. external)?

The schemes that make up the CCSL are as follows:

- Certified Cloud Service – TUV Rhineland
- CSA Attestation – OCF Level 2
- CSA Certification Level 2
- CSA Self-Assessment – OCF Level 1
- EuroCloud Self-Assessment (ECSA Self-Assessment)
- EuroCloud Star Audit Certification (ECSA Audit)
- Payment Card Industry Data Security Standard (PCI DSS) v3.2
- LEET Security Rating Guide
- AICPA SOC 1
- AICPA SOC 2
- AICPA SOC 3

The Cloud Certification Schemes Metaframework (CCSM) is an extension of the CCSL designed to provide a high-level mapping of security requirements of the customer to security objectives in existing cloud security schemes.

The first version of the CCSM was released in 2014 and can be accessed from the following URL: https://resilience.enisa.europa.eu/cloud-computing-certification/ list-of-cloud-certification-schemes/cloud-certification-schemes-metaframework.

There are 27 CCSM security objectives that the customer can select to cross-reference against. A resultant comparison matrix might look something like Table 11.1.

TABLE 11.1 A comparison matrix

CCSM security objective	Certified Cloud Service – TUV Rhineland	CSA Attestation OCF Level 2	EuroCloud Self-Assessment	ISO/IEC 27001 Certification
Risk Management	X	X	X	
Cloud Data Security	X	X	X	
Cloud Software Security	X	X	X	X
Cloud Monitoring and Log Access	X	X	X	X

CSA Security, Trust, and Assurance Registry (STAR)

The CSA STAR program, initiated in 2011, appeared as demand for a single consistent framework for evaluating cloud providers developed. Several other frameworks were floating around, but there was no single source where customers could go and see how a cloud provider rated with regard to the framework.

The CSA STAR program was designed to provide an independent level of program assurance for cloud consumers. It is based on three levels of assurance, covers four offerings, and consists of a comprehensive set of cloud-centric control objectives.

The CSA STAR is a complementary registry of security controls provided by popular cloud computing offerings and is designed for users to assess cloud providers, security providers, and advisory and assessment service firms as part of their vendor management due diligence in choosing providers.

The CSA STAR consists of the two following components:

Cloud Controls Matrix (CCM) A list of security controls and principles appropriate for the cloud environment, cross-referenced to other control frameworks such as COBIT, ISO standards, and NIST pubs. You can download a copy of the current CCM from CSA at `https://downloads.cloudsecurityalliance.org/assets/research/cloud-controls-matrix/CSA_CCM_v.3.0.1-10-06-2016.xlsx`.

Consensus Assessments Initiative Questionnaire (CAIQ) A self-assessment performed by cloud providers, detailing their evaluation of the practice areas and control groups they use in providing their services. You can download a copy of the current CAIQ from CSA at `https://cloudsecurityalliance.org/download/consensus-assessments-initiative-questionnaire-v3-0-1/`. You can also review completed CAIQs and certifications for various cloud providers in the CSA's STAR registry online at `https://cloudsecurityalliance.org/star/#_registry`.

The CSA STAR program also consists of three levels based on the Open Certification Framework (see Figure 11.3):

FIGURE 11.3 The Cloud Security Alliance Open Certification Framework

Level One: Self-Assessment   Requires the release and publication of due diligence assessments against the CSA's *Consensus Assessment Initiative Questionnaire and/or Cloud Matrix (CCM)*

Level Two: CSA STAR Attestation   Requires the release and publication of available results of an assessment carried out by an independent third party based on CSA CCM and ISO 27001:2013 or an AICPA SOC 2

Level Three: CSA STAR Continuous Monitoring   Requires the release and publication of results related to the security properties of monitoring based on the CloudTrust Protocol

There have been several iterations of the CCM, with the most recent and default being CCM v3.0.1 effective October 2016.

Much like the SOC reports discussed in Chapter 10, these levels are representative of varying degrees of compliance with the framework. Involving independent third-party assessors can be quite expensive, and only large providers can usually absorb the cost as they typically also have a large investment in their security infrastructure.

Supply Chain Risk

When evaluating supply chain risk, the customer should be thinking of disaster recovery and business continuity: What happens if something goes south with one or more of these vendors on which your business depends? You might also look at it like a network where interdependencies are everywhere. You cannot afford to have any major outages, so you build in redundancy where it makes good sense. The same is true of the supply chain. Remember the old saying, *don't put all your eggs in one basket.*

Some common supply chain risks are:

- Financial instability of provider
- Single points of failure
- Data breaches
- Malware infestations
- Data loss

Even more common than folks would like to think are natural disasters. What if the datacenter of your cloud provider is destroyed by an act of nature like the tsunami in Japan several years ago?

As you are aware you cannot, nor should you attempt to, reduce all risks. Some are simply too large. When risks are too large to remove, you need to look to other means such as transferring the risk or avoiding the risk. Risk can be avoided by not engaging in the activity. Insurance is one form of transferring some of the risk. This is often done in situations where the likelihood of a disaster is rather small but the consequences could be catastrophic, such as in the event of a fire or tornado.

ISO 28000:2007 defines a set of security management requirements, including those that must be applied to all parties within a supply chain. However, the responsibility of ensuring the suitability of each vendor in the supply chain for meeting those requirements and enforcing them up and down the supply chain is squarely on the shoulders of the contracting organization. In other words, if you pay someone else to perform a service that in any way might affect your customers, you are obligated to ensure that the entities you've paid are subject to governance equivalent to what you've promised your customers and that those entities are following that governance. ISO 28000:2007 also provides for a certification against certain elements that relate to supply chain risk:

- Security management policy
- Organizational objectives
- Risk management practices
- Documented practices and records
- Supplier relationships
- Roles, responsibilities, and authorities
- Organizational procedures and processes

As the standard grows in popularity with cloud providers, it will in all likelihood be more widely adopted in the future. Much like the STAR Registry, ISO certification gives the consumer some level of assurance that the appropriate controls are in place to secure data and privacy.

Summary

In this chapter we discussed a number of issues dealing with risk and risk management. We examined risk frameworks, contracts, service-level agreements, and certifications that help in assuring cloud customers that sound security practices are in place and that they can rely on their provider.

Exam Essentials

Ensure that you have a good grasp of the models, frameworks, and standards discussed in this chapter.   This includes ISO standards, NIST standards, and ENISA.

Be familiar with data management roles.   Make sure you understand the various data roles and the activities and responsibilities of each.

Make sure you have a thorough understanding of all the elements of the service-level agreement (SLA).   Understand how SLAs apply to cloud computing.

Be sure to understand the three levels of the CSA Security, Trust, and Assurance Registry (STAR) Open Certification Framework. Be sure to understand the three levels of the CSA STAR Open Certification Framework.

Written Labs

1. Go to the CSA website and read the detailed description of the CSA STAR program at `https://cloudsecurityalliance.org/star/`. Be sure you understand the three levels in the Open Certification Framework. Then attempt to identify at least three cloud service providers who have met the requirements and write down their names.

2. Go to the following URL and watch the video demo of the CSA CloudTrust Protocol (CTP): `https://cloudsecurityalliance.org/group/cloudtrust-protocol/`.

3. Name and describe at least two major risk management frameworks.

4. Describe the primary difference between risk appetite and risk tolerance.

5. Name at least two important factors in reviewing an SLA.

Review Questions

You can find the answers in Appendix A.

1. Which is the lowest level of the CSA STAR program?
   A. Continuous monitoring
   B. Self-assessment
   C. Hybridization
   D. Attestation

2. Which of the following is a valid risk management metric?
   A. KPI
   B. KRI
   C. SLA
   D. SOC

3. Which of the following frameworks focuses specifically on design implementation and management?
   A. ISO 31000:2009
   B. HIPAA
   C. ISO 27017
   D. NIST 800-92

4. Which of the following frameworks identifies the top 8 security risks based on likelihood and impact?
   A. NIST 800-53
   B. ISO 27000
   C. ENISA
   D. COBIT

5. The CSA STAR program consists of three levels. Which of the following is not one of those levels?
   A. Self-assessment
   B. Third-party assessment-based certification
   C. SOC 2 audit certification
   D. Continuous monitoring–based certification

6. Which ISO standard refers to addressing security risks in a supply chain?
   A. ISO 27001
   B. ISO/IEC 28000:2007
   C. ISO 18799
   D. ISO 31000:2009

7. Which of the following is *not* a risk management framework?

   A. NIST SP 800-37

   B. European Union Agency for Network and Information Security (ENISA)

   C. Key risk indicators (KRI)

   D. ISO 31000:2009

8. Which of the following best define risk?

   A. Threat coupled with a breach

   B. Vulnerability coupled with an attack

   C. Threat coupled with a threat actor

   D. Threat coupled with a vulnerability

9. Which of the following is not a part of the ENISA Top 8 Security Risks of cloud computing?

   A. Vendor lock-in

   B. Isolation failure

   C. Insecure or incomplete data deletion

   D. Availability

10. Which of the following is a risk management option that halts a business function?

   A. Mitigation

   B. Acceptance

   C. Transference

   D. Avoidance

11. Which of the following best describes a cloud carrier?

   A. A person or entity responsible for making a cloud service available to consumers

   B. The intermediary who provides connectivity and transport of cloud services between cloud providers and cloud consumers

   C. The person or entity responsible for keeping cloud services running for customers

   D. The person or entity responsible for transporting data across the Internet

12. Which of the following methods of addressing risk is most associated with insurance?

   A. Transference

   B. Avoidance

   C. Acceptance

   D. Mitigation

13. Which of the following components are part of what a CCSP should review when looking at contracting with a cloud service provider?

    A. The physical layout of the datacenter

    B. Background checks for the provider's personnel

    C. Use of subcontractors

    D. Redundant uplink grafts

14. A data custodian is responsible for which of the following?

    A. The safe custody, transport, storage of the data, and implementation of business rules

    B. Logging access and alerts

    C. Data content

    D. Data context

15. Which of the following is *not* a way to manage risk?

    A. Enveloping

    B. Mitigating

    C. Accepting

    D. Transferring

16. Which of the following is not a risk management framework?

    A. Hex GBL

    B. COBIT

    C. NIST SP 800-37

    D. ISO 31000:2009

17. Which of the following is not appropriate to include in an SLA?

    A. The number of user accounts allowed during a specified period

    B. Which personnel are responsible and authorized among both the provider and the customer to declare an emergency and transition the service to contingency operation status

    C. The amount of data allowed to be transmitted and received between the cloud provider and customer

    D. The time allowed to migrate from normal operations to contingency operations

18. What is the Cloud Security Alliance Cloud Controls Matrix (CCM)?

    A. An inventory of cloud service security controls that are arranged into separate security domains

    B. An inventory of cloud services security controls that are arranged into a hierarchy of security domains

    C. A set of regulatory requirements for cloud service providers

    D. A set of software development life cycle requirements for cloud service providers

19. Which of the following is not one of the types of controls?

    A. Transitional

    B. Administrative

    C. Technical

    D. Physical

20. Which of the following is not an example of an essential internal stakeholder?

    A. IT analyst

    B. IT director

    C. CFO

    D. HR director

Appendix

A

Answers to the Review Questions

Chapter 1: Architectural Concepts

1. B. Programming as a Service is not a common offering; the others are ubiquitous throughout the industry.

2. D. Virtualization allows scalable resource allocation; broadband connections allow users to have remote access from anywhere; cryptographic connections allow for secure remote access. Smart hubs aren't widely used in cloud offerings.

3. A. Service-level agreements (SLAs) specify objective measures that define what the cloud provider will deliver to the customer.

4. C. Security is usually not a profit center, and is therefore beholden to business drivers; the purpose of security is to support the business.

5. D. Lack of access is an availability issue.

6. B. CASBs don't usually offer BC/DR/COOP services; that's something offered by cloud providers.

7. D. The data on magnetic swipe cards isn't usually encrypted.

8. B. Risks, in general, can be reduced but never eliminated; cloud service, specifically, does not eliminate risk to the cloud customer, because the customer retains a great deal of risk after migration.

9. B. Backups are still just as important as ever, regardless of where your primary data and backups are stored.

10. B. There are no written laws that require a cloud customer to remain with a certain cloud provider.

11. B. This is the definition of vendor lock-out.

12. B. This is a nonsense term used as a red herring.

13. C. Under current law, the data owner is responsible for any breaches that result in unauthorized disclosure of PII; this includes breaches caused by contracted parties and outsources services. The data owner is the cloud customer.

14. B. The business impact analysis is designed to ascertain the value of the organization's assets, and learn the critical paths and processes.

15. A. This is the definition of a private cloud model.

16. B. This is the definition of a public cloud model.

17. D. This is the definition of a community cloud model.

18. B. PaaS allows the cloud customer to install any kind of software, including software to be tested, on an architecture that includes any desired OSs.

19. C. SaaS is the most comprehensive cloud offering, requiring little input and administration on the part of the cloud customer.

20. A. IaaS offers what is basically a hot/warm DR site, with hardware, connectivity, and utilities, allowing the customer to build out any kind of software configuration (including choosing OSs).

Chapter 2: Design Requirements

1. B. When we gather information about business requirements, we need to do a complete inventory, receive accurate valuation of assets (usually from the owners of those assets), and assess criticality; this collection of information does not tell us, objectively, how useful an asset is, however.

2. B. The business impact analysis gathers asset valuation information that is beneficial for risk analysis and selection of security controls (it helps avoid putting the ten-dollar lock on the five-dollar bicycle), and criticality information that helps in BC/DR planning by letting the organization understand which systems, data, and personnel are necessary to continuously maintain. However, it does not aid secure acquisition efforts, since the assets examined by the BIA have already been acquired.

3. D. In IaaS, the service is bare metal, and the customer has to install the OS and the software; the customer then is responsible for maintaining that OS. In the other models, the provider installs and maintains the OS.

4. C. In PaaS, the provider supplies the hardware, connectivity, and OS; the customer installs and maintains applications. In IaaS, the customer must also install the OS, and in SaaS, the provider supplies and maintains the applications.

5. B. SaaS is the model in which the customer supplies only the data; in the other models, the customer also supplies the OS, the application, or both.

6. B. The contract codifies the rights and responsibilities of the parties involved upon completion of negotiation. The RMF aids in risk analysis and design of the environment. An MOU is shared between parties for a number of possible reasons. The BIA aids in risk assessment, DC/BR efforts, and selection of security controls.

7. D. Layered defense calls for a diverse approach to security.

8. A. A process is an administrative control; sometimes, the process includes elements of other types of controls (in this case, the access control mechanism might be a technical control, or it might be a physical control), but the process itself is administrative. Keystroke logging is a technical control (or an attack, if done for malicious purposes, and not for auditing); door locks are a physical control; and biometric authentication is a technological control. This is a tricky question.

9. A. A firewall is a technological control. The safe and extinguisher are physical controls, and firing someone is an administrative control.

10. D. Fences are physical controls; carpets and ceilings are architectural features, and a door is not necessarily a control: the lock on the door would be a physical security control. Although you might think of a door as a potential answer, the best answer is the fence; the exam will have questions where more than one answer is correct, and the answer that will score you points is the one that is *most* correct.

11. D. All of these activities should incorporate encryption, except for profile formatting, which is a made-up term.

12. A. We don't want to improve default accounts—we want to remove them. All the other options are steps we take to harden devices.

13. B. Updating and patching the system helps harden the system. Encrypting the OS is a distractor. That would make the OS/machine impossible to use. Video cameras are a security control, but not one used to harden a device. Background checks are good for vetting personnel, but not for hardening devices.

14. A. Homomorphic encryption hopes to achieve that goal; the other options are terms that have almost nothing to do with encryption.

15. B. Senior management decides the risk appetite of the organization.

16. C. This is the definition of the term.

17. B. Reversal is not a method for handling risk.

18. D. Although all the other options are ways to harden a mobile device, two-person integrity is a concept that has nothing to do with the topic, and, if implemented, would require everyone in your organization to walk around in pairs while using their mobile devices.

19. D. Although the rest of the options are good tactics for securing devices, we can't remove all admin accounts; the device will need to be administered at some point, and that account needs to be there.

20. C. Option C is the definition of risk—and risk is never preventable: it can be obviated, attenuated, reduced, and minimized, but never completely prevented. A risk may be everlasting or transient, indicating that risk itself is not limited to being either.

Chapter 3: Data Classification

1. B. All the others are valid methods of data discovery; user-based is a red herring with no meaning.

2. C. All the others might be included in data labels, but we don't usually include data value, since it is prone to change frequently, and because it might not be information we want to disclose to anyone who does not have need to know.

3. B. All the others might be included in data labels, but we don't include delivery vendor, which is nonsense in context.

4. D. All the others might be included in data labels, but multifactor authentication is a procedure used for access control, not a label.

5. D. All the others are data analytics methods, but "refractory iterations" is a nonsense term thrown in as a red herring.

6. B. The data owner is usually considered the cloud customer in a cloud configuration; the data in question is the customer's information, being processed in the cloud. The cloud provider is only leasing services and hardware to the customer. The cloud access security broker (CASB) only handles access control on behalf of the cloud customer, and is not in direct contact with the production data.

7. C. In legal terms, when "data processor" is defined, it refers to anyone who stores, handles, moves, or manipulates data on behalf of the data owner or controller. In the cloud computing realm, this is the cloud provider.

8. A. Policy drives all programs and functions in the organization; the organization should not conduct any operations that don't have a policy governing them. Penalties may or may not be an element of policy, and severity depends on the topic. Multifactor authentication and homomorphic encryption are red herrings here.

9. D. All the elements except adjudication need to be addressed in each policy. Adjudication is not an element of policy.

10. B We don't have physical ownership, control, or even access to the devices holding the data, so physical destruction, including melting, is not an option. Overwriting is a possibility, but it is complicated by the difficulty of locating all the sectors and storage areas that might have contained our data, and by the likelihood that constant backups in the cloud increase the chance we'll miss something as it's being overwritten. Cryptoshredding is the only reasonable alternative. Cold fusion is a red herring.

11. A. Copyrights are protected tangible expressions of creative works. The other answers listed are answers to subsequent questions.

12. B. Patents protect processes (as well as inventions, new plantlife, and decorative patterns). The other answers listed are answers to other questions.

13. D. Confidential sales and marketing materials unique to the organization are trade secrets. The other answers listed are answers to other questions.

14. D. Confidential recipes unique to the organization are trade secrets. The other answers listed are answers to other questions.

15. C. Logos and symbols and phrases and color schemes that describe brands are trademarks. The other answers listed are answers to other questions.

16. C. The DMCA provision for takedown notices allows copyright holders to demand removal of suspect content from the web, and puts the burden of proof on whoever posted the material; this function has been abused by griefers and trolls and overzealous content producers. The OSP exemption providers a safe harbor provision for web hosts.

The decryption program prohibition makes DeCSS and other similar programs illegal. Puppet plasticity is a nonsense term used for a red herring.

17. B. The U.S. Patent and Trademark Office accepts, reviews, and approves applications for new patents. The USDA creates and enforces agriculture regulation. OSHA oversees workplace safety regulations. The SEC regulates publicly traded corporations.

18. C. DRM solutions use all these methods except for dip switch validity, which is a nonsense term.

19. D. The United States does not have a single, overarching personal privacy law; instead, the U.S. often protects PII by industry (HIPAA, GLBA, FERPA, and so forth.). All EU member countries adhere to the Data Protection Regulation. Argentina's Personal Data Protection Act cleaves to the EU Regulation, as does Japan's Act on the Protection of Personal Information.

20. B. DRM tools should include all the functions listed except for self-destruction, which might hurt someone.

Chapter 4: Cloud Data Security

1. B. Data discovery is a term used to describe the process of identifying information according to specific traits or categories. The rest are all methods for obscuring data.

2. D. SIEM does not intend to provide any enhancement of performance; in fact, a SIEM solution may decrease performance because of additional overhead. All the rest are goals of SIEM implementations.

3. B. DLP does not have anything to do with elasticity, which is the capability of the environment to scale up or down according to demand. All the rest are goals of DLP implementations.

4. B. DLP solutions may protect against inadvertent disclosure. Randomization is a technique for obscuring data, not a risk to data. DLP tools will not protect against risks from natural disasters, or against impacts due to device failure.

5. A. DLP tools can identify outbound traffic that violates the organization's policies. DLP will not protect against losses due to performance issues or power failures. The DLP solution must be configured according to the organization's policies, so bad policies will attenuate the effectiveness of DLP tools, not the other way around.

6. C. AES is an encryption standard. Link encryption is a method for protecting communications traffic. One-time pads are an encryption method.

7. A. DLP tools need to be aware of which information to monitor and which requires categorization (usually done upon data creation, by the data owners). DLPs can be implemented with or without physical access or presence. USB connectivity has nothing to do with DLP solutions.

8. B. In order to implement tokenization, there will need to be two databases: the database containing the raw, original data, and the token database containing tokens that map to original data. Having two-factor authentication is nice, but certainly not required. Encryption keys are not necessary for tokenization. Two-person integrity does not have anything to do with tokenization.

9. D. Data masking does not support authentication in any way. All the others are excellent use cases for data masking.

10. A. DLP can be combined with DRM to protect intellectual property; both are designed to deal with data that falls into special categories. SIEMs are used for monitoring event logs, not live data movement. Kerberos is an authentication mechanism. Hypervisors are used for virtualization.

11. B. ITAR is a Department of State program. Evaluation assurance levels are part of the Common Criteria standard from ISO. Digital rights management tools are used for protecting electronic processing of intellectual property.

12. A. EAR is a Commerce Department program. Evaluation assurance levels are part of the Common Criteria standard from ISO. Digital rights management tools are used for protecting electronic processing of intellectual property.

13. B. Cryptographic keys should not be stored along with the data they secure, regardless of key length. We don't split crypto keys or generate redundant keys (doing so would violate the principle of secrecy necessary for keys to serve their purpose).

14. D. We should do all of these except for requiring multifactor authentication, which is pointless in key management.

15. A. The physical security of crypto keys is of some concern, but guards or vaults are not always necessary. Two-person integrity might be a good practice for protecting keys. The best answer to this question is option A, because it is always true, whereas the remaining options depend on circumstances.

16. D. All of these things should be considered when creating data archival policies, except option D, which is a nonsense term.

17. B. The other options are the names of the phases, but out of proper order.

18. B. Data loss, leak prevention, and protection is a family of tools used to reduce the possibility of unauthorized disclosure of sensitive information. SIEMs are tools used to collate and manage log data. AES is an encryption standard.

19. B. Object-based storage stores data as objects in a volume, with labels and metadata. Databases store data in fields, in a relational motif. A CDN stores data in caches of copied content near locations of high demand.

20. D. Object-based storage stores data as objects in a volume, with labels and metadata. File-based is a cloud storage architecture that manages the data in a hierarchy of files. Databases store data in fields, in a relational motif.

Chapter 5: Security in the Cloud

1. D. Elasticity is the name for the benefit of cloud computing where resources can be apportioned as necessary to meet customer demand. Obfuscation is a technique to hide full raw datasets, either from personnel who do not have need to know or for use in testing. Mobility is not a term pertinent to the CBK.

2. D. This is not a normal configuration and would not likely provide genuine benefit.

3. B. Background checks are controls for attenuating potential threats from internal actors; external threats aren't likely to submit to background checks.

4. B. DRM and DLP are used for increased authentication/access control and egress monitoring, respectively, and would actually decrease portability instead of enhancing it.

5. A. Dual control is not useful for remote access devices, because we'd have to assign two people for every device, which would decrease efficiency and productivity. Muddling is a cocktail preparation technique that involves crushing ingredients. Safe harbor is a policy provision that allows for compliance through an alternate method than the primary instruction.

6. D. The cloud provider's resellers are a marketing and sales mechanism, not an operational dependency that could affect the security of a cloud customer.

7. A. State notification laws and the loss of proprietary data/intellectual property pre-existed the cloud; only the lack of ability to transfer liability is new.

8. A. IaaS entails the cloud customer installing and maintaining the OS, programs, and data; PaaS has the customer installing programs and data; in SaaS, the customer only uploads data. In a community cloud, data and device owners are distributed.

9. C. NIST offers many informative guides and standards, but nothing specific to any one organization. The cloud provider will not have prepared an analysis of lock-out/lock-in potential. Open source providers can offer many useful materials, but, again, nothing specific to the organization.

10. B. Malware risks and threats are not affected by the terms of the cloud contract.

11. C. DoS/DDoS threats and risks are not unique to the public cloud model.

12. B. Hardened perimeter devices are more useful at attenuating the risk of external attack.

13. C. ISP redundancy is a means to control the risk of externalities, not internal threats.

14. D. Scalability is a feature of cloud computing, allowing users to dictate an increase or decrease in service as needed, not a means to counter internal threats.

15. C. Conflict of interest is a threat, not a control.

16. A. Metered service allows cloud customers to minimize expenses, and only pay for what they need and use; this has nothing to do with BC/DR.

17. C. Cryptographic sanitization is a means of reducing the risks from data remnance, not a way to minimize escalation of privilege.

18. B. Attackers prefer Type 2 hypervisors, because the OS offers more attack surface and potential vulnerabilities. There are no Type 3 or 4 hypervisors.

19. B. Vendor lock-in is the result of a lack of portability, for any number of reasons. Masking is a means to hide raw datasets from users who do not have need to know. Closing is a nonsense term.

20. C. Software developers often install backdoors as a means to avoid performing entire workflows when adjusting the programs they're working; they often leave backdoors behind in production software, inadvertently or intentionally.

Chapter 6: Responsibilities in the Cloud

1. A. In IaaS, the cloud provider only owns the hardware and supplies the utilities. The customer is responsible for the OS, programs, and data. In PaaS and SaaS, the provider also owns the OS. There is no QaaS. That is a red herring.

2. D. While the provider might share any of the other options listed, the provider will not share administration of security controls with the customer. Security controls are the sole province of the provider.

3. B. The contract between the provider and customer enhances the customer's trust by holding the provider financially liable for negligence or inadequate service (although the customer remains legally liable for all inadvertent disclosures). Statutes, however, largely leave customers liable. The security control matrix is a tool for ensuring compliance with regulations. HIPAA is a statute.

4. D. The SOC 3 is the least detailed, so the provider is not concerned about revealing it. The SOC 1 Types 1 and 2 are about financial reporting, and not relevant. The SOC 2 Type 2 is much more detailed and will most likely be kept closely held by the provider.

5. B. The SOC 3 is the least detailed, so the provider is not concerned about revealing it. The SOC 1 Types 1 and 2 are about financial reporting and not relevant. The SOC 2 Type 2 is much more detailed and will most likely be kept closely held by the provider.

6. C. Sarbanes-Oxley was a direct response to corporate scandals. FERPA is related to education. GLBA is about the financial industry. HIPAA is about health care.

7. B. Removing antimalware agents. Hardening the operating system means making it more secure. Limiting administrator access, closing unused ports, and removing unnecessary services and libraries all have the potential to make an OS more secure. But removing antimalware agents would actually make the system less secure. If anything, antimalware agents should be added, not removed.

8. C. Video surveillance will not provide meaningful information and will not enhance trust. All the others will and do.

9. B. The customer does not administer on behalf of the provider. All the rest are possible options.

10. B. SOC 2 deals with the CIA triad. SOC 1 is for financial reporting. SOC 3 is only an attestation by the auditor. There is no SOC 4.

11. C. SOC 2 deals with the CIA triad. SOC 1 is for financial reporting. SOC 3 is only an attestation by the auditor. There is no SOC 4.

12. C. The provider may share audit and performance log data with the customer. The provider will most likely not share any of the other options, since they reveal too much information about the provider's security program.

13. A. The customer always owns the data and will therefore always have access to it. The customer will never have administrative access to the security controls, regardless of the model. The customer may or may not have administrative control over user permissions. The customer only has administrative power over the OS in an IaaS model.

14. D. Security is always contingent on business drivers and beholden to operational needs. The virtualization engine does not dictate security controls, and the hypervisor may vary (depending on its type and implementation). The SLAs do not drive security controls; they drive performance goals.

15. B. The customer currently always retains legal liability for data loss, even if the provider was negligent or malicious.

16. A. Knowledge of the physical layout and site controls could be of great use to an attacker, so they are kept extremely confidential. The other options are all red herrings.

17. B. Open source software is available to the public, and often draws inspection from numerous, disparate reviewers. A DBMS is not reviewed more or less than other software. All software in a production environment should be secure. That is not a valid discriminator for answering this question. Proprietary software reviews are limited to the personnel employed within the offices of the software developer, which narrows the perspective and necessarily reduces the amount of potential reviewers.

18. D. Firewalls do use rules, behavior analytics, and/or content filtering in order to determine which traffic is allowable. Firewalls ought not use random criteria, because any such limitations would be just as likely to damage production efforts as enhance them.

19. C. A honeypot is meant to draw in attackers but not divulge anything of value. It should not use raw, production, or sensitive data.

20. C. Vulnerability assessments can only detect known vulnerabilities, using definitions. Some malware is known, as are programming flaws. Zero-day exploits, on the other hand, are necessarily unknown, until discovered and exercised by an attacker, and will therefore not be detected by vulnerability assessments.

Chapter 7: Cloud Application Security

1. B. The other answers all list aspects of SOAP.

2. B. The other answers are all possible stages used in software development.

3. D. The other answers all include aspects of the STRIDE model.

4. C. All the possible answers are good, and are, in fact, correct. C, however, is the most complete and therefore the best answer.

5. B. Again, all of these answers are actually correct, but B is the best answer, because it is the most general, includes the others, and is therefore the optimum choice. This is a good example of the type of question that can appear on the actual exam.

6. C. Options A and B are also correct, but C is more general and incorporates them both. D is incorrect, because sandboxing does not take place in the production environment.

7. B. Options A and C are also correct, but included in B, making B the best choice. D is incorrect, because we don't want unauthorized users gaining access.

8. A. In a trusted third-party model of federation, each member organization outsources the review and approval task to a third party they all trust. This makes the third party the identifier (it issues and manages identities for all users in all organizations in the federation), and the various member organizations are the relying parties (the resource providers that share resources based on approval from the third party).

9. B. Option A is incorrect, because it refers to a specific applications security elements, meaning it is about an ANF, not the ONF. C is true, but not as complete as B, making B the better choice. D suggests that the framework contains only "some" of the components, which is why B (which describes "all" components) is better.

10. C. All the answers are true, but C is the most complete.

11. B. Remember, there is a one-to-many ratio of ONF to ANF; each organization has one ONF and many ANFs (one for each application in the organization). Therefore, the ANF is a subset of the ONF.

12. B. Option C is also true, but not as comprehensive as B. A and D are simply not true.

13. B. Option B is a description of the standard; the others are not.

14. C. Options B and D are also correct, but not as comprehensive as C, making C the best choice. A is not correct; we don't want to encrypt data if we're using the data for testing or display purposes, the common uses of masked data.

15. A. We don't use DAM in place of encryption or masking; DAM augments these options without replacing them. We don't usually think of the database interaction as client-server, so A is the best answer.

16. C. WAFs detect how the application interacts with the environment, so they are optimal for detecting and refuting things like SQL injection and XSS. Password cracking, syn floods, and ransomware usually aren't taking place in the same way as injection and XSS, and they are better addressed with controls at the router and through the use of HIDS, NIDS, and antimalware tools.

17. D. Option D is the best, most general, and most accurate answer.

18. C. The other answers are true of SOAP.

19. B. We do the testing prior to deployment, so A and C are incorrect. D is simply a distractor.

20. A. Options B and C are incorrect, because a sandbox is not in the production environment. D is incorrect in that sandboxing does not prevent code from running.

Chapter 8: Operations Elements

1. A. There are four tiers of the Uptime Institute's datacenter redundancy rating system, with 1 being the lowest and 4 the highest.

2. C. The other answers are distractors.

3. A. The three common types of security training are initial, recurring, and refresher.

4. A. Repudiation is an element of the STRIDE model; the rest of the answers are not.

5. C. Resiliency is not an element of the STRIDE model; all the rest of the answers are.

6. B. Team-building has nothing to do with SAST; all the rest of the answers are characteristics of SAST.

7. D. Binary inspection has nothing to do with DAST, and it is not really a term that means anything in our industry (although it could be interpreted as a type of code review, more related to SAST); all the rest of the answers are characteristics of DAST.

8. A. Keystroke logging is not a characteristic of secure KVM design; in fact, secure KVM components should attenuate the potential for keystroke logging. All the rest of the answers are characteristics of secure KVM components.

9. C. Emergency egress redundancy is the only aspect of datacenters that can be expected to be found in datacenters of any tier; the rest of the answers list characteristics that can be found only in specific tiers.

10. B. Regardless of the tier level or purpose of any datacenter, design focus for security should always consider health and human safety paramount.

11. B. Parity bits and disk striping are characteristic of RAID implementations. Cloud-bursting is a feature of scalable cloud hosting. Data dispersion uses parity bits, but not disk striping; instead, it uses data chunks and encryption. SAN is a data storage technique, but not focused on resiliency.

12. A. Cross-training offers attenuation of lost contingency capabilities by ensuring personnel will be able to perform essential tasks, even if they are not primarily assigned to those positions in a full-time capacity. Metered usage is a benefit for cloud customers associated with ensuring value for payment, but not resiliency. Proper placement of HVAC temperature measurement and raised floors both aid in optimizing component performance but are not practically associated with resiliency. This is a difficult question, and it could be read in ways that would suggest other correct answers.

13. C. Changing regulations should not result in lack of availability. All the other answers have caused DoS outages.

14. C. Security training documentation can be used to show that personnel have received adequate, pertinent training to a suitable level, which demonstrates due diligence—that is, effort in furtherance of due care. All the other answers are beneficial to the resiliency and durability of the datacenter, but they are not methods for demonstrating due diligence. This is a difficult question, and it could be read in ways that would suggest other correct answers.

15. D. The location of many datacenters—rurally situated, distant from metropolitan areas—may create challenges for finding multiple power utility providers and ISPs, as those areas just aren't usually served by multiple vendors. Expense is not usually a concern; economies of scale make costs acceptable as part of the pricing structure. Personnel deployment doesn't usually affect access to either type of connection. The carrying medium has nothing to do with challenges for finding multiple providers and is not even a common industry term.

16. D. The height of dropped ceilings is not a security concern, except in action movies. The rest of the answers are all aspects of physical security that should be taken into account when planning and designing a datacenter.

17. B. The Brewer-Nash model is also known as the Chinese Wall model.

18. B. Type II hypervisors run via the OS on the host machine; this makes them attractive to attackers, as both the machine and the OS offer potential attack vectors. Cat IV and converged are not terms associated with hypervisors. Bare-metal hypervisors (Type I) are less preferable to attackers, as they offer less attack surface.

19. C. Data dispersion uses parity bits, data chunks, and encryption. Parity bits and disk striping are characteristic of RAID implementations. Cloud-bursting is a feature of scalable cloud hosting. SAN is a data storage technique but not focused on resiliency.

20. D. Security training should not be boring; you want attendees to be enthused so that they pay attention, which enhances recall of the material, elevating security for the organization. All the other answers are characteristics of good security training.

Chapter 9: Operations Management

1. C. The full test will involve every asset in the organization, including all personnel. The others will have lesser impact, except for D, which is a red herring.

2. A. The tabletop testing involves only essential personnel and none of the production assets. The others will have greater impact, except for D, which is a red herring.

3. C. Liquid propane does not spoil, which obviates necessity for continually refreshing and restocking it and might make it more cost-effective. The burn rate has nothing to do with its suitability, unless it has some direct bearing on the particular generator the datacenter owner has chosen. The various relative prices of fuel fluctuate. Flavor is a distractor in this question and means nothing.

4. B. Frustrated employees and managers can increase risk to the organization by implementing their own, unapproved modifications to the environment. The particular interval changes from organization to organization.

5. B. A datacenter with less than optimum humidity can have a higher static electricity discharge rate. Humidity has no bearing on breaches or theft, and inversion is a nonsense term used as a distractor.

6. D. The UPS is intended to last only long enough to save production data currently being processed. The exact quantity of time will depend on many variables and will differ from one datacenter to the next.

7. C. Generator power should be online before battery backups fail. The specific amount of time will vary between datacenters.

8. B. Automated patching is much faster and more efficient than manual patching. It is, however, not necessarily any less expensive than manual patching. Manual patching is overseen by administrators, who will recognize problems faster than automated tools. Noise reduction is not a factor in patch management at all.

9. C. Checklists serve as a reliable guide for BC/DR activity and should be straightforward enough to use that someone not already an expert or trained in BC/DR response could ostensibly accomplish the necessary tasks. Flashlights and call trees are certainly useful during BC/DR actions, but not for the purpose of reducing confusion and misunderstanding. Control matrices are not useful during BC/DR actions.

10. B. A datacenter that doesn't follow vendor guidance might be seen as failing to provide due care. Regulations, internal policy, and the actions of competitors might all inform the decision to perform an update and patch, but these are not necessarily directly bearing on due care. This is a difficult, nuanced question, and all the answers are good, but option B is the best.

11. A. Regulators are not involved in an organization's CMB; all the rest are.

12. D. Print spooling is not a metric for system performance; all the rest are.

13. B. While the other answers are all steps in moving from normal operations to maintenance mode, we do not necessarily initiate any enhanced security controls.

14. A. If the CMB is receiving numerous change requests to the point where the amount of requests would drop by modifying the baseline, then that is a good reason to change the baseline. None of the other reasons should involve the baseline at all.

15. B. A UPS can provide line conditioning, adjusting power so that it is optimized for the devices it serves and smoothing any power fluctuations; it does not offer any of the other listed functions.

16. A. All deviations from the baseline should be documented, including details of the investigation and outcome. We do not enforce or encourage deviations. Presumably, we would already be aware of the deviation, so "revealing" is not a reasonable answer.

17. A. The more systems that be included in the baseline, the more cost-effective and scalable the baseline is. The baseline does not deal with breaches or version control; those are the provinces of the security office and CMB, respectively. Regulatory compliance might (and usually will) go beyond the baseline and involve systems, processes, and personnel that are not subject to the baseline.

18. C. Joint operating agreements can provide nearby relocation sites so that a disruption limited to the organization's own facility and campus can be addressed at a different facility and campus. UPS and generators are not limited to serving needs for localized causes. Regulations do not promote cost savings and are not often the immediate concern during BC/DR activities.

19. D. The Uptime Institute dictates 12 hours of generator fuel for all cloud datacenter tiers.

20. C. While hard drives may be useful in the kit (for instance, if they store BC/DR data such as inventory lists, baselines, and patches), they are not necessarily required. All the other items should be included.

Chapter 10: Legal and Compliance Part 1

1. D. Forensic analysis is the least challenging of the answers provided as it refers to the analysis of data once it is obtained. The challenges revolve around obtaining the data for analysis due to the complexities of international law, the decentralization of data storage or difficulty knowing where to look, and identifying the data owner, controller, and processor.

2. A. Legal controls are those controls that are designed to comply with laws and regulations whether they be local or international.

3. D. Plausibility, here, is a distractor and not specifically relevant to cloud forensics.

4. D. The value of data itself has nothing to do with it being considered a part of contractual PII even though it may have value associated with it.

5. B. Mandatory breach reporting is the *best* example of regulated PII components. The rest are generally considered components of contractual PII.

6. D. Quality is not associated with security in the way that confidentiality, integrity, and availability are.

7. A. As discussed in the chapter, the primary advantage of external audits based on the choices given would be that of independence. External audits are typically more independent and therefore lead to more effective results.

8. C. SOX was passed primarily to address the issues of audit independence, poor board oversight, and transparency of findings.

9. A. The SAS 70 was a report used in the past primarily for financial reporting and was oftentimes misused in the service provider context. The SSAE 16 standards and subsequent SOC reports are its successors.

10. A. The SOC 1 report focuses primarily on controls associated with financial services. While IT controls are certainly part of most accounting systems today, the focus is on the controls around those financial systems.

11. D. The SOC 3 report is more of an attestation than a full evaluation of controls associated with a service provider.

12. A. The primary purpose of the gap analysis is to begin the benchmarking process against risk and security standards and frameworks.

13. D. The AICPA is the organization responsible for generating and maintaining what are the Generally Accepted Accounting Practices in the United States.

14. A. FERPA deals with data protection in the academic industry, HIPAA in the medical industry, and SOX for publicly traded corporations.

15. C. Wholesalers or distributors are generally not regulated, although the products they sell may be.

16. B. An SOC Type I report is designed around a specific point in time as opposed to a report of effectiveness over a period of time.

17. D. An SOC Type II report is designed around a period of time as opposed to a specific point in time.

18. C. The right to be forgotten is about the individual's right to have data removed from a provider at any time per their request. It is being tried in the EU at the moment but does not yet apply here in the United States.

19. A. The right to audit should be contained in the client service-level agreement (SLA).

20. D. Options A, B, and C are reasons leading up to the creation and passage of SOX.

21. C. The most important aspect of GLBA was the creation of a formal information security program.

22. D. Financial controls are not addressed by HIPAA.

23. A. The doctrine of the proper law refers to how jurisdictional disputes are settled.

24. A. The Restatement (Second) Conflict of Law is the basis used for determining which laws are most appropriate in a situation where conflicting laws exist.

25. D. The Stored Communication Act, passed in 1995, is old, in bad need of updating, and unclear with regard to newer technologies.

Chapter 11: Legal and Compliance Part 2

1. B. The lowest level is Level 1, which is self-assessment, Level 2 is an external third-party attestation, and Level 3 is a continuous-monitoring program. Hybridization does not exist as part of the CSA STAR program.

2. B. KRI stands for key risk indicator. KRIs are the red flags if you will in the world of risk management. When these change, they indicate something is amiss and should be looked at quickly to determine if the change is minor or indicative of something important.

3. A. ISO 31000:2009 specifically focuses on design implementation and management. HIPAA refers to health care regulations, NIST 800-92 is about log management, and ISO 27017 is about cloud specific security controls.

4. C. ENISA specifically identifies the top 8 security risks based on likelihood and impact.

5. C. The SOC 2 report is not a part of the CSA Star program. It is a totally different audit reporting standard developed by the AICPA.

6. B. ISO /IEC 28000-2007 applies to security controls in supply chains. The others are cloud computing standards by have little to do with supply chain management.

7. C. Key risk indicators are useful, but they are not a framework. ISO 31000:2009 is an international standard that focuses on designing, implementing, and reviewing risk management processes and practices. NIST SP 800-37 is the Guide for Implementing the Risk Management Framework (RMF), a methodology for handling all organizational risk in a holistic, comprehensive, and continual manner. European Union Agency for Network and Information Security (ENISA) identifies 35 types of risks organizations should consider but goes further by identifying the top eight security risks based on likelihood and impact.

8. D. The best definition of risk is that of a threat coupled with a vulnerability.

9. D. The ENISA Top 8 Security Risks of Cloud Computing does not include availability, even though it is certainly a risk that could be realized.

10. D. Avoidance halts the business process, mitigation entails using controls to reduce risk, acceptance involves taking on the risk, and transference usually involves insurance.

11. B. A cloud carrier is the intermediary who provides connectivity and transport of cloud services between cloud providers and cloud customers.

12. A. Avoidance halts the business process, mitigation entails using controls to reduce risk, acceptance involves taking on the risk, and transference usually involves insurance.

13. C. The use of subcontractors can add risk to the supply chain and should be considered; trusting the provider's management of their vendors and suppliers (including subcontractors)

is important to trusting the provider. Conversely, the customer is not likely to be allowed to review the physical design of the datacenter (or, indeed, even know the exact location of the datacenter) or the personnel security specifics for the provider's staff. "Redundant uplink grafts" is a nonsense term used as a distractor.

14. A. A data custodian is responsible for the safe custody, transport, and storage of data, and the implementation of business roles.

15. A. Enveloping is a nonsense term, unrelated to risk management. The rest are not.

16. A. Hex GBL is a reference to a computer part in Terry Pratchett's fictional Discworld universe. The rest are not.

17. B. Roles and responsibilities should be included in the contract, not the SLA; a good method to determine whether something might belong in the SLA at all is figuring out whether a numerical value is associated with it—in this case, the element involves names and offices (roles), not numerical values, so it's immediately recognizable as something that isn't appropriate for the SLA. Options A and C are explicitly defined by exact numbers and are just the sort of aspects that belong in the SLA. Option D, the amount of time allowed to transition between normal and contingency operations, is also an explicit numerical value, but it is not a recurring event, regularly anticipated during each period of performance (or shouldn't be, anyway; if your cloud provider is fluctuating between normal and contingency ops every performance period, you should probably find a new provider), so this is something that can be defined once in the contract, and if the provider fails to perform in the (hopefully rare) event it needs to be evaluated, then the provider is in breach, and there should be remedies available other than the SLA. This is not an easy question, and understanding the nuances can be difficult.

18. A. The CSA CCM is an inventory of cloud service security controls that are arranged into separate security domains, not a hierarchy.

19. A. Transitional is not a term we associate with types of controls; the rest are.

20. A. An IT analyst is generally not high enough of a position to be able to provide quality information to other stakeholders. However, the IT director would be in such a positon, as would the others.

Appendix B

Answers to the Written Labs

Chapter 1

1. The Cloud Security Alliance website provides a lot of helpful information. Be sure after watching the video to check out the white papers and all of the helpful resources.

2. Answers will vary. Some good possible responses are
   - "The business might be concerned with unauthorized disclosure due to negligence or malice on the part of the cloud provider."
   - "The business may be attracted to the dramatic cost-savings offered by cloud computing."
   - "The business may want to transition from a cumbersome legacy environment into something more flexible and modern."

3. The three cloud computing service models include IaaS, PaaS, and SaaS, and some of their common advantages and disadvantages include (but are not limited to) the following:
   - IaaS:

     Advantages: Reduced capital investment; increased redundancy for BC/DR; scalability

     Disadvantages: Reliant on cloud provider for security; retain responsibility for maintaining OS and apps
   - PaaS

     Advantages: Multiple OS platforms to utilize, making it particularly good for testbed and software development purposes; all the advantages of IaaS

     Disadvantages: Reliant on cloud provider for updating OSs; retain responsibility for maintaining apps
   - SaaS

     Advantages: Cloud provider is responsible for all infrastructure, OSs, and apps; all the advantages of PaaS

     Disadvantages: Lose all administrative control; may not have any insight into security

Chapter 2

1. The Business Impact Analysis Worksheet is fairly straightforward and easy to use.

2. For this lab, I chose the Marketing department, but any department or function can be analyzed.

3. For this lab, I chose the general loss of systems due to any and all possible reasons.

4. My worksheet, still in progress, looks like Figure B.1.

FIGURE B.1   Business Impact Analysis Worksheet

Business X - Fashion Clothing

✓ **Ready** Business.

Business Impact Analysis Worksheet

Department / Function / Process ___Marketing___

Operational & Financial Impacts

Timing / Duration	Operation Impacts	Financial Impact
start of fall line	loss of end customers	up to $20M
>72 hours from trade show	loss of distributors	up to $10M
	loss of market share	up to $10M

Considerations (customize for your business)

Timing: Identify point in time when interruption would have greater impact (e.g., season, end of month/quarter, etc.)

Duration: Identify the duration of the interruption or point in time when the operational and or financial impact(s) will occur.
- < 1 hour
- >1 hr. < 8 hours
- > 8 hrs. <24 hours
- > 24 hrs. < 72 hrs.
- > 72 hrs.
- > 1 week
- > 1 month

Operational Impacts
- Lost sales and income
- Negative cash flow resulting from delayed sales or income
- Increased expenses (e.g., overtime labor, outsourcing, expediting costs, etc.)
- Regulatory fines
- Contractual penalties or loss of contractual bonuses
- Customer dissatisfaction or defection
- Delay executing business plan or strategic initiative

Financial Impact
Quantify operational impacts in financial terms.

ready.gov/business

Chapter 3

1. The NIST guidelines are helpful and easy to understand. Appendix D.1 provides a handy format that you can use for your devices.

2. Results should look like the example listed in 800-88, D.1:

    Example Statement of Cryptographic Erase Features

    1. **Make/Model/Version/Media Type:** Acme hard drive model abc12345 version 1+. Media type is Legacy Magnetic media.

    2. **Key Generation:** A DRBG is used as specified in SP 800-90, with validation [number].

    3. **Media Encryption:** Media is encrypted with AES -256 media encryption in Cipher Block Chaining (CBC) mode as described in SP 800-38A. This device is FIPS 140 validated with certificate [number].

4. **Key Level and Wrapping:** The media encryption key is sanitized directly during Cryptographic Erase.

5. **Data Areas Addressed:** The device encrypts all data stored in the LBA-addressable space except for a preboot authentication and variable area and the device logs. Device log data is retained by the device following Cryptographic Erase.

6. **Key Lifecycle Management:** As the MEK moves between wrapped, unwrapped, and rewrapped states, the previous instance is sanitized using three inverted overwrite passes.

7. **Key Sanitization Technique:** Three passes with a pattern that is inverted between passes.

8. **Key Escrow or Injection:** The device does not support escrow or injection of the keys at or below the level of the sanitization operation.

9. **Error Condition Handling:** If the storage device encounters a defect in a location where a key is stored, the device attempts to rewrite the location and the Cryptographic Erase operation continues, reporting success to the user if the operation is otherwise successful.

10. **Interface Clarity:** The device has an ATA interface and supports the ATA Sanitize Device feature set CRYPTO SCRAMBLE EXT command and a TCG Opal interface with the ability to sanitize the device by cryptographically erasing the contents. Both of these commands apply the functionality described in this statement.

Chapter 4

1. This white paper on preventing data leaks is just one of the many useful resources that ISACA provides. Be sure to explore others when you have the time.

2. An outstanding response would look something like this:

   According to the ISACA white paper on DLC solutions, operational risks involved in implementing DLC might include:

   - Improperly set DLP tools. This is fairly obvious. The data owner must define the rules and categories associated with the organization's data, or the DLP solution won't work in the manner intended. In fact, misconfigured DLP tools might actually harm the IT environment by adding extraneous overhead or responding to a significant amount of false positives.

   - Improperly sized network DLP module. If the DLP solution isn't correctly scoped for the organization's IT environment, it might miss a significant portion of network traffic, and data that should be prevented from leaving the organization's control might be allowed to go, because the tool didn't even inspect it.

   - Excessive reporting and false positives. See the first item; the rules and characteristics of suspect data have to be properly set by the data owner, and the tool has to understand the rules sufficiently to block only that data that fails, instead of blocking legitimate traffic.

   - Conflicts with legacy environment. Interoperability will always be a concern for any new tool, including DLP.

- Changes in process of infrastructure that affect DLP ability to function properly. The rules and identification capabilities for the DLP solution need to be updated as the environment changes; there is no "one-size-fits-all" DLP mechanism.

- Improperly placed DLP modules. See the second point; the DLP tool might miss suspect traffic if it's placed in the wrong network location to monitor that traffic.

- Undetected failure of DLP modules. Like any other toolset, if the DLP mechanisms aren't monitored and maintained properly, and failure goes undetected, the organization will end up having a false sense of security.

- Improperly configured directory services. The DLP tools can only create an accurate audit chain when there is sufficient traceability in the environment to support that effort.

Chapter 5

1. If possible, be sure to use the cloud providers' actual contracts when you do this. Discrepancies can exist between their marketing materials and contracts, and the contract is what is legally binding in the event of a later problem between you and the cloud provider.

2. Answers will vary. Be sure to record the URLs where you got the materials so you can refer back to them. Also, keep in mind that backup, pricing, and portability needs will vary from organization to organization. There is no one-size-fits-all solution.

Chapter 6

1. The Cloud Security Alliance's STAR program is widely used. You should be sure to fully understand STAR.

2. This is the questionnaire that registered cloud providers fill out. It includes information on how they handle various aspects of security.

3. This is an important document. It tells you a lot about how a cloud provider provides its services. Take some time to really consider what the information in this document means, particularly in the context of your organization's needs.

4. The registry lists various cloud providers who have each registered with the CSA.

5. If you have time, it would be a good idea to download several completed questionnaires for different providers and compare them, too.

6. Answers will vary. An outstanding response will look like this:

   I chose to review the [name of specific product] from [name of specific provider]. The three issues that came to my attention are:

   1. This provider is charging customers for malware and vulnerability scans. These should probably be functions included with the price of the service, instead of additional costs.

2. The provider's response about collecting/creating metadata on its customers is vague and leaves room for doubt about what specific information it gathers on customer behavior. They say that the customer owns their virtual machines and that the provider doesn't access or collect the customer's data. Does the provider truly not have any idea how customers are using the service?

3. The provider is securing ecommerce transactions with SSL; it would be better if TLS was used instead.

Chapter 7

1. Answers will vary. An outstanding response would look something like this:

   "I use Microsoft's Office 365, an SaaS. The APIs include my browser (Mozilla's Firefox), and any plugins necessary to run the various 365 suite of applications; these can include some Java implementations, Microsoft's own specific plug-ins for Firefox (Microsoft Office 2010, Silverlight, and Windows Live Photo Manager), and any other multimedia APIs used for including material in Office work products (possibly including the plug-ins for Adobe Acrobat and the Widevine tools from Google). There may be other plug-ins and add-ons that Firefox uses to manipulate data while 365 is running."

2. The cloud software development life cycle is extremely similar to other SDLCs. A couple of the major differences to note are the importance of inspecting secure remote access and strong authentication for development of apps that will be used in the cloud.

3. Answers will vary. The cloud application architecture includes many components. These include, but are not limited to, the following: APIs, tenant separation, cryptography, sandboxing, and application virtualization.

4. An identity management provider will be in charge of provisioning, maintaining, and deprovisioning identities on behalf of the cloud customer. This might include providing secure remote access, managing crypto-keys, and federation of multiple resource providers.

Chapter 8

1. Answers will vary. An example might look like this:

   "The application I am using as a theoretical sample is a database of information regarding dogs. The primary key will be each dog's RFID chip number, and all other fields will describe characteristics of the dogs, such as weight, color, owner information (including contact data such as email and home address), and so forth. The organization (data owner) is a dog food and toy manufacturer, and it uses this database for targeted marketing to groups of dog owners. The organization's staff (the user base) accesses the database through web portals."

2. STRIDE is comprised of Spoofing identity, Tampering with data, Repudiation, Information disclosure, Denial of service, and Elevation of privilege. Using this model helps you quickly identify many possible points of failure.

3. Answers will vary. An example:

The database might be subject to these three kinds of threats:

- **Tampering with data:** SQL injection. A malicious user (either internal or external) might try to enter SQL commands in data fields as a means to corrupt the data or affect the overall system.

- **Controls:** Field validation should be included so that the program can detect SQL commands in data fields and not accept them.

- **Information disclosure:** Dog owner PII. Because the owners' PII is included in the database (email and home addresses), the organization should be careful to reduce the likelihood of the PII being disclosed to unauthorized parties, including the organization's employees who do not have a need to know that data.

- **Controls:** Employ masking/obfuscation techniques so that unauthorized users do not see the PII content in those specific fields, but instead see blank spaces or Xs.

- **Denial of service:** DDOS. Because access to the database is via the Web, a DDOS attack against the servers could hinder user access to the data.

- **Controls:** Deploy and utilize strong network security tools, such as properly configured routers, firewalls, and IDS/IPS systems, and ensure redundancy of all Internet connections (including DNS nodes).

Chapter 9

1. Answers will vary. Possible choices might include Kohler, Honda, Cummins, Subaru, and Hitachi.

2. Answers will vary. Be sure to compare the specifications for the generators you chose against the hypothetical loads you imagine for you data centers against the ASHRAE standards.

3. Answers will vary. You should use the listed criteria (load, price, fuel) to justify your choice of preferred generator. The ASHRAE guidance is fairly detailed regarding specific ranges, based on the type, age, and location of the equipment. As you compare the generators, it is important to determine which guidance is most applicable to your facility and take into account any guidance and recommendations from the manufacturers regarding ambient ranges affecting performance parameters for their specific products.

Chapter 10

1. Laws are dictated by legislatures and enforced by government. Regulations are any constraints binding the organization; these can include laws or they might also be contractual in nature. Standards are prescribed modes for certain types of activity; sources include industry bodies, certifying entities, or internal guidelines within organizations themselves.

2. HIPAA now includes a number of rules that have been developed to address a range of issues. The two most often referred to are the Privacy Rule and the Security Rule. The Privacy Rule deals with the necessity to protect patient data (ePHI), and the Security Rule deals with supporting the CIA Triad in a medical organization.

3. The SOC 1 report addresses only financial reporting activity and is of no interest to IT security practitioners. The SOC 2 describes IT security controls and comes in two types, Type 1 and Type 2. Type 1 covers the architecture and control framework design, whereas Type 2 is a review of the actual controls as implemented. The SOC 3 report is only an attestation that one of the other reports (SOC 1 or SOC 2) has been performed, without any detail.

Chapter 11

1. The CSA Star program and Open Certification Framework have been widely adopted. While many cloud providers meet their requirements, not all have, so it is still important to confirm this.

2. This video of the CloudTrust Protocol is just one of many useful resources provided by the Cloud Security Alliance. Be sure to explore their website in detail.

3. Answers will vary and might include NIST's 800-37 (Risk Management Framework), COSO, and COBIT.

4. Risk appetite and risk tolerance are two terms that are very similar and are often used synonymously. The difference is nuanced. An organization's risk appetite and risk tolerance can be looked at as reflecting their attitude toward the benefits and levels of danger that a particular risk poses.

5. Answers will vary and might include throughput, per-use prices, the customer's business drivers, BC/DR considerations, portability, and more.

Index